THERAPEUTIC ALLIANCE IN INTEGRATIVE ADDICTIONS-FOCUSED PSYCHOTHERAPY AND COUNSELING

T0399721

THERAPEUTIC ALLIANCE IN INTEGRATIVE ADDICTIONS-FOCUSED PSYCHOTHERAPY AND COUNSELING

Enhancing Outcomes and The Recovery Process

By

GARY G. FORREST, EdD, PhD

*Licensed Clinical Psychologist
and Executive Director
Psychotherapy Associates, PC and
The Institute for Addictive Behavioral Change
Colorado Springs, Colorado*

CHARLES C THOMAS • PUBLISHER, LTD.
Springfield • Illinois • U.S.A.

Published and Distributed Throughout the World by

CHARLES C THOMAS • PUBLISHER, LTD.
2600 South First Street
Springfield, Illinois 62704

© 2021 by CHARLES C THOMAS • PUBLISHER, LTD.

ISBN 978-0-398-09356-3 (paper)
ISBN 978-0-398-09357-0 (ebook)

Library of Congress Catalog Card Number: 2020057763 (print)
2020057764 (ebook)

With THOMAS BOOKS *careful attention is given to all details of manufacturing
and design. It is the Publisher's desire to present books that are satisfactory as to their
physical qualities and artistic possibilities and appropriate for their particular use.*
THOMAS BOOKS *will be true to those laws of quality that assure a good name
and good will.*

Printed in the United States of America
MM-C-1

Library of Congress Cataloging-in-Publication Data

Names: Forrest, Gary G., author.
Title: Therapeutic alliance in integrative addictions-focused psychotherapy
and counseling: enhancing outcomes and the recovery process/ by Gary
G. Forrest.
Description: Springfield, Illinois : Charles C. Thomas, Publisher, Ltd.,
[2021] | Includes bibliographical references and index.
Identifiers: LCCN 2020057763 (print) | LCCN 2020057764 (ebook) | ISBN
9780398093563 (paperback) | ISBN 9780398093570 (ebook)
Subjects: LCSH: Drug abuse counseling. | Eclectic psychotherapy.
Psychotherapist and patient.
Classification: LCC RC564 .F68 2021 (print) | LCC RC564 (ebook) | DDC
362.29/186--dc23
LC record available at https://lccn.loc.gov/2020057763
LC ebook record available at https://lccn.loc.gov/2020057764

ACKNOWLEDGMENTS

This text is dedicated to my patients and their families, over the course of some fifty years of addictions-focused clinical practice.

I can't even begin to count the number of colleagues, friends, and significant others in my life who have contributed to my personal development and well-being over the course of my life span. This textbook is devoted to my wife Sandy, daughter Sarah Forrest, son-in-law Dr. Rob Ochsner, granddaughters Della and Morgan Ochsner, daughter Allison Forrest, son-in-law Josh Parrill, granddaughter August Olivine Parrill, the Della-Giustina family, and my many colleagues, patients and lifelong friends over the course of my lifetime. My experience as the Clinical Director of the Ft. Gordon, GA and Ft. Carson, CO Alcohol and Drug Rehabilitation Programs has also played a significant role in my development. I have been fortunate to have been involved with incredible professional colleagues during my private practice group experiences over the course of 1976-2021.

I want to acknowledge the support and ongoing involvement of my family and our extended families related to all the extended summer vacations that we spent at various beaches on the South Carolina and Georgia beaches. These vacations provided me with the opportunity to write several books between 1975 and 2002. Our family and extended families have also supported and contributed mightily to the success of our nationally recognized annual Psychotherapy Associates, PC "Addictive Disorders, Behavioral Health and Mental Health" Winter Symposium which has been held here in Colorado Springs, CO between 1974 and 2020. This event began with 58 attendees, and has grown to over 1,500 participants. We have trained thousands of behavioral health professionals, and provided thousands of scholarships enabling addictions and behavioral health clinicians to participate in this training and educational event over the years. We also thank our more recent Educational Supporters and Exhibitors for their help with making this event possible for so many people.

My previous office secretary, Mackenzie Kniesche, also contributed to the completion of this text, and my wife Sandy and our friend and colleague Larry Ritterband conducted a great deal of the work involved with putting on our annual Winter Symposium during the process. A special thanks to Jen Ochsner, who contributed to the process of preparing this text and who manages the Psychotherapy Associates group. Finally, I want to especially thank Bruce Carruth, PhD, Tim Gust, PhD, and Michael Thomas for their exceptional editorial work and assistance with this book. Unlike my earlier texts that were generally written and edited within the course of a year or perhaps two, this book was completed over the course of four or five years and required considerable editorial work. Thanks to all of you, and I certainly hope the professionals who read this text find it useful in their practices and clinical work with the spectrum of addictive disordered persons.

BOOKS BY THE AUTHOR, DR. GARY G. FORREST, EdD, PhD

1. *The Diagnosis and Treatment of Alcoholism* (1975; Revised Second Edition, 1978)
2. *How to Live with a Problem Drinker and Survive* (1980)
3. *Confrontation in Psychotherapy with the Alcoholic* (1982)
4. *Alcoholism, Narcissism and Psychopathology* (1983)
5. *Alcoholism and Human Sexuality* (1983)
6. *Intensive Psychotherapy of Alcoholism* (1984)
7. *How to Cope with a Teenage Drinker* (1984)
8. *Alcoholism and Substance Abuse: Strategies for Clinical Intervention* (Eds.), with T.E. Bratter (1985) Book of the Year via Behavioral Health Book Club
9. *Guidelines for Responsible Drinking* (1987)
10. *Substance Abuse, Homicide and Violent Behavior* (with R.H. Gordon) (1990)
11. *Chemical Dependency and Antisocial Behavior: Psychotherapy and Assessment Strategies* (1995, 1996)
12. *Countertransference in Chemical Dependency Counseling* (2002)
13. *Self-Disclosure in Psychotherapy and Recovery* (2010, 2012)
14. *See Jason Aronson, Publishers, Inc. "Master Works Series" including the author's books.
15. *Therapeutic Alliance in Integrative Addictions-Focused Psychotherapy and Counseling: Enhancing Outcomes and Recovery* (2021)

WHAT OTHERS ARE SAYING
ABOUT THIS BOOK

"In consideration of the current push from insurances to provide evidence-based treatment, Dr. Forrest provides great evidence for why, as practitioners of mental health, we need to remain aware of the importance of the therapeutic alliance regardless of the treatment used. He coined the term "alliance universality" to demonstrate the ongoing relevance of relationship throughout all mental health treatment. This book is a fantastic reminder of the importance of building our relationships first!"

Dr. Emily Rademan

"Dr. Forrest provides a clear and compelling argument for the value of the therapeutic working alliance in this engaging and accessible book. After examining both the elements and the impact of the therapeutic alliance across a range of approaches and client populations, this important text addresses the critical need to leverage the impact of the alliance when working with clients who have addictive disorders. Based on his rich clinical and scholarly experience, Dr. Forrest thoroughly discusses the issues that add complexity to the working alliance in addictive disorder counseling, and then provides illustrated practical examples of the power of the therapeutic alliance from the first help-seeking phone call through late-stage conclusion of services. This book fills an important gap in the treatment of addictive disorders by emphasizing the impact and power of relationship and alliance in facilitating human change. It is an extremely valuable resource for addiction health care service providers."

Cindy Juntunen, PhD

"Dr. Forrest has given us a definitive manuscript on the meaning of the therapeutic alliance in psychotherapy, and particularly as that alliance relates to effective treatment of people with addictive disorders. His work is also an indispensable reference for others who are researching the arena of the therapeutic relationship and alliance. The therapeutic alliance with addicted patients has long been an interest of Dr. Forrest and a subject upon which he has extensively written. Chapter 7 in this manuscript encapsulates and summarizes his lifelong study of this issue. . . . This manuscript benefits both the "beginner" therapist and the advanced practitioner. It is also a valuable resource for anyone contemplating research in the area. Finally, it reminds us all that, despite the wide range of approaches to psychotherapy, the relationship between two individuals remains the basic building block of change."

Bruce Carruth, Ph.D.
San Miguel de Allende, GTO, México

"Understanding the power of relationship - the power of the therapeutic alliance - is vital to our work in the field of substance use and addictive behavior disorders. Technique and strategies cannot take the place of a meaningful relationship; our clients heal and recover through the power of relationship. Dr. Gary Forrest offers a compelling argument for developing a therapeutic alliance, with meaningful suggestions and strategies for decreasing inevitable tensions that can occur in any professional psychotherapeutic relationship. His discussion on psychonoxious behaviors is a useful perspective and reminder to all of us on what not to do. Professionals and service providers, who work with clients struggling with addictions, would benefit from reading and applying the recommendations put forth by Dr. Forrest in this book."

Mita M. Johnson, EdD, NCC, LPC, LMFT, LAC

"Once again Dr. Forrest has done it! He has given us a book that summarizes what experienced therapists have known for many years – that the relationship is the paramount fixture in the mechanism known as the therapeutic process. While the focus of this text is directed at substance abuse treatment, the knowledge gained through it can be easily applied to the treatment of any mental health disorder. This is very much an academic and educational approach to the subject, for me it resonates my memories of the literature written by R.D Lange, Sidney Jourard, Carl Rodgers, and Irvin Yalom all of whom felt that the therapeutic relationship was paramount to treatment success."

Michael Wilbourn, Psy.D. Director of Behavioral Health Services,
Peak Vista Community Health Centers

"Gary Forrest is an outstanding clinician and prodigious author of books and articles on addiction. This book continues his lifelong journey of analyzing, theorizing, and treating addicts. It is the culmination of his successful winter conferences attended by thousands of mental health professionals over the past forty plus years. In this book he presents his philosophy and his psychology of treating the individual who needs help with their unfortunate addictions to alcohol and other drugs. I set up the first U.S. Army inpatient program in Germany in the 1970's using one of his first books on treatment of alcohol addicts. I have also used his various books to set up one of the first methadone programs for the VA in 1972. So, I was thrilled to get to know him, firsthand and refer patients to him, when I moved to Colorado Springs. This current tome is especially relevant to the young clinician on theory and treatment of the addictive individual."

Elliot Cohen, M.D
Life Member, American Psychiatric Association

FOREWORD

The word alliance has many shades of meaning, but all of them imply a close association, a connection, close similarity, affinity, or in some way joined together. A therapeutic alliance means that the therapist and the patient have entered into a relationship that serves as the foundation to achieve an acceptable and appropriate accomplishment. The alliance between patient and therapist has been a foundational component for successful psychotherapy since the early days of Freudian practice and, in fact, even before that. Transference and countertransference can provide the basis for the therapeutic or working alliance. And so, a *working* transference is both a fact and an activity or a series of activities that permeate the entire therapeutic progression. The efficacy of the alliance is independent of the theory and method used by the helper. Still, the therapists' interventions are proven techniques and skills. It is important to realize that the relationship buttresses the therapist's interventions. Consequently, the alliance is not static. Something happens as a result of it. Interventions change and clients change their behavior. Communication often becomes less guarded and even direct at times. Far from petrified, this process becomes tangible and concrete throughout Dr. Gary Forrest's book, a work that is nothing less than epic and monumental.

The author further describes how the alliance implies efforts to achieve a targeted outcome, a process that fits with the current requirement for treatment planning and to reach a higher level of patient mental health. When Carl Rogers formulated empathy, positive regard and genuineness as the cornerstones for reaching a more fulfilling level of mental health for the patient, he and his followers gave the world a developmental process that has inspired therapists on virtually every continent. In his classic interview with *Gloria,* Rogers spontaneously demonstrates empathy, positive regard and genuineness and truly sees the client's point of view in a congruent and authentic manner. And yet, Rogers was not a passive observer. As the alliance developed and flourished in this classic therapy session, toward the closing Rogers poignantly remarked, "Perhaps the person you're not being honest with is yourself." This seemingly simple intervention illustrates not only genuineness and the growth of the trusting relationship but also the fact

xiv   *Therapeutic Alliance in Integrative Addictions-Focused Psychotherapy*

that Rogers could comfortably make a statement that would probably not be appropriate in the early stages of the therapy session. The relationship was secure enough that it not only would not be damaged by this direct observation, but it would be strengthened.

Dr. Forrest emphasizes the universality of the alliance with a wide range of scenarios in which for instance, cognitive behavioral therapy embraces the central role of the alliance. Moreover, so significant and universal is the therapeutic alliance that research studies cited by Dr. Forrest have validated its use with children, adults, families, and in group therapy.

Even in the text, Dr. Forrest illustrates the appropriate use of self-disclosure. He cites his willingness to engage a patient who, intoxicated for 13 years, would probably have been voted "least likely to succeed" by individuals in the world of recovery. After lengthy therapy the patient made the decision to turn his life around and followed through on it for decades until his death. Dr. Forrest relates that even today, he is moved when he recalls this patient. So significant is this case that I want to cite it in its entirety. In Chapter 7 he states,

> . . . this patient was seen in therapy on a weekly basis for some 13 months prior to his military discharge. The client was acutely intoxicated at each of his weekly therapy sessions over the initial 9 months of his "therapy", and each session lasted no more than 10 to 15 minutes. As the author (Dr. Forrest) supportively and repeatedly attempted to explain to the patient the requirement of coming to sessions sober. Jim was also referred to attend group therapy and participate in the various recommended adjunctive treatment activities. Some 9 months later, the patient arrived for his first sober therapy session, began attending weekly group therapy, and was seen in marital therapy, and he sustained alcohol abstinence until the time of his retirement and for the duration of his life, which encompassed 12 years. He graduated from college during that time, remained married, became employed as an addictions counselor in the VA Hospital system, and (I) continued to receive Christmas cards with a lengthy "family" letter every year until the patient passed away. Each correspondence credited (me) and "our sessions" with "saving" his life. At the time, as I write this case study, Jim remains one of the "least likely to succeed" patients that I have ever treated within the context of nearly 50 years of addictions specific practice; nonetheless, the memories of our extremely difficult and unusual experience over the course of some 13 months still evokes significant personal emotions—ultimately very positive emotions for myself as well as his family. An obviously positive but unusual alliance eventually did evolve within the rather bizarre dynamics associated with this case.

The above case illustrates the efficacy of the therapeutic alliance as well as one of the many forms it can take. It changes with each patient, but the statement central to all therapy is, "I care about you and I will continue to work with you, to struggle to understand you and to accept you."

As you read this book, one additional issue is how could this excellent resource be used? The thoroughness, practicality and scholarship of Dr. Forrest's work provide its users with many benefits. I suggest that it be used as a text for training mental health and addiction specialists. It can also be a text for seasoned professionals and for in-servicing experienced therapists. Consequently, students and anyone seeking to become credentialed as licensed mental health professionals or addiction specialists will gain a deeper level of knowledge beyond what any formal education can provide. Professionals who wish to self-evaluate and grow in their transparency levels or who seek added skill in expressing accurate empathy would do well to apply the suggested principles in their own lives.

Finally, a word about the author: Many people are enriched by the scholarship of Gary Forrest, his willingness to consult with them and his genuineness and warmth shown to anyone he encounters.

ROBERT E. WUBBOLDING, EdD

PREFACE

This textbook examines a multiplicity of clinical issues associated with the role of the therapeutic alliance within the context of Integrative Addictions-Focused Psychotherapy and Counseling. These issues are associated with enhancing therapeutic outcomes and recoveries specific to patient populations manifesting the spectrum of substance abuse problems and addictive-brain disease.

Each chapter in this text examines the various evidence-based ingredients in the alliance relationship that foster successful patient outcomes and recoveries. Effective and successful psychotherapy relationships develop and evolve within the basic context of human relationships. Experienced and skilled therapists and counselors generally agree that the therapeutic relationship involving alliance dynamics constitutes one of the most, or perhaps the most salient single variable, impacting virtually every facet of psychotherapy, counseling and the therapeutic process and outcome. The reader will appreciate the evidence-based science presented throughout every chapter in this book relating to therapeutic outcomes and patient recoveries.

This work also reflects the author's clinical experience specific to addictions psychotherapy and counseling work over the course of some 50 years of clinical practice with addictive-disordered patients. These facets of the text also reflect the author's prior professional addictions treatment-related textbooks and professional articles dealing with addictions. Finally, this book includes a wealth of therapeutic vignettes, case studies, clinical information, treatment strategies, modalities, and diagnostic issues that will enhance counselors' and therapists' skill set, resulting in improved therapeutic outcomes. The therapeutic alliance constitutes the heart and soul of therapeutic change, growth, and recovery.

This book is written for all professional addictions—therapists, counselors, psychologists, social workers, physicians, nurses, residential and intensive outpatient care directors, as well as staff personnel involved in any form of addictions treatment. Many of these professional addiction treatment clinicians and counselors have very limited knowledge related to the impact of the therapeutic alliance factor involved in integrative addictions-focused psychotherapy work. The information that is presented in this text will significantly enhance and improve therapeutic outcomes in virtually all addictions specific treatment care settings.

Gary G. Forrest, EdD, PhD

CONTENTS

Page

Preface xiii

Chapter

1. Introduction 3

2. Psychotherapy Relationships That Heal: Implications for
   Addictions-Focused Psychotherapists and Counselors 13

3. The Therapeutic Alliance 26

4. Alliance Ingredients in Effective Psychotherapy and Counseling
   Relationships 51

5. Ancillary Therapist-Patient Alliance Dynamics in Effective
   Psychotherapy and Counseling Relationships 81

6. Psychopathology, Psychodynamics and Alliance Dynamics in
   Integrative Addictions-Focused Psychotherapy and Counseling
   Relationships 125

7. Alliance Dynamics and the Process of Effective Addictions-
   Focused Integrative Psychotherapy and Counseling Work 159

8. A Review of the Norcross-Wampold Clinical Practice Guidelines
   and Conclusions Pertaining to Evidence-Based Psychotherapy
   Relationships 292

9. Clinical Practice Suggestions and Recommendations for
    Addictions-Focused Therapists, Counselors and Treatment
    Providers 300

10. Alliance Universality: The Heart and Soul of Change and
    Recovery 315

References and Bibliography 329
Index 353

THERAPEUTIC ALLIANCE IN INTEGRATIVE ADDICTIONS-FOCUSED PSYCHOTHERAPY AND COUNSELING

Chapter 1

INTRODUCTION

Psychotherapy and counseling take place within the basic context of human relationships. The importance and perceived relevance of the psychotherapeutic relationship between various "schools" or approaches to the process and outcomes of psychotherapy vary considerably. However, most practicing psychotherapists and clinicians agree that the therapeutic relationship constitutes one of the most salient, if not the single most important, variable impacting virtually every facet of the psychotherapeutic process and outcome.

Experienced psychotherapists who have been formally educated, trained and supervised to practice therapy and counseling within the broad parameters of particular therapeutic approaches or models such as psychoanalysis, cognitive behavioral therapy, reality therapy, rational-emotive therapy, client-centered (person-centered) therapy, DBT or EMDR may actually tend to utilize and manifest similar therapeutic behaviors, relational dynamics, cognitions, and verbal exchanges or "styles" within the context of their therapeutic relationships. Indeed, most experienced practicing psychotherapists utilize a rather eclectic model of therapy in their clinical work. However, psychotherapy process and outcome studies involving therapists representing divergent therapeutic models and approaches have historically reported that particular and consistent therapist characteristics or ingredients consistently predict treatment outcomes (Bedics et al., 2015; Bergin and Garfield, 1971; Eubanks-Carter, Muran and Safran, 2015; Farber, Brink, and Raskin, 1996; Friedlander, 2015; Forrest 1978, 2016; Laska, Gurman and Wampold, 2014; Norcross, 2002, 2010, 2011; Tillman, 2013; Truax and Carkhuff, 1967). This body of evidence-based psychotherapy outcome literature indicates that specific therapist-patient relationship qualities or ingredients consistently predict the success, failure, and global outcomes pertaining to psychotherapy relationships in general.

As will be discussed in Chapter 3 of this book, the primacy of the therapeutic relationship as a core vehicle for constructive change in psychotherapy has remained at the heart of psychotherapy literature since the inception of Freudian Psychoanalysis. The psychotherapist, psychotherapy relationship and therapeutic alliance continued to be viewed by contemporary clinicians as the primary vehicle for constructive growth and change within the context of the psychotherapy process. The development and historic evolution of the therapeutic alliance as a primary construct and ingredient in psychotherapy is examined early in this text. Physicians, psychologists, counselors and other health care specialties have also historically recognized and emphasized the important role of the "doctor-patient" relationship consistently impacts the practice of medicine and the "healing arts" (Ochsner, 2013; Prince et al., 2016; Wiprovnick and Kuerbis, 2015).

Historic and contemporary psychotherapy relationship-based research and clinical studies have in large measure included (1) individual psychotherapy investigations, and (2) a diversity of patient sub-populations, (3) receiving therapy in a diversity of care settings or environments, and (4) the patients in these studies have received psychotherapy with therapists manifesting a diversity of education and training skills, experience, theoretical-orientations, multicultural backgrounds, and other demographic characteristics. These studies involve actual patients but also include analogue-based psychotherapy investigations. Many, if not most, of the past few decades include diverse, generally very good experimental designs, and methodologically sound data pertaining to the process and outcome of therapy (Cook et al., 2015; Duncan, Miller, Wampold and Hubble, 2010; Friedlander et al., 2014; Norcross, Beatles and Levant, 2006; Norcross, VandenBos and Freedheim, 2011; Norcross et al., 2010; Wiprovnick, Kuerbis and Morgenstern, 2015; Laska, Gurman and Wampold, 2014; Gelso and Hayes, 1998; Horvath et al., 2011; Bedics et al., 2015).

Since Zetzel (1956) first studied the therapeutic alliance concept, clinicians and researchers have continued to examine a myriad of psychotherapy alliance-focused process and outcome therapeutic relationship issues. These publications have generally continued to evince more sophisticated research designs and methodologies as well as increasingly complex and diverse facets of therapy. Therapeutic alliance related studies also continue to include a strong focus on individual psychotherapy as well as a diversity of therapeutic models and modalities. A number of well-designed and fascinating psychotherapy studies involving the alliance have recently been generated by very skilled academic clinicians within the context of graduate school settings. These recent studies include a wide range of therapeutic models, approaches, patient populations, treatment settings and other variables (Cook et al., 2015; Escudero et al., 2012; Friedlander et al., 2014; Gelso and Bhatia, 2012; Han and O'Brian, 2014; Tillman, 2013; Ulvenes et al., 2012).

Psychotherapy alliance evidence-based research and clinical investigations clearly and consistently indicate that the alliance is a crucial ingredient in the process and outcome of therapy (Bedics et al., 2015; Friedlander, Heatherington, Escudero and Diamond, 2011; Friedlander et al., 2014; Gelso and Hayes, 1998; Horvath, Fluckiger, Del Re and Symonds, 2011; Laska, Gurman and Wampold, 2014; Norcross, 2002; Norcross, VandenBos and Freedheim, 2013; Prince et al., 2016; Shirk, Karver, and Brown, 2011; Tillman, 2013).

The general evidence-based conclusion that alliance-related psychotherapy process and outcome efficacy also tends to transcend many demographics pertaining to the psychotherapy relationship and certainly supports the position of Norcross and Lambert (2011) debunking the historical "cultural wars in psychotherapy" precept. This mind set has long attempted to suggest that psychotherapy outcome is largely impacted by therapist theoretical orientation and/or the specific modality of therapy. The above authors astutely remind therapists that patient variables may contribute a greater impact on psychotherapy outcomes than the therapy relationship or specific treatment modality. They also point out that the combination of therapist, patient, therapeutic relationship, treatment modality and therapy context interactively shape and determine the process and outcome of all psychotherapy relationships.

In contrast to the thousands of alliance-related psychotherapy investigations that have been conducted with diverse patient populations over the past six decades, (Horvath et al., 2011), relatively fewer and rather limited studies involving alliance-related psychotherapy process and outcome therapy studies have been generated involving substance abusing and addictive disordered patients. However, there are notable recent exceptions to this finding which suggest an ever growing and evolving clinical as well as research interest in addictive disorders focused psychotherapy and alliance dynamics related to the process and outcome of addictions psychotherapy and counseling as well as other addictions related treatment modalities and variables (Auerbach et al., 2008; Barber et al., 2006; Barber et al., 2001; Cook et al., 2015; Darchuk, 2007; Faw et al., 2005; Flicker et al., 2008; Friedlander et al., 2011; Friedlander et al., 2014; Prince et al., 2016; Robbins et al., 2008; Raytek et al., 1999; Ritter et al., 2002; Shaw and Murray, 2015; Szapocznik et al., 1988; Wiprovnick, Kuerbis and Morgenstern, 2015).

As a practicing clinical psychologist and therapist with an active addictions specialized practice for over forty years, this author has long maintained a keen interest in the psychotherapy alliance related literature. Several of my earlier books and publications (Forrest, 1975-2019) have emphasized the paramount importance of the therapeutic relationship and more specifically, the working and productive therapeutic alliance, as a crucial ingredient in the process and outcome of effective addictions psychotherapy work. These publications have also examined the conceptual alliance ingredients, definitional, and therapist-patient relational parameters of the working and productive alliance in integrative addictions-focused psychotherapy work (Forrest, 1975-2019).

Within the context of this author's clinical practice publications related to the compelling relevance of the alliance in extended integrative addictions-focused psychotherapy and counseling work within a private practice setting, it was somewhat disheartening to re-read the following statement from an earlier text (Forrest, 1975); "until quite recently, very little research effort has been directed at the psychotherapy enterprise with alcoholic patients." However, this same text included an appropriate, encouraging and contextually contemporary comment made by Freud (1953) nearly one hundred years ago; "as you know, we have never prided ourselves on the completeness and finality of our knowledge and capacity. We are just as ready now as we were earlier to admit imperfections of our understanding and to learn new things and to alter our methods in any way that can improve them (i.e., treatments and matters of effective patient care) (p. 92). From the author's vantage point, Freud's statement might have been found in the pages of the Alcoholics Anonymous Big Book, contemporary or historic self-help or therapy group dialogue, a clinical staff meeting, a contemporary academic faculty meeting or in a diversity of behavioral health oriented treatment settings spanning the course of the last one hundred years.

This book was developed with the basic goal of providing addictions psychotherapists, counselors, clinicians and treatment providers with an enhanced awareness and more in-depth appreciation of the alliance impact and relevance within the context of all forms of addictions psychotherapy, counseling and treatment. Experienced addictions therapists consciously recognize that their therapeutic relationships with addictive disordered persons generally impact their patients and themselves in many constructive ways. Practicing clinicians also experience these realties on an hourly and daily basis throughout the duration of their careers. This text will also enhance the therapeutic armamentarium, general clinical practice skills, and sensitivity of addictions psychotherapists as they become more alliance-focused within the context of their therapy relationships in all care and recovery settings.

Alliance related addictions-focused psychotherapy literature and information can increasingly enhance the evolving effectiveness of addictions psychotherapy and counseling work as well as the addictions treatment industry. The general body of alliance related psychotherapy studies and literature generated to date has no doubt unknowingly involved significant numbers of addictive disordered persons who were never identified as manifesting primary or secondary additive disorders at the time of their inclusion in many clinical investigations and publications. Addictions therapists in particular will appreciate the "speculative" nature of this position upon further reflection.

The author's global review of the alliance related literature for this book reveals that the majority of psychotherapy and counseling patient populations involved in this particular area of investigation have also included a broad spectrum of persons manifesting a spectrum of co- occurring disorders and conflicts including childhood anxiety disorders, adolescent adjustment difficulties, various psychiatric disorders (adolescents and adults), aggressive and antisocial patterns of behavior, parenting problems, depression, marital and family problems, spousal abuse, child abuse, sexual abuse and trauma, and various other adjustment and emotional difficulties. These clinical realities are addressed in-depth and explored within the therapist-patient alliance context throughout this text.

As noted earlier, a somewhat limited number of alliance focused publications also include patient populations manifesting various specific addictive disorders, patterns of addictive brain disease and substance abuse or dependence. With regard to the various clinical and research populations included in the alliance focused literature, it is very important to note that demographic and epidemiological studies involving a wide variety of mental health disorders including adult and adolescent depression, anxiety disorders, bipolar and major depression, personality disorders, schizophrenia and major mental illness, OCD, and other patient subpopulations consistently report over 40 to 60+ percent of these diagnostic categories manifest at least one comorbid addictive disorder and/or substance use disorder (DSM-IV, 1994; DSM-V, 2014; ICD-10, 2015).

Addictive disorder related behaviors and pathology frequently precipitate the process of patient treatment engagement, diagnostic assessment, psychotherapy involvement, and other forms of medical and behavioral health care engagement upon the part of thousands of American people each year. Many of these individuals manifest florid alcohol dependence, polysubstance dependence, and/or polysubstance abuse in combination with comorbid schizophrenia, personality disorders, bipolar disorder, generalized anxiety disorder, and various other forms of co-occurring psychopathology or biopsychosocial dysfunction. It should be noted that addictive disordered clinical populations also include severe and chronically mentally ill persons, prison populations, sex offenders and victims, domestic violence perpetrators and victims, suicidal persons, chronic pain patients, enraged or homicidal individuals, and virtually all age groups, minority groups, and a diversity of people in any given population of human beings through the world (Forrest, 2019).

These combined clinical demographic realities pertaining to addictive disordered and mental health disordered populations certainly provide grist for practicing addictions psychotherapists and other health professionals to anticipate that 40-60 percent of their patients manifest, or are at risk for developing, a complex addictive disorder involving one or more comorbid mental health disorders. Patients who present with a prior diagnosis involving a mental health disorder have also frequently been given an addictive disorder diagnosis by earlier treatment providers or they may have a more recent history of addictive disorder diagnosis with comorbid mental health disorder. Patient self-disclosure and the therapist's clinical acumen (Forrest, 2002, 2012) are essential to the therapist's ability to accurately assess and provide appropriate diagnoses and care for persons manifesting complex and co-occurring disorders. These clinical realities also exist with all of the seemingly univariant diagnostic patient categories as well. The evolving psychotherapeutic process frequently reveals complex and complicated underlying clinical diagnostic realities as the therapeutic alliance and relationship unfolds within the course of ongoing addictions psychotherapy and counseling work.

In short, the evidence-based psychotherapy alliance data rather compellingly demonstrate the paramount importance of the alliance within the context of addictions psychotherapy and counseling relationships. This realm of psychotherapy and counseling research and clinical practice needs to be more fully and thoroughly examined within the specific context of addictions therapy and treatment. Thus, the content of this book may foster future integrative research and practice investigations pertaining to addictions psychotherapy, counseling and various alliance dynamics in academic, institutional, clinical and all behavioral health care settings.

Psychotherapy can be a powerful and efficacious instrument for global constructive behavioral health change and recovery on the part of persons manifesting every form of addictive brain disease. From a variety of perspectives, the world community has long been plagued with a variety of profound biopsychosocial problems and conflicts associated with our collective addictive disordered populations. Economic instability and uncertainty, perpetual war, anxiety, mental health and mental illness, political corruption and ineptness, poverty and joblessness, health and health care, crime, violence, suicide, homicide, domestic violence and family depression, legal and financial issues, marital-relational conflicts, sexual dysfunction, trauma and every other facet of human interaction has been adversely and collectively impacted by the addictive disorders and mental health disorders. These complex and collective interactive biopsychosocial processes include a concurrent loss of our basic capacity for sustained healthy human relatedness, effective communication, peace, authentic being, and intimacy. The therapeutic alliance represents a potentially significant and curative vehicle for patient change and growth related to many, if not all, realms of human functioning.

Chapter 2 examines the issues of counseling and psychotherapy efficacy: does therapy really help or heal people? This chapter addresses the history and various facets of treatment successes and failures as well as evidence-based psychotherapy outcome studies over the past 60 years. The author also addresses important therapy issues related to addiction-specific treatment outcomes and various factors which impact both successful and unsuccessful therapy outcomes among addictive-disordered patients. Most behavioral scientists or therapists involved in addiction-focused therapy and treatment work clearly realize that many addictive-disordered patients also benefit and recover as a result of their various therapy and treatment experiences.

As noted earlier, Chapter 3 provides an in-depth review of the history, definitions, and evolution of evidence-based psychotherapy research and clinical data pertaining to the alliance construct in the practice of psychotherapy. Readers will appreciate the aggregate of data and information presented in this chapter demonstrating the therapeutic impact of the key alliance ingredients in the process and outcome of effective psychotherapy and counseling relationships. Alliance ingredients play a crucial role in shaping the process and outcome of most psychotherapy relationships; however, it is also emphasized that the therapeutic process and outcome can also be powerfully influenced by a diversity of patient-therapist related variables, therapy approaches or modalities, environment or setting, random events, and other variables as well.

The fourth chapter in this text addresses specific therapeutic alliance related ingredients in effective counseling and psychotherapy. These essential therapeutic alliance ingredients in large measure consistently result in positive therapeutic outcomes. This chapter explores the extensive body of psychotherapy research evidence associated with these constructs and ingredients: 1) therapist non-possessive warmth or positive regard, 2) therapist empathy, 3) therapist genuineness, or authenticity, 4) therapist concreteness, and (5) communication style. The various roles, uses, impact and dynamics associated these core alliance ingredients in successful integrative addictions-focused counseling and psychotherapy work are also discussed in the chapter.

Chapter 5 elucidates the limited research and clinical literature pertaining to ancillary therapist patient alliance dynamics and factors that impact the process and outcome of effective integrative addictions-focused counseling and psychotherapy. These ancillary ingredients include a diversity of dynamics and factors including transference, countertransference, self-disclosure or transparency, relapse, patient readiness, motivation and commitment to change, alliance rupture and repair work, "common everyday life" events, and the random realities associated with daily living. Definitions, descriptions, history, and both clinical and research data pertaining to these psychotherapy constructs are also discussed in this chapter.

Chapter 6 addresses alliance related psychodynamics and psychopathology dynamics associated with integrative addictions-focused psychotherapy and counseling work. The general aggregate of clinical histories and symptoms that patients manifesting severe addictive disorders often present with often include a diversity of complicating and complex difficulties which may also result in a variety of problematic psychotherapy alliance process and outcome dilemmas, difficulties, and challenges for addictions-focused therapists as well as general relational interactions with other care providers. Many of these issues are also discussed in the chapter.

Chapter 7 of this text provides an extensive and in-depth examination of the various Early Stage, Middle, Stage, and Late Stage therapy alliance dynamics involved in efficacious addictions-focused integrative psychotherapy and counseling work. This chapter also includes twenty-five sections related to the therapeutic alliance in integrative addictions-focused psychotherapy and counseling associated with therapy outcomes and the recovery process. An additional segment of Chapter 7 deals exclusively with the specific issue of termination in psychotherapy with addictive disordered patients. This segment of the chapter provides a great deal of very recent evidence-based research dealing with termination in psychotherapy.

Chapter 7 also includes a wealth of rich therapy vignettes and case studies which demonstrate the various clinical issues that are addressed in each segment of the chapter.

Each stage of therapy in Chapter 7 addresses a diversity of clinical practice issues related to addictions-focused integrative psychotherapy and counseling, including etiology, diagnosis, models of therapy, transference and countertransference, relapse, resistance, addiction-focus, interpretation, affect regulation, projective identification, exercise, medication management, alliance rupture and repair work, self-help care, confrontation, patient co-morbid psychopathology, and the genetic reconstruction process. These factors and therapist-patient dynamics continually impact every facet of the therapeutic alliance, relational course of therapy and therapy outcomes.

The eighth chapter includes a verbatim review of the Norcross-Wampold research conclusions and clinical practice guidelines (2011) pertaining to evidence-based psychotherapy relationships. All practicing addictions psychotherapists, counselors, and clinicians will benefit significantly from reading this chapter. Addictions-focused psychotherapy and counseling students, trainees, practicing clinicians, and addictions program directors also need to be cognizant of the data and practice guidelines included in the Norcross-Wampold evidence-based psychotherapy practice review.

Several alliance related education, training, supervision, and practice guidelines for addictions-focused psychotherapists and counselors are discussed in Chapter 8. The suggestions and practice guidelines that are elucidated in this chapter stem from the author's long and extensive practice history involving consultation, training, and supervision of addictions therapists and counselors practicing in residential, intensive outpatient, medical and detox, college and university, hospital, industrial, mental health center, correctional, legal, DUI/DUID settings, drug courts, private practice settings, and EAP programs.

Chapter 9 examines and discusses the overall context of the Norcross-Wampold (2011) clinical practice guidelines and conclusions related to evidence-based psychotherapy relationships presented in Chapter 8. Chapter 9 addresses and outlines several clinical practice guidelines and recommendations for all contemporary addiction therapists, clinicians and treatment providers. Several of these addictions-focused therapy and treatment provider guidelines mirror the content of Chapter 8, and as Norcross and Wampold (2011) indicate, "practice divisions, mental health organizations as a whole, administrators or mental health centers are encouraged to attend to the relational features of their services. Researchers are also encouraged to examine various facets of the therapeutic relationship and treatment outcomes." This chapter also provides comments on "what works" and "what does not work" in addictions-focused psychotherapy and addictions treatment programs.

The final chapter in this text (Chapter 10) addresses the Alliance Universality construct within the context of psychotherapy studies in general as well as the context of addictions-focused psychotherapies and various other diverse patient populations manifesting a wide range of clinical histories and diagnoses. In short, the author (Forrest, 2019) indicates in this chapter that the 70-year empirical data base pertaining to a wide range of alliance related factors compellingly demonstrates the universal relevance and salient role of the alliance in virtually all forms of counseling and psychotherapy. The alliance or therapeutic "bond," and the human relationship dimensions of therapy constitute the bedrock foundation for constructive human growth, adaptive change, and successful psychotherapy outcomes.

Finally, this chapter clearly supports the validity of the evidence-based Alliance Universality construct vis a vis the extensive 70-year alliance specific therapy studies and empirical investigations that are examined throughout Chapter 11. As Escudero, Friedlander and Heatherington (2001) indicate, "of the many technique- and relationship-related factors that account for change in successful psychotherapy, the working alliance is undoubtedly the most robust" (p. 138). More recently, Cook, Heather and McCambridge (2015) report that their study supports rating of working alliance as important in explaining differences in outcome following treatment for alcohol problems, and perhaps for differences in the mechanisms of effect of different treatments (p. 380).

The working and productive therapeutic alliance represents a potential royal road to improve addictions-focused psychotherapy, counseling, and other addiction specific treatment outcomes and the recovery process.

The text clearly delineates the powerful integrative impact of alliance, therapist behaviors and qualities, patient variables and multi-variant factors that shape and determine the process and outcome of all psychotherapy relationships. The information presented in this text clearly debunks historic and contemporary belief systems or models which purport the singular or most salient causative factor associate with poor outcomes and treatment failure in addictions psychotherapy rests primarily with patients.

This book is the first to comprehensively explore the therapeutic alliance in the practice of integrative addictions-focused psychotherapy and counseling. As such, this work represents a starting point in this particular area of psychotherapy practice. Much of the content that has been incorporated into this book has been gleaned from the substantial prior research efforts of clinical and academic psychologists who have systematically investigated a multitude of psychotherapy alliance related dynamics over the course of forty years. As noted earlier, the clinical and research efforts of such individuals have included limited studies involving addictions psychotherapy and counseling and information from these works have also been incorporated into this text.

This book will be a very important resource and tool for all practicing addictions psychotherapists, counselors, and addictions treatment providers. The wealth of alliance-based research data and clinical information in this text will also provide grist for clinical researchers, students, trainees, supervisor and graduate academic faculty involved in psychotherapy and treatment research, and clinical practice work involving addictive disordered persons.

Chapter 2

PSYCHOTHERAPY RELATIONSHIPS THAT HEAL: IMPLICATIONS FOR ADDICTIONS-FOCUSED PSYCHOTHERAPISTS AND COUNSELORS

INTRODUCTION

This chapter re-visits the long-standing issue of psychotherapy efficacy: simply stated, "does psychotherapy and counseling really help and heal patients?" Many related questions have surrounded this general topic since the advent of psychoanalysis, and although the basic general scientifically-based answer to this question has resoundingly remained "yes" for some seventy years or more, these issues continue to be met with varying levels of public as well as professional skepticism.

This essential question continues to impact patients, therapists, and the American health care professions, and every facet of the American behavioral health system including the realm of addictive disorders, mental health care, the health care and treatment industry. Ancillary questions pertaining to psychotherapy efficacy involving a diversity of behavioral health patient sub-populations, "how and why" therapy benefits particular patient groups and diagnostic categories, "cost-effectiveness" of therapy and treatment, patient needs for hospitalization or residential care, duration of treatment, and outcome and effectiveness related to different therapeutic approaches or models seem to remain unanswered both within and outside of the behavioral health care industry. Psychotherapy "failures" and poor therapeutic outcomes have also remained germane to the ever evolving and underlying skepticism related to basic questions of treatment efficacy and outcomes. It is important to realize that the general matter of treatment efficacy has been and will continue to remain (Weiss, 2015) an essential component in every form of evolving health care practice.

Psychotherapy can and does "heal" many people who manifest a wide variety of human problems or disorders. The content of this chapter includes a discussion of the psychotherapy relationship and general evidence-based literature pertaining to the healing and constructive change data related to the process and outcome of therapy. The implications of this extensive body of psychotherapy evidence-based research and clinical literature for addictions psychotherapists, counselors, clinicians and all behavioral health care treatment providers are also discussed in this chapter.

THE PSYCHOTHERAPY RELATIONSHIP AS A VEHICLE FOR CONSTRUCTIVE PERSONALITY GROWTH AND BEHAVIOR CHANGE

Psychoanalysis represents the most widely recognized historic form of psychotherapy practiced in the United States and throughout much of the modern world over the past one hundred years. Freud and the Neo-Freudians (Fenichel, 1945; Freud, 1912; Horney,1936; Sullivan, 1953) developed and utilized psychoanalysis as a medical instrument and vehicle for healing or curing "emotionally disturbed" people. Every school or model of psychotherapy and counseling developed since the advent of psychoanalysis and psychodynamic psychotherapy has been directed toward this same essential goal; helping human beings constructively change, grow and modify complex and diverse human problems.

Psychotherapy relationships involve a psychotherapist and patient or client. The single most essential ingredient or vehicle for constructive change within the context of the therapeutic process and outcome process most often involves the therapist-patient relationship. Obviously, exceptions to this generalized position can and do occur. For example, basic life circumstances impacting the therapist or patient and therapeutic relationship, internally or externally, can result in any number of consequences effecting the process and outcome of psychotherapy. Geographic moves, health issues including loss of health insurance, family matters, death or divorce, and a myriad of "real life" realities may significantly impact the process and outcome of psychotherapy.

It is important to note that various therapeutic approaches and models generally involve differing therapeutic styles, interventions and actions which may contribute to significantly different therapist-patient relationship interactions and dynamics within the context of the therapeutic process. These factors also directly impact therapeutic outcome (Forrest, 2012, 2016, 2019). Psychotherapy relationships involving person-centered, psychoanalytic and psychodynamic, and rational emotive or EMDR therapists and their clients may differ very significantly with regard to various relationship dynamics occurring simply within the contexts of treatment, duration, frequency, cost of care, level of therapist-patient feelings and personal involvement, and even outcome-assessment methods. Nonetheless, psychotherapy always takes place within the context of a rather unique intimate human encounter involving the therapeutic alliance and the psychotherapy relationship process. This reality even applies to the practice of contemporary virtual and on-line psychotherapy relationships (Dillon, 2014, 2016).

The author (Forrest, 1975) historically defined psychotherapy and counseling interchangeably, as a "particular form of human interactional process involving at least two individuals, one of which is experiencing significant difficulty in the process of daily living, and another who, by virtue of professional training and select life experiences, is potentially capable of helping facilitate positive behavioral growth or change upon the part of the person experiencing difficulties" (p. 7). Many psychotherapy definitions have been developed and utilized by therapists and clinical researchers representing different "schools" and models of psychotherapy practice over the past seventy years (Rogers, 1942, 1951, 1957; Truax and Carkhuff, 1967; Garfield and Bergin, 1971; Gelso and Hayes, 1998; Hayes, Gelso and Hummel, 2011; Norcross, 2002; Norcross, Vanden Bos and Freedheim, 2011). Some definitions pertaining to the psychotherapy relationship (Gelso and Carter, 1985, 1994; Norcross, 2011) have utilized operational definitions and qualities in their evidence-based psychotherapy investigations. Again, the various relational dimensions and qualities of the therapist-patient relationship form the crux of psychotherapy definitions and studies. Gelso and Carter (1994) define the therapy relationship as "the feelings and attitudes that therapist and client have toward one another, and the manner in which these are expressed." Many therapists include behavioral, cognitive, and other dimensions in their personal definitions of the psychotherapy construct.

Psychotherapy is also consistently defined by the clinical practice behaviors, therapy interventions, verbal, cognitive and social transactions, feelings and other interpersonal and intrapersonal processes that take place in the ongoing context of the therapeutic relationship. These dynamic relational realities are shaped and developed vis-à-vis the therapist's clinical training, education, supervision and practice as well as his or her "real life" experiences. Likewise, each patient brings his or her unique "real life" learning experiences, and global experiential being to the therapeutic relationship. These therapist-patient relational realities provide a glimpse at the window of complexity involved in the process of attempting to understand, identify, and internally experience the particular vicissitudes of the psychotherapy experiences which truly facilitate adaptive patient personality growth and change.

As noted earlier in this chapter as well as Chapter 1, psychotherapy facilitated healing, change and recovery always occurs as a function of multiple interactive therapist, patient, therapy relationship, technique related, environmental and sometimes random chance variables. This combination of psychotherapy interaction variables appears to consistently produce significant therapy facilitated improvement and constructive change in 65–70 percent of psychotherapy cases involving diverse patient-therapist sub-populations (Eysenck, 1967; Duncan, Miller, Wampold and Hubble, 2010; Norcross, 2002; Truax and Carkhuff, 1967). Chapter 1 also describes the overall scope and general alliance focused content of this text.

Psychotherapy research evidence has historically indicated that therapy also produces "for better or worse" patient outcomes (Eysenck, 1967; Forrest, 1974-2019; Garfield and Bergin, 1971; Truax and Carkhuff, 1967). Indeed, based upon the psychotherapy evidence-based research of the past half-century it is reasonable to assume that roughly two-thirds of psychotherapy patients will benefit from therapy while one-third will either evidence no change or actually deteriorate as a function of treatment. The identified therapist qualities and ingredients which in large measure predictably result in constructive therapeutic outcomes are identified, described and discussed at length in Chapters 3, 4, and 5. The therapeutic alliance and therapist-related alliance qualities that significantly impact the "for better or worse" dynamics surrounding the efficacy and issues related to psychotherapy outcomes are also addressed in these chapters. Many contemporary practicing integrative addictions-focused therapists, counselors, and clinicians have a very limited knowledge of the evidence-based psychotherapy and counseling literature pertaining to the process and therapy outcomes related to addictions specific therapies, treatment models and modalities.

ADDICTIONS PSYCHOTHERAPY, HEALING AND RECOVERY IMPLICATIONS

Addictions psychotherapy, counseling and treatment constitutes a relatively new and evolving profession within the psychotherapy, mental health and behavioral health professions. Substance abuse and addictive disorder treatment providers and programs are no longer segregated or separate components of the American national or state and local level behavioral health care systems.

The 1980s and 1990s ushered in a national integration of the mental health, behavioral health and addictive disorders health care systems. Professional addictions psychotherapy, counseling and treatment focused educational training programs also began to develop within the framework of traditional academic undergraduate and graduate counseling and psychology settings. Specific addictions psychotherapy and counselor training programs were significantly expanded and developed at the state regulatory agency level in the 70s and 80s. Within the context of the rather profound nationwide social and cultural changes that were occurring within the American health care industry at this juncture came the growing collective realization that addictive disordered persons (1) constituted a major patient population in America, (2) various addictive disorders either directly caused and/or were related to the development of a multitude of medical, mental health and social problems, (3) the national "cost" in health care dollars pertaining to the growing American problems of drug abuse, dependency and the addictive and mental health disorders were an interrelated "problem" involving billions of dollars, and (4) as a function of the ever-growing collective awareness of these inter-related realities associated with the American "drug epidemic," more treatment programs were developed that began to utilized new and different treatments, created thousands of addictions-specific jobs, professional addiction career opportunities and occupations evolved, and finally (5) larger numbers of addictive disordered persons were treated, benefitted from treatment, and probably through media-generated recovery stories of persons involving alcoholism, drug dependence and abuse, eating-disorders, nicotine dependence, gambling addictions, sexual addiction and other addictive brain disease related behaviors created a confluence or zeitgeist pertaining to the reality that addictions psychotherapy and other treatments can, in fact, heal, help and constructively impact people manifesting a diversity of addictive disorders.

Addictions-focused psychotherapy and treatments frequently "work," and akin to treatment interventions for other health disorders, diseases and illnesses, addictions psychotherapy and other treatments may result in relatively different outcomes related to different therapy approaches, care provider skills and programs, also within the recent collective realization that patient related characteristics significantly impact psychotherapy treatment outcomes and effectiveness.

The impact of social media and the explosion of information and education technology over the past fifteen years have dramatically enhanced the awareness level of the American and world-wide communities about addictions, mental health, and virtually every other facet of human behavior and interaction. A major component of this process includes the awareness that there are many forms of effective treatment available for a multitude of human health disorders, illnesses and diseases.

Addiction psychotherapists, clinicians and treatment providers experience the realities of patient change and recovery on a regular basis. It is also important for addictions-focused counselors, therapists and patients to clearly realize that there are many varieties of therapy and therapeutic change facilitating methodologies that they can utilize to initiate and sustain the addiction recovery process. Some addictions-focused psychotherapists and counselors as well as residential, intensive out-patient treatment, and other care-setting providers continue to maintain a treatment ideology which basically supports a "one treatment approach fits all alcoholics and addicts," or individuals manifesting other severe addictive brain diseases. Collegial education, training, supervision, and therapist networking experiences are viable alternatives that can be used to enhance therapist and treatment program provider skills, awareness, knowledge, efficiency, and motivation for patients to sustain care and recovery. Patient-specific treatment interventions need to be a key ingredient in all forms of addictions-focused psychotherapy and counseling work as well as general behavioral health care services.

Addictions counselors and therapists practice in a diversity of treatment settings. Therapists also encounter a diversity of addictive-disordered patients within the confines of different treatment settings. For example, therapists and counselors who practice mainly within "detox" and court-ordered treatment settings frequently work with addictive-disordered persons manifesting multiple, chronic or complex debilitating illnesses as well as a diversity of biopsychosocial problems. A significant number of these patients may be imminently terminal. Clinicians who are involved in the psychotherapy and ongoing treatment of acutely disturbed and extremely difficult patients on a daily basis for protracted periods of time need to consistently be reminded by supervisors and colleagues of the basic truth that recovery and treatment can, in fact, "work." This truism applies to different segments of all addictive-disordered patient populations. Therapists working in these setting also need to remind themselves of these realties on a regular basis. Interestingly, many psychotherapists who have practiced in these more difficult clinical environments for 3 or 4 years, or even twenty or more years, have an uncanny ability to recall in detail some of their individual patients who had literally been at "death's door" on countless occasions, and perhaps been engaged in numerous treatment programs over the course of 10 or 20 years, who subsequently then experienced a particular or unknown life changing treatment experience with a therapist which eventually resulted in an addictive free and functional lifestyle that continued for the duration of their lives. Uncommon positive outcomes or perhaps relative "miracles" can and do take place involving the most difficult and conflicted psychotherapy patients. Some of these patients are treated in the most impoverished and limited treatment environments. Patients who sometimes return to "detox" facilities in 24–72 hours in the same state they manifested prior to their last treatment episode may eventually recover following numerous subsequent treatment episodes a decade later. However, many of the "revolving door" patients also die in a few days, weeks, or months following release from care.

Paradoxically, psychotherapists and other staff members who work in "detox" facilities infrequently experience short-term physical and psychological changes and relative "miracles" that accompany a few days of patient alcohol and drug abstinence. The other "side" of this paradox can be the reality that many of these improved patients will eventually continue to relapse and deteriorate.

Addictions-focused psychotherapists that practice with "specialty" patient populations involving attorneys and judges, physicians, pharmacists, dentists, nurses, psychologists or other behavioral health providers, corporate executives, airline pilots, airline or railroad personnel, teachers, college or university faculty, and other professional addictive disordered patient subpopulations experience the various concrete and consistent realities associated with their personal experiences of constructive and successful or "curative" psychotherapy and counseling outcomes on a consistent daily practice basis. Indeed, it is very reasonable to anticipate high (85–90%) successful therapy related outcomes specific to these particular patient populations. However, it is also very important to point out within the context of treatment outcome effectiveness related to professional patient populations as a group, these patients are routinely required by their professional organizations and various local, state, and national regulatory agencies to become actively involved in very comprehensive, highly monitored, structured and very expensive recovery care regimens that often encompasses 3–5 years of mandated, consistent highly structured ongoing therapy and multifaceted care.

Clinicians who work in residential, intensive out-patient, extended care, and DUI/DUID addictions treatment program settings also consistently experience many of the realities associated with constructive change related to addictions-focused therapy work, education and treatment. Most addictive disordered persons who complete a 28 day or 90 day residential treatment program evince very significant global change over the course of their treatment experiences. Physical appearance and medically induced constructive change (i.e., blood pressure, pulse, cholesterol levels, blood studies, etc.) psychological test results, interpersonal behaviors, family relationships, attitudes, diverse behaviors, and patterns of thinking and emoting may change rather dramatically within the context of 28–90 days; sometimes, these constructive benefits of psychotherapy and treatment can be quite apparent in only a few days!

Psychotherapists and counselors who are also "recovering" persons providing counseling and therapy services in any addictions or behavioral health setting have their personal recovery, treatment and therapy experiences as an internal well-spring and internal frame of reference pertaining to the many realties of change and recovery. Recovering addictions therapists may also experience personal and patient recovery related transference and countertransference/transference issues within the context of their psychotherapy relationships with addictive-disordered persons (Forrest, 1997–2019) in any treatment setting. As a result of these dynamics, recovering addictions-focused therapists and counselors can potentially use their personal recovery journey process as a therapeutically useful tool for continued self-healing and change as well as a potentially very useful therapeutic vehicle for facilitating patient growth and change within the context of their psychotherapy work with patients.

In this context, non-recovering addictions psychotherapists and counselors also frequently experience a myriad of therapy relationship dynamics related to the matter of lacking a personal history of substance abuse or addiction. Although this facet of the addictions treatment industry has evolved and changed radically over the past twenty years, a significant number of additive-disordered patients continue to prefer working in therapy with therapists who are themselves "recovering" addicts. Treatment programs no longer require or principally select clinical and other program staff according to this singular therapist or staff characteristic. Many non-recovering addictions counselors and therapists appear to be more open to the use of multiple integrative treatment strategies in their psychotherapy relationships with patients. Younger, well trained but relatively inexperienced addictions therapists can (1) bring personal energy, patient-investment, optimism, new and diverse clinical skills, and the openness and expectations that synergize patient involvement and motivation for recovery and change that result in changes that reinforce both patient and therapist commitment to, (2) the real healing and recovery process that can and does take place through the medium of efficacious ongoing psychotherapy and counseling relationships as well as the integrative care process.

EXPECTATION, PERSUASION, HEALING AND RECOVERY

Several decades ago, Jerome D. Frank's original text on persuasion and healing (Frank, 1965; Frank and Frank, 1991) examined the profound impact that physician persuasion, expectations, and other behaviors can play in the process of patient healing. This seminal publication continues to impact the general behavioral health, psychotherapy and helping professions. The therapeutic expectations of integrative addictions-focused psychotherapists and clinicians can impact patients in many constructive as well as potentially destructive ways. Effective addictions-focused therapists consistently and persistently expect their patients to recover and improve. They are also consistently committed to the process of therapeutically motivating

(Laska, Gurman and Wampold, 2014; Miller and Rollnick, 2013; and Philips and Wennberg, 2014), their patients to change, and they manifest the necessary therapeutic skills, training and acumen that includes a broad repertoire of recovery fostering techniques and skills. Persuasion, in one form or another, remains an important and relevant dimension of the psychotherapy healing process (Frank and Frank, 1991).

Therapists are role models for patients within the context of the therapeutic relationship as well as the life process. Efficacious psychotherapy relationships with addictive disordered persons entail active therapist attempts to teach and educate, expect, persuade, motivate, and experientially model a multiplicity of behaviors, self-perceptions, thoughts, beliefs, feelings, expectations, values, social skills and life-skills that foster the process of constructive patient change, growth, healing and recovery.

Addictive disordered patients and addictions-focused psychotherapists sometimes initially experience a sense of overwhelming apprehension associated with the multitude of patient problems and morass of difficulties they are facing as the therapeutic process begins to unfold. Importantly, even the most hopeless and severely conflicted patients can sometimes learn to begin the healing process via an hour by hour, day by day, one conflict issue at a time therapeutic approach. Experienced therapists tend to have developed a number of clinical practice based survival skills which enhance their personal therapeutic effectiveness, persistence, motivation, and patient healing expectations while working with exceedingly difficult addictive-disordered persons manifesting clinical histories involving very limited or unsuccessful treatment episodes, and who have perhaps experienced as many as 20–50 or more treatment episodes. Therapist self-care remains a particularly crucial ingredient in long-term successful psychotherapy work involving severely disturbed clinical populations including patients manifesting addictive brain disease.

In concert with this data, information and the precepts delineated within the context of this chapter focusing on psychotherapy relationships that facilitate constructive behavioral change, growth, healing and recovery involving addictive disordered patients, the author would especially encourage practicing psychotherapists, counselors, residential program directors, clinical directors, and other key behavioral health professionals involved in integrative addictions-focused treatment settings to collect ongoing program or provider outcome efficacy assessment data. In most cases, this information should be made available to program staff, persons considering entering psychotherapy or residential, IOP, extended care, or other forms of addictions-focused and behavioral health care modalities. This clinical data base does not necessarily need to involve highly sophisticated research designs or models, but can provide realistic feedback and a realistic care expectancy information framework for therapists, patients and their families and program staff relative to many practical treatment related matters.

Integrative addictions-focused behavioral health programs and providers have historically tended to resist collecting and making clinical outcome data available to perspective patients, former patients, the general public and even clinical staff members. Developing a relatively simple ongoing outcome treatment data collection and outcome assessment model does involve additional therapist and program staff time, expense, and an inherit set of potential risk factors. Nonetheless, addiction-focused psychotherapists and counselors in private practices settings as well as clinical directors, and supervisors providing services in small or large residential addictions programs, including professionals in diverse behavioral health care settings, can develop any number of brief Likert-scale based pre-post measures of patient status, change dimensions, and other treatment process-outcome specific measures. Follow-up phone calls or questionaries at 3, 6, and 12–18 months intervals may also be beneficial, and random or limited selection of patients for inclusion in the outcome data collection process further simplify this task.

Addiction-focused psychotherapists, counselors and treatment providers need to be very aware and cognizant of the efficacy, qualitative and evidence-based healing dimensions of their work. Therapists also need to disclose (Forrest, 2012) the various realities associated with these matters to their patients, potential patients and persons seeking information pertaining to addictions treatment and recovery. Patients need to be informed about the various realities surrounding psychotherapy, addictions care, treatment efficacy and relapse risk when they initiate care, and these issues often need to be re-visited by the therapist and patient throughout the therapy process.

Psychotherapists, addictions treatment programs, and recovery environments can produce self-enhancing, patient enhancing, program enhancing as well as over-all healing and enhanced treatment outcomes vis a vis the consistent use of psychotherapy, various treatment modalities, recovery and healing information! In this regard, it is imperative that addictions-focused therapists and clinicians be knowledgeable about the efficacy and healing dimensions of psychotherapy in general, and generally cognizant and knowledgeable about the efficacy and outcomes of their personal psychotherapy and counseling relationships with patients. These factors can provide further therapist and patient self-motivation for individual growth and change, enhance the psychotherapy contextual capacity for change, and foster a relational learning and healing milieu which may additionally generalize to include colleagues and the treatment program staff. These transactions often prove energizing for all parties and they both reinforce and synergize healing potential.

Integrative addictions-focused psychotherapists assume the primary responsibility for initiating and consistently utilizing therapeutically enhancing practice information and an effective therapist skill set within the context of their evolving therapy and counseling relationships.

SUMMARY

Psychotherapy relationships involving a diversity of patient sub-populations, including addictive-disordered persons, consistently result in significant constructive change and growth for many persons who engage in therapy. Psychotherapy and counseling evidence-based outcome studies have long reported that 65–70 percent of persons who received psychotherapy and counseling services benefit significantly from their therapy experiences (Bergin and Garfield, 1971; Cook et al., 2015; Truax and Carkhuff, 1967; Norcross, 2002, 2010; Norcross et al., 2011).

Many practicing integrative addictions-focused psychotherapists, clinicians and treatment providers continue to have little or very limited knowledge pertaining to the general evidence-based psychotherapy outcome literature and research as well as evidence-based addictions focused alliance therapy counseling and psychotherapy outcome data. Addictions-focused therapists need to be generally knowledgeable about treatment programs, therapy modalities, duration of care, and other efficacy and outcome related variables that pertain to the repertoire of possible treatments and care modalities related to the various addictive disorders.

Information, data, and resources related to the facets of addictions-focused psychotherapy and treatment are included in this chapter. As noted in the chapter, a multiplicity of different psychotherapy approaches, treatments, and interventions can facilitate constructive therapy-related outcomes. The psychotherapy relationship remains a principal vehicle for constructive change within the various forms and environments in which addictions treatment and recovery occur. Patient change always takes place as a function of multiple and interactive patient, therapist, relationship, situational and environmental factors. As explained throughout this text, certain identifiable and consistent therapist qualities or ingredients constitute the core conditions related to the constructive behavioral change and growth that usually takes place within the context of efficacious psychotherapy relationships. However, as noted earlier in this chapter, psychotherapy and counseling relationships also can result in "for better or worse" outcomes. Many of the divergent factors related to these realities and the evolution of addictions therapy and care are also addressed in this chapter.

The healing impact of psychotherapy and other treatments for the addictive disorders can be associated with factors such as therapist characteristics, patient addictive disorder specific factors, including motivation for change and attachment dynamics as well as related factors such as duration of treatment, economic factors, vocational and occupational status, multicultural and ethnic issues, religious affiliation, gender issues, and random chance. As American and Western culture become progressively plagued with the ever-growing biopsychosocial maladies associated with the addictive disorders, a variety of integrative addictive-disorder specific therapy strategies, treatments, interventions, and healing or recovery driven models have been developed to help these patients.

In addition to the evolving evidence based approaches to addictions-focused psychotherapy and counseling practice as well as every other variety of modern health care therapy, health providers continue to rely upon the alliance and therapeutic relationship as essential vehicles for change; the healing nature of relational non-possessive warmth, empathy, genuineness, concreteness, expectation, persuasion, love, motivation, self-disclosure, attachment, and every other conceivable facet of the healing process takes place within the basic context of the therapeutic alliance relationship. This is the essence of all effective psychotherapy and counseling relationships.

The potential implications for addictions therapists and counselors pertaining to the psychotherapy relationship and patient healing that were touched upon in this chapter are basic and limited, but paradoxically limitless when viewed within the context of 100 or 10,000 psychotherapy relationships. As noted earlier, therapists need to periodically remind themselves that every psychotherapy session with every patient represents a potential therapeutic experience which can foster constructive patient change and growth, and from time to time may even save or radically improve a human life—or with time, perhaps one hundred or even hundreds of lives!

Very early in my professional career as a clinical psychologist, I developed an ongoing friendship and collegial relationship with a Catholic priest by the name of Father Joseph C. Martin. Father Martin always had a profoundly therapeutic impact on the audiences that he lectured to, and his lectures and presentations were always about alcoholism, addictions and recovery—filled with recovery stories—and healing stories.

Father Martin eventually committed himself to the process of building a residential chemical dependency treatment center, and though many years of personal recovery, incredibly hard work, and no doubt "divine intervention" mixed with the support, dedication and love of many others as well as millions of donated and borrowed dollars, Father Martin's Ashley residential treatment program became a reality. Twenty-five years later and thousands of patients later, from throughout the United States and the world, Father Martin's Ashley recovery center continues to provide healing and recovery services for addicted persons. And, there are literally hundreds of other addictions specific and behavioral treatment centers, programs, and stories like this throughout the United States.

Integrative addictions-focused psychotherapists and counselors need to remain cognizant and aware of the ever present powerful and potentially life changing constructive impact their therapeutic relationships and therapeutic alliances can effect in their patients. Therapist growth, constructive change, and self-healing can also be a byproduct of this process.

Chapter 3

THE THERAPEUTIC ALLIANCE

INTRODUCTION

The history, evolution, definitional and relational parameters of the therapeutic alliance are examined in this chapter. Recent research evidence pertaining to the alliance and psychotherapy outcome is also discussed in the chapter. Alliance related research and clinical evidence pertaining to diverse therapeutic approaches is also examined in the chapter with related therapeutic practice guidelines. The therapeutic alliance is a potentially therapeutic ingredient effecting constructive change in all psychotherapy relationships.

Psychotherapy relationships have remained a focal construct of discussion and research in the counseling and psychotherapy literature for over one-hundred years, and therapist-patient relationship behaviors and dynamics have always been viewed by most practicing therapists as essential therapeutic ingredients impacting the course and outcomes of therapy.

Alliance is a relatively new concept in the substance abuse and integrative addictive disorders focused psychotherapy literature, and encompasses terms such as "working alliance," "helping alliance," "working and productive alliance," "therapeutic alliance," "caring alliance," "bond," and simply "alliance" (Forrest, 1984–2017; Horvath et al., 2011).

The concept of Therapeutic Alliance was used in the title of this text due to the widespread and generalized use and recognition of this construct in the professional psychotherapy literature over the past sixty years. This author (Forrest, 2019) has historically used the "working and productive therapeutic alliance" concept pertaining to addictions-focused specific psychotherapy relationships. In this context, the working and productive therapeutic alliance was consciously used in reference to the level of effort, work and commitment that therapists and patients *both* invest in efficacious intensive psychotherapy relationships that result in successful therapeutic outcomes. Working and productive therapeutic alliances "work" in the sense of producing constructive and measurable patient change.

The author (Forrest, 1984-2019) has also consistently reported that working and productive therapeutic alliances involving patients manifesting addictive brain disease are frequently precarious, and alliance conflicts and ruptures frequently occur within the context of relationships involving this patient population. Conflicts and ruptures can occur at any juncture in the process of integrative addictions-focused psychotherapy work. This particular dynamic of addictions-focused psychotherapy work poses an ever-present set of therapeutic relationship and alliance related vulnerabilities pertaining to therapists and patients. In sum, a working and productive therapeutic alliance involving addictive-disordered persons is never an "absolute given" or "guarantee" for successful therapeutic outcomes. This is an arena in which a repertoire of patient behaviors as well as therapist behaviors unendingly impact the ongoing therapeutic process and ultimate psychotherapy outcome!

Readers will appreciate the scope and diversity of clinical research evidence-based alliance data and practice-based information that is reviewed in this chapter. The evolving professional interest and investigative alliance path was initiated by a number of psychotherapy meta-analysis studies that began in the 1960's (Truax and Carkhuff, 1967); and well into the mid-1970s (Horvath et al., 2011). Horvath et al., (2011) report that a recent (2009) electronic database search produced over 7,000 items including terminology references pertaining to words including alliance and therapeutic alliance. Psychotherapy practice implications related to this body of data and information are also included in this chapter and throughout the entire book.

Much of the alliance-based psychotherapy literature has remained focused upon various facets of the individual psychotherapy relationship (Ulvenes et al., 2012; Bedics et al., 2015; Fisher et al., 2016). This information and data are presented in the chapter as well as recent alliance literature and research evidence-based findings pertaining to other therapeutic treatment modalities. Alliance information data and research findings involving family therapy, couples or conjoint marital therapy, and group work are also addressed in this chapter. Several recent studies involving different addictive-disordered patient populations and the working alliance are also included in the chapter (Auerbach et al., 2008; Barber et al., 2000; Miller and Rollnick, 2002).

In sum, the broad content and scope of Chapter 3 will greatly enhance addictions-focused psychotherapists, counselors, and other behavioral health treatment providers in-depth understanding and awareness of the various healing and curative dynamics that are related to the therapeutic alliance. As Ulvenes et al. (2012) and others point out, the alliance appears to be a very important factor that impacts the process and outcome of psychotherapy independent of therapy model, orientation or modality. Hopefully, the information and data examined in this chapter will also enhance therapist alliance-related sensitivity, skill level, and practice acumen strategies for all therapist populations involved in addictions-focused psychotherapy work as well as general patient populations.

This chapter will also serve as a prelude to the elucidation and discussion of the essential therapist alliance characteristics and ingredients in consistently efficacious psychotherapy relationships. These therapist alliance conditions are explored in depth in Chapters 4 and 5.

HISTORY AND EVOLUTION OF THE ALLIANCE IN PSYCHOTHERAPY

Evolving psychotherapy relationship literature including Freud's early discussions and publications (1912-1913, 1958) pertaining to transference dynamics in psychoanalysis may be conceptually viewed as the origin of the alliance construct used in contemporary psychotherapy (Horvath et al., 2011). Prior to the early 1940s, the clinical practice-based therapist-patient relationship dynamics associated with literature and research had been aimed at "scientifically" understanding and identifying if, how, and why psychotherapy "works" as well as elucidating the central ingredients or causative factors resulting in effective psychotherapy relationships. The early publications of Carl R. Rogers (1942, 1951, 1957) synergized the clinical and evidence-based psychotherapy process and outcome studies. Roger's publications examined and elucidated various aspects of the development of both the counselling and psychotherapy relationship. Rogers (1951, 1957) also developed the client-centered therapy approach, and even described the "necessary and sufficient conditions" for constructive therapeutic change. Rogers (1957) indicated that the "necessary and sufficient conditions" for therapeutic change included (1) the client being in a "state of incongruence," (2) the client and therapist being in "psychological contact," and (3) "the therapist being congruent or integrated in the relationship," (4) experiencing "positive regard for the client," and (5) maintaining "an empathic understanding of the clients' internal frame of reference" (p. 96). However, as noted earlier, Freud's early discussions and publications (1912, 1913, 1958) pertaining to patient-analyst transference dynamics in psychoanalysis may be conceptually viewed as the origin of the alliance construct in contemporary psychotherapy. Horvath et al. (2011) point out that Freud recognized patient transference reactions resulted in premature therapy terminations or "fleeing from therapy," as well as patient transference reactions involving the patients' capacity to resist in the therapeutic process, dealing with disturbing therapeutic issues, and collaborating with the analyst to, in effect, produce a successful psychoanalytic outcome. These authors (Horvath et al., 2011) also indicate that Freud explained the transference contradiction by proposing the "presence of a positive or unobjectionable transference which binds the client to the person of the therapist and assists the patient to treatment despite the increased levels of anxieties" (p. 96).

The Freudian transference concept is generally referred to as "displaceable energies" (Levy and Scala, 2012), as the emotions and feelings which evolved in the analytic relationship and were related to the analyst who played no role in the origin of these feelings and cognitions. Freud and Breuer (1988) and Freud (1895) also described how patients transfer unconscious feelings and beliefs involving various persons from their pasts to their doctor (or therapist). These distorted transference dynamics were resolved or no longer occurred with a successful psychoanalysis. Resolution of the transference neurosis was believed to be tantamount to the successful psychoanalytic treatment of neurosis. As Gelso and Bhatia (2012) suggest, it has "always seemed to us that transference phenomena occur in virtually all close relationships." This author (Forrest, 1984, 1985, 2002) fully concurs with this positon, and this position is certainly consistent with the various other facets of Freudian psychoanalysis that pertain to the profound importance and relevance of the therapeutic alliance and transference dynamics in contemporary psychotherapy relationships.

Zetzel (1956) first used the alliance construct in contemporary psychotherapy literature. p. 10. Several other authors (Bordin, 1975, 1979, 1989, 1994; Greenson, 1967; Luborsky, 1976; Sterba, 1934) also contributed to the early psychotherapy and dynamically-oriented therapy alliance literature.

The author's (Forrest, 1975, 1985) early texts dealing with the psychotherapy of alcoholism and addictive disorders consistently emphasized and explored the medium of the psychotherapy relationship as a (1) primary vehicle for constructive therapeutic change, (2) methodology for exploring and resolving therapist-patient relationship dynamics pertaining to premature treatment terminations, (3) reducing patient flight from therapy, as well as anxiety and trauma related to narcissistic injury issues, and (4) generally enhancing "working and productive therapeutic alliance" dynamics specific to this patient population. Addictions psychotherapy specific definitions and information related to these alliance issues are also discussed in later chapters of this book.

Bordin's (1979), as well as Freud's (Fried/Ander et al., 2011; Pinsof and Catherall, 1986) use of the pan theoretical working alliance concept evolved from the earlier work of Greenson (1965) involving a collaborative therapist-patient therapeutic effort to effect constructive patient change and growth.

Development of the working alliance (Horvath et al., 2011) was facilitated by three processes: "(1) agreements on the therapeutic goals, (2) consensus on the tasks that make up therapy, and (3) a bond between the client and therapist" (p. 10). The working alliance also evolves and changes throughout the course of therapy, and is subject to various client-therapist stresses that take place during therapy. Early stage therapy goal consensus and agreement between the client and therapist is crucial to the process of alliance development as well as the therapeutic relationship bond.

More recent conceptualizations of the alliance concept also focus upon the conscious aspects of the therapist-patient therapy relationship (Bordin, 1994; Hatcher and Barends, 2006; Horvath et al., 2011; Ulvenes et al., 2012) rather than "unconscious" dynamics. Recent research and clinical alliance related literature and alliance definitions also focus on the collaborative therapist-patient tasks and the "working" dynamics that impact the therapeutic relationship as well as the process and outcome of therapy. As noted by Ulvenes et al. (2012) and Norcross (2011), recent research and clinical interest in the alliance is probably related to the pan-theoretical nature of this construct and its "well-documented and robust relationship with the outcome of psychotherapy." The alliance clearly represents a manifestation of the mutually active therapist-patient investment and collaborative effort to help facilitate constructive patient change in psychotherapy.

The psychotherapy literature and research involves numerous studies and publications which employ a diversity of definitions, models and instruments utilizing different assessment measures and conceptualizations of the alliance construct (Forrest, 2016). It is important that therapists and counselors realize these divergent realities as they attempt to incorporate alliance-related information and evidence-based treatment interventions into their clinical practice work with all patient populations. Alliance measures de facto define what the researcher means by the term "alliance" in the absence of a basic shared definition of the psychotherapy construct (Horvath et al., 2011).

There are also many similarities and common denominators associated with the meaning and interpretation of the alliance construct, but there are significant differences among contemporary and historic clinicians as well as research findings pertaining to these matters (Gaston et al., 1995; Hatcher and Barends, 2006; Horvath et al., 2011; Ulvenes et al., 2012). Finally, clinicians need to realize that the definitional parameters of alliance are additionally or perhaps ultimately defined by a diversity of psychometric tools and instruments which have been developed to assess the alliance construct. Finally, alliance research-based assessment results are always interpreted by the clinicians and researchers who conduct psychotherapy alliance investigations. Practicing clinicians subsequently must personally interpret these factors within the scope of their clinical practice experiences.

In spite of this mosaic of limitations and dynamics related to the history, research-evidence, and practice of alliance-focused psychotherapy, Ulvenes et al. (2012) report that the most recent meta-analysis on the working alliance in individual psychotherapy identified nearly 200 independent studies that investigated the relationship between alliance and outcome, supporting its well-documented and robust relationship with the outcome of psychotherapy.

Practicing addictions psychotherapists and graduate level academic training programs need to be very cognizant of this line of practice-related science and investigation, and initiate studies and training efforts pertaining to a diversity of alliance related issues associated with addictions-focused specific psychotherapy, training, treatment and clinical interventions.

As noted by Farber and Doolin (2011), Rogers' impact on the evolution of psychotherapy practice during the late 1950s through the early 1970s effected the supposition and belief that the therapeutic relationship per se was the "critical factor in determining therapeutic success." During the mid-60s to mid-70', Truax and Carkhuff (1967) conducted extensive clinical research and published a wealth of articles and books pertaining to the assessment and impact of Roger's "core conditions" involved in the process and outcome of psychotherapy. Truax (1966, 1971) and others (Truax and Carkhuff, 1967; Truax and Lister, 1971; Truax and Wargo, 1966; Truax and Mitchell, 1971) also played a major role in the process of operationally re-defining Roger's original "necessary and sufficient conditions" model for constructive therapeutic change into three essential psychotherapy relationship constructs: (1) non-possessive warmth (positive regard), (2) empathy, and (3) genuineness. Truax and Carkhuff (1967) also indicted that concreteness was an additional ingredient in effective psychotherapy. These authors subsequently developed psychometric assessment instruments to assess a wide repertoire of psychotherapy relationship behaviors and process-outcome variables.

Based upon an extensive review of the psychotherapy outcome research evidence during this time frame, Meltzoff and Kornreich (1970) concluded: "Far more often than not, psychotherapy of a wide variety of types and with a board range of disorders has been demonstrated under controlled conditions to be accompanied by positive changes in adjustment that significantly exceed those that can be accounted for by the passage of time alone" (p. 73).

The evolution of psychotherapy relationship research and clinical literature between 1980 and today continues to examine a multiplicity of facets associated with the Rogerian constructs of non-possessive warmth, empathy and genuineness as well as many other therapeutic relationship dynamics (Bratter and Forrest, 1985; Forrest, 1984-2019; Gelso and Hayes, 1998; Norcross, 2002, 2010; Patterson, 1984; Strupp, 1973; Ulvenes et al., 2012).

As noted earlier in this chapter, Freudian psychoanalysis initiated the focus upon therapist-patient relationship dynamics that interactively impact the process and outcome of psychoanalysis. Virtually all contemporary clinicians and counselors utilizing a diversity of treatment models, modalities, and practicing in many different therapy settings involving a diversity of patient populations recognize the paramount role of the therapeutic alliance in their professional work. The earliest conceptualizations of the therapeutic alliance share this Freudian background.

ALLIANCE DEFINITIONS

As noted earlier, Zetzel (1956) was an early originator of the alliance concept, and generally employed this construct in reference to the conscious aspects of psychotherapy relationships between therapists and patients which facilitate patient relational attachment to the person of the therapist resulting in a therapeutic relationship which persists and remains sustainable in spite of the various anxieties and stresses associated with the therapeutic process. Furthermore, this alliance relationship between the therapist and patient plays a central role in the process of effecting constructive patient change in psychotherapy. In short, the working alliance fosters successful therapy outcomes.

Luborsky (1976) developed a two-stage alliance concept indicating that the initial stage of this model involves (1) developing the patient's belief that the therapist is a "potent source of help" or instrument for constructive change, and (2) therapist development of a therapy relationship characterized by warmth, support and caring. These dimensions of the alliance create a "secure holding relationship within which the work of therapy can begin" (Horvath et al., 2011).

Luborsky's second stage, or "type two" alliance involved the "client's" investment and faith in the therapeutic process itself, a commitment to the core concepts undergirding the therapy process as well as a willing investment of her or himself to share the ownership for the therapy process."

Bordin's (1979) pan-theoretical "working alliance" concept departed from the psychodynamic precepts underlying the alliance construct that was developed earlier by Greenson (1965). The Bordin alliance construct definition incorporated a number of very contemporary and widely used psychotherapy practice strategies: (1) establishing a collaborative therapeutic relationship or stance, i.e., the alliance, between the therapist and patient, and (2) alliance development is facilitated by three additional core processes: "agreements on the therapeutic goals, consensus on the tasks that make up therapy, and a bond between the client and therapist" (Horvath et al.

2011, p. 10). These authors also note that Bordin indicated different therapeutic models or approaches would emphasize or stress the importance different components of the therapeutic alliance.

Horvath et al. (2011) also indicate that Bordin later (1994) modified his concept of the "working alliance" indicating that the "alliance was centrally the achievement of a collaborative stance in therapy." Bordin (1994) also characterized the working alliance "as an ever changing or dynamic relationship" that evolves throughout the psychotherapeutic process. The "working alliance" is not static by nature and the therapist plays a significant role in the therapeutic process of managing and repairing alliance stressors or potential ruptures during the course of therapy. Therapist and patient alliance collaboration aimed at the resolution of such stressors may contribute significantly to patient growth and change via the therapeutic process.

Conscious collaborative consensus and "working together" dynamics of the alliance and the more global psychotherapeutic relationship encompass the core contemporary definitional parameters of the alliance construct. Indeed, as Horvath et al. noted (2011), the "alliance represents an emergent quality of partnership and mutual collaboration between therapist and client." The psychotherapy relationship as well as the specific therapist-patient alliance within the context of the therapeutic process are no longer perceived as being solely therapist driven "treatments" or essentially therapist determined human processes. A myriad of patient and therapist factors clearly impact and effect every aspect of the alliance as well as the process and outcome of the psychotherapy relationship.

It should be noted that very recent alliance investigations and meta-analysis alliance-therapeutic outcome studies involving diverse patient populations as well as many therapeutic models consistently utilize or report that the Bordin definitional model had been employed in most of these publications (Fisher et al., 2016; Friedlander et al., 2011; Horvath et al., 2011; Safran et al., 2011; Shirk et al., 2011; Tryon and Winograd, 2011; Ulvenes et al., 2012).

The author's descriptions and definitional parameters of the alliance construct within the context of integrative addictions-focused psychotherapy work (Forrest, 1984-2019) incorporate the essential Bordin (1975, 1979, 1985, 1994) definition emphasizing (1) the ongoing collaborative nature of the therapist-patient alliance, (2) shared therapist-patient therapeutic goal setting, including goals and tasks such as drug abstinence, patient honesty, openness, and self-disclosure in therapy, and (3) patient-therapist commitment to the ongoing work of the psychotherapy process (Forrest, 1997), related to therapist and patient collaboration and commitment to resolve a diversity of potential stressors and alliance rupture facilitating behaviors including such events such as relapse, hospitalization, severe marital dysfunction, health issues, suicide attempts, and other destructive or extreme alliance disruptive behaviors can be essential ingredients for successful therapy outcomes and recovery. Thus, the author has historically emphasized the importance of the essential therapist and patient ingredients (Forrest, 1978-2019) that contribute to the establishment and maintenance of "working and productive" therapeutic alliances in addictions-focused psychotherapy while also emphasizing the unendingly fragile nature of the alliance in addictions-focused therapy. Working and productive therapeutic alliances involving months or years of recovery, and global adaptive adjustment change can be and is infrequently terminated via patient relapses that may result in incarceration, death or other extreme adverse outcomes. Financial problems, job loss, and loss of health insurance, and a myriad of other factors can also be external realities that adversely impact the alliance or result in alliance ruptures and therapy terminations in integrative addictions-focused psychotherapy and counseling work.

As noted earlier, addiction-focused therapists conceptualize the working and productive therapeutic alliance as encompassing the therapist's (and patient's) "basic belief and awareness that (1) addictive disordered persons can benefit from psychotherapy, (2) psychotherapists and patients expect (and are committed to the process) to terminate the use of addictive substances and modify or extinguish the behavioral repertoire which maintains and supports the addiction process, and (3) recognize that recovering patients/persons grow and change in a myriad of ways which are often tangential to the addiction process" (Forrest, 1985, p. 320). Furthermore, working and productive therapeutic alliances involving patients manifesting addictive brain disease evolve as a process; "They do not simply occur as a function of several hours of therapist-patient contact—the therapist and patient need to be equally committed to the process of creating a therapy relationship (alliance) that becomes a potent and meaningful vehicle for change—"mutual trust, respect, concern and goals are essential ingredients of the therapeutic alliance" (Forrest, 1984, 1997, 2019).

This author Forrest (2019) also indicates that the "basic humanness" and "relatedness" of the therapeutic alliance can be curative. Furthermore, the author indicates that the "cement of the productive and working therapeutic alliance involves the patients' ability to remain committed to the psychotherapeutic process—the therapeutic alliance is based upon the therapist's fundamental comfortableness with addictive-disordered persons—the simple capacity to like addicted persons, and the therapeutic alliance is also nurtured and strengthened in relation to the therapist's consistent communication of respect and dignity for the patient" (pp. 55–57). The therapeutic alliance is constructed via the development of mutual trust, respect, concern, work, and commitment to the evolving recovery goals, tasks and bond that are central to the therapeutic process.

Therapist "core" conditions or central ingredients in the development and maintenance of the working and productive therapeutic alliance with addictive disordered patients are defined and delineated in-depth in Chapter 4. These essential therapist qualities or ingredients are central to the alliance and efficacious therapeutic outcomes with diverse patient populations as well as utilizing diverse treatment intervention modalities.

ALLIANCE, PSYCHOTHERAPY IMPACT, AND EFFICACY

As discussed earlier in this chapter and briefly in Chapters 1 and 2, psychotherapy outcome and efficacy studies have historically reported that psychotherapeutic treatment results in significant positive patient change and successful therapeutic outcomes in approximately 70 percent of cases (Eysenck, 1967; Truax and Carkhuff, 1967).

Very recent alliance focused psychotherapy evidence-based or efficacy related meta-analysis studies and reviews (Fisher et al., 2016; Horvath et al., 2011; and Wiprovnick, Kuerbis and Morgenstern, 2015) generally conclude that "diverse therapist's provided similar beneficial effects to psychotherapy clients." These authors also report that "perhaps the most potent force responsible for the sustained growth of interest in the alliance has been the consistent finding of a moderate but robust relationship between the alliance and treatment outcome across a board spectrum of treatments in a variety of client/problem contexts" (Horvath et al., 2011, pp. 9–10). Ulvenes et al. (2012) indicate that the most recent meta-analysis study on the "working alliance" in individual psychotherapy (Horvath et al., 2011) involved nearly 200 independent investigations involving the alliance-therapy outcome relationship. These authors (Ulvenes et al., 2012) reported an "aggregate correlation between alliance and outcome of .275—which is a moderate to large effect." They also note the "importance of the alliance as a therapeutic factor," but also point out that a number of nonspecific psychotherapy factors also impact the alliance outcome relationship. The alliance outcome relationship may be impacted by (1) "the therapist's ability to form the alliance," (2) patient characteristics that are facilitative of forming a relationship (i.e., patient social skills, attachment style), (3) an appropriate match of therapist and patient characteristics, or (4) earlier symptom change (i.e. "before the alliance was measured" (Ulvenes et al., 2012, p. 291).

Baldwin, Wampold and Imel (2007) indicate that therapists do vary in their capabilities to form alliances with their patients, and also therapists who establish strong patient alliances produce better psychotherapy outcomes than therapists who establish weaker alliances with their patients. These authors further indicate that the patient's "contribution to the alliance did not affect the outcome of therapy." It should be noted that the therapist's alliance development skills and ability has been consistently found to be related to positive therapy outcomes in a variety of care settings (Zuroff et al., 2010; Bedics et al., 2015). The Horvath et al. (2011) alliance literature review included foreign studies (Italian, German, French, and English), various alliance measures and outcome measures, types of treatments, and publication sources. These alliance based investigations and publication's did include substance abuse patient populations and treatment.

Horvath et al. (2011) summarized the alliance-therapy outcome evidence data as follow: "this result strongly supports the claim that impact of the alliance on therapy outcome is ubiquitous irrespective of how the alliance is measured, from whose perspective it is evaluated, when it is assessed, the way outcome is evaluated, and the type of therapy involved. The quality of the alliance matters" (p. 13). Ulvenes et al. (2012) concurs with this conclusion, noting "despite the ambiguities in the literature, it appears that the therapist is critical to making the alliance therapeutic, and thus attention must be paid to what the therapist does to form an alliance that is therapeutic" (p. 292).

Additional research data (Ackerman and Hilsenroth, 2003; Hilsenroth and Cromer, 2007) pertaining to therapist alliance development strategies and techniques found that certain behaviors and characteristics facilitate the alliance development process. These therapist alliance development characteristics and behaviors include support, reflection, activity or active involvement, accurate interpretations, affirmation, understanding and attending to the patients' personal experiences, encouraging emotional expression, and in-depth exploration of therapeutic material. Hilsenroth and Cromer (2007) report similar early stage alliance development findings. These authors also note that "it is never too early for clinicians to attempt to adopt these attitudes and interventions" (p. 210).

Within the context of a recent investigation involving individual therapy and therapist actions, bond (alliance), and outcome (Ulvenes et al., 2012; Wiprovnick, Kuerbis and Morgenstern, 2015), these authors astutely comment on the general alliance research evidence presented thus far in this chapter as follows: "the relationship between therapist actions, the alliance, and outcome are unfortunately not straightforward. It may be problematic to assume that therapist characteristics and actions that are associated with the alliance are also important to therapeutic outcome based on the fact that the alliance is related to outcome. It could be that some therapist characteristics and actions might predict the alliance but not predict outcome—that is, the characteristics and actions might predict a part of the alliance that is not related to outcome" (p. 292). These authors also note that there is a "lack of research that has examined therapist actions, alliance, and outcome simultaneously in therapy."

The Ulvenes et al. (2012) study involved cognitive therapy and brief dynamic therapy involving DSM-IV-R cluster C personality disordered patients. The patient sample in this study did not include current substance abuse or eating disordered persons. These investigators found that the "relationship among therapist actions, bond (alliance) and outcomes in psychotherapy differ depending on the therapeutic approach. Therapist avoidance of affect was found to be positively related to formation of the bond (alliance), as rated by the patients in both short-term dynamic psychotherapy and cognitive therapy" (p. 296). The patients in this investigation "found the focus on affect to be problematic in terms of feeling bonded to their therapist; however, the avoidance of affect (or alternately, the focus on affect) functioned very differently in the two treatments. In STDP, although a focus on affect detracted from the bond, this focus resulted in a reduction of symptoms, and the part of the bond not related to a focus on affect was predictive of outcome. However, in CT, the portion of the bond not related to a focus on affect was unrelated to outcome, and a therapist focus on affect was counterproductive" (p. 296).

These authors (Ulvenes et al., 2012) provide several other conclusions and findings associated with their recent alliance related investigation: (1) differences between STDP and CT were consistent with theoretical and empirical evidence, (2) the bond, "most likely the alliance more generally, may well function differently in different therapies," and with different patient populations, (3) the alliance as a "common factor may be misleading in the sense that although the importance of the alliance may be common, the manner in which it interacts with the specific treatment to achieve benefits may not be common," (4) for STDP therapy patients "the bond predicts outcome and affective work leads to positive outcomes," and (5) in the "context of the bond, avoiding affective material in CT led to better outcomes, which is the opposite of what was found in STDP" (pp. 296–298). Interestingly, in STDP therapy the "bond predicts outcome and the bond is also related to the therapist being distant or avoiding affect, but the therapist being distant and avoidant of affective material is not predictive of the outcome" (p. 296). In this context, the authors speculate that the therapist's avoidance of affect "may help the patient like the therapist or therapy better, but it does not help the patient get better." Paradoxically, this aspect of therapist alliance related behavior is "predictive of the bond and the bond is predictive" of therapeutic outcomes (pp. 296–298).

Thus, the role of the alliance or "bond" in therapy may ultimately depend upon the type of treatment modality and patient characteristics or sub-population—specific treatment and patient variables may interactively impact the outcome salience of the alliance in all therapies.

Horvath et al. (2011) summarize the findings of their alliance in individual psychotherapy investigation and provide therapeutic practices guidelines as follows: "The positive relation between quality of the alliance and diverse outcomes for many different types of psychological therapies is confirmed in this meta-analysis" (p. 15). These authors indicate that the "development and fostering of the alliance is not separate from the interventions therapists implement to help their clients, the distinguishing feature of the alliance is the focus on therapy as a collaborative enterprise, the development of a "good enough" alliance early in therapy is vital for therapy success, in the early phases of therapy, modulating the methods of therapy (tasks) to suit the specific client's needs, expectations and capacities is important in building the alliance, therapist and client perceptions of the alliance, particularly early in treatment, do not necessarily match the strength of the alliance, within or between sessions, often fluctuates in response to a variety of in-therapy factors, therapist non-defensive responses to client negativity or hostility are critical for maintaining a good alliance, and therapist contributions to the quality of the alliance are critical. Therapists who are good at building a strong alliance tend to have better alliances with most of their clients. The reverse is true, and this finding suggests that alliance development is a skill and/or capacity that therapists can and should be trained to develop" (p. 15).

ALLIANCE, PSYCHOTHERAPY MODELS, APPROACHES, AND DIVERSE PATIENT POPULATIONS

The alliance or therapeutic bond has been referred to as a "pervasive predictor of intervention response" by Wampold (2001), and early client perceptions of the alliance predict "retention and outcome in pharmacological and behavioral treatments" for substance abuse (Barber et al., 1999; Dundon et al., 2008; Fisher et al., 2016). These authors also note that research also "suggests an influence of early client rated alliance on nondrinking outcomes, such as improved psychiatric functioning." Meier, Barrowclough and Donmall (2005) indicate the therapeutic bond is a consistent predictor of client engagement and retention in substance abuse treatment. A strong early alliance may additionally provide a compensatory therapeutic effect or impact for client's manifesting low initial self-efficacy (Ilgen et al., 2006).

ALLIANCE IN CHILD AND ADOLESCENT PSYCHOTHERAPY

The therapeutic alliance construct has been associated with adolescent and child psychotherapy literature for some sixty-five years (Freud, 1946); however, alliance research dealing with these clinical populations remains quite limited relative to the adult alliance related to evidence-based clinical and research studies. According to Shirk, Karver and Brown (2011), Anna Freud (1946) observed that an "affectionate attachment" between the child and therapist is a prerequisite for all later work in child therapy (p. 17). These authors also note that A. Freud's (1946) position establishes "enduring differentiation of alliance components" between alliance (bond) and work, emotional and collaborative relationships, and indicates that the bond is a catalyst for facilitation on the work of therapy rather than being the essential curative factor in psychotherapy.

Play therapists (Axline, 1947; Shirk and Russell, 1996) have viewed the therapy relationship as an essential ingredient in affective psychotherapy, and have also emphasized the importance of the therapist's capacity to effect constructive change vis a vis the process of providing Roger's (1957) essential core conditions or "active ingredients" for therapeutic change (empathy, genuineness, and positive regard) within the context of therapist-child therapy relationships. Shirk, Karver, and Brown (2011) indicate that the "emotional bond," then appears to be a core component of alliance with children, and also note "this view has taken root in recent approaches to assessing the alliance in child and adolescent therapy—a central component of alliance, especially with older children and adolescents, consists of agreements regarding treatment goals and the methods for accomplishing them" (p. 17). The Shirk, Karver and Brown (2011) assessment of "alliance-outcome relationships" via their meta-analysis study involving 16 existing studies related to child and adolescent therapy resulted in the following findings: (1) "current meta-analysis of prospective studies of individual alliance-outcome associations yielded an effect that is quite comparable to results obtained in adult literature, (2) these results strengthen the claim that the alliance is an important predictor of treatment outcome in child and adolescent therapy, (3) a marginally stronger association between alliance and outcome for children than for adolescents, (4) the alliance is a robust predictor of outcomes with preadolescent children, (5) a trend for alliance-outcome associations appears to be stronger in behavioral than non-behavioral therapies, (6) there was some variability in alliance-outcome associations across types of treated problems, however only the difference between the eating disorder sample and both substance abuse and mixed problems samples proved to be reliable, (7) it was somewhat surprising to find such a small association between alliance and outcome with substance abusing youth, and finally, (8) it is not clear if this result reflects unique difficulties with alliance assessment with substance abusing youth, or an accurate estimate of the limited contribution of alliance to outcome with substance-abusing teens" (pp. 21–22).

These authors (Shirk, Karver, and Brown, 2011) also provide the following therapeutic practice alliance guidelines and general information pertaining to child and adolescent psychotherapy: (1) " alliance is an important predictor of youth therapy outcomes and may very well be an essential ingredient that makes diverse child and adolescent therapies work, (2) alliances with both youth and their parents are predictive of treatment outcomes—psychotherapists need to attend to the development of multiples alliances, not just to the alliance with the youth, (3) parents and youth often have divergent views about treatment goals, (4) maintenance of a positive alliance over time predicts successful outcomes with youth—alliance formation is not simply an early treatment task, it is a recurrent task, and (5) youth are likely to have a limited understanding of therapy—early alliance formation with youth requires the therapist to balance active listening to the youth with providing an explicit frame work for understanding therapy processes (roles, framework, tasks, relevance), and overemphasizing the later to the exclusion of the former appears to interfere with alliance formation with adolescents" (p. 22).

Child and adolescent therapists who treat addictive disordered youth, and/or their addictive disordered parents in diverse clinical settings (i.e., divorce custody cases, residential and out-patient settings, private practice, correctional settings, etc.) can enhance their therapeutic outcomes significantly by integrating these alliance facilitating measures within their general practice work.

ALLIANCE IN CONJOINT AND FAMILY THERAPY

The importance of alliance in couples or conjoint therapy and family therapy has also been long recognized but this particular psychotherapy construct has also received less clinical and research attention than the realm of individual psychotherapy.

As described by Friedlander et al., (2011, 2014), Pinsof and Catherall (1986), the Bordin (1979) alliance construct can be applied to the "goals, tasks and bonds of three interpersonal facets of the alliance in family treatment (self-with-therapist, other-with-therapist, and group-with therapist)" (p. 25). This alliance model incorporates individual, couple and family bonds, goals, tasks and how the couple or family unit responds to the treatment process. Obviously, couples and family alliances are far more complex than individual therapy alliances; couples and family alliances also present a much wider and complex spectrum of psychotherapy process and outcome investigative arenas than individual therapy alliances. Friedlander (2015) has examined relational strategies related to alliance rupture repair work and supervisor training skills in couple and family therapy. Alliance-focused training has also been addressed by Eubanks-Carter, Muran and Safran (2015).

Friedlander et al., (2011) recently completed a meta-analysis investigation of 24 couple and family therapy alliance studies. Seven of these studies involved couples therapy, including two group studies, and seventeen involved family therapy in which "at least a portion of the treatment" was conducted conjointly. This investigation involved over 1,460 clients and involved a number of treatment models: cognitive-behavioral therapy, functional family therapy, emotion-focused therapy, psychoeducational family therapy and "treatment as usual."

The Friedlander et al. (2011) meta-analysis study and other studies (Friedlander et al., 2014, 2015) provide many clinically useful alliance-related conjoint and family therapy related findings that will be useful for family and marital therapists. With regard to alliance and treatment retention, these authors report that "good outcomes depend upon attendance, and retention in family therapy is challenging—especially families with drug-abusing adolescents—the composite index of CFT (couple and family therapy), that is, an average of all family members' alliances, is not predictive of retention or outcome" (p. 29). The authors also indicate that research with adolescents manifesting externalizing problems ("acting out") or anorexia indicate that parental but not youth alliances predict treatment completion (Pereira, Lock and Oggins, 2006; Shelef and Diamond, 2008). Investigations of externalizing adolescents also "indicate that both children's and the parents' alliances with the therapist discriminated dropout from completer families." Unbalanced alliances tend to be related to higher dropout rates, family role and other complex factors (Robbins et al., 2008). Friedlander et al. (2011) also note that "therapist experience has not been systematically manipulated in any study;" however, Raytek et al. (1999) reported that therapist experience "was positively associated with the alliance in conjoint alcoholism treatment for couples," noting that more experienced therapists tended to be "more active, more responsive to client initiated topics, better at managing couples negativity, and more flexible" than less experienced therapists.

Couples therapy outcome studies pertaining to alliance and gender indicate that the man's alliance "tends to be more strongly associated with outcome" in both group marital therapy and couples therapy (Bourgeois et al., 1990; Symonds and Horvath, 2004). However, women's alliances can be the stronger predictor of outcome and factors such as male resistance to therapy involvement and women have a "relatively higher commitment to therapy and ability to work toward positive change regardless of the relative strength of their relationship with the therapist" (Symons and Horvath, 2004).

The Friedlander et al. (2011) study involving couple and family therapy outcomes data indicates that "family role emerged as the most consistent but complex potential moderator." These authors report the following alliance research evidence pertaining to family therapy outcomes: (1) "adolescents (but not parents) observed alliance with the therapist predicted early weight gain, whereas parents alliance later in therapy was associated with the teen's over-all weight gain in a study of family therapy for anorexia nervosa, (2) in a study of family treatment for adolescent substance abuse, observer measures but not self-report measures of adolescents' alliances predicted post treatment outcomes, whereas parent measures did not, (3) adolescent alliance predicted outcome only in cases in which the parent-therapist alliance was moderate to strong, (4) in a study of outpatient psychotherapy 'as usual' that combined individual and conjoint parent-teen sessions, youths' alliances predicted outcomes (youth symptom improvement, family functioning) as reported by all family members, whereas parents' alliances predicted fewer outcomes and only their own (i.e. not their children's) ratings of treatment success" (p. 30).

As indicated earlier in this chapter, different treatment approaches or models may impact the alliance-outcome relationship as well as patient characteristics and diagnostic features. Studies involving behavioral family therapy for schizophrenia have found that only "relatives' observed" alliances predicted patient reoccurrence of symptoms, patient's alliances predicted "less rejection by relatives, and less care burden" (Smerud and Rosenfarb, 2008). These findings suggest that the alliance in one family subsystem may interactively impact others or the entire system constructively. Additional studies report that cognitive behavior therapy and multidimensional family therapy comparative research evidence pertaining to the treatment of adolescent substance abusers indicated that CBT alliances were not associated with outcome. Multidimensional family therapy alliances for both substance abusing youth and parental alliances were related to therapy outcomes. Early-stage therapy "parental comfortableness" in the initial family therapy session predicted later therapy perceptions of therapeutic improvement. These studies (Friedlander et al., 2011; Friedlander et al., 2008a, 2008b, 2008c; Hogue et al., 2006; Smerud and Rosenfarb, 2008) demonstrate that alliance dynamics and psychotherapy outcome efficacy can be significantly related to therapeutic models and methods of therapy.

Friedlander et al. (2011) indicated that the couples and family alliance clinical literature "focuses almost exclusively" on therapist behavior but also note that "all client behavior" impacts the alliance. These authors report that "alliance-related behavior cuts across therapy approaches and formats, like successful clients in individual therapy, successful family members form a close, trusting bond with their therapists and negotiate (and renegotiate) treatment and tasks—clients who have a shared sense of purpose listen respectfully to one another, validate each other's perspective (even when they disagree), offer to compromise, and avoid excessive cross-blaming, hostility, and sarcasm. Family members who feel safe and comfortable in therapy and are emotionally expressive, ask each other for feedback, encourage one another to open up and speak frankly, and share thoughts and feelings, even painful ones, that have never been expressed at home" (p. 30).

Client alliance characteristics and behaviors in couples therapy do suggest that while psychiatric symptoms do not impact the alliance, factors such as less marital conflict and higher couple relationship trust do result in the formation of stronger alliances (Knobloch-Fedders et al., 2004; Johnson and Talitman, 1997; Mamodhoussen et al., 2005). Knobloch-Fedders et al. (2004) also found that alliance formation differs between men and women with enhanced male alliance development being related to recalled positive family of origin experiences. For males, marital conflict resulted in a later therapy negative alliance impact. For women, "sexual dissatisfaction was negatively associated with the alliance throughout therapy, and women's family of origin distress contributed to a split alliance early in the process" (Friedlander et al., 2011, p. 30).

The complexity of couples and family therapy alliances is reflected by additional studies (Thomas, Werner-Wilson and Murphy, 2005; Friedlander et al., 2011) indicating that "men were less likely to agree with the therapist on the goals for treatment when their partners made negative statements about them, whereas women tended to feel more negatively about therapy tasks when they were challenged by their partners" (p. 30). However, men and women formed a "stronger alliance with the therapist when their partners self-disclosed, and both felt more distant from the therapist when their partners challenged or made negative comments about them." Both patient and therapist self-disclosure (Farber, 2006; Forrest, 2012, 2016) have been found to play an important role in alliance formation and positive therapeutic outcomes.

Lambert and Friedlander (2008) report that "parental differentiation of self-predicted stronger perceived alliances" in early-stage community-based family therapy. These authors (Friedlander et al., 2011) also indicate "parents who reported being generally less emotionally reactive tended to feel safer and more comfortable in conjoint family therapy, diagnosis or presenting problem may also matter, for example, in family based therapy for anorexia nervosa, teens with relatively more weight and eating concerns found it particularly difficult to establish an alliance with the therapist, and the nature of adolescents' emotional problems played no role in alliance development in a study of multidimensional family therapy for drug-abusing adolescents where there was no variability in teens' alliance related behavior based on pretreatment externalizing or internalizing behaviors" (p. 31).

Friedlander et al. (2011) conclude their review of the alliance research pertaining to couples and family therapy as follows: (1) "the current body of research on alliance in couples and family therapy is small but solid, diverse client populations and therapy approaches have been sampled, (2) the finding that alliances predict treatment retention and outcome over and above specific therapy methods strengthens the case for the unique contribution to relationship variables in couples and family therapy, and (3) there are limitations in this body of work (i.e., alliance assessment instruments, timing of measurements, sample sizes, etc.)" (p. 31). These authors also note that "most" of the family therapy alliance research focuses on "families of drug-abusing, externalizing adolescents, thus limiting the generalizability of this data to families involving other populations of family therapy adolescents and children. They further point out that alliances in family therapy involving adults (and/or youths) manifesting major mental illness may involve "different dynamics" and attachment style may "moderate the alliance-outcome relationship" in couples and family therapy.

Importantly, Friedlander et al. (2011) provide the following alliance therapeutic practice guidelines for couples and family therapists: (1) "the therapeutic alliance is a critical factor in the process and outcome of couples and family therapy, and therapists need to be aware of what is going on within the family system while monitoring the personal bond and agreement on goals and tasks with each family member (while directly addressing and repairing problematic alliances), (2) shared sense of purpose within the family, a particularly important dimension of the alliance, involves establishing overarching systemic goals, (3) creating a safe space is critical, particularly early on in therapy, (4) evaluating the alliance based on observation is a skill that can be taught, and (5) each person's alliance matters, and alliances are not interchangeable, clinicians should build and maintain strong alliances with each party, and depending on the family's dynamics, the whole alliance is more than the sum of its parts" (p. 31).

ALLIANCE OR COHESION IN GROUP THERAPY

Recent (Burlingame, McClendon, and Alonso, 2011; Ulvenes et al., 2012) research and clinical studies of group psychotherapy have examined the impact of relationship dynamics on the various processes and outcomes of group therapy. Group therapy relationship constructs including alliance, cohesion, group climate, group dynamics and therapeutic bond (Wiprovnick, Kuerbis and Morgenstern, 2015) have been investigated and utilized in these studies. According to Burlingame, McClendon and Alonso (2011) "cohesion is the most popular" in the contemporary group therapy literature, and this construct has also become synonymous with the "therapeutic relationship" in group therapy.

These authors also clearly delineate several cohesion construct definitions, problems and challenges limiting the utility associated with these group therapy relationship constructs. A diversity of methods, instruments, and behavioral definitions have been used to assess the therapeutic relationship in group therapy. As Hornsey et al. (2009) note "just about anything that has a positive valence (with outcome) has been interpreted at some point as an index of cohesion." However, after reviewing the group therapy cohesion literature, Burlingame, McClendon and Alonso (2011) conclude that this body of evidence "supports two fundamental dimensions of cohesion: relationship structure and relationship quality." This body of evidence included nine measures of cohesion and "all assess horizontal cohesion between members and their group, while fewer than half focus on the member's relationship with the leader (vertical); affective bond is universally assessed by all measures while the task cohesion is assessed by a third of the measures" (p. 34).

The relationship structure dimension of group therapy cohesion comprises the direction and function of the relationship, and vertical cohesion refers to "a group member's perception of the group leader's competence, genuineness and warmth." Horizontal cohesion describes "a group member's relationship with other group members and with the group-as-a-whole." Functionally, task cohesion "indicates that members are drawn to the group to accomplish a given task or goal," while affective cohesion "indicates members feel connected because of the emotional support the group experience affords" (Burlingame et al., 2011; Dion, 2000, p. 35).

The relationship quality dimension of the cohesion construct includes (Burlingame et al., 2004; Burlingame et al., 2011) a "two-factor" definition of the therapeutic relationship in group therapy: (1) belonging and acceptance factors (cohesion and member-leader alliance), and (2) interpersonal work factors (group working alliance, individual working alliance, and group climate) (p. 35). These authors report that additional cohesion related group therapy studies found the two-dimensional model revealed "positive bond, positive work, and negative relationship factors explained how members perceived the quality of the relationship in both nonclinical and clinical groups, positive bond described the affective relationship members felt with their leader (vertical cohesion) and in member-to-member relationships (horizontal cohesion), positive work equally captured the tasks and goals of the group while negative relationship captured empathic failure with the leader and conflict in the group" (p. 35). The authors further conclude after reviewing several other cohesions in group therapy investigations that "these studies support structure and quality as the two fundamental dimensions of cohesion."

Based upon their review of five additional published group therapy meta-analysis studies (Burlingame, McClendon and Alonso, 2011), these authors report that "past reviewers have concluded that cohesion has shown an overwhelmingly positive relation with patient improvement;" however, the results of the authors' meta-analysis differed with "only 43 percent of the studies posting a statistically significant correlation." Nonetheless, the "overall conclusion from forty studies published across a four-decade span is a positive relation between cohesion and outcome." It should also be noted that fifty-eight percent of these group therapy cohesion studies were published after 2000, and over a fourth of the studies appeared before 1990 (pp. 35–36).

Another more recent investigation conducted in Germany (Dinger and Schauenburg, 2010) involving over 300 "mixed diagnosis adults treated on a psychodynamically-oriented impatient psychotherapy unit" found that "higher levels of cohesion as well as an increase in cohesion over the life of the group were associated with greater symptom improvement" (p. 35).

The Burlingame, McClendon and Alfonso (2011) meta-analysis group therapy data and evidence-based findings support the following therapeutic practices: (1) "cohesion is reliably associated with group outcome when outcome is defined as reduction in symptom distress or improvement in interpersonal functioning; this association was found for groups across different settings (inpatient and outpatient) and diagnostic classifications, (2) cohesion is most strongly involved with patient improvement in groups using an interpersonal, psychodynamic or cognitive-behavioral orientation, (3) group leaders emphasizing member interaction, irrespective of theoretical orientation, post higher cohesion-outcome links than groups less focused on process, thus, it is important to encourage member interaction, (4) cohesion explains outcome regardless of the length of the group, but is strongest when a group lasts more than twelve sessions and is comprised of five to nine members, cohesion requires sufficient member interaction and time to build, and (5) younger group members experience the largest outcome changes when cohesion is present within their groups (fostering cohesion will be particularly useful for therapists working in college a counseling centers and with adolescent populations)" (pp. 39–40). These authors further conclude that "cohesion is integrally related to the success of group therapy, and the research has identified specific behaviors that enhance cohesion." However, it is important that addictions therapists and other practicing clinicians recognize the presence of various research design and methodology limitations associated with psychotherapy process and outcome studies involving the therapeutic alliance as well as all other psychotherapy constructs. The clinical evidence and empirical alliance related psychotherapy literature presented in this chapter clearly demonstrates that the therapeutic relationship has "healing qualities" (Norcross and Lambert, 2011), but as Ulvenes et al. (2012) and virtually all of the other psychotherapy researchers and clinicians contributing to the alliance literature and empirical science presented in this chapter acknowledge that the bond or alliance may be differently impacted by a diversity of therapy models, patient diagnosis, attachment, situational, demographic and multicultural factors. For example, Ulvenes et al. (2012) and Orellana and Gelso (2013) found that (1) "psychotherapy with cluster C personality disordered clients involving the relationship bond and outcomes differed depending on therapeutic approach, and (2) therapist avoidance of affect was found to be positively related to formation of the bond (rated by patients in cognitive therapy and short-term dynamic psychotherapy); that is, patients in the study found the focus on affect to be problematic in terms of feeling bonded to their therapist, while in STDP a focus on affect detracted from the bond, but this focus resulted in a reduction of symptoms and, as well, the part of the bond not related to a focus on affect was predictive of outcome" (p. 296).

Gelso and Bhatia, 2012; Gelso and Samstag, 2008; and Orellana and Gelso, 2013 have in effect, proposed that the therapeutic relationship consists of three components: (1) the working alliance, (2) the transference countertransference matrix, and (3) "the real relationship." Real relationship, alliance, transference and countertransference related psychotherapy studies involving psychotherapy trainees reflect the complex interactive impact of therapist, patient and psychotherapy process and outcome construct variables that characterize all psychotherapy studies.

In view of these realities, the author would encourage integrative addiction-focused psychotherapists and clinicians to actively incorporate the wealth of alliance-focused psychotherapy process and outcome information included in this chapter and text with an ever present and vigilant cognitive awareness of the multifaceted therapist-patient-psychotherapy, model-treatment milieu, diversity of individual and relational factors which consistently impact our therapeutic relationships with persons manifesting a broad spectrum of addictive disorders.

A common and very real example of this over-riding clinical reality facing addiction-focused therapists might involve any addictive disordered middle-aged patient manifesting a clinical history of protracted alcohol dependence, cocaine dependence, opioid dependence or polydrug dependence with co-morbid bi-polar disorder, panic disorder, severe anorexia nervosa, borderline personality disorder or complex trauma. These patients also commonly manifest clinical histories (Forrest, 1978–2017) involving severe and chronic relational dysfunction, attachment difficulties and interpersonal failure, as well as abandonment, and for sexual and psychological trauma related issues which interactively impact their active addictive disease process, and frequently limit their capacity for early or ongoing working alliance formation. These realities may also directly and significantly impact the addiction therapist's capacity for fostering the process of alliance development in a myriad of ways.

However, in the author's clinical experience involving hundreds of addictive disordered patients manifesting complex co-morbid diagnoses and psychopathology, it can be surprising to find a number of these persons can and eventually do develop working and productive therapeutic alliances. These persons may also actualize profound global adjustment and life changes during the therapeutic process and their ongoing recovery process. A key ingredient in the successful psychotherapy (Forrest 1975–2019) of all addictive disordered patients including the most complex clinical cases almost always begins with (1) the alliance, the multimodal and integrative care fostered ability of the patient to establish and sustain substance abstinence within the context of the ongoing psychotherapy process, and therapeutic relationship and (2) the patients capacity to sustain an ongoing commitment to both the therapeutic process as well as eventually sustaining an ongoing personal commitment to the work and tasks of the ongoing alliance process and the evolving recovery process. For many addictive disordered patients, these sustained goals, tasks, work and commitments eventually encompass a herculean life-long multifaceted process.

SUMMARY

The therapeutic alliance is a crucial ingredient in the process and outcome of psychotherapy and counseling relationships involving addictive-disordered patients and most, if not all psychotherapy relationships involving a broad spectrum of patient populations manifesting a diversity of behavioral health and emotional or mental health disorders (Bedics et al., 2015; Cook et al., 2015; Wampold and Imel, 2015; Forrest, 2018). In the historic as well as recent clinical, educational, training and consultation experiences of the author, many addictions counselors and psychotherapists remain basically unaware of the potentially profound relevance and impact of the alliance in the process and psychotherapy outcome relationship involving addictive-disordered persons.

This chapter provides a wealth of research evidence, clinical practice information, guidelines and alliance-related psychotherapy process and outcome data pertaining to a multiplicity of patient populations, treatment models and approaches, and therapist-patient factors. The historic definitional and evolutional parameters of the alliance construct that are discussed in this chapter along with the consistent and rather compelling process and outcome evidence-based findings and information that has evolved over the past fifty years will greatly enhance integrative addictions-focused therapists' and clinicians' awareness of the outcome enhancing impact of the working and productive alliance in their therapeutic work. The alliance specific therapeutic skills and practice guidelines provided in the chapter will not only facilitate more successful therapy outcomes, but may also be utilized by supervising and training addictions therapists to potentially enhance trainee as well as over-all addiction and behavioral health program efficacy and care outcomes. Finally, the alliance information that has been presented in this chapter many stimulate better research and practice efforts related to a broad spectrum of addictive-disordered therapeutic and treatment modalities as well as a wide array of addictive disordered patient populations and other patient populations.

As noted earlier in this chapter and, throughout the chapter, clinical and research psychotherapy alliance literature clearly indicates (1) the therapeutic relationship has "healing qualities," and (2) the alliance appears to be a critically important factor that impacts the process and outcome of psychotherapy independent of therapy model, therapist orientation or treatment modality (Cook et al. 2015; Norcross and Lambert, 2011; Ulvenes et al. 2012). The evolution of alliance-based clinical and empirical literature encompasses the initial work of Freud (1912, 1958) to the work of Fenichel (1945), and Greenson (1967) who described the working alliance as a "natural relationship between patient and analyst," to Zetzel (1956) and Bordin (1979) as well as the various contemporary authors included in the chapter. The global body of psychotherapy relationship-alliance literature presented in this chapter robustly and consistently indicates that the alliance is simply and complexly a crucial ingredient in psychotherapy.

Gelso's (2011) excellent article on "emerging and continuing trends in psychotherapy titled "Views from an editors' eye," focuses on six major trends in psychotherapy over the past decade. All of these trends encompass a core integrative shift; "the increasing integration of techniques and the therapeutic relationship, increasing focus on theoretical integration, increasing efforts at research-practice integration, increases in more specific, integrative reviews, integration of biological, neuroscience understandings, and integration of diversity and cultural considerations into psychotherapy" (p. 182). These observations and trends stem from the author's editorship experiences and observations associated with the American Psychological Association Psychotherapy journal between 2004–2010.

The alliance evidence data and information discussed in this chapter reflects many of the recent diversity-oriented trends that are discussed in the

Gelso article, and these trends have certainly been paralleled within the clinical practice context of integrative addictions-focused psychotherapy, counseling and treatment programs over the past several years. Interestingly, clinicians and therapists also need to integratively remain ever aware of Yalom's (2002) caution as we continue our integrative evolutionary psychotherapy science and neuroscience process from questions of "nature and nurture" which are "now obsolete—the answer is that of course both nature and nurture influence who we are and how we feel and behave—it is backed by the hardest scientific evidence—genes alone, provide only part of the reason for the development of mental illness" (p. 7). The same "may be said of all behavior. The newest neurobiological evidence not only demonstrates how neurobiology affects intrapsychic events and behavior, but how experiences, including the psychotherapy relationship, effect and change the structure of the brain" (Cappas, 2005; Divino and Moore, 2010, p. 7).

Yalom (2002) also notes "it's never the specific content that cures": "Remember, that ancient archaic frameworks (alchemical, magical, shamanistic, theological, libidinal, phrenological, astrological) used to do the trick too! Any cogent explanation (that is an explanation attuned to the person-cultural-historical context of the individual) offers relief though making sense of previously inexplicable feelings. Naming and understanding lead to a sense of control particularly when they are matched with the patient's educational, cultural, and intellectual background.

The truly instrumental factor is process the nature of the therapeutic relationship—the intellectual task of psychotherapy is primarily by a procedure that keeps therapist and patient locked together in some mutually relevant and interesting task while *the real healing force, the therapeutic relationship is percolating and gaining strength*" (pp. 9–10).

The working and productive therapeutic alliance provides a very "real healing force" within the context of the therapeutic relationship in all forms of addictions psychotherapy work and efficacious clinical practice work. However, it must also be remembered that the alliance and "real psychotherapy relationship" process and outcome always remain impacted by a multiplicity of unending interactive therapist, patient, relationship, situational, and environmental variables. The alliance always remains a potential powerful vehicle for constructive patient growth and change within the evolving psychotherapy relationship process.

The "real relationship" (Orellana and Gelso, 2013) and general "working alliance" related empirical psychotherapy evidence has "consistently shown that therapist effects dwarf the contribution made by the perennially popular treatment models and techniques, accounting for 5–9 times more variance in outcome" (Miller et al., 2015; Wampold and Imel, 2015).

Chapter 4

ALLIANCE INGREDIENTS IN
EFFECTIVE PSYCHOTHERAPY AND
COUNSELING RELATIONSHIPS

The psychotherapy literature of the past century and now into the second decade of the new millennium encompasses an ever-evolving diversity of therapy theories models and approaches as "schools" of therapy. A diversity of different therapeutic techniques and methods are generally utilized and employed by therapists and counselors who have been trained and practice psychotherapy and counseling as cognitive behavioral therapists, reality therapists, interpersonal therapists, hyper therapists, gestalt therapists, rational emotion therapist, psychoanalysts, EMOR therapists, thought-field therapist, client (person) centered therapists and grief solution focused therapist. This list of therapy "specialties": can be greatly expanded to include sex therapists, psychodynamic psychotherapists, behavioral therapists, Reichian and Jungian therapists and many others, as well as group therapists, family therapists, couple therapists, and child and adolescent therapists.

During the past several decades, increasing number of behavioral clinicians and therapists tends to practice within the confines of specialty areas including select patient populations (i.e., people manifesting mood disorders, major mental illness, substance abuse and addictions, eating disorders, anxiety disorders, learning disorders, personality disorders, cognitive disorders, autism spectrum disorders, etc.).

The ever-evolving interactive matrix of these various psychotherapy practice realities also includes an evolving and equally complex system of individual psychotherapy practitioners beliefs, skill, levels, training, supervision and actual practice experiences, patient outcomes, and various together variables (demographics, multi-cultural, environmental, etc.) which ultimately slope, determine and impact every facet of the therapists behavior and being pertaining to the basic ingredients that facilitate the process and outcome of effective psychotherapy. This changing and interceptive dynamic process never remains static, and continually impacts the therapist-patient-therapy relationship from the first to the last session.

A very large and significant segment of the empirical psychotherapy process outcome literature that has been produced over the past sixty years clearly demonstrates the primary importance of several putative therapist ingredients in effective psychotherapy. These therapist characteristics and qualities are frequently referred to in psychotherapy literature as the "central ingredients" a "core condition of essential ingredients" for successful therapy outcomes. Carol Rogers (1942; 1951; 1957) and several of his students and other Rogerian Therapists (Mitchell et al., 1973; Truax and Carkhuff, 1967: Truax, 1971; Truax and Mitchell, 1971; Truax and Wargo, 1966) continued to investigate and coordinate the empirical relationships between other relatively well defined and measured essential Therapist characteristics and positive therapeutic outcomes.

It should also be noted that Rogers's global impact upon the training and practice of psychotherapy imitated a rather genealogical realization and belief that the therapeutic relationship "per se was the critical factor in determining therapeutic success." This belief system has generally evolved and changed within the psychotherapy training and practice literature over the past two or three decades, but many practicing clinicians, therapist and research-academic therapists continue to use the therapeutic relationship per se to be one of the most fundamental ingredients in the therapeutic process outcome equation. Therapists academic psychotherapy educator, and supervisors also practice therapy theories various contemplating virtual reality and internet information technology mediums many differ significantly with more tradition and therapists who practice and provide academic as well as clinical training or supervision with regard to a number of matters pertaining to the saliency of the therapeutic relationship as an essential ingredient in successful therapy outcomes.

This chapter examines the following empirically-based therapist alliance ingredients or qualities consistently facilitate the process of successful psychotherapy outcomes: non-possessive warmth or positive regard, empathy, genuineness or influence, and concreteness or effective communication.

The impact and roles of therapist-patient transference, counter reference, self-disclosure, relapses, alliance ruptures and repair work patient readiness and notation, commitment to the recovery process, capacity for vigorous honesty and ancillary alliance dynamics in additions psychotherapy and counseling will be examined in Chapter 5.

NON-POSSESSIVE WARMTH OR POSITIVE REGARD

Therapist non-possessive warmth, more recently referred to in the psychotherapy literature as "positive regard," was one of the initial ingredients proposed by Carl Rogers (1957) as a component of the tripartite "necessary and sufficient conditions for therapeutic change." Empathy and geniuses (congruence) comprised the other essential therapist ingredients that resulted in successful therapeutic outcomes.

The empirical psychotherapy success-outcome research and literature that Roger's model for therapeutic change has synergized thousands of related psychotherapy publications, and directly impacted psychotherapy training and practice programs for over fifty years. As not by Foster (2007) and Foster and Doolin (2011), the Rogerian influence on clinical practice has been "incorporated into the psychotherapeutic mainstream with minimal awareness or explicate acknowledgement—Therapist of varying persuasions, even those form Theoretical camps that had traditionally emphasized more technical factors, have begun to acknowledge the importance of the relationship" (p. 58). Farber and Doolin (2011) also provided examples of how very contemporary as well as instinct behavioral therapists, cognitive-behavior therapist, psychotherapists, and self-psychology therapists emphasize the importance of empathy, support, positive regard and "relational" dynamics in effective psychotherapy relationships.

Roger's earliest publications indicating the core precepts of client-centered therapy (Rogers, 1942, 1951, 1957) encompassed non-possessive warmth, empathy and geniuses. This model also stressed the importance of therapist respect and conveying a sense of dignity for clients. Rogers believed that the therapist, ability to constantly therapeutic manner which conveyed a sense of non-possessive warmth, empathy, active caring, positive regard and genuine Therapists being within the context of the therapeutic relationship (alliance) resulted in personality growth, change and the capacity for clients to actualize their optimal human potential. Rogerian non-possessive warmth or positive regard was definitionally characterized as "real spontaneous praising; you can call that quality acceptance, you can call it caring, you can call it non possessive love" (Shostrom, 1965). The positive regard terminology that was employed by Farber and Doolin (2011) in their extensive review of the historic and current empirical research findings included the "general constellation of attitudes encompassed" in the Rogerian non=possessive warmth psychotherapy outcome information revised in this chapter.

As Farber and Doolin (2011) point out, defining and precisely defining the therapeutic qualities related to therapist non-possessive warmth, empathy and geniuses were difficult for Roger's (1951) himself: the therapists attempts to "provide deep understanding and acceptance of the attitudes consciously held at the moment by the client" are only accomplished by the therapists struggle to achieve the client's internal frame of reference, to gain the center of his own perceptual field, and see with him as receive." Rogers acknowledged that it was :virtually impossible for any therapist to provide constant closes of unconditional positive regard," noting: "from a clinical and exponential point of view, I believe the most accurate statement is that the effective therapist expresses unconditional positive regard for the client during many moments of his contact with him, yet from time to time he experiences only a conditional positive regard—and perhaps at times a negative regard, though this is not likely in effective therapy—in this sense unconditional positive regard exists as a matter of degree in any relationship" (p. 101).

These authors also indicate that "most investigations" of the effects of non-possessive warmth or positive regard have utilized the Barnett-Lennard Relationship Inventory or the Truax Relationship Questionnaire (BLRI, 1964, 1978; Truax and Carkhuff, 1967) and they also point out that therapist positive regard has been investigated with instruments designed to assess the therapeutic alliance.

The Farber and Doolin (2011) extensive general review of historic and contemporary investigations work involving numerous studies which examine the relationship between therapist positive regard or non-possessive warmth and psychotherapy outcome included the following findings: (1) the first review of the relationship between positive regard and therapy outcome (Truax and Carkhuff, 1967) taken from their classic text toward effective counseling and psychotherapy included ten studies "from which conclusions could be drawn on the effects of positive regard alone." Eight of these investigations "supported the Hypothesis that non-possessive warmth is significantly associated with therapeutic improvement," (2) the Bergin and Garfield (1971) text *Handbook of Psychotherapy and Behavior Change* chapters by Truax and Mitchell (1971) involving the results of twelve studies including non-possessive warmth reported "the evidence was quite strong in regard to the positive relationship between warmth and therapeutic outcome," (3) follow-up studies by Mitchell, Bozarth and Krauft (1977) involving eleven investigations concluded "at most four of these studies supported the finding of therapist non-possessive warmth resulted in better outcomes," while a review of twenty-three investigations by Orlinsky and Howard (1978) found that "approximately two-thirds of the studies indicated a significant positive association between therapist warmth and therapeutic outcome," and (4) another Orlinsky and Howard (1986) review of eleven studies evaluating the effect of therapist support and therapist information related to the process and outcome of psychotherapy reportedly although six of the twenty-five (separate findings) are significantly positive findings none are negative"—the authors also identified" ninety-four findings in the association between therapist information and outcome, with more than half demonstrating a significant relationship between these sets of variables." These authors additionally reported "the proportion of positive findings across all outcome categories when therapist warmth and acceptance are observed from the patient's process perspective," and therapist affirmation precept encompasses "aspects of acceptance, non-possessive warmth and/or positive regard." They pointed out that, again, well over fifty percent (56%) of the one-hundred and fifty-four results were positive based on patient perspective), sixty-five percent of positive therapeutic outcomes" (Orlinsky et al., 1994, pp. 27–376), and (5) finally the Farber and Lane (2001) sixteen study review of positive regard and psychotherapy outcome found that "no post-1990 study reported a negative relationship between positive regard and outcome." These authors found an even split between positive and non-significant effects; they also reported that "the majority of nonsignificant relationships occurred when an objective rater (rather than the therapist or patient) evaluated therapeutic outcome," and when patients "rated both the therapist's positive regard and treatment outcome, a positive association between these variables was especially likely" (p. 60).

Farber and Doolin (2011) conclude from the non-possessive warmth positive regard psychotherapy outcome research received within the context of these historic publications and empirical evidence, as well as their recent meta-analysis review of 18 studies (1) in no patient characteristics were significant moderators in our analysis of the date; "they also hypothesize that select patient characteristics or factors were not addressed in these studies and they likely do impact the therapist's provision of positive regard and the extent to which this increases the likelihood of therapeutic success." They also note that therapist behaviors are a "function of the various individual and diagnostic characteristics that constitute the patient populations they work with" (pp. 58–62). This author (Forrest, 1985, 2002, 2013) has indicated the therapist's "simple comfortableness," and "ability to like his or her addicted patients" tends to foster the development of successful treatment relationships with these individuals. Patient warmth, receptiveness to treatment, motivation for therapy and recovery, empathy, genuineness and self-disclosure, capacity for intimacy, attachment and multi-cultural issues and various other therapist patient relational realities continuously impact both therapist and patient capacities for the employment, development, and maintenance of the mutual levels of non-possessive warmth, empathy, genuineness and other nonspecific variables that are so important for the establishment and maintenance of efficacious therapeutic alliances which consistently foster successful treatment.

It is very important to point out that the Farber and Doolin (2011) outcomes provide a detailed description of the methodology, procedures, and limitations and caveats related to their meta-analysis investigation of therapist positive regard (non-possessive warmth) and therapeutic outcome. These general issues were also addressed by most of the psychotherapy researchers who founded the various other studies revised in this chapter and text. Farber and Doolin (2011) astutely point out that "positive regard has been studied primarily within the realm of client-centered therapy, an orientation that no longer attracts the attention of many prominent researchers; "they also note, "There have been very few studies of positive regard within the past twenty years—We believe the concept of positive regard hasn't so much gone away in recent years as it has been folded into newer concepts in the field, particularly, measures of the therapeutic alliance (p. 62).

The author's experience is fully congruent with this viewpoint. In this regard and within the addiction and psychotherapy arena, the client-centered therapy orientation has and continues to remain essentially unrecognized and is infrequently utilized in addictions focused clinical practice. However, the more recent guises of motivational interviewing, mindfulness, and the supportive therapies are exceptions to the generalization. Cognitive-behavioral therapy approaches (RET, DBT, REBT, Reality Therapy, brief therapies, solution focused therapy, relapse prevention counseling, EMDR, etc.) have been utilized far more frequently in the general addiction focused research and treatment outcome literature over the last few decades. Addiction-focused conjoint marital or relational therapy, family, and group therapies also generally utilize cognitive behavioral and short-term or brief therapy interventions and other approaches.

Within the explicit realm of individual addictions psychotherapy work, the author (Forrest, 1975, 1994) indicated many years ago:

> regardless of therapy orientation, the medium of the therapist-patient transaction remains the essential point of behavioral change and growth—in the absence of a meaningful relationship (successful) psychotherapy as a process simply cannot take place. While all therapists essentially rely upon the patient-therapist relationship as a vehicle for constructive and relational change and growth; what actually takes place within this encounter is in part determined by the theoretical orientation and training of the therapist as well as conscious patient related factors. While research has indicated that the theoretical orientation of therapists tends to dissipate with experience. Research has also rather clearly indicated that certain types or forms of therapist behavior are consistently related to positive patient growth and personality growth—this seems to be the case regardless of patient diagnosis or psychopathology. Rogers (1952 was one of the pioneers in relationship-oriented therapy, and through his client-centered approach to psychotherapy the systematic investigation of therapist qualities was initiated. Truax and Carkhuff (1967) in a rather convincing summary of the research,

identify these essential therapist ingredients in the effective psychotherapeutic enterprise; accurate empathic understanding of the patient, non-possessive warmth and therapist genuineness or authenticity—Therapists who consistently respond to their patients with high levels of these facilitative conditions tend to help effect significant positive behavioral change upon the part of their patients—Therapists unable to provide adequate levels of these facilitative conditions have been shown to constantly produce minimal or even negative therapeutic effects. (p. 77)

A second variable in the therapeutic relationship involves therapist communication of non-possessive warmth for the patient. Basically, this concept relates to the therapist's warm acceptance of the patient (both expressions and feelings) without any conditions. The therapist accepts what *is,* rather than being concerned with was *should be.* The failures and depression of the patient, as well as his or her successes, are shared by the therapist—it has been asserted in the literature (Truax and Carkhuff, 1967) that warmth is a precondition for the therapist to accurately perceive the inner feelings and experiences of the patient, as well as a precondition for the patient's trust and self-exploration. (p. 78)

As noted by the author (Forrest, 1984, 1985, 1987):

core conditions of the therapeutic alliance facilitate recovery; however, the essential therapist ingredient in effective alcoholism (additions focused) intensive psychotherapy constitute the necessary but not always sufficient conditions for creating adaptive personality and behavioral change. The working and productive therapeutic alliance involves many strategic therapist actions behaviors, strategies and interventions—the successful intensive psychotherapy of alcoholism and other addictive disorders demands that the therapist exudes consistent therapeutic empathy" (p. 57). The author (Forrest, 1985) has also stressed that 'productive and working therapeutic alliances' evolve as a process; they are not established within a matter of two or three therapy hours. While the initial therapy hours represent a critically important barometer of therapist-patient potential for establishing a working and productive therapeutic alliance, it takes several sessions to develop (and maintain) the therapy relationship into a meaningful and effective vehicle of change. There are numerous other essential ingredients in the process of effective psychodynamically oriental psychotherapy with addicts and substance abusers." (pp. 320–321)

Finally, within the context of addictions psychotherapy the author (Forrest, 1997) indicates that:

key ingredients in the development and maintenance of a working and productive therapist alliance include non-possessive warmth, empathy, genuineness and concreteness—These therapeutic qualities (characteristics) pertain to the therapist's ability to (1) acceptable alcoholic patient conditionally, (2) to be affectively and cognitively attuned to the patient's feelings, experiences and behaviors, (3) communicate effectively to the patient an understanding of this awareness, and (4) be open to his or her own experience within the therapeutic encounter. Furthermore, the therapist is able to honestly and genuinely express his or her feelings, beliefs, and experiences with the patient. The psychotherapist is a 'real person' within the therapeutic encounter—effective therapists are able to consistently provide high levels of these therapeutic ingredients throughout the course of their psychotherapy relationships with primary alcoholics. (pp. 56–57)

The author also adds that the therapist's ability to communicate a sense of respect and dignity, for the patient, and effectively manage potential alliance ruptures throughout the course of addictions focused psychotherapy, are central to effective psychotherapeutic work and successful outcomes with addictive-disordered patients (Forrest, 1984, 1997, 2013, 2016).

These issues as well as a diversity of additional addictive disorder focused psychotherapy relationships, alliance, and process outcome clinical practice dynamics and guidelines will be examined in-depth in Chapter 5 of this book. The great deal of the clinical practice information in Chapter 5 is derived directly from the diverse and extensive clinical addictions-specific practice experiences of this author and his earlier addictive-disorders psychotherapy and treatment publications.

The Doolin and Farber (2011) analysis of therapist positive regard and psychotherapy outcome includes the following psychotherapy conclusions and psychotherapy practice recommendations and guidelines:

(1) The psychotherapist's ability to provide positive regard is significantly associated with therapeutic success—indicating a moderate relationship— it is a significant but not exclusive part of the process outcome equation, (2) Therapist provision of positive regard is strongly indicated in practice (at a minimum, it *sets the stage* for other mutative integrations and, at least in some cases, may be sufficient by itself to effect positive change), (3) There is virtually no research-driven reason to withhold positive regard, (4) positive regard serves many valuable functions across the major forms of psychotherapy, (5) positive regard may be particularly important in situations where a non-minority therapist is working with a minority client, (6) therapists cannot be content with feeling good about their patients but instead should ensure that their positive feelings are communicated to them, (7) therapists need to monitor their positive regard and adjust it as a function for the need of particular patients and specific clinical situations; the research demonstrates that therapists vary in the extent to which they are able to convey positive regard to their patients, and clients vary in the

extent to which they need, elicit, and/or benefit from a therapist's positive regard—we suspect that the inevitable ruptures in the therapeutic alliance that occur over the course of therapy are the result not only of therapist's technical errors but also of the therapist's occasional inability to demonstrate minimally facilitative levels of positive regard and support. (pp. 62–63)

EMPATHY

Therapy empathy has remained a focal topic of psychotherapy outcome investigations and clinical practice publications since the advent of Carl Roger's early client centered therapy work. Indeed, Rogers (1942, 1951, 1957, 1980) identified therapist empathy as being one of the "necessary and sufficient" therapeutic conditions for effective psychotherapy to occur. As noted earlier in this chapter, the Rogerian conditions for constructive therapeutic change (non-possessive warmth or positive regard, empathy and genuineness) have generated thousands of scientific investigations pertaining to the process and outcome of psychotherapy over the past fifty years. However, these intense clinical and research interest in these therapeutic constructs is diminished significantly during the 1980s and early 1990s due to "intense scrutiny" by psychotherapy researchers related to the notion of "universal effectiveness" associated with these constructs (Forrest, 2016). The past ten to fifteen years have included a regeneration of scientific interest and investigation associated with the impact of these therapist qualities on the process and outcome of psychotherapy. The evolution of biological, behavioral science and evolving newer therapeutic methods of treatment have fostered the growth and regeneration of scientific and clinical research involving these constructs as they relate to many facets related to the process and outcome of therapy.

Rogers (1980) defined empathy as "the therapists' sensitive ability and willingness to understand the client's thoughts, feelings and struggles from the client's point of view—it is this ability to see completely through the client's eyes, to adopt his frame of reference" (p. 85). Furthermore, "it means entering the private perceptual world of others—being sensitive, moment to moment, to the changing felt meanings which flow in the other person. It means sensing meanings of which he or she is scarcely aware" (p. 142).

Elliot et al. (2011) further define and characterize empathy as "a higher-order category, under which different subtypes, aspects, and models can be tested. For example, we find it useful to distinguish between three main modes of expressing therapeutic empathy; first, for some therapist's empathy is primarily the establishment of *empathic* rapport. The therapist exhibits a compassionate attitude toward the client and tries to demonstrate that he or she understand the client's experience, often in order to set the context for effective treatment. Second, *communicative attunement,* consists of an active, ongoing effort to stay attuned on a moment-to-moment basis with the client's communications and unfolding experience. Client-centered and experienced therapists are most likely to emphasize this form of empathy. The third mode, *person empathy* or experience-near understanding of the client's world, consists of a sustained effort to understand the kinds of experiences the client has had, both historically and presently, that form the background of the client's current experiencing—These three modes of empathic expression are not mutually exclusive, and the differences are a matter of emphasis" (p. 44).

Truax and Carkhuff (1967) indicate that Bordin (1955) "heavily stressed the role of the therapeutic triad of empathy, warmth and genuineness as central attributes of an effective counselor." Bordin (1955) further states "one of the things he (the therapist) is trying to understand is the inner life and experience of another person. In order to fully understand what it means to be hopeless or to be in a rage, and how it feels when some other person turns away from you when you feel helpless or when you feel another person tells you to calm down when you feel in a rage, the observer (therapist) must draw upon his own experience. Doing this seems to be a central part of the idea of empathy to assist us in understanding other people—this (empathy) is most fully achieved when an observer (therapist) is sufficiently involved to be able to make full use of his own emotional experience, and, at the same time, sufficiently detached to be able to differentiate his own experience from those of the other person" (p. 120).

Truax and Carkhuff (1967) define accurate empathy as "involving more than just the ability of the therapist to sense the client or patient's "private world" as if it were his own. It also involves more than just his ability to know what the patient means. Accurate empathy involves both the therapist's sensitivity to current feelings and his verbal facility to communicate this understanding in a language attuned to the client's current feelings.

These authors (Truax and Carkhuff, 1967) further indicate that "it is not necessary—indeed it would seem undesirable—for the therapist to *share* the client's feeling in any sense that would require him to feel the same emotions. It is instead an appreciation and a sensitive awareness of those feelings. At deeper levels of empathy, is also involves enough understanding of patterns of human feelings and experience to sense feelings that the client only partially reveals. With such experience and knowledge, the therapist can communicate what the client clearly knows as well as meanings in the client's experience of which he is scarcely aware—at a high level of accurate empathy the message "I am with you" is unmistakably clear—the therapist's remarks fit perfectly with the client's mood and content. Such empathy is communicated by both the language used and all of the voice qualities, which unerringly reflect the therapist's seriousness and depth of feeling. At a low level of accurate empathy, the therapist may go off on a tangent of his own or may misinterpret what the patient is feeling. At a very low level he or she may be so preoccupied and interested in his or her intellectual interpretations that he is scarcely aware of the client's "being." The therapist at this low level of accurate empathy may even be uninterested in the client or concentrating on the intellectual content of what the client says rather than what he "is" at the moment, and so may ignore or misunderstand the client's current feelings and experiences" (p. 46).

According to Truax and Carkhuff (1967):

> *the* central ingredient of the psychotherapy process appears to be the therapist's ability to *perceive and communicate,* accurately and with sensitivity, the feelings of the patient and the meaning of those feelings. At the higher levels of accurate empathy, the therapist unerringly responds to the client's full range of feelings in their exact intensity, whether be communicates this in the form of 'reflection of feeling,' 'depth reflections,' or sensitive 'interpretations.' At the highest levels of accurate empathy, the therapist's response expands the patient's verbal, gestural and content hints into full-blown, sensitive, but still native verbalizations of feelings or experiences—This means that the therapist has to a great degree successfully assumed the *internal frame of reference* of the patient. (p. 285)

Rogers and Truax (1966) further note that "to sense the client's bewilderment, anger, love or fear as if it were the therapist's own feeling is the critical perceptive aspect of empathic understanding—in being empathic, the therapist can be seen as assuming the role of the patient, and in that role initiating the process of self-exploration as if he were the patient himself—it is in this sense that the therapist, through trial identification, becomes the "other self" or "alter ego" of the client" (p. 286). Truax (1961a) indicates "within a modest range, the more frequently the therapist responds to the client even if only with an "um-hmm," the greatly the likelihood that a high level of accurate empathy will be perceived and communicated—research also indicates that the specificity or concreteness of the therapist's response is related to both the level of accurate empathy and the level of patient engagement in process" (p. 287). In short, the intensity and intimacy of the relationship itself, because of the intense focus of the therapist on the client, makes possible the moment-to-moment contact necessary for accurate empathic understanding (Truax and Carkhuff, 1967).

Barrett-Lennard (1980) operationally defined empathy within the context of three different dimensions: that of the therapist (empathic resonance), the observer (expressed empathy), and the client (received empathy).

The author (Forrest, 1975) originally defined empathy within the context of individual psychotherapy work with alcoholic patients as "accurate empathic understanding—Accurate empathy refers to the ability of the therapist to be both affectively and cognitively attuned to what the patient is currently feeling and experiencing, and to communicate to the patient an understanding of these feelings. Furthermore, the therapist who is accurately empathic (Truax and Carkhuff, 1967) explores the more latent cues expressed by voice, posture and content" (p. 78).

Forrest (1975) also noted "it is felt that these essential therapist ingredients have a very cogent bearing upon the therapeutic enterprise with alcoholic patients—indeed, a primary prerequisite to the therapeutic process with alcohol-addicted individuals is the presence of a therapist who can offer consistently high levels of these facilitative conditions within the therapeutic context" (pp. 78–79). Effective psychotherapists are able to "consistently provide high levels of non-possessive warmth, empathy, and genuineness throughout their treatment relationships with addictive patients, and there are numerous other essential ingredients in the process of dynamically oriented psychotherapy with addicts and substance abusers—however, these "core" conditions are essential to successful psychotherapy" (Forrest, 1985, p. 321).

It is also essential to the process of successful psychotherapy with addicted persons that "the therapist simply be comfortable with addicts—therapists who are able to like their addicted patients tend to be successful in their treatment relationships with these individuals" (Forrest, 1985).

The recent extensive meta-analysis study by Elliott et al. (2011) investigating the relationship between empathy and psychotherapy outcome found that empathy is a "moderately strong predictor of therapy outcome." This study included fifty-nine independent investigation samples involving three thousand and ninety-nine patients. This study also reported that (1) "the empathy-outcome relation held equally for different theoretical orientations "with" considerable nonrandom variability," (2) "client and observer perceptions of therapist empathy predicted outcomes better than therapist perceptions of empathic accuracy measures," and "the relation was strongest for less experienced therapists" (p. 43).

Earlier reviews by Barrett-Lennard (1981) and Gurman (1977) indicated that "therapist-related empathy neither predicted outcome nor unrelated with client-rated or observer-rated empathy." However, Bogart et al. (2002) found that "therapist-rated empathy did predict outcome, but at a lower level than client or observer ratings" (Elliott et al., 2011, p. 44). Gurman (1977) also reviewed more than twenty therapist empathy studies and reported that empathy correlated .62 with congruence, .53 with non-possessive warmth (position regard), and .28with unconditional positive regard. This data suggests that one primary or global factor may impact all of these therapeutic ingredients and that it is difficult to differentiate between these therapeutic relationship factors. However, it should also be noted in this regard that other investigations have identified empathy as a separate therapeutic efficacy factor, and recent investigators (Elliott, et al. 2011) view "new empathy as a relationship component that is both conceptually distinct and part of a higher-order relationship construct."

The historic seminal empathy publications of Truax (1961) and Barrett-Lennard (1962) found that "accurate empathy, warmth (or unconditional positive regard), and genuineness were all found to be significantly associated with the patient's engagement in the process of therapy, self-revelation, and self-exploration—these findings suggested that of the three, the therapist's accurate empathy and genuineness (or self-congruence) were by far the most important for patient behavior" (p. 83). Barrett-Lennard (1962) found that "experienced therapists were perceived as offering significantly higher levels of empathy, warmth and congruence than less experienced therapists" and among "more disturbed patients there was a positive relationship to therapeutic outcome."

Truax (1961-G) also examined therapist levels of accurate empathy in hospitalized psychiatric patients who showed "clear improvement on a variety of personality tests" and found that "the psychotherapists whose patients improved on the test rated consistently higher on accurate empathy than those with test-deteriorated outcomes—furthermore, the therapists' level of accurate empathy did not tend to vary throughout the six months of intensive psychotherapy" (p. 84). Another Truax (1963) study involving fourteen "schizophrenic patients who were seen in intensive psychotherapy for periods ranging from six months to four and one-half years" reported a correlation between accurate empathy and case outcome of .77; patients in this study who showed deterioration received "virtually no deeply empathic responses" from their therapists. Accurate empathy measures correlated .54 with non-possessive warmth measures, and .49 with measures of therapist genuineness—warmth and genuineness correlated .25, indicating that between six and thirty per cent of the variation in one measure is common to another" (p. 86).

Truax data (1962) also indicated that the "highest moments of accurate empathy obtained throughout the interviews were more predictive of therapeutic outcome compared to cases with relatively lower "highest" moments, and by contrast, there was no relationship between the level of lowest moments of accurate empathy and case outcome." Several studies (Truax and Carkhuff, 1963) indicate that "therapist level of empathy does not tend to vary systematically across time in therapy with patients."

Truax and Carkhuff (1967) examine the results of numerous investigations which examine a multiplicity interaction effects and associations between the essential facilitative conditions for effective psychotherapy (non-possessive warmth, empathy, and genuineness) and psychotherapy outcome. These authors (Truax and Carkhuff, 1967) also present a comprehensive didactic and experiential training model that can be utilized within the context of counselor and therapist training and supervision programs to significantly enhance the counselor or therapist's ability to consistently provide high levels of the essential therapeutic ingredients which also consistently produce successful psychotherapy outcomes. The bulk of this data continues to be rather compelling some forty years after much of it was initially published.

The contemporary study of Elliot et al. (2011) examining the impact of empathy on therapeutic outcome and involved a sample of two hundred and twenty-four separate tests of empathy-outcome association, age-related into fifty-nine different samples of clients from 57 studies and encompassing a total of 3,599 clients:

> reports several therapist mediating factors and client factors associated with therapist empathy and therapeutic outcome. Within the context of this study, the authors indicate that consistent with recent affective neuroscience research, "research in both developmental psychology and in psychotherapy has found relations between various measures of cognitive complexity, such as those perspective-taking or abstract ability, and empathy. With respect to affective stimulation and emotional regulation, therapists who were open to conflictual, countertransferential feelings were perceived as more empathic by clients" (p. 46). Also, the degree of similarity between therapist and client influences the level of empathy, as does the similarity and familiarity between the target of empathy and the empathizes in neuroscience studies of mirror neurons.

Another important factor is therapist non-linguistic and paralinguistic behavior. This encompasses "therapists' posture, vocal quality, ability to encourage exploration using emotion words, and not talking too much, giving advice, or interrupting" (p. 46). Related to these findings, a "qualitative study of clients' experience of empathy" by Myers (2000) found that "interrupting, failing to maintain eye contact, and dismissing the clients' position while imposing the therapist's own position were all perceived as unemphatic; conversely, being nonjudgmental, attentive, open to discussion of any topic, and paying attention to details were perceived as empathic" (pp. 173–185).

Both clinical and research evidence suggest out-patient or client factors also clearly impact the level of therapist empathy. Beutler et al. (1990) indicated "patients who are highly sensitive, suspicious, poorly motivated, and reactive against authority perform relatively poorly with therapists who are particularly empathic, involved, and accepting" (p. 279).

As the author (Forrest, 1984, 1985, 2002, 2012, 2013) has consistently noted, addictive-disordered patients often present and continue to manifest the very characteristics that Beutler et al. (1986) describe, and some addictive-disordered patients can also negatively impact the therapists' capacity to provide high level therapeutic conditions vis-à-vis their manipulative, angry, dishonest, denial-based, and even combative personality and characterological styles. Thus, addictive disordered patients manifesting co-morbid borderline personality disorder, antisocial personality disorder, bi-polar disorder and other diagnoses facilitate a diversity of therapist and psychotherapy relationship impediments and challenges related to the therapist's capacity to provide facilitative therapeutic interventions. These common patient realities and others have historically facilitated the reluctance of many psychotherapists, physicians and other health providers to enter into the realm of addictions-related psychotherapy and health care (Forrest, 1985, 2002, 2013).

However, as Elliott et al. (2011) and others have indicated (Duan and Hill, 1996; Martin, 2000) when therapists are "truly empathic they attune to their clients' needs and accordingly adjust how and how much they express empathy, especially, when clients are experiencing negative in-session reactions to their therapists or shame-ridden vulnerability." Experienced addictions therapist well recognize that they will infrequently be faced with the various clinical realities that can be associated with therapeutic and other office encounters with acutely intoxicated or psychotic patients who, at the very least, "challenge" the limits of their empathy skills and therapeutic *armamentarium!* The juxta positioned therapeutic realities of these patients, therapeutic interactions and moments generally prove to be exceedingly difficult for all therapists practicing with a diversity of patient populations in a diversity of psychotherapy and treatment settings.

Importantly, empathy and psychotherapy outcome investigators consistently point out the various methodological and research limitations associated with their investigations, and as Elliot et al. (2011) note the "key question of whether empathy is causally related to therapeutic outcome-as opposed to being merely correlated, it cannot be answered unequivocally from a meta-analysis of process-outcome studies. However, these authors also point out that several additional causal modeling studies (Anderson et al., 2009); Burns and Nolen-Hoeksema, 1992) investigating empathy and outcome and empathy or comparable variables separate from therapy support the position that the evidence they (Elliott et al., 2011) have presented. It is "clearly compatible with a causal model implicating therapist empathy as a mediating process leading to client change. The authors do discuss additional caveats and limitations associated with their study and other psychotherapy process and outcome investigations.

The authors (Elliott et al., 2011) further indicate that "empathy is a medium-sized but variable predictor of outcome psychotherapy. The most robust evidence is that clients' perceptions of feeling understood by their therapists relate to outcome. This repeated finding, in both dozens of individual studies and now in multiple meta-analyses, lead to a series of clinical recommendations" (p. 47).

Elliott et al. (2011) provide the following empathy specific recommendations and psychotherapy practice guidelines for therapists:

(1) an empathic stance on the part of the therapist is in essential goal of all psychotherapists, regardless of theoretical orientation, treatment format, and severity of patient psychopathology, (2) it is important for psychotherapists to make every effort to understand their clients, and to demonstrate this understanding through responses that address the perceived needs of the client—the empathic therapists' primary task is to understand experiences rather than words. Empathic therapists do not parrot clients' words back or reflect only the content of those words; instead, they understand overall goals as well as moment-to-moment experiences, (3) therapist responses that accurately respond to and carry forward the meaning in the client's communication are useful. These responses can take various forms—empathic understanding responses convey understanding of client experiences—empathic affirmations are attempts by the therapists to validate the client's perspective—empathic evocative responses try to bring the client's experience alive using quick, evocative, concrete, connotative language and often have a problem solving quality—empathic conjectures attempt to get at what is implicit in clients' narratives but not yet articulated—They are similar to interpretation but do not attempt to provide the client with new information, rather they are guesses grounded in what the client has presented, (4) empathic therapists assist clients to symbolize their experience in words, and track their emotional responses so that clients can deepen their experience and reflexively examine their feelings, valves and goals—to this end, therapists attend to what is not said, (5) empathy entails individualizing responses to particular patients. For example, certain fragile patients may find the usual expressions of empathy too intrusive, while hostile patients may find empathy too directive—Therapists therefore need to know when—and when not to respond empathically, (6) There is no evidence that accurately predicting clients' own views of their problems or self-perceptions is effective. Therapists should assume neither that they are mind readers nor that their experience of understanding the client will be matched by the client feeling understood—Empathy should always be offered with humility and held lightly, ready to be corrected, and finally (7) because research has shown empathy to be inseparable from the other relational conditions, therapists should seek to offer empathy in the context of positive regard and genuineness. Empathy will not be effective unless it is grounded in authentic caring for the client. We encourage psychotherapists to value empathy

as both an "ingredient" of a healthy therapeutic relationship as well as a specific, effective response that promotes strengthening of the self and deeper exploration. (pp. 47–48)

Therapist accurate empathic understanding is a core ingredient that is empirically and consistently fosters successful psychotherapy relationships that involve a diversity of patient populations, therapy modalities and therapist approaches, and treatment settings. Historic and contemporary accurate empathy studies (Shapiro and Gust, 1974; Truax and Carkhuff, 1967; Truax and Lister, 1921; Ulvenes et al., 2012) supporting the consistent body of this research over the past fifty years have included hospitalized chronic schizophrenics, depressives, college students, juvenile delinquents, substance abusers, anxiety disordered patients who were treated by a diversity of therapists utilizing a variety of treatment modalities within the context of a diversity treatment settings. The therapist's skill and ability to be consistently empathic in psychotherapy also may vary as a result of any number of factors, but as Truax and Carkhuff, 1967) also clearly demonstrated—accurate empathy and training specific to the core ingredients of effective psychotherapy can also significantly enhance therapist's dislike related to providing these conditions within their counseling and therapeutic relationships with clients.

GENUINENESS

As touched upon earlier in this chapter, Rogers (1957) initially indicated that the "necessary and sufficient conditions for therapeutic change involved the client who was in a "state of incongruence," a client and therapist who were in "psychological contact, and a therapist who was "congruent or integrated in the relationship" and experiencing "a positive regard for the client 'as well as' an empathic understanding of the client's internal frame of reference" (p. 96). As Kolden et al. (2011) note, two facets of congruence include the therapist's personal integration in the relationship, or "he is freely and deeply himself, with his experience accurately represented by his awareness of himself" (p. 65). Secondly, congruence or genuineness refers to "the psychotherapist's capacity to communicate his or her experience with the client to the client—the aim is not for the client to indulge in indiscriminate self-disclosure or ventilation of feelings—he or she must not deceive the client about his or her feelings—neither empathy nor regard can be conveyed unless the therapist is perceived as genuine" (Kolden et al., 2011, p. 65) Client centered therapists (Rogers, 1942, 1951, 1957; Rogers and Dymond, 1954), existential therapists and "third force" therapists of the 1950s and 60s

(May 1958, 1973) as well as Neo-Freudian analysts (Fromm-Reichmann, 1950, 1959; Gendlin and Geist, 1962) emphasized the importance and therapeutic aspects of therapist over therapeutic modality and self-issues in the therapeutic encounter. May (1958) states that "the relationship of the therapist and patient is taken as a real one—the therapist being not merely a shadowy reflector but an alive human being who happens, at that hour, to be concerned not with his own problems but with understanding and experiencing, so far as possible the being of the patient; and the therapist is assumedly an expert, but if he is not first of all a human being, his expertness will be irrelevant and quite possibly harmful—the therapist is what Socrates named the 'mid-wife'—completely *real* in "being there," but being there with the specific purpose of helping the other person to bring to birth something from within himself" (pp. 80–82).

Truax and Carkhuff (1967) note that "the therapist, within the relationship be himself integrated, genuine, and authentic seems most basic to therapeutic outcome—the counselor or therapist must be a real person in the encounter, presenting himself without defensive phoniness, without hiding behind the facade of the professional role—the current conceptualization of genuineness (or authenticity or congruence) requires the therapist's personal involvement; he is not simply 'doing his job' as a technician—the therapist's capacity for openness and personal freedom in the therapeutic encounter offers, in part, a model for the client to follow in moving toward openness and freedom to be oneself" (p. 329).

Jourard (1964) states:

> if therapists are themselves in the presence of the patient, avoiding compulsiveness to silence, to reflection, to interpretation, to impersonal technique, and kindred character disorders, but instead are striving to know their patient, involving themselves in his situation, and then responding to his utterances with their patients. They employ their powers in the service of their patient's well-being and growth. (p. 62)

Jourard (1964) further concludes:

> (1) the closest therapists can come to eliciting and reinforcing real-self behavior in their clients is by manifesting real-self behaviors themselves, (2) when therapists are committed to the task of helping clients grow, they function as whole persons, not as disembodied intellects, computers, or reinforcement programmers, (3) in the presence of a man or woman who is of good will, even the most defensive will self-disclose, (4) no patient can be expected to drop all of his or her defenses or fully disclose or reveal himself or herself *except* in the presence of someone whom he or she believes is for them, (5) therapy proceeds through *honest* responses between the client

and counselor, (6) to be transparent to the client, to have nothing of one's experience in the relationship that is hidden, is basic to effective psychotherapy, (7) if a therapist hides his being from the client, he is engaging in the same behavior that generated symptoms in the clients, (8) therapist openness serves gradually to relieve the client's distrust, (9) by being open and letting themselves *be* in the therapy relationship and also letting clients be, therapists provide clients with a role-model for personal growth, and (10) a therapeutic relationship (or alliance) can change the therapist as much as it does the client. (Forrest, 2012)

Rogers et al. (1967) have also generally defined congruence or genuineness as the therapist openly "being the feelings and attitudes which at the moment are flowing within him." These authors also include the importance of the therapist "not hiding behind a professional role or "holding back feelings that are obvious" in the therapeutic encounter.

The author (Forrest, 1984, 1985, 1997) has defined genuineness an addictions psychotherapy as the therapist's ability to "be open to his or her own experience within the therapeutic encounter. Furthermore, the therapist is able to honestly and genuinely express his or her own feelings, beliefs, and experiences with the patient—the psychotherapist is a "real person" within the therapeutic encounter—the therapist needs to interact with patients in a manner that conveys a deep sense of dignity, respect and worth for the patient" (pp. 56–57).

Genuineness has been defined in the contemporary psychotherapy literature by Kolden et al. (2011) as "the therapist is mindfully genuine in the therapy relationship, underscoring present personal awareness as well as genuineness or authenticity." These authors also stated that "congruence thus involves mindful self-awareness and self-acceptance on the part of the therapist as well as a willingness to engage and tactfully share perceptions. Therapist genuineness has remained an important construct in many psychotherapy theoretical orientations and therapy models, and psychotherapy constructs such as the therapist *real relationship* (Gelso and Carter, 1985; Gelso and Hayes, 1998; Orellana et al., 2013) corroborating the "healing qualities" of genuineness and congruence within the context of the therapeutic encounter. Genuineness is defined by Gelso and Carter (1994) as "the ability to and willingness to be what one truly is in the relationship." Therapist genuineness has also been definitionally associated with therapist characteristics such as authentically, transparency, self-disclosure, rigorous honesty, real person, openness, and non-phoniness (Jourard, 1964; Forrest, 1970, 1984, 2002, 2012; Gelso and Hayes, 1998; Greenson, 1967; Truax and Carkhuff, 1967).

Kolden et al. (2011) note that in contemporary psychotherapy literature, genuineness is "frequently considered the most important of the three

Rogerian facilitative conditions." Lietaer (1993) defines genuineness with the parameters of a two component internal and external model involving (internal) "the therapist's own internal experiencing with the client—to the extent that therapists are able to be in touch with their own experience they may be termed congruent," and the second component (external) refers to "the therapists ability to reveal their experience to their clients—this is termed transparency—it is not measuring to share every aspect of their experience but only those that they feel would be facilitative of their clients' work. Transparency is always used in an empathic climate" (Watson et al., 1998, p. 9).

Kolden et al. (2011) also indicate that the definitions of congruence have been expanded to include *therapeutic presence* and refer to an interview quote of Rogers in this context:

> over time, I think I have become more aware of the fact that in therapy I do use myself. I recognize that when I am intensely focused on a client, just my presence seems to be healing—perhaps it is something around the edges of those conditions (non-possessive warmth, empathy and genuineness) that is really the most important element of therapy—when myself is clearly, obviously present. (Baldwin, 1987, pp. 29–30)

Therapeutic *presence* implies a "dual levels of mindful awareness whereby the therapist balances contact with his or her own experience and contact with the client's experience to maintaining a place of internal and external connection" (Kolden et al., 2011).

Greenberg and Watson (2005) indicate that the "communicative aspects of congruence involve the ability to translate intrapersonal experience into certain types of interpersonal response," and a congruent response involves the therapists' ability to convey to the client attitudes of intention of being helpful, understanding, valuing, respecting and being nonintrusive or nondominant." Within this context, Kolden et al. (2011) state that congruence (or genuineness) is "more than avoiding formality on the one hand, or phoniness on the other; it entails the therapist's attentive recognition and nonjudgmental acceptance of feelings, perceptions, and thoughts, both positive and negative" (p. 127).

As noted by Kolden et al. (2011) the earliest and most frequently utilized measures of therapist genuineness in psychotherapy include the Barrett-Lennard Relationship Inventory (BLRI, 1959), Truax Relationship Questionnaire (TRQ, 1967), Carkhuff (1969) scale of genuineness, and more recently the Real Relationship Inventory (Gelso et al., 2005).

Truax and Carkhuff (1967) found in studies of group psychotherapy with hospitalized patients and other patient populations that accurate empathy, warmth or unconditional regard and genuineness were "all found to be significantly associated with the patients' engagement in the process of therapy, self-revelation and self-exploration; however, of the three, the "therapists' accurate empathy and genuineness or self-congruence were by far the most important for the patient behavior." However, a study by Truax (1965) investigating the generality of these three psychotherapy ingredients via their relationship to group psychotherapy involving "chronic hospitalized mental patients" indicated that "the therapist's genuineness was, surprisingly, in direct opposition to the prediction. There was a uniform tendency on all sub-scales (MMPI) for the patients who had received *relatively low* levels of therapist genuineness to show greater improvement than those receiving high levels. "These findings on the therapists' genuineness are well reportedly "in sharp contrast to the previous findings in individual psychotherapy" (pp. 225–228a).

Gendlin and Geist (1962) also found that "instances of extremely low genuineness in the therapist may invalidate the effects of higher levels of other conditions offered by him—Thus, in effect, the measurement of genuineness alone may serve only to indicate the deleterious effects when its level is low" (Truax and Carkhuff, 1967, p. 87). This investigation also involves group psychotherapy patients from the Wisconsin Schizophrenia project. Truax and Carkhuff (1967) report numerous other group and individual psychotherapy studies involving "institutionalized juvenile delinquents "as well as a diversity of other patient populations also were treated in various settings' (i.e., college students, mental health clinics, etc.) having treatment outcomes consistently indicating "higher" (therapeutic) conditions in therapy were associated with positive changes, while low conditions were associated with negative or deteriorative changes. With outpatients, the data suggest that warmth is most important, genuineness less important, and empathy least important.

The recent extensive meta-analytic review of empirical evidence pertaining to the relationship between therapist genuineness (congruence) and client psychotherapy outcomes (Kolden et al., 2011) was "previously reviewed by at least ten sets of researchers." These authors provide specific references to these earlier authors and studies dating between 1970 (Meltzoff and Kornreich, 1970) and 1994 (Orlinsky et al., 1994). Twenty additional articles addressing therapist genuineness and client therapy outcomes identified by Klein et al. (2002) and another five "potential articles" were evaluated in the recent met-analytic investigation conducted by Kolden et al. (2011).

Kolden et al. (2011) provides extensive and detailed methodological information related to the design, data analysis and findings related to their recent meta-analysis investigation of the therapist genuineness—client psychotherapy outcomes relationship. Their research procedure "resulted in fourteen articles reporting sixteen studies" that were also included in the meta-analysis. The overall "weighted effect size" for genuineness (congruence) with psychotherapy outcome was .24. This over-all effect size for genuineness is considered a "small to medium effect" (Cohen, 1988) and "accounts for six percent of the variance in treatment outcome." According to Kolden et al. (2011) "this provides evidence for congruence (genuineness) as a noteworthy facet of the psychotherapy relationship." However, the authors also indicate this finding must be "cautiously interpreted," as publication bias favors significant results; thus, this effect size may be an overestimation of the congruence-outcome relationship in psychotherapy—at the same time, "this effect size could also be an underestimation as we used the conservation assumption of treating unreported, a nonsignificant result as zero" (p. 68).

Kolden et al. (2011) also found that client-rated outcome produced a "significantly higher effect size than therapist-rated outcome." However, their finding may also affect the "fact that with congruence (genuineness) and outcome were more often assessed from the client perspective, and assessed with the observation that relations within this perspective (the client-related process and client-related outcome) are often more robust." Additional methodological and phenomenological factors may have also influenced their findings. The authors also found a "positive relation between therapist clinical experience and the genuineness-psychotherapy outcome effect size" (pp. 69–70).

The Kolden et al. (2011) meta-analytic study also examined several additive clients, and treatment factors related to therapist genuineness and therapist outcome. The authors do point out most of the studies included in their investigation were published prior to 1990 when "client descriptive information was seldom reported" and thus, limit the results of this study. The authors do report that client education "moderated the magnitude of the congruence (genuineness)—outcome relation—as education decreased, the congruence-outcome relation increased. Clients with less education were most likely to demonstrate a greater congruence-outcome relation, in other words, therapist genuineness (congruence) is more important for outcome with less educated clients" (p. 68). Client age "as a continuous variable" was not a significant moderator; however, adolescent vs. adult did moderate the genuineness outcome relation. Studies examining the genuineness-therapy outcome relation with adolescent populations "attained a significantly higher effect size than those using adult clients—Thus, it appears that therapist congruence (genuineness) may be more important for outcome in adolescent clients" (pp. 68–69).

The authors (Kolden et al., 2011) indicate that their investigation found that therapist theoretical orientation does impact the genuineness effect size, and they also "speculated that congruence (genuineness) is more important for outcome in a present-oriented, problem-focused therapy orientation in contrast to psychodynamic approaches—this meta-analytic study found that eclectic, client-centered and interpersonal theoretically-oriented therapists "attained significantly higher effect sizes than those characterized as psychodynamic" (p. 70).

Therapist genuineness outcome effect sizes also showed significant differences among different therapeutic settings: "school counseling centers, impatient settings, and mixed settings had a significantly higher effect size than outpatient mental health settings, and school counseling centers also had a significantly higher effect size than mixed settings." Finally, with regard to the effect of psychotherapy modality (group vs. individual therapy) on the genuineness therapy outcome association, "group therapy studies obtained a higher effect size than those examining individual therapy—congruence (genuineness) may be more important for outcome in group therapy." The authors further note that the higher group therapy genuineness-outcome effect size findings "might have more to do with the characteristics of the clients involved (in the studies) than the format pattern "(individual vs. group therapy) given that adolescents and inpatients were highly represented in the group therapy condition" (Kolden et al., 2011, pp. 67–70).

Kolden et al. (2011) also address the role of patient genuineness and various other interpersonal and intrapersonal factors as well as therapist-patient relationship dynamics that impact psychotherapy outcomes, client perceptions, beliefs, needs, responses and desire for therapist genuineness. Patients and therapists may be impacted by a diversity of factors that include diagnostic characteristics, multicultural, ethnic and gender or racial matters, socioeconomic, educational, age, religious, and occupational influences. Zane et al. (2004) suggest that a congruence (genuineness) "match between the client and therapist may be of great consequence" for the psychotherapy relationship. Kolden et al. (2011) state that:

> a client who has greater needs and expectation for congruence is likely to find comfort and satisfaction (an emotional hand/therapeutic alliance) with a highly congruent (genuine) therapist—These clients require a therapist to be comfortable and at ease, "real and genuine," say tactfully what he or she is feeling and thinking, naturally express honest, authentic impressions, not avoid, hide, hold back, or fail to be direct when the "elephant in the room" requires confrontation. Clients in a congruent therapy relationship learn that they are capable and worthy of time and attention, that they matter as a person with strengths and weaknesses, regrets as well as hopes and dreams for the future—Therapist commitment to truthfulness promotes client acceptance of the problems they face as well as efforts to change. (p. 69)

The authors of this extensive meta-analytic study of the relationship between therapist genuineness and client psychotherapy outcome (Kolden et al., 2011) site several limitations of their research:

> studies not limited to clients in need of change, low levels or restricted ranges of genuineness, different rating perspectives, varying qualifications and/or training of raters, sampling methods, small sample sizes, paucity of recent studies examining the congruence-outcome association and the lack of any randomized controlled trials investigating the causal impact of congruence. (p. 69)

The authors also note that it is important "not to overgeneralize," pointing out that "positive findings for genuineness/congruence have appeared primarily in studies investigating client-centered, eclectic, and interpersonal therapies—as such, researcher bias is one possible explanation for our results—congruence/genuineness may not be as potent a change process in all types of therapy nor with all kinds of clients (p. 69).

However, the authors finally conclude that:

> the finding of a small to medium effect size in the present quantitative review and affirmative impressions from our previous qualitative review (Klein et al., 2002) lead us to reaffirm our previous conclusion that the evidence is likely to be more strongly supportive than appears at first glance of a positive relation between genuineness and psychotherapy outcome—a consistent pattern of positive findings is quite unlikely to be explained by study flaws. (pp. 69–70)

Kolden et al., (2011) also provide the following therapist clinical practice recommendations for fostering therapeutic genuineness:

> (1) Therapists must first embrace the idea of striving for genuineness with their clients. This involves acceptance of and receptivity to experiencing with the client as well as willingness to use this information in discourse. The congruent (genuine) therapist is responsible for his or her feelings and reactions and this "ownership of feelings is specified—This experimental stance serves an attachment function (bonding) as well as a role (guides behavior) for the therapy relationship, (2) therapists can mindfully develop the intrapersonal quality of congruence (genuineness), (3) therapists can model congruence (genuineness)—congruent (genuine) responding may well involve considered therapist self-disclosure of personal information and life experiences—It could also entail therapist articulation of thoughts, feelings, opinions, pointed questions, and feedback regarding client behavior. Congruent responses are not disrespectful, overly intellectualized, or insincere and though they may involve irreverence. They are authentic and consis-

tent with the therapist as a real person with lies, dislikes, beliefs, and opinions as well as a sense of humor—genuine therapist responses are cast in the language of personal pronouns, (4) the maintenance of congruence requires that therapists be aware of instances when congruence falters, (5) It is important for therapist to identify and become aware of their congruence (genuineness) style and to discern the differing needs, preferences and expectations that clients have for congruence—effective therapists will modify and tailor their congruence style according to client presentation (i.e., culture, age, education), (6) Congruence (genuineness) may be especially important in younger, less educated, and perhaps less sophisticated clients (i.e., adolescents, college students, young adults). The congruent (genuine) therapist communicates acceptance and the possibility of engaging in an authentic relationship, something needed, but not easily expected from the often formal and authoritarian adults in the lives of these clients, and (7) congruence appears to be especially apparent in psychotherapy with more experienced (often older) practitioners. Perhaps therapists come to relax the pretense of role bound formality and give themselves permission to genuinely engage their clients as they gain experience, confidence and maturity—moreover, experienced therapists may recognize and more carefully discern a clients' need for relational congruence (genuineness and authenticity). (p. 70)

The author (Forrest, 2012, 2013) would modify the Kolden et al. (2011) sixth therapist recommendation that "the congruent therapists communicated acceptance and the *possibility of engaging in an authentic relationship,*" to the "congruent addictions-focused therapists *always* attempts" to communicate acceptance and the personal relational qualities or ingredients that are essential for the client to engage in an authentic and potentially healing human relationship with the therapist. In accord with this modified stance and as an older therapist with the clinical experiences of several hundreds of patients over the course of some forty-five years of practice, this author is in complete agreement with the final recommendation and observations Kolden et al., (2011) provide in their recent article!

As noted earlier in this section of the chapter, Truax and Carkhuff (1967) indicate that "the therapist, within the (therapeutic) relationship, be himself (or herself) integrated, genuine, and authentic seems most basic to therapeutic outcome. Without such genuineness, a trusting relationship could scarcely exist—the counselor or therapist must be a real person in the encounter, presenting himself (herself) without defensive phoniness, and without hiding behind the façade of the professional role" (p. 329). This therapeutic stance is generally consistent with the diversity of congruence-genuineness therapy outcome evidence-based studies that have been examined in this chapter, and over the course of more than fifty years. Therapist genuineness plays a key role in the therapeutically interactive process involving the various other ingredients that effect efficacious positive therapeutic outcomes.

CONCRETENESS

The therapist's ability to effectively *communicate* with the patient has long been recognized as a key clinical component of effective and productive psychotherapy relationships. Truax and Carkhuff (1967) also emphasized the importance of the therapist's capacity to consistently communicate with the patient in a concrete or mutually understandable manner. These authors examine the historic emphasis that a diversity of widely recognized therapists representing a spectrum of theoretical orientations have made related to the matter of the relevancy of therapist communication concreteness and successful or efficacious psychotherapy outcomes. For example, Rogers (1957) specifies that the "therapist's ability to communicate empathic understanding and unconditional positive regard for the patient, and his being a congruent or genuine person in the relationship, are both "necessary and sufficient" conditions for (positive) therapeutic change" (pp. 95–103). The therapist is "deliberately realistic and non-partial in his concrete relationship with the patient—he is fully aware of the therapeutic assignment of talking to the patient in terms the patient can understand and accept. Freudian interpretations mostly follow a common-sense vocabulary hardly different from other schools" (p. 27).

Truax and Carkhuff (1967) review the historic clinical and research psychotherapy works of therapists such as Alexander (1956), Bordin (1995), Brammer and Shostrom (1964), Fiedler (1955), Fromm-Reichmann (1948, 1952), McGowan and Schmidt (1962), Menninger (1958), and Sullivan (1954) emphasizing the importance of effective concrete therapist communication in psychotherapy. In this general review involving several schools of therapy, Cameron (1963) highlights this construct in psychoanalysis and all forms of expressive psychotherapy, noting "true expressive psychotherapy is carried out by both patient and therapist alike in ordinary terms—the good psychotherapist always adopts some of the patient's own terms in their communication, always doing this without artificiality, condensation, or facetiousness. When a patient says approvingly, "you speak my language," this may well be a sign that the therapist is reaching the patient in a common-sense, personal level" (p. 40). In his effort to facilitate effective communication, the therapist strives to understand the patient's behavior by observing how he behaves, thinks and expresses emotions, by formulating ideas as to why the patient behaves as he does.

As Rogers and Truax (1966) suggested, the "order in which the three essential therapeutic conditions (non-possessive warmth, empathy and genuineness) are considered is especially significant because of their "interlocking nature;" for example, Truax and Carkhuff (1967) indicate:

> accurate empathy involves more than just the ability of the therapist to sense the client or patient's "private world" as if it were his own. It also involves more than just his ability to know what the patient means. Accurate empathy involves both the therapist's sensitivity to current *feelings* and his verbal facility to (concretely) communicate this understanding in a language attuned to the clients' current feelings. (p. 46)

Truax and Carkhuff (1967) further report that their research findings suggest that "the person" (whether a counselor, therapist or teacher) who is "better able to communicate warmth, genuineness, and accurate empathy is more effective in interpersonal relationships no matter what the goal of the interaction" (p. 151). These authors also indicate that their research demonstrates the

> positive effects of therapist concreteness and specificity and the negative effects of therapist ambiguity reflect the role of labeling—in a sense, the facilitation, through empathic responses to the patient's self-labeling, is akin to the patient's own development of insight into 'what leads to what' in his current existence because it aids his discrimination of precisely 'what leads to what.' Thus, the general experimental research implies that an effective therapist would be one who selectively reinforces self-concepts that have a positive value for interpersonal relating (by providing greater intensity of the essential therapeutic conditions for the patient in an understandable and concrete manner). (p. 157)

The author (Forrest, 1978. 1982, 1984, 1995, 1997, 2002, 2012 and 2014) has repeatedly emphasized the therapeutic utility and crucial importance of therapist concreteness as an essential catalyst for communicating the therapists' experience of non-possessive warmth, empathy, genuineness and authenticity to the patient. Effective interactive therapist communication and these therapeutic qualities or ingredients always remains a primary vehicle for constructive change in the process of intensive psychotherapy with addictive-disordered patients.

The patient's capacity to communicate concretely (Forrest, 1995, 2012, 2013, 2014), openly, honestly and effectively *with* the therapist also remains an important and essential ingredient in the therapeutic outcome equation process. Indeed, the capacity for consistent effective communication, openness involving honesty, and mutual understanding remains a basic ingredient in all forms of constructive human social interaction—including all forms of psychotherapy.

SUMMARY

As indicated throughput this chapter, a very consistent and protracted body of psychotherapy process and outcome evidence-based research data indicate that the therapist's ability to consistently provide high levels of non-possessive warmth or positive regard, empathy, genuineness or authenticity and concreteness within the context of the therapeutic alliance and psychotherapy relationship predictably result in successful psychotherapy outcomes.

This chapter builds upon the historical clinical practice-based conceptualizations of the alliance construct as well as the historic and contemporary evidence-based psychotherapy process and outcome research findings that have evolved over the past sixty years that were presented in Chapter 3. It is of great significance that the research and clinical evidence of the past and present continue to robustly indicate that therapist non-possessive warmth, empathy, and genuineness constitute the essential or core conditions that result in constructive patient change and contribute greatly to successful psychotherapy outcomes. The information and data presented in Chapters 3 and 4 consistently support and reflect these findings.

Non-possessive warmth, more recently referred to as "positive regard" (Farber and Doolin, 2011) was included as one of Roger's (1957) initial "necessary and sufficient conditions for (successful) therapeutic change." Therapist empathy and genuineness were Roger's other necessary ingredients that provided constructive therapeutic change.

These original clinical constructs resulted in the publication of several thousand psychotherapy research-based publications which consistently validated their roles in therapeutic practice outcome efficacy. A multiplicity of research tools and psychometric instruments have also been developed to assess these relatively specific therapist qualities over the past six decades. Many graduate programs and academically based researchers and their graduate students in counseling and clinical psychology programs as well as counselor education programs, social work programs, psychiatry departments, veteran's administration facilities, and other mental health training and treatment facilities throughout the United States have also contributed to the science and research evidence supporting the roles and efficacy of the core therapist ingredients in therapy between 1960–2020.

This chapter provides a detailed and comprehensive review of the historic and developmental evidence-based psychotherapy process outcome research pertaining to the therapist qualities of non-possessive warmth, empathy, and genuineness between 1960 and 2020. As noted earlier in this review, the therapeutic constructs, examination of research findings, and conclusions of hundreds of psychotherapy researchers who have detailed their research evidence, studies, methodology and their conclusions and interpretations related to their research evidence. It should also be noted that most of the psychotherapy researchers who have contributed to this body of psychotherapy process and outcome investigation have openly acknowledged and pointed out the various methodological limitations that are associated with their studies. The author has included in this chapter many of the difficulties and limitations that Rogers (1957), Truax and Carkhuff (1967), and most of the other practice-based clinicians, academic based clinicians, students, and psychotherapy researchers have consistently identified pertaining to their psychotherapy process-outcome publications.

The concept of therapist concreteness (Truax and Carkhuff, 1967) was not initially one of Roger's "necessary and sufficient" conditions for effective therapy. However, the clinical importance of therapist-patient communication within the context of the alliance and therapeutic relationship has long been examined in the clinical literature and also frequently noted in empirical-based therapy studies. Truax and Carkhuff (1967) stress the importance of the therapist's ability to communicate the therapeutic qualities of non-possessive warmth, empathy and genuineness in a manner that each patient understands, experiences and internally responds to. This form of therapeutic communication incorporates (accurate empathy) both the therapist's sensitivity to *current* feelings and his "verbal facility to concretely communicate this understanding in a language attuned to the client's current feelings." The chapter examines a number of other facets of effective therapist communication.

The ideas and construct content included in this chapter pertaining to non-possessive warmth, empathy, and genuineness provide a strong underpinning for the universality and generally profound relevance related to the therapist. The alliance and therapy relationship variables in all therapy and treatment relationships potentially involve all patient populations being treated in a wide variety of treatment settings via a multiplicity of treatment models or methods. With regard to these specific matters, a great deal of further complex alliance and psychotherapy research pertaining to these specific therapist and alliance qualities as well as a myriad of other therapy process-outcome and alliance factors need to be investigated. Certainly, more research is indicated pertaining to patient qualities including non-possessive warmth, empathy, genuineness, concreteness and several other specific areas of psychotherapy investigation which are discussed in Chapter 5. *Patient* therapeutic qualities, therapy setting, different therapeutic models and approaches, and diagnostic issues impact the alliance as well as a diversity of therapy alliance, process and outcome factors that need to be more fully examined.

In spite of the various caveats associated with the "universal effectiveness" of non-possessive warmth, empathy, and genuineness espoused by many clinicians, the body of evidence-based psychotherapy data and information presented in Cjhapters 3 and 4 clearly support this contention in a compelling manner. All addictions therapists and treatment providers, as well as other behavioral health clinicians, need to remain aware of the powerfully constructive and always potentially healing therapeutic impact of these therapist qualities within the context of the therapeutic alliance.

Within the context and scope of the historic alliance, therapeutic relational dynamics, and essential therapeutic ingredients related to efficacious psychotherapy relationships it is essential that all practicing counselors, therapists, addictions psychotherapists and behavioral health professional recognize that the most recent empirical research evidence consistently and rather compellingly supports the findings reported in this chapter (Bedics et al., 2015; Campbell et al., 2015; Cook and McCambridge, 2015; Fischer et al., 2016; MacFarlane, Anderson and McClintock, 2015; Miller et al., 2015; Prince et al., 2016; Wiprovnick and Kuerbis, 2015). Clinical evidence and clinical practice reports and publications also continue to endorse the enduring relevance, effectiveness and role of the alliance and psychotherapy relationship in effective psychotherapy work.

Chapter 5

ANCILLARY THERAPIST-PATIENT ALLIANCE DYNAMICS IN EFFECTIVE PSYCHOTHERAPY AND COUNSELING RELATIONSHIPS

INTRODUCTION

This chapter examines a diversity of ancillary therapist-patient alliance dynamics and factors that can significantly impact the course of both effective and ineffective psychology relationships. In some cases, the dynamics or the realities associated with them may actually become the primary factors that determine and influence the process and outcome of any therapeutic relationship . . . for better, worse, or relationships simply ended with an undetermined outcome.

The myriad of dynamics associated with patient transference continually influence the therapeutic alliance, psychotherapy relationship, and both the process of and the outcome of all counseling and therapy experiences. Definitions and descriptions of transference, historic clinical perspectives or transference, and transference related addictions psychotherapy dynamics are elucidated in this chapter. Patient transference reactions impact, influence and are manifested in all forms or models of psychotherapy and counseling, and involve all patient populations being treated in a diversity of treatment settings.

Therapists countertransference dynamics and reactions were also explored in this light. Historic definitions, designations, and clinical observations pertaining to the impact and dynamics of therapist countertransference in general psychotherapy practice go well as addictions focused therapeutic which are explained in this chapter. Differing levels and dynamics of therapist countertransference continually influence and occur within the context of all therapy and counseling relationships involving diverse clinical populations and treatment settings.

Therapist self-disclosure and transparency or authenticity dynamics have continued to be a point of discussion and controversy in the psychotherapy literature for over one-hundred years. However, in the advent of Client-Centered therapy (Rogers, 1942, 1951, 1957) and various other models of psychotherapy have been developed over the ensuring six decades. Therapist self-discipline has generally been viewed as an important and often very effective therapeutic tool that therapists can utilize to help foster adequate patient behavioral change and constructive growth. Some of the research and clinical data pertaining to self-discipline in psychotherapy included in this chapter has touched upon or discussed in the Chapters 3 and 4 of this text. This chapter also includes the authors (Forest, 2012) work pertaining to counselor and therapist self-disclosure in the context of addiction psychotherapy work. Therapist self-disclosure in addictions therapy sometimes result in unpredictable client responses, and alliance disequilibrium, and anxiety. However, therapist disclosures also frequently facilitate patient openness, foster alliance cohesion and client attachment, and synergize healthy patient learning as noted earlier in the text patient openness, self-disclosure, honestly, and truth telling are also essential ingredients in alliance development and effective therapy outcomes. Yet, as Han and O'Brien (2014) point out it is always impossible to know in advance how a particular therapist disclosure will impact a particular client at any juncture in the therapeutic process.

As noted in the self-disclosure section of this chapter, therapist's always need to utilize conscious awareness, appropriate timing and sensitivity when self-disclosing. Therapists need to utilize self-disclosures judicially and always in the service of client growth and awareness rather than as an attempt to meet or resolve self-directed and self-motivated needs. Therapist's self-disclosure always remains a somewhat thorny mechanism related to client and therapist-related change, and addiction therapists need to remain ever cognizant of the realities in their therapeutic work with addictive disorder persons.

Patient and sometimes therapist relapses during the process of therapy can result in any number of very impactful alliance consequences this chapter addresses a multiplicity of issues pertaining essentially relapse may occur at any junction in the therapeutic process to psychotherapy relationships involving addictive disregarded persons. The various realities of associated with psychotherapy terminations, legal entanglements, severe health issues, patients commitments to psychiatric units, detox centers and residential treatment program are discussed in this chapter.

As the author notes, "it is highly unrealistic" for therapists to expect addictive-disordered patients entering therapy to never relapse or return to a fully-functioning life style. Recovering therapists and counselors can also experience relapses which significantly impact the therapeutic alliance, patients and themselves directly in a myriad of unpredictable but unusually corrosive ways.

The concept of rupture implies a "dramatic breakdown" in therapy "in theory; however, ruptures vary in intensity, and therapist-patient misunderstanding and communication difficulties, therapeutic impasse, or empathetic failure may also characterize alliance ruptures. However, as told in the chapter alliance ruptures or stressors may also be related to disagreements that the tasks of therapy, conflicts related to treatment goals, and strains in the patient-therapist bond (Bordin, 1979). These episodes of tension or breakdown in the collaborative patient-therapist relationship may occur independent of the therapeutic model or approach. Successful alliance repair and fosters the clients' ability to actively participate in an adaptive resolution of alliance conflicts.

This section of the chapter also eliminates several recent evidence-based clinical alliance-rupture and repair work factors of dynamics related to both general psychology practice (Escudero et al. 2012; Friedlander et al. 2014; Safran, Muran and Eubanks-Carter, 2011), and specific addiction-focused psychotherapy related therapist strategies. Addiction-focused alliance rupture and repair practice suggestions and guidelines (Forrest, 1997, 2014) are also included in the chapter.

Practicing therapists and counselors discover very early in their clinical practice work that relatively "common everyday lifestyle" factors and dynamics impact the therapeutic alliance and psychotherapy relationships in a myriad of profound or very significant ways. As indicated earlier in the chapter, the potentially profound alliance factors involve a myriad of everyday life events or circumstances ranging from the sudden death of the patient or therapist, to loss of health insurance, or perhaps a job, geographical moves, divorce and accidents. Alliance ending or changing can also precipitates a diversity of circumstantial reactions, consequences, or even potentially life changing dynamics effecting both therapist and patient.

TRANSFERENCE

Transference has been defined (Marmarosh et al. 2012) as "the degree to which the client is dealing with material that is overtly or covertly related to the therapist. This material must be a manifestation of, or displacement from an early important relationship. The previous person (or transference source), however, need not be mentioned; he or she may be inferred because of, for example, the presence of distortion, strong affect, inappropriate affect, and so forth" (p. 364). More recently, Gelso and Bhatia (2012) also provide the following "working definition" of transference as "representing the patient's experience and perceptions of the therapist that are shaped by the patient's own psychological structures and past, involving carryover from and displacement onto the therapist's feelings, attitudes, and behaviors belonging rightfully in earlier significant relationships." These authors also note that the therapist, "no matter how neutral, does contribute to the transference experience, creating some degree of co-construction" (p. 385).

Gelso and Hayes (1998) indicate that "to varying degrees, transference occurs and affects process and outcome in all psychotherapies, regardless of theoretical orientation." Gelso and Bhatia (2012) also state that leading theoreticians of "just about all major theoretical counseling and psychotherapy orientations acknowledge that transference exists in all therapies" (p. 384). These authors refer to the work of Rogers (1951), Pearls (1958), May (1983), Brown (1994), Kelly and Greene (2010), Rabinovich and Kacen (2009), and Sullivan (1954) in this context.

Anderson and Przybylinski (2012) state that transference "occurs in all types of psychotherapies regardless of approach." According to Anderson and Przybylinski (2012), transference occurs when a significant-other representation is activated by a new person, usually through subtle resemblance to this significant other." These authors also suggest that transference processes "emerge in everyday life in normal individuals and not only in clinical populations nor specific interventions in treatment" (pp. 370–372). They further point out that Sullivan (1953) indicated that "another person may be perceived or evaluated based on relational learning acquired in actual interactions with past significant others so that he or she then potentially recreates patterns from prior relationships anew." Sullivan's "dynamisms" (1954) also reflect the "relationship and typical interpersonal interactions that occur with the significant other." Horney (1939) viewed transference in terms of the "problematic interpersonal patterns" which she referred to as "neurotic trends" (p. 371).

Marmarosh (2012) defines transference as the "degree to which the client is dealing with material that is overtly of covertly related to the therapist." This material must be a manifestation of or displacement from an early important relationship. The previous person (or transference source), however, need not be mentioned; he or she may be inferred because of, for example, the presence of distortion, strong affect, inappropriate affect, and so forth (p. 364).

Levy and Scala (2012) elucidate the contextual development of the transference concept and then define transference as a "tendency in which representational aspects of important and formative relationships (such as with parents and siblings) can be both consciously experienced and/or unconsciously ascribed to other relationships—this fundamentally unconscious process also occurs in relationships between therapists and patients, and although there may be real aspects to this experience, it often represents a distortion or cognitive bias" (p. 392). These authors also note that transference can be "reality based" and involves individual differences in terms of degree, rigidity, awareness and other dynamics related to the patient and therapist relationship.

As Levy and Scala (2012) further indicate, it was Freud (1905/1963) who elaborated upon and synthesized the concept of transference as being generally regarded as the "similes that replaced some earlier person by the person of the physician, some were found to be more ingenuously constructed by the patient—by cleverly taking advantage of some real peculiarity in the physician's person or circumstances and attaching themselves to that" (p. 391). Freud (1912) also described transference as a source of resistance in psychotherapy and believed that the therapist resolution of the patient's transference neurosis constituted a "cure" in psychoanalysis. Freud viewed (Levy and Scala, 2012) transference as the "central mechanism of therapeutic change, and saw the central task of psychoanalysis as the establishment, interpretation, and resolution of transference" (p. 391).

Gelso and Bhatia (2012) provide a rather extensive review of the recent empirical research evidence pertaining to transference in non-analytic therapies and conclude that "in both quantitative and qualitative studies involving samples of behavior therapy, cognitive therapy, and cognitive-behavior therapy, as well as in samples of theoretically heterogeneous psychotherapies, transference indeed seems to exist and show itself in the treatment hour" (p. 386). A plethora of transference related psychotherapy studies support this position (Arachtingi and Lichtenberg, 1998, 1999; Beach and Power, 1996; Bradley, Heim and Westen, 2005; Horowitz and Moeller, 2009; Gelso et al., 2005; Tellides et al., 2008).

An early investigation involving mostly behavior therapy (Ryan and Gizynski, 1971) reported "these patients hardly stopped talking about issues in the relationships between themselves and their therapists—time and again, it seemed that just as in psychodynamic psychotherapy, elements of the transference intruded into these therapies" (p. 6). Interestingly, these authors also reported "it was surprising to observe how infrequently the therapists were aware of such phenomena (transference) or how little importance they attributed to them." Even when there was clear evidence for "strong sexual and dependent feelings for their therapists, these feelings were never explored, including when they threatened to jeopardize otherwise successful treatments" (pp. 6–7).

Schaeffer (2007) concludes: "there is no question that *all* therapists and clients transfer functions and roles they or others played in the past to each other. There is no question that non-analytic therapists much identify transference and countertransference as soon as possible. There is no question that they must diagnose them accurately and give serious consideration to interpreting them to appropriate clients so that, rather than be controlled by them, they can control them, and benefit from the major contributions they can make to variables responsible for positive outcomes—otherwise, the double-edged swords of transference and countertransference will cut their way through what is working and enable variables responsible for negative outcome to gain a stronghold" (p. 11).

Readers are especially encouraged to examine the recent and historic transference focused psychotherapy investigations of Gelso and Bhatia (2012) for a more thorough examination of the many impactful evidence-based facets of transference on the process and outcomes of psychotherapy.

The author (Forrest, 1984, 1997, 2002, 2012, 2014, 2017) has written extensively about a diversity of transference related dynamics that are related to the therapeutic alliance as well as the process and outcome of psychotherapy relationships involving addictive-disordered patients. In a very early text (Forrest, 1975), it was noted that "constructive change is not possible in the absence of a transference relationship—perhaps more than anything else, the alcoholic needs to establish a meaningful relationship with a significant other human being" (p. 88).

The author also (Forrest, 1984, 1999) indicated that transference dynamics and conflicts often become "overtly and acutely manifest during the middle stages of intensive psychotherapy—transference is a Freudian concept that refers to the patient's distorted or neurotic responses to the psychotherapist and the psychotherapy relationship. In essence, transference encompasses the patient's parataxic early-life experiences and emotions that primarily stem from parental and family interactions. The patient begins to relate to the therapist as a father figure, mother, or significant other—obviously, the patient's historic authority conflicts, affective conflicts, behaviors, cognitive distortions, generalized neurotic struggles, and eventually addictive disordered brain disease issues are exacerbated as a result of the transference phenomenon in (addictions) psychotherapy" (p. 82).

According to this author (Forrest, 1999), the "alcoholic's transference distortions are usually repressed and relatively well-controlled during the initial weeks of therapy—however, after a few months of involvement in intensive psychotherapy, most patients begin to evince a rather acute transference reaction" (pp. 82–83). The therapeutic resolution of the transference neurosis (Freud, 1953; Gelso and Bhatia, 2012; Kernberg, 1975; Masterson, 1981) is believed to constitute the essence of effective treatment. Traditional psychoanalysts (Fenichel, 1945) emphasized that a therapeutic "cure" can only be affected through the successful therapeutic resolution of the transference neurosis.

The middle stages of intensive addictions-focused psychotherapy (Forrest, 1985, 1997, 2012, 2019) involve the therapeutic resolution of transference dynamics that are consistently associated with the patient's (1) avoidance defense system (denial, distortion, projection, defensiveness and resistance), (2) authority conflicts, (3) control issues, and 4) narcissistic disturbance. As noted earlier, transference dynamics and conflicts frequently become overly and acutely manifest during this stage of intensive addictions-focused psychotherapy. During this stage of therapy, many patients begin to consciously resent the therapist as an authority figure, feel controlled by the therapist, therapeutic relationship and recovery process, and also feel angry about continuing feelings of being out of control. The patient's bipolar narcissism begins to emerge in the form of an exaggerated sense of egocentricity, self, mastery, and a vacillating sense of complete inadequacy and worthlessness. Any number of narcissistic related struggles involving the patient and therapist may unfold during the middle stage of therapy.

Therapists also need to consciously recognize that the therapeutic relationship spontaneously and never endingly contributes to the development of a transference neurosis. The intimacy, dependency, regression, symbiosis, change process, authority-power dynamics and many other vicissitudes of the intensive psychotherapy relationship facilitate the evolving emergence of transference dynamics throughout the course of addictions-focused psychotherapy.

Addictions-focused therapists additionally need to consistently and sensitively point out, discuss, confront and interpret these various transference dynamics *as they occur* in addictions therapy. It is imperative that addictions therapists do not personally deny and avoid these important patient-therapist dimensions of the therapeutic process. Therapist scotomization of the therapeutic process dynamics can precipitate a diversity of psychonoxious phenomena. Importantly, the therapist needs to explore and help the patient understand and resolve important sources of patient transference and resistance within the framework of the working and productive therapeutic alliance—i.e., how the patient feels about self, the therapist, the therapeutic process, and other issues associated with the therapeutic alliance per se, whenever transference becomes manifest during each stage of addictions-focused psychotherapy work (Forrest, 1984, 1997, 2002, 2014, 2017).

There are several therapist roles and intervention strategies that can help addictive-disordered patients resolve their transference conflicts during the ongoing process of intensive psychotherapy and recovery: (1) first of all, addictions therapists need to allow the transference relationship to develop. Transference dynamics reveal many of the patient's most basic conflicts, personality and adjustment problems. Therapists should not avoid or suppress the patient's transference pathology and conflicts with the patient while initially maintaining a therapeutic alliance stance involving support, empathy and sustaining technical neutrality (2) secondly, it is imperative that the therapist sustain a working and productive therapeutic alliance context involving his or her consistent identification, interpretation and examination of the patient's transference conflicts, and finally, (3) the therapist needs to consistently help the client distinguish between the transference realities of the past and those that are, in reality, now occurring within the context of the present psychotherapy relationship and alliance involving the therapist and client. The therapist also needs to consistently differentiate himself or herself from the patient's transference images and distortions within the here and now context of the current therapeutic alliance.

The author (Forrest, 1984, 1997, 2002) has previously noted that very few addictive-disordered clients develop a classic transference psychosis during the process of ongoing intensive addictions-focused psychotherapy. However, focused transference work in therapy with this patient population can always foster and enhance alliance conflicts, possible alliance ruptures, and relapse risks for these patients (Forrest, 1997, 2012). Thus, therapists must remain every vigilant, empathetic, supportive, and consistently sensitive to these realities throughout the course of therapy. Addictions therapists need to realize "full-blown," acute, and out of control severe relapse within the context of intensive psychotherapy work with addictive-disordered persons. These episodes precipitate the equivalent of a brief or transient chemically induced acute psychotic episode. In this context, the therapist's continued ability to sustain a working and productive therapeutic alliance framework with the patient remains essential to the process of (1) helping addictive-disordered persons both modify their transference-related and more global relational conflicts, and (2) reducing, preventing, and/or clinically managing the probability of catastrophic patient relapses during the course of the intensive addictions psychotherapy process.

Transference dynamics remain unendingly present in all of our life-long human interactions and relationships. Patient transference dynamics can be evident within the patient's initial interactions with office staff as well as the therapist. The relatively unique transference dynamics that each client brings to the therapeutic relationship and therapeutic alliance are a function of the relatively limitless experiential history and core human experiences of the client. Client transference dynamics are also significantly shaped and influenced by the relatively unique and multifaceted characteristics of each therapist and each therapeutic alliance.

The early stages of the psychotherapy relationship spontaneously contribute to the development of the patient's transference neurosis involving intimacy, anxiety, regression, symbiosis, control, and parenting or authority-power dynamics associated with early life narcissistic injury (Forrest, 1983,

1997, 2012). These transference dynamics tend to evolve and change during the middle stages of therapy, and during the later stages of successful therapy cases (Forrest, 1997, 2014, 2018). The patient's transference dynamics and therapeutic stance "generally reflect a very positive transference reaction to the therapist and therapeutic relationship. These transference dynamics generally reflect the patient's sense of respect, empathy, object-identification and emulation, incorporation and internalized values. Patient transference related self-transferential cognitions, behaviors, affects, perceptions and precepts also tend to be consistently much more positive during the later stages of successful addictions-focused psychotherapy."

COUNTERTRANSFERENCE

The concept of countertransference was originally developed by Freud (1910) and was described as "arising in the physician as a result of the patient's influence on his unconscious feelings, and have nearly come to the point of requiring the physician to recognize and overcome this transference in himself."

Gelso and Hayes (2007) indicate that four models of countertransference have evolved over the past sixty or seventy years. Hayes, Gelso and Hummel (2011) further report that the classical Freudian definition of countertransference refers to "the therapist's unconscious, conflict-based reaction to the patient's transference—unresolved conflicts originating in the therapist's childhood are triggered by the patient's transference and are acted out by the therapist." The authors also point out that advocates of this position see "little or no benefit to countertransference—they do not generally believe countertransference can be used to enhance understanding or to promote therapeutic gains" (pp. 88–89).

The totalistic model of countertransference (Little, 1951) represents "all of the therapist's reactions to the patient—reactions are important, all should be studied and understood," and, thus, countertransference became "more and more as potentially beneficial to therapy, if therapists studied their reactions and used them to further their understanding of patients" (p. 88).

The complementary model of countertransference (Hayes, Gelso and Hummel, 2011) views the therapist's reactions as "a complement to the patient's style of relating—that is, the patient exhibits certain 'pulls' on the therapist." However, these authors (Hayes, Gelso and Hummel, 2011) also note that the "well-functioning therapist does not act out Lex Talionis (an eye for an eye, a tooth for a tooth)," as others often react to the patient. This therapeutic position "fosters understanding the patient's interpersonal style of relating and for the effective framing of therapeutic interventions" (pp. 88–89).

Finally, the relational model views countertransference as mutually constructed by the patient and therapist—the needs, unresolved conflicts, and behaviors of *both* are believed to contribute to countertransference in psychotherapy. Understanding and therapeutic work by *both* the patient and therapist pertaining to countertransference dynamics can also help facilitate constructive therapeutic change and growth for the patient and therapist.

These differing conceptualizations of countertransference in contemporary therapy are used interchangeably, sometimes in a contradictory fashion, and all of these models manifest limitations.

Hayes, Gelso and Hummel (2011) also reviewed recent and historic empirical research pertaining to countertransference, noting "its management, and the relation of both to psychotherapy outcome—three meta-analyses are presented, as well as studies that illustrate findings from the meta-analyses." Based upon three meta-analysis studies, the authors report (1) "countertransference reactions are related inversely and modestly to psychotherapy outcome, (2) countertransference management factors that have been studied to date play little to no role in actually attenuating countertransference reactions, and (3) managing countertransference successfully is related to better therapy outcomes" (pp. 88–94).

These authors (Hayes, Gelso and Hummel, 2011) also indicate that countertransference is "modestly associated with less desirable psychotherapy outcomes, and that effective countertransference management is associated with fewer countertransference reactions," inferring that effective countertransference management enhances psychotherapy outcomes. The authors note that this general finding is supported by other studies indicating that "excellent therapist" and supervisor ratings of "trainee therapeutic excellence" in comparison with "therapists in general" show the excellent therapists are rated more favorably on countertransference management ability than therapists in general (Latts, 1996; Van Wagoner et al., 1991, p. 94).

In this context, Hayes, Gelso and Hummel (2011) point out that countertransference management is "largely up to therapists—there are certain patients who are difficult for most therapists to work with, and these patients are likely to evoke countertransference reactions that are challenging to manage. For example, patients with borderline features often evoke rage, and it may be difficult to produce change in these patients—patients who have poor prognoses are more likely to prompt countertransference reactions—both patient and therapist contribute to countertransference" (p. 94).

More recently, Orellana and Gelso (2013) define countertransference as "the therapist's internal and external reactions that are shaped by the therapist's past or present emotional conflicts or vulnerabilities" (p. 12). Hayes, Gelso and Hummel (2011) also suggest a number of therapeutic practices related to the empirical research evidence related to countertransference:

Therapist reactions can be useful when they inform his or her work; when acted out, these reactions are likely to be a hindrance, countertransference that is acted out in the session can be so damaging, an inverse relation between real relationship and countertransference behaviors has been theorized—research has indeed demonstrated a negative relationship between countertransference behavior in a session and the working alliance, and thus, effective psychotherapists can work at preventing such acting-out and must manage internal countertransference reactions in a way that benefits the work, several therapist behaviors appear to be a useful part of this process, i.e., using self-insights and self-integration, the therapist's struggle to gain self-understanding and work on his or her own psychological health, including boundary issues with patients are fundamental to managing and effectively using one's internal reactions, self-integration underscores the importance of the therapist resolving his or her own major conflicts, which, in turn, points to the potential value of personal therapy and clinical supervision for psychotherapists, the value of a therapist's admission that a mistake was made and that it was the therapist's conflicts that were the source (when countertransference has already been acted-out in a session), and the empirical evidence suggests that theory in conjunction with personal awareness is a key to the therapeutic use of countertransferenc. (Orellana and Gelso, 2013; Hayes, Gelso and Hummel, 2011, pp. 94–96)

Forrest (1982, 1984, 1997, 2002, 2016) has addressed and defined countertransference within the context of addictions psychotherapy work as "the therapist's inappropriate and neurotic reactions to the patient and the psychotherapy relationship—the psychotherapeutic process sometimes exacerbates the psychotherapist's unresolved infantile and family of origin conflicts. Thus, the therapist begins to interact neurotically with the patient as he or she did with early-life significant others. Countertransference reactions can result in psychonoxious psychotherapy, poor therapeutic outcomes or failures" (p. 84).

Forrest (2002) also indicates that (1) "countertransference conflicts can be related to the unconscious and preconscious behaviors and beliefs that the therapist models in the psychotherapeutic relationship, and (2) therapist countertransference distortions are frequently manifestations of over-determined 'rescuing' during the early stages of intensive addictions psychotherapy" (p. 95). Countertransference can be related to:

the process of suicidal acting-out and successful suicides in psychotherapy with alcoholics and chemically dependent patients—a basic psychodynamic consideration in therapeutic work with alcoholic patients, as with other addictive-disordered patients, has to be with our (the therapist's) countertransference distortion related to rescuing or saving the patient—addicts entering treatment are often depressed, overwhelmed, and literally 'begging for help.' As such, the alcoholic sets the therapist up for assuming a rescuing position—as a result, counselors and therapists tend to construct highly dependent relationships with their patients in which superficial or early stage sobriety and behavioral change depend upon the ongoing rescuing transactions of the therapist. Ultimately, such a psychotherapy alliance suffers a possibly irreversible impasse—in fact, the addicted patient may be killed by this form of ongoing therapeutic transaction. (pp. 85, 115)

The author's early (Forrest, 1992) elucidation of psychonoxious therapist confrontation styles of transactions suggest that these therapist transactions and behaviors sometimes evolve vis a vis the countertransference distortions of the therapist—anger, rejection, and patient dislike form the nuclear core of the therapist's pathological confrontations—iatrogenic confrontation strategies tend to evolve from the therapist's feelings of frustration, anger, and, at times, acting-out and poorly controlled rage.

Forrest (1979, 1992, 1997) has also indicated that the interpersonal style of addictive-disordered patients tends to generate countertransference distortion, and as countertransference intensifies over the course of therapy, the therapist may unwittingly sabotage the therapeutic alliance via an active movement or role shift into that of a primary persecutor.

Several other clinicians (Bratter and Forrest, 1985; Culbreth and Borders, 1999; Forrest, 2002; Levin, 1991; Weiss, 1994) have reported that chemically dependent patients can be (1) very difficult to treat, and (2) tend to evoke intense and personally disturbing emotions in the therapist—such intensive affective, cognitive and behavioral reactions are often cogent examples of countertransference.

Levin (1991) believes that countertransference is always present in the counseling relationship and that it is essential for counselors to be aware of countertransference feelings;

> otherwise, they will be acted out, to the detriment of the treatment—in the broad sense it (countertransference) tell us something about ourselves and something about the patient. Our feelings while working with patients provide us with data about our own mental processes and unresolved conflicts, and with vital data about patients' mental processes and their effects on people; they are a unique source of information, providing us with insight not otherwise available. (p. 267)

Weiss (1994) astutely observes that countertransference feelings emerge in various forms between patients and health service providers other than psychotherapists. Weiss (1994) also notes that countertransference can be associated with the tendency of medical school and psychiatric departments to "inadvertently disown" alcoholic patients, resistance toward treating substance abusers, and the professional misconception that alcoholic and sub-stance abusers are impossible to treat. Weiss further states that countertransference toward the alcoholic patient can reverberate throughout an institution, noting that alcoholics often arouse feelings of discouragement, anger, chaos, anxiety, and regression in the clinician. Indeed, institutions as well as therapists are vulnerable to unconscious countertransference reactions toward addicts, substance abusers and addictive-disordered persons in general.

Searles (1987) indicates that countertransference refers to the "attitudes and feelings, only partly conscious to the analyst toward the patient," noting that, "countertransference gives one one's most reliable approach to the understanding of patients of whatever diagnosis." Searles also emphasizes that any diagnostic formulation should begin with studying the therapist's emotional reactions in the relationship between the patient and the interviewer (therapist).

Blum (1987) defines analytic countertransference as a "counter reaction to the patient's transference which is unconscious and indicative of the analyst's own unresolved intrapsychic conflicts." Blum additionally indicates that analysts:

> (1) are vulnerable to all human frailties, to conflict and regression, (2) may have neurotic reactions to any aspect of the patient and not only to the transference, (3) the personal life ('agenda') of the analyst may be associated with vulnerability to countertransference reactions and/or the extension of his personal problems with his professional work, (4) countertransference is often related both to the specific features of the patient's transference and to the analyst's character pathology, (5) the chronically angry analyst will be prone to acute and specific negative countertransference, (6) too much therapeutic zeal and rescue fantasies, loss of therapeutic interest and concern with boredom, or subtle devaluation of the patient's efforts at mastery, and silence or speech changes (pitch, pressure, syntax) can be indicators of countertransference, and (7) countertransference reactions to termination are common. (pp. 88–93)

Contemporary therapists and analysts generally view countertransference as an inevitable and even desirable facet of the psychotherapy and psychoanalytic relationship (Forrest, 2002, 2012, 2016; Hahn, 2000; Slakter, 1987; Tansey and Burke, 1989). Brenner (1977) notes that countertransference is not necessarily harmful or destructive to the therapeutic process as well as

> ubiquitous and inescapable, just as in transference—countertransference is the transference of the analyst (therapist) in an analytic (psychotherapy) sit-

uation. Becoming an analyst (therapist) practicing analysis (psychotherapy), necessarily involves, for each individual therapist, derivatives of that therapist's childhood conflicts. There is nothing pathological or neurotic in this. It is, in fact, as inevitable for the profession of analysis (psychotherapy) as it is for the choice and practice of any other vocation. Instances of countertransference which interfere with analysis (therapy) are examples of pathological or neurotic compromise formation. (p. 44)

Forrest (2012, 2014) would additionally emphasize that being a therapist involves potential countertransference related derivatives associated with every facet of the therapist's lifespan developmental and experiential process.

Within the countertransference context, Tansey and Burke (1989) point out that "all therapists work well with certain types of patients and less, or even poorly, with others." Likewise, Sullivan (1953) refers to "difficulties in living" and indicates "we are all much more simply human than otherwise," and Ferenczi (1950), Fromm-Reichmann (1950) and other early analysts emphasized that the analyst or counselor is a "human being." Reik (1948) states, "the psychoanalyst is a human being like any other, and not a god. There is nothing superhuman about him. In fact, he has to be human. How else could he understand other human beings." If he were cold and unfeeling, a "stuffed shirt," as some plays portray him, he would be an analytic robot or a pompous, dignified ass who could not gain entry to the secrets of the human soul (p. 154).

Contemporary counselors and therapists who routinely provide online, telephonic, virtual, and other non-traditional counseling and psychotherapy services (Dillon, 2013, 2014) also tend to report preliminary anecdotal clinical as well as evidence-based data (Escudero, Friedlander, and Heatherington, 2011) supporting the efficacy of these cutting-edge therapeutic modalities. However, the roles of countertransference, therapy outcomes, transference therapy outcomes, and various other dimensions of the psychotherapy relationship continue to be empirically and clinically investigated, understood, and evaluated (Maroda, 1994; Yeh and Hayes, 2011).

Forrest (2002, 2012, 2014, 2018) and other clinicians indicated that therapist disclosure of countertransference material is currently viewed as both clinically appropriate and therapeutic. This author (Forrest, 2002) generally

> advocates sharing of countertransference material with clients, and guidelines for the therapeutic management of this complex and sometimes difficult or thorny task are outlined—countertransference can also be used as (1) a diagnostic tool, (2) a barometer of client change or index of ongoing treatment progress, and (3) a vehicle for enhancing counselor self-awareness and client self-awareness and facilitating both client and counselor personal growth and education. In contrast to the viewpoints and interpretations of

the early analysts, countertransference can always be a potential well-spring for constructive therapist and patient growth and change in virtually all psychotherapy relationships. (pp. 82–83)

The author (Forrest, 2002) also notes that psychonoxious confrontation styles of transactions frequently evolve from the countertransference distortions of the therapist. Anger, rejection and feelings of dislike may form the nuclear core of the therapist's pathologic countertransference behaviors. However, the katagogic or neurotic countertransference reactions of the therapist are also frequently exacerbated by the denial, avoidance, narcissism, resistance or regressive behaviors, acting-out, angry, and iconoclastic attitudes and other behaviors of chemically dependent patients. The pathologic anger and confrontational style of the addictive-disordered patient may also fuel the therapist's countertransference reactions, and patient relapse or multiple relapses may also trigger regressive countertransference reactions upon the part of therapists. Thus, countertransference dynamics can ultimately result in successful or unsuccessful psychotherapy outcomes (Hayes, Nelson, Fauth, 2015). Forrest (2002) has also indicated that "many therapists wisely avoid working with chemically dependent persons due to a keen awareness of their personal negative feelings and reactions to these patients." With regard to clinical practice guidelines for working with addictive disordered clients, the author further states

> it is clinically and ethically important for therapists to be aware of countertransference dynamics that (1) impede the therapist's ability to function in an optimally therapeutic fashion (with any given individual client or patient sub-population), (2) contribute to the therapist's inability to initiate or sustain a productive and efficacious psychotherapy relationship with particular patients or subgroups, or (3) impact the process of therapy in a parataxic fashion—therapist's need to be firm in their refusal to initiate treatment relationships with persons who fall into the second category. However, personal therapy and active supervision may make it possible for the therapist to work effectively with some patients who initially provoke strong countertransference reactions that fall within the scope of categories one and three. (pp. 20–21)

Forrest (2002) also notes that many substance abusers may have an "uncanny ability to feed the therapist's narcissistic needs early in the therapeutic process ('honeymoon phase of therapy'), but these patients also may relapse during the early or middle stages of intensive psychotherapy which may also result in a rupture of the therapeutic alliance. In these situations, it is 'absolutely imperative' that the therapist controls his or her personal countertransference reactions involving direct feelings of anger, rage, rejection and retaliation against the patient. Therapists need to remind themselves that they cannot control their addictive-disordered clients, and it is the patient who must assure the lion's share of work and responsibility for initiating and sustaining the recovery process. However, it may periodically be necessary for the therapist to exert control over a patient vis a vis the use of hospitalization or other appropriate interventions, but it is impossible and countertransferentially inappropriate for clinicians to consistently attempt to control their addictive-disordered clients" (pp. 21–22).

Finally, Forrest (2002, 2018) consistently indicates that these patients can also be "extremely demanding, dependent, parasitic, seductive, angry, manipulative, dishonest, and simply difficult to work with in psychotherapy. Authority conflicts, early life narcissistic injury and trauma, anxiety, intimacy and identity conflicts, and antisocial behaviors may all fuel the therapist's countertransference conflicts in psychotherapy work with this patient population" (p. 24).

Counselors and therapists may benefit from examining the extensive exploration of countertransference in counseling and therapeutic work with addictive-disordered clients via Dr. Forrest's earlier Countertransference in Chemical Dependency Counseling text (2002). This book provides historical perspectives and definitions of countertransference, and specifically examines several countertransference dynamics related to the process of chemical dependency counseling, the alliance, and psychotherapy work. This book also directly addresses a diversity of countertransference related therapy dynamics related to countertransference ethics, gender and multicultural realities, managed care, client co-morbidity, diagnosis, relapse prevention, counselor education and training, and therapist supervision.

As noted earlier, it is very important for contemporary therapists and especially addictions clinicians to recognize and consistently utilize their countertransference based experiential self-awareness and clinical skills to foster healthy patient change, awareness, and growth within the context of the ongoing therapeutic alliance relationship. Healthy countertransference awareness and efficacious clinician management can contribute greatly to the feelings, cognitions, behaviors, communications and therapeutic alliance dynamics which ultimately facilitate both patient and therapist growth and change.

The therapist's constructive uses of his or her ongoing countertransference reactions always remains a potentially powerful catalyst for positive patient change and recovery. Countertransference distortion of the malignant management and expressions of therapist countertransference consistently impact clients and therapeutic outcomes adversely, and thus, as Carruth (2002) affirms, "countertransference is inherently neither good nor bad, neither right nor wrong; it is just part of the mix that is the intimate, therapeutic contact between two people—that does, however, need to be recognized and addressed as such."

As indicated earlier in this discussion of countertransference in the realm of psychotherapy with addictive disordered clients (Forrest, 2002; Hayes, Gelso and Hummel, 2011; Maroda, 1994), both clinical and meta-analytic evidence strongly suggests that countertransference acting out is therapeutically psychonoxious, and effective counselor management of countertransference likely facilitates positive therapeutic outcomes. Carruth (2002) astutely indicates that:

> very few of us have escaped the pervasive impacts that addiction wreaks on individuals and their families. None of us have escaped the attitudes and perceptions our culture holds for the alcoholic or drug addict—as therapists and counselors, all of us have been affected, for better or worse, by the behaviors of our addicted clients. Thus, our countertransferential responses—the attitudes, values, beliefs, and expectations we bring from our history into the therapy office and unconsciously project onto the client—are significant importance in our work with chemically dependent people.
>
> Chemically dependent patients have a unique ability to provoke our own history—also, of course, in this field, where so many of the care providers are recovering addicts themselves, a counselor's experience of his or her own recovery cannot help but affect how the counselor relates to the recovery needs of the client—surprisingly little scientific study has been devoted to the topic of countertransferential dynamics with chemically dependent patients.

SELF-DISCLOSURE

Self-disclosure in psychotherapy has remained a rather controversial topic among therapists and counselors since the advent of Freudian psychoanalysis in the late 1800s (Forrest, 2018). As indicated earlier in this chapter, Freud's (1912/1958) psychoanalytic model viewed self-disclosure upon the part of the analyst, and in particular disclosure of countertransference material by the therapist, to be detrimental to therapy. Therapeutic self-disclosures were viewed as evolving from the therapist's neurosis. This model of psychoanalytic thought no longer permeates the psychodynamic and psychoanalytic approaches to therapy. Various other models of counseling and psychotherapy which have evolved over the past seventy years have increasingly incorporated the acceptance, use and potentially significant therapeutic benefits that are associated with therapist and client disclosure and transparent interactions within the context of psychotherapy relationships (Forrest, 2002, 2012, 2018; Jourard, 1964).

Carl Rogers and the Rogerian or client-centered model of counseling and psychotherapy (Rogers, 1942, 1951, 1954, 1957, 1958) extolled the relevance, uses, and constructive therapeutic impact of therapist authenticity, genuineness, transparency and self-disclosure in psychotherapy. Therapists were encouraged to be open to their own experience in the therapeutic encounter, and this process also involved the open and honest expression of these feelings and emotions to the patient. Self-disclosure is an essential ingredient in therapist genuineness, and effective therapists are "real persons" who wear no masks in their "real therapeutic alliances and relationships" with patients (Forrest, 1983, 1984, 2002, 2012, 2018).

The client-centered therapy research that evolved from the early clinical publications of Carl Rogers precipitated a wealth of empirical investigations related to the essential ingredients in effective psychotherapy during the late 1960s (Truax and Carkhuff, 1967). This general arena of psychotherapy and counseling research now spans some seventy years. The history and evolution of this psychotherapy research and clinical literature was presented in a rather extensive and detailed manner earlier in this text.

Clinical research literature (Farber, 2003, 2006; Forrest, 2012; Knox and Hill, 2003) focusing on therapist and patient self-disclosure in psychotherapy and counseling has remained an ongoing focal component in the academic, research, and practice of psychotherapy. Client-centered or person-centered counselors and therapists, existential and humanistic therapists, dynamically-oriented and cognitive-behavioral therapists, and numerous researchers and practicing therapists utilizing various models of therapy (conjoint marital therapy, family therapy, group therapy, self-help care, etc.) have explored, investigated and written about many diverse facets of self-disclosure in counseling and psychotherapy. The bulk of this literature and research has continued to stem from the works of academic clinicians and graduate school faculty in counseling and clinical psychology, counselor education, social work, and various behavioral health settings (Farber, 2006; Farber and Sohn, 2007; Forrest, 1970, 1984, 2002, 2012, 2018; Hill and Knox, 2001, 2013; Hill et al., 1989; Hountras and Forrest, 1970; Jourard, 1964, 1971; Jourard and Lasakow, 1958; Meltzoff and Kornreich, 1970; Orellana and Gelso, 2013; Truax and Carkhuff, 1967).

In brief, psychotherapy researchers investigating the effects of therapist self-disclosures in psychotherapy involving mostly individual therapy and a diversity of patient populations, treatment settings, diagnoses, and various research design models (analogue studies, actual therapy sessions, university counseling centers, psychiatric and mental health facilities, private practice, etc.), report consistent research evidence indicating that therapist or counselor self-disclosures generally enhance therapeutic outcome efficacy. For example, Hill and Knox (2001) reviewed eighteen analogue studies of therapist self-disclosure in individual therapy and found that "14 reported positive perceptions of self-disclosure, 3 reported negative perceptions, and 1 reported mixed findings" (p. 413). An earlier investigation by Truax and Carkhuff (1967) reported that among psychiatric patients, as early as the second interview, level of patient self-disclosure provides a "reasonably accurate" prediction of therapy outcome. Forrest (1978, 1994) found that self-disclosure among alcoholic military patients predicted treatment outcome, and that initially high disclosing military patients more frequently entered individual and group therapy, persisted in treatment, and sustained prolonged sobriety more often than lower self-disclosing military alcoholics.

Hill and Knox (2001) also note that "therapists who self-disclosed in a moderate or non-intimate way have been viewed more favorably and have elicited more client self-disclosure than therapists who did not disclose at all, who disclosed a lot, or who disclosed very intimate material," and non-clients typically perceive therapist disclosure positively (p. 413). These authors further report that "clients gave their highest rating to helpfulness and had the highest subsequent experiencing levels (i.e., involvement with their feelings) to therapist self-disclosures, and therapists gave the lowest ratings of helpfulness to self-disclosures, perhaps because disclosure made them feel vulnerable" (p. 414). Hill et al. (1989) indicate "reassuring disclosures were viewed as more helpful than challenging disclosures in terms of both client and therapist helpfulness ratings, and subsequent client experiencing levels." Knox et al. (1997) conducted a qualitative analysis of client perceptions of the effects of helpful therapist self-disclosure in actual long-term therapy and found that therapist self-disclosure fostered client insight and also made the therapist seem more real and human. Furthermore, these therapist self-disclosure factors help clients feel more normalized, reassured, and helped clients feel better, served as a model for positive change, and reinforced client self-disclosure and honesty in therapy (pp. 274–283).

However, it should be noted that therapist self-disclosure research has also suggested that the distal or ultimate therapeutic outcome effects the therapist self-disclosure on therapeutic outcome includes mixed results (no relationship, negative and positive effects (Hill and Knox, 2001)). To the contrary, Peterson (2002) reviewed an earlier small study by Wells (1994) reporting that therapist self-disclosure resulted in "generally negative results" and concluded that:

> all 8 participants in this study reported some degree of disappointment, disillusionment, or surprise—however, 6 of the 8 participants described a range of positive and negative emotions following the disclosure, and 4 of the participants reported that the disclosure helped them perceive their therapist as involved, trusting, and understanding—thus, half of the clients in this

investigation did report some positive effects associated with therapist self-disclosure. (pp. 21–31)

Kirschenbaum and Jourdan (2005) summarize several decades of research evidence pertaining to the efficacy and outcomes of individual psychotherapy involving the client-centered or person-centered therapeutic approach, and indicate that this body of research data clearly demonstrates that:

> (1) when therapists consistently provide high levels of the 'core conditions' of effective psychotherapy (non-possessive warmth, empathy, and genuineness) within the context of the therapeutic relationship, and (2) when the client perceives these essential therapeutic alliance qualities at least to a minimal degree within the therapeutic encounter, then (3) clients generally evidence constructive personality change and growth. (pp. 43–44)

Kirschenbaum and Jourdan (2005) also noted "much of the latest research on psychotherapy outcome has demonstrated that, rather than particular approaches, it is certain common factors in the therapy relationship" that account for therapeutic change. They also add that "certain types of self-disclosure by the therapist may be helpful, too much or inappropriate self-disclosure may be harmful" (p. 44).

As noted by Kolden et al. (2011), therapist genuineness or congruence has remained a highly valued and integral therapist quality throughout the history of psychotherapy. Rogers (1957) referred to the therapist's personal being in the therapeutic encounter, indicating "he is freely and deeply himself, with his experience accurately represented by his awareness of himself." The genuineness construct in psychotherapy has also long encompassed such terms as authenticity, openness, therapist real relationship, transparency, congruence, self-disclosure and real person. Kolden et al. (2011) indicate that in the current psychotherapy literature, genuineness is "frequently considered the most important of the three Rogerian facilitative conditions." These authors (Kolden et al., 2011) include the following recommendations for clinical practice related to fostering congruence or genuineness: "therapists can model congruence—congruent responding may well involve considered self-disclosure of personal information and life experiences. It could also entail articulation of thoughts and feelings, opinions, pointed questions, and feedback regarding client behavior. Congruent responses are honest—they are authentic and consistent with the therapist as a real person with likes, dislikes, beliefs, and opinions, as well as a sense of humor—congruence appears to be especially apparent in psychotherapy with more experienced (often older) practitioners" (p. 70). Thus, these various facets of effective therapist behavior and responding encompass a multiplicity of therapist self-disclosure related dynamics and behaviors.

Clinicians have long espoused the relevance and importance of therapist authenticity and self-disclosure in effective counseling and psychotherapy relationships. Jourard (1964, 1968) examined a diversity of therapist and client issues related to self-disclosure in counseling and psychotherapy as well as many other forms of human interaction, concluding among other things, that (1) "therapy proceeds through *honest* responses between the client and counselor, (2) to be transparent to the client, to have nothing of one's experience in the therapeutic relationship that is hidden, is basic to effective psychotherapy, (3) if a therapist hides his or her being from the client, he or she is engaging in the same behavior that generated symptoms for the client, and (4) a therapeutic relationship can change the therapist as much as it does the client" (Forrest, 2012, p. 13).

Bridges (2001) identifies several sources of therapeutic gain associated with therapist self-disclosure including "opening up space for deep therapeutic engagement between the therapist and patient, enhancing self-perception, affective experiences and the relational connection (alliance)." She further states that:

> intentional self-disclosure is a valuable tool in a therapeutic relationship that facilitates exploration, introduces new perspectives on self in relationship, and conveys to the patient the possibility of creating new, healing object relationships—therapist self-disclosure may be a helpful vehicle to make conscious unconscious affect or relational dynamics that influence the treatment and benefit the patient's development—the therapist's intentional self-disclosures can lend to unexpected growth-fostering clinical opportunities. (Forrest, 2012, pp. 11, 17)

It is also of paramount importance to point out that Bridges (2001) states that "as (addiction) therapists reveal feelings and aspects of themselves, they, too, feel vulnerable and exposed to the scrutiny of patients." Forrest (2012) indicates, "in reality, counselors and clients continually self-disclose and self-reveal in counseling and psychotherapy relationships, and these transactions often (1) provoke mutual anxiety, (2) stir discomfort upon the part of one of the participants, or (3) cause disequilibrium within the therapeutic alliance. And yet, the mutually self-disclosing dialogues and interactions between therapist and client can constitute the communicative and relational nexus for constructive growth and change upon the part of both participants" (p. 18).

It is simply impossible to know in advance (Han and O'Brien, 2014) how the therapist's or the client's self-disclosures will impact the therapist, client, therapeutic relationship and therapeutic processes. Virtually all therapists and researchers who have extensively explored and examined the concept of therapist self-disclosure or transparency in psychotherapy caution clinicians about the various sources of therapist, client and alliance parameters and vulnerabilities which can be associated with the uses of therapist self-disclosures in psychotherapy. In this context, Forrest (2010, 2018) encourages all addictions therapists to further explore the works of many professional researchers, clinicians and academics included in this chapter pertaining to therapist-client self-disclosure in psychotherapy. In sum, therapist self-disclosure is clearly as essential but potentially complicated pathway to relational change. Counselors and therapists need to keep these realities and caveats in mind during their therapeutic work.

RELAPSE

Relapse remains an ever-present reality that pertains to the ongoing care, treatment and outcomes associated with a myriad of health conditions and diseases. These various human conditions pertain to every disease and illness ranging from the common cold to various cancers, diabetes, mental health, and addictive brain disease. For example, it is not uncommon for people to receive a successful treatment, and then, after varying intervals of time, experience a recurrence or "relapse" of their disease process. Many, if not most, people who are diagnosed with a depressive disorder, major mental illness, cancer, heart disease, or a severe addictive disorder, experience repeated episodes of relapse with their specific disease or disorder.

The relapse process can be predicted with reasonable medical accuracy for some diseases and conditions, and yet relapse remains highly unpredictable for other disorders and diseases. Relapse appears to be especially difficult to predict relative to addictive brain disease and many, if not most, psychiatric and psychological disorders.

Prior to the early 1980s, addictions counselors as well as alcoholics and other addicted persons tended to refer to relapses as "slips," "falling off the wagon," "regressive phenomenon," or "massive regressions" (Forrest, 1975–1984).

Forrest (1975, 1983, 1984, 1997) has also provided earlier in-depth clinical examination of relapse within the context of intensive alcoholism psychotherapy work, noting that:

> relapse of massive regression may occur at any time during the process of intensive addictions-focused psychotherapy—however, in the clinical experience of the author, relapse seems most likely to occur between the third and sixth, and tenth and thirteenth months of therapy—this bimodal relapse distribution pertains to the psychotherapy of primary alcoholic patients who are motivated to recover and committed to the psychotherapeutic process. Alcoholics who are not motivated or in various other ways 'not ready' for

treatment tend to experience multiple relapses very early in therapy, and frequently terminate the psychotherapy relationship prematurely. (p. 114)

Furthermore, the author (Forrest, 1984, 1997) indicates:

it is highly unrealistic for the therapist to expect the alcoholic to enter therapy and simply never drink again, as well as change adaptively in many other areas of living. Most of these patients do experience a massive regression or several relapses while in treatment—relapse is not tantamount to treatment failure—quite simply, it is always very difficult to overcome or resolve, and an alcoholic-facilitated massive regression within the context of intensive psychotherapy can actually be a therapeutic learning experience for both patient and therapist. Therapists may be able to deter a relapse on some occasions by actively interpreting and confronting the patient's unconscious or preconscious processes that are operating to reinforce further drinking. Therapists need to help their patients re-examine their program of recovery and most patients stop 'working,' modify their program of recovery, or unconsciously being planning a relapse event several weeks prior to relapse. Patients also tend to report that various other factors have contributed to relapse events. (pp. 114–115)

The author has also explored the various roles of therapist counter-transference dynamics related to patient relapse (1984, 2002, 2016), noting "the psychotherapist needs to make every effort to be proactively involved in the patient's attempts to recover and continue in treatment at these junctures (relapse episodes). Juxtaposed to these issues, the therapist should avoid over-determined attempts to rescue patients from a relapse—these individuals (alcoholics and addicts) potentially develop the capacity to learn about self as a function of relapse while in therapy, and relapse can also be a basic ingredient in the process of integratively accepting self as being alcohol dependent. Relapse in therapy also helps some alcoholics face the unreality of their personal fantasies and irrational cognitions associated with returning to 'social drinking'" (pp. 115–116).

Few relapses are limited to "a couple of drinks." A drinking relapse frequently involves florid loss of control of one's drinking behavior as well as a profound regression into various other pathologic behaviors, affect, family and marital interactions and dynamics, and various other life dynamics that may also include legal, career, financial, and potential life and death health matters. Continued intoxication precipitates an acute exacerbation of the alcoholic's maladaptive behaviors, cognitions, feelings, and global adjustment style.

Therapists and patients need to fully comprehend the ever-present potentially catastrophic consequences of relapse. Whenever an alcoholic relapses, for whatever set of reasons, he or she has actualized a very destructive and possible life-threatening choice. For these reasons, the therapist must make every effort to help patients circumvent the relapse process, and this may involve active intervention in the event of relapse. Some patients may need to be hospitalized, referred and/or transported to a detox facility or residential chemical dependency treatment program, or infrequently, medically committed to an appropriate inpatient treatment facility by the therapist.

Unlimited sources of learning and growth potential can be associated with relapse, and relapse sometimes occurs within the context of very productive and effective psychotherapy relationships and treatment programs. When relapse takes place within the context of intensive psychotherapy and a working and productive therapeutic alliance, it is important for the therapist to (1) "actively reinforce the patient's commitment to the treatment process, (2) supportively point out to the patient that relapse does not mean that the patient has failed or that therapy is ineffective or 'not working,' but rather a relapse can be and is a primary symptom of the addictive brain disease process involving alcoholism, (3) remain (therapist) *self-aware* of these same realities, (4) systematically explore the global antecedents of 'triggers' associated with the patient's relapse, and therapeutically explore and clarify the reality of these relapse precipitating factors with the patient, (5) elucidate and therapist-patient therapeutic alliance dynamics that may have operationally impacted the relapse process immediately prior to the actual relapse episode, (6) explore and identify specific behavioral, cognitive, interpersonal and other alternatives to drinking and relapse related to potential future situations that can be used but the patient as deterrents to relapse, and (7) implement short-term ancillary therapeutic measures such as intensified self-help involvement and/or more active sponsorship, initiate possible medication associated alternatives (i.e., Naltrexone, Vivitrol, Antabuse, SSRI's, etc.), and intensive outpatient (IOP) or residential treatment, family or conjoint marital (couples) therapy or patient engagement in an intensive relapse prevention program" (Forrest, 1997, p. 117).

Therapist experience, skill and acumen are required for the effective clinical management of diverse forms of relapse involving a wide range of addictive disordered patients manifesting various individual differences.

It is helpful for the therapist to view relapse as a process that can occur at any juncture in the therapeutic relationship. Relapse involves antecedent, process and outcomes that are relatively specific to each patient, therapist, and psychotherapy relationship. The author (Forrest, 1984, 1997) has also noted that relapse during the middle and later stages of intensive addiction-focused psychotherapy work can be particularly destructive and can threaten or actually result in a rupture of the therapeutic alliance.

While patients tend to manifest relatively unique relapse patterns, styles and responses, the general consequences and dynamics associated with severe relapses occurring during the later stages of a working and productive therapeutic alliance generally damage the basic integrity of the working alliance. These relapses may result in an almost immediate alliance rupture or in some cases involve herculean rupture repair work upon the part of both therapist and patient. However, these relapse events may constructively precipitate adaptive learning and changes that ultimately result in the patient's ability to sustain life-long abstinence and recovery.

The early seminal work and publications of Gorski and Miller (Gorski, 1976; Gorski and Miller, 1979, 1982, 1986) pertaining to relapse prevention counseling, relapse dynamics, the relapse process, and various other clinical facets of relapse in addictive disease continue to impact and shape the counseling behaviors and care strategies of contemporary addiction therapists and counselors as well as residential, intensive outpatient (IOP) programs, and other addiction-focused care providers. The intensive relapse training workshops and seminars that Gorski provided for hundreds, if not several thousand alcoholism and drug treatment centers and programs, clinicians and counselors, hospitals, mental health facilities, state alcohol and substance abuse programs, military programs and health care providers, and academic or educational providers between the late 1970s and 2014 clearly attests to the continuing profound relevance and impact of relapse within the addiction treatment industry.

Gorski's original work has continued to evolve and expand to include opioid dependence and prescription drug abuse, eating disorders, sexual addictions and the entire gamut of addictive brain disease. The body of training, education and publications that Gorski's contemporary colleagues have produced over the past decade (Grinstead, 2014, 2016; Grinstead and Cabaret, 2018) specific to opioid and prescription drug dependence clearly indicates that relapse prevention counseling and psychotherapy skills will continue to be an essential component of the addiction therapist's armamentarium. Relapse prevention training and education also continue to be integral components of virtually all residential and IOP programs throughout the United States. Relapse prevention counseling and education is included in DUI offender programs, private practice addiction counseling and therapy programs, and virtually all models or approaches used in the treatment of addictive disorders.

It should be noted that the seminal evidence-based research and academically-generated relapse prevention, counseling and education publications of Marlatt and Gordon (1985), Marlatt and Witkie-witz (2010), Miller and Rollnick (2002), and Miller, Sovereign, and Kregel (1988) have contributed greatly to the awareness, uses and practice of relapse counseling skills and strategies by contemporary addiction therapists and clinicians over the past two decades. The contributions of Marlatt, Miller, Prohaska, and other academically-based research psychologists and clinicians have exerted a profoundly positive influence upon university and college communities, and the general American behavioral health care community related to the various facets of brain disease. Relapse realities and dynamics pertaining to the addictive brain diseases are certainly included in the spheres of awareness, understanding and educational impact specific to addiction counselor education, training, supervision, and practice in America.

The Gorski and Miller (1986) text, *Staying Sober: A Guide for Relapse Prevention,* examines the concept and clinical characteristics of addictive disease, irrational or "mistaken" beliefs about recovery and relapse, the warning signs of relapse, motivation and treatment, the relapse process, the relapse syndrome, and relapse prevention planning as well as family dynamics in relapse.

Gorski and Miller (1986) indicate that

> (1) many relapsed persons are victims of 'mistaken beliefs' and have relapsed because they do not know how to prevent relapse—they blame themselves for past relapses and believe they are hopeless, (2) relapse is a complex process, (3) relapse is a problem that applies to a variety of addictions and the same relapse prevention methods can be used with a variety of addictions, (4) the process of relapse begins before addictive use starts (people can become dysfunctional in sobriety without drinking or using), (5) the relapse process includes attitudes and behaviors that lead to active addictive using, (6) the relapse process is the movement away from recovery, (7) recovery from addictive disease starts with accepting the fact that you cannot safely use alcohol or mood altering drugs, but abstinence alone is not enough, (8) it is necessary to correct the physical, psychological, and social damage to health caused by addiction, and also necessary to learn to live a healthy and productive life without the need for alcohol or other drugs or addictive behaviors, (9) relapse and recovery are intimately related, and relapse 'tendencies' are a normal and natural part of the recovery process, (10) when the sobriety-based symptoms of addiction become severe enough a person begins to become dysfunctional even though not drinking or using ('dry drunk'), this constitutes the relapse syndrome, and (11) it is possible to interrupt the relapse syndrome before serious consequences occur by bringing the warning signs of relapse that you are experiencing into conscious awareness. This is relapse planning. (pp. 31–36)

The Gorski and Miller (1986) relapse model includes an examination of post-acute withdrawal dynamics, developmental stages of recovery, "mistaken" or irrational beliefs about recovery and relapse, components and causative factors related to the relapse process, relapse prevention planning, and other clinical issues pertaining to relapse in addictive disease. Their essential steps of relapse prevention include:

> (1) Stabilization: get control of yourself, (2) Self-Assessment: find out what is going in your head, heart, and life, (3) Relapse Education: learn about relapse and what to do to prevent it, (4) Warning Sign Identification: make a list of your personal relapse warning signs ('triggers'), (5) Warning Sign Management: learn how to interrupt signs before you lose control, (6) Inventory Training: learn how to become consciously aware of warning signs as they develop, (7) Review the Recovery Program: make sure your recovery program is able to help you to manage your warning signs ('triggers'), (8) Involvement of Significant Others: teach others how to work with you to avoid relapse, and (9) Follow-Up: update your relapse prevention plan regularly. (pp. 157–158)

Gorski and Miller (1986) additionally indicate that "recovery from addiction must be an active process, recovering persons must work a daily program of recovery, they must remind themselves daily that they are suffering from an addiction, and they must have an active recovery program that provides guidelines for effective and productive living" (p. 129). Furthermore, the authors postulate that "(1) recovery from addiction is like walking up a down escalator. It is impossible to stand still, (2) loss of control post-acute withdrawal symptoms result in the Relapse Syndrome (RS=PAW-Symptom Management), (3) the relapse process does not only involve the act of taking a drink or using drugs, it is a progression that creates the overwhelming need for alcohol and/or other drugs, (4) it is possible to interrupt the relapse progression before the warning signs are obvious, and (5) the relapse syndrome is the sobriety-based disease of addiction" (pp. 129–135).

These authors (Gorski and Miller, 1986; Gorski and Grinstead, 1986) further elucidate the Relapse Progression (change→stress→denial→PAW→behavior change→breakdown in social structure→loss of control and judgment→loss of behavioral control→option reduction→acute degeneration→ addictive use), provide strategies for Interrupting the Relapse Syndrome (Internal Dysfunction involving thought impairment, emotional impairment, memory problems, sleep problems and coordination problems; External Dysfunction involving denial return, avoidance and defensiveness, crisis building, immobilization, and confusion and overreaction; loss of control involving depression, loss of behavioral control, recognition of loss of control, option reduction, and relapse episode), and as briefly discussed earlier, provide extensive steps involving Relapse Prevention planning and training.

Grinstead (2014, 2016) has developed a contemporary model of relapse prevention for chronic pain management and opioid addiction that both incorporates and expands upon the earlier relapse work of Gorski and Miller

(1986). The Grinstead relapse prevention model (2014, 2016) for this specific clinical population is referred to as the Addiction-Free Pain Management Treatment System. The American and world-wide epidemic of opioid and prescription drug abuse and addiction over the past decade clearly demonstrates the lethality and multifaceted adverse consequences associated with relapse. As Grinstead notes, approximately fifty-eight percent of the over thirty-eight thousand drug overdose deaths in the United States in 2010 involved pharmaceutical drugs (75.2% opioids, 29.4% benzodiazepines). In addition, hundreds of thousands of emergency room visits related to opioid and benzodiazepine medications have occurred over the past decade, and this rate of ER visits involving prescription drugs continues to rise at alarming rates (90-100 percent increase per approximate five-year time intervals for the past 15 years). This data also makes it very clear that chronic pain is a major public health problem in the United States, and the cost of this American health "problem" in recent years ranges between 500–700 billion dollars per year, involves approximately 120 million Americans and equals about $2,000 for every person in the United States. Furthermore, ninety percent of pain patients use opioids (Grinstead, 2014, 2016).

Grinstead's comprehensive addiction free pain management treatment system model (2014, 2016) incorporates common co-occurring disorders (addiction, chronic pain, anxiety, depression, PTSD, eating disorders, etc.), proactive patient involvement, pain management, stress, didactic education and training, recovery skills, training, and education and relapse prevention training. This relapse prevention model identifies paths from remission to relapse (i.e., "relapse triggered by exposure to addictive/rewarding drugs, relapse triggered by exposure to stressful experiences involving brain stress circuits"), the Relapse Cycle (i.e., "commitment to stabilize and the recovery process, return to denial, stopping personal growth process, return to old thinking, stress and problems return, return of old behaviors, social isolation, increased problems, addictive thinking returns, loss of control occurs, and relapse takes place" (p. 13). Relapse with prescribed medications may be related to elective dental procedures, elective surgical procedures, painful injuries, painful medical conditions, and mismanaged chronic pain.

The core clinical process involved in Grinstead's (2014, 2016) relapse prevention for chronic pain management and opioid addiction model include: cognitive-behavioral-affective therapy, effective medical management interventions, and use of proactive pain management intervention using non-pharmacological interventions. This multimodal model utilizes assessment, motivational, relapse prevention, and recovery strategies to deter patient engagement in the relapse cycle and also deter potential future relapses. The model also delineates transitional medical procedures (i.e., spinal cord stimulation, lumbar sympathetic blocks, facet joint injections, etc.), non-pharmacological approaches (i.e., meditation and yoga, massage therapy, physical therapy, acupuncture, chiropractic care, prayer, pet therapy and self-help groups, etc.) and passive versus proactive tools. Treatment and pain management stages, outcome treatment goals, and the patient relapse prevention therapy workbook are used to sustain the ongoing recovery process. Relapse prevention therapy remains an ongoing component in Grinstead's approach to relapse prevention for chronic pain management and opioid dependence.

The relevance and global impact of relapse on every facet of the psychotherapy process, outcome and therapeutic alliance cannot be understated within the context of intensive individual psychotherapy work with addictive disordered persons. This basic postulate applies to virtually every addiction specific treatment modality utilized to treat the addictive disorders as well as most, if not all, of the continuum of behavioral and mental health disorders.

The specter and unpredictable consequences of patient relapse within the context of intensive individual addiction-focused psychotherapy can profoundly impact the patient, therapist, therapeutic alliance and outcome of the therapeutic process. Relapse can also be tantamount to a "for better or worse" experience within the various parameters of addictions psychotherapy work. Experienced and skilled addictions counselors and therapists need to be consistently cognizant of these realities.

ALLIANCE RUPTURE AND REPAIR IN ADDICTIONS THERAPY

Safran, Muran, and Eubanks-Carter (2011) indicate that one of the "most consistent findings emerging from the psychotherapy research is that the quality of the therapeutic alliance is a robust predictor of outcome across a wide range of different treatments and that, conversely, weakened alliances are correlated with unilateral termination by the patient." These authors note that the term "rupture" may imply a "dramatic breakdown" in therapy, ruptures "vary in intensity from relatively minor tensions, which one or both of the participants may be only vaguely aware of, two major breakdowns in collaboration, understanding, or communication" (p. 80). Misunderstanding, therapeutic impasse, or empathetic failure may also characterize an alliance rupture.

The Safran, Muran, and Eubanks-Carter (2011) conceptualization of alliance rupture follows Bordin's (1979) model which indicates that ruptures in the alliance consist of (1) disagreements about the tasks of therapy, (2) disagreement about treatment goals, or (3) strains in the patient-therapist bond.

Ruptures in the therapeutic alliance have been defined as "episodes of tension of breakdown in the collaborative relationship between patient and therapist," and deterioration in the quality of the relationship may occur frequently regardless of therapeutic approach (Eubanks-Carter, 2011; Escudero et al., 2012). Successful alliance "repair" reportedly fosters the client to experience a mature or adaptive resolution of interpersonal conflict (p. 80).

Escudero et al. (2012) also indicate that "ruptures vary in intensity, frequency, and duration; they can be conceptualized on a continuum ranging from slight fluctuations which are difficult to observe, to significant problems in the relationship, marked by the client's direct expression of negative affect, resistance to the psychotherapist's influence attempts, or premature termination." These authors further state that due to the "common occurrence of alliance strains across psychotherapy approaches, the importance of recognizing and repairing ruptures from in-session behavior cannot be overemphasized" (p. 26).

In clinical practice, managing and repairing ruptures can be challenging, if not difficult, as a result of several factors. Clients "are not always willing or able to indicate discomfort or disagreement with the psychotherapist, and studies have shown that recognition of alliance strain is difficult, even for experienced therapists—for example, 65 percent of clients indicated avoiding certain topics, and in only 45 percent of cases, the therapists were aware that the client was hiding negative feelings" (Escudero et al., 2012, p. 26).

These authors also report that a "substantial body" of individual psychotherapy research has identified two major categories of client behavior associated with alliance strain: "Confrontation and Withdrawal—ruptures marked by confrontation are characterized by the client's aggressive and accusatory expressions of disagreement, whereas withdrawal ruptures are marked by the client's disengagement from the psychotherapist, the therapeutic tasks, or from his or her own internal experience." Furthermore, behaviors signaling confrontation ruptures include complaints about the psychotherapist's competence or about the progress and activities of the psychotherapy (process); withdrawal markers, by contrast, are more akin to passive-resistance, including denial, changing the subject, talking about extraneous matters, intellectualization, and so forth. The authors also state that "the clearest ruptures to observe are those that pertain directly to the working alliance, that is, disagreement between client and therapist about the goals or tasks of psychotherapy or tension in the emotional bond" (p. 27).

Successful repair of a ruptured alliance can involve direct interventions (i.e., eliciting clients' feelings, and then explicitly resolving disagreements about the therapy goals and tasks) or direct interventions (i.e., changing or reframing the tasks and goals to be more acceptable to the client).

Safran, Muran, and Eubanks-Carter (2011) describe the following rupture and repair interventions that can be utilized by therapists:

(1) outlining the therapeutic rationale at the beginning of treatment can play an important role in developing the alliance at the onset, reiterating the rationale throughout treatment can help to repair a strained alliance, (2) changing tasks or goals, the therapist responds to ruptures resulting from disagreements about tasks or goals by modifying his or her behaviors in a fashion that feels meaningful to the patient, (3) clarifying misunderstandings at a surface level—the therapist responds in a non-defensive fashion and acknowledges that he or she can see how the patient might have felt upset by what he or she said or expressed, (4) exploring relational themes associated with the rupture, the process of clarifying factors leading to a rupture can lead to an exploration of relational themes, (5) linking alliance rupture (or strains) to common patterns in a patient's life, resolving a rupture can involve explicitly exploring the link between the rupture that occurs in the session and some situation in the patient's life (or a pattern of repetitive dysfunctional lifestyle behavior, Forrest, 2012), and (6) new relational experience, it can be useful for the therapist to act in a way that he or she hypothesizes will provide the patient will an important new relational experience without explicitly exploring the underlying meaning of the interaction. This repair intervention can be particularly important when the patient has difficulty exploring the therapeutic relationship in the here-and-now" (pp. 81–82)

These authors (Safran, Muran, and Eubanks-Carter, 2011) provide the following therapeutic alliance related research-supported rupture repair guidelines:

(1) Practitioners should be aware that patients often have negative feelings about psychotherapy or the therapeutic relationship that they are reluctant to broach for fear of the therapist's reactions; thus, it is important for therapists to be attuned to subtle indications of ruptures in the relationship when they suspect that a rupture has occurred, (2) it is probably helpful for patients to express negative feelings about therapy to the therapist should they emerge or to assert their perspective on what is going on when it differs from the therapist, (3) it is important for therapists to attempt to respond in an open or non-defensive fashion, and to accept responsibility for their contribution to the interaction as opposed to blaming the patient for misunderstanding or distorting, (4) it also proves important for therapists to empathize with their patient's experience and to validate them for broaching a potentially divisive topic in a session, (5) in some forms of treatment, the primary intervention may consist of the therapist changing the tasks or goals of treatment without necessarily explicitly addressing the rupture with the patient, (6) in other forms of treatment, resolving alliance ruptures may involve more in-depth exploration of what is transpiring between the therapist and patient as well as in-depth exploration of the patient's experience, and (7) preliminary evidence suggests that in some approaches,

it may prove useful for the therapist to explicitly establish a link between the rupture event and characteristic interpersonal patterns in the patient's life. However, caution needs to be exercised in the decision to pursue this alternative as a growing body of evidence indicates that frequent transference interpretations linking what is taking place in the therapeutic relationship to other relationships in the patient's life can exert negative effects— quality (not quantity) of the interpretation(s) and the relational meaning of the interpretation in the context of the emergent therapeutic relationship appears to make the difference between a positive and negative effect on the patient. (p. 86)

Alliance rupture and repair work in couples, family, and group therapy are much more complex than in individual therapy.

The empirical alliance and specific alliance rupture and repair literature of the past 15 years reveals a diversity of findings and evidence related to these issues as they pertain to various treatment modalities, patient sub-populations, and outcomes. For example, couple and family studies involving drug-abusing adolescents (Friedlander et al., 2011) found that the composite couple-family therapy index (merging of all family members' alliances) was not predictive of therapy retention of outcome. However, research studies involving adolescents with externalizing problems and anorexia (Robbins et al., 2008) report that "parents (but not patients) alliances predicted treatment completion, and with externalizing adolescents both for the children's and parent's alliances with the therapist discriminated dropout from complete families, and unbalanced alliances tend to negatively relate to treatment retention." Therapist experience was positively associated with the alliance in conjoint alcoholism treatment for couples, and with respect to gender, the man's alliance in conjoint alcoholism treatment for couples, and with respect to gender, the man's alliance tends to be more strongly associated with outcome in both group marital therapy and couples therapy. Family therapy of adolescent substance abuse studies (Shelef et al., 2005) indicate that "observer measures (but not self-report measures) of adolescent's alliance predicted post treatment outcomes, whereas parent measures did not; moreover, adolescent alliance predicted outcome only in cases in which the parent-therapist alliance is moderate to strong. It is also interesting that there is no evidence that therapist gender, race/ethnicity, or therapist-family ethnic match factors in the strength of alliance moderations of couple and family therapy alliance-outcome association" (Friedlander et al., 2011, pp. 29–30).

The Safran, Muran, and Eubanks-Carter (2011) meta-analytic investigation identified three studies that defined rupture-repair episodes based on "session to session fluctuations in alliance scores" and "examined the relation between the presence of these episodes and outcome." A fourth study examined rupture and repairs "that occurred within the first six sessions," and a study involving Cluster C personality disorder clients reported finding the "relation between the rupture-repair episodes and outcome" indicated that "higher rupture intensity was associated with poor outcome measures of interpersonal functioning, and rupture and repair was predictive of retention in treatment." The aggregated correlation of these studies (including 148 clients) indicated that "the presence of rupture-repair episodes was particularly related to good outcome" (pp. 81–84).

A second meta-analytic study (Safran, Muran, and Eubanks-Carter, 2011) involving the impact of rupture resolution training or supervision on patient outcome in eight studies, including 376 clients found that "rupture resolution training/supervision led to significant patient improvement." The authors further concluded "results indicate rupture resolution training/supervision leads to small but statistically significant patient improvements relative to treatment by therapists who did not have such training" (p. 82).

This author (Forrest, 2014) would encourage all addictions therapists to examine the Safran, Muran, Eubanks-Carter (2011) and Escudero et al. (2012) studies closely, as well as the Escudero et al. (2011), Smith-Hansen et al. (2011), Johansen, Lumley, and Caro (2011), and Friedlander et al. (2014) studies pertaining to e-SOFTA video training and research pertaining to alliance-related behaviors. This arena of alliance-based investigations represents one of the very important evolving and emergent domains in psychotherapy research, practice, and counselor/therapist training, supervision, and education.

Forrest (1984, 1985, 1997, 2002, 2012, and 2013) has written and lectured about various facets of the "working and productive" therapeutic alliance in the explicit realm of addictions psychotherapy and counseling for many years, indicating that *Alliance Rupture and Repair Work with Addictive-Disordered Clients* encompasses a significant component of the ongoing therapeutic process. Alliance ruptures frequently occur in the initial early therapy with patients manifesting substance abuse disorders, and ruptures which result in patient unilateral therapy terminations.

Patient related alliance-rupture facilitating factors and dynamics may include denial and avoidance defense system dynamics, forced or coercion-based therapy involvement, lack of motivation, severe co-morbid psychopathology, intimacy disturbance, relapse, cognitive impairment or limitations, cost/economics of care, care setting, non-compliance of rejection of shared therapist-treatment goals or tasks, and various other transference-relational dynamics. Addicts and substance abusers may also reject or disagree with the therapist's approach or immediate care recommendations very early or at other junctures in the therapeutic process. Therapists are frequently confronted with the clinical need to facilitate immediate detoxification, hospitalization, and medical care during the initial therapy sessions with these patients. Such transactions are often met with patient anger or initial rejection which may result in terminations, and "therapeutic ruptures" can be "tantamount to therapeutic termination and failure" at any juncture in the therapeutic process with addictive-disordered persons. These transactions can be precipitated by a wide diversity of factors and dynamics.

A multiplicity of therapist related variables impacts the therapist's capacities to recognize, initiate, and facilitate rupture repair work and defer full-blown alliance ruptures in addictions therapy. The therapist's capacity to feel comfortable with actively drug dependent and recovering addicts in combination with his or her capacity to provide patients with a consistent therapeutic relationship involving high levels of non-possessive warmth, empathy, genuineness, and concreteness remains an ever-present red-thread ingredient in efficacious rupture repair work. The therapist's awareness, understanding, and personal understanding of various transference, countertransference, relational and other process variables that continually impact and shape the therapeutic alliance are also key ingredients in effective therapeutic rupture and repair work.

Finally, the relational dynamics that compromise the patient-therapist relationship and therapeutic alliance mending process impact every facet of rupture and rupture repair wok dynamics and treatment outcome (Forrest, 2016).

ADDICTION-FOCUSED PSYCHOTHERAPY ALLIANCE RUPTURE AND REPAIR PRACTICE SUGGESTIONS AND GUIDELINES

1. Addiction therapists need to sustain a vigilant sensitivity and awareness pertaining to alliance fluctuations and nuances very early in the therapeutic relationship and throughout the ongoing course of therapy. Early stage therapy shapes the alliance, and they use of therapist unconditional positive regard and patient support during the process of developing essential tasks, goals, and the structural components of the therapeutic process are essential to the process of establishing and maintaining a working and productive therapeutic alliance with addictive disordered persons.

2. Addiction therapists and their clients need to discuss the relatively fixed or changing and evolving nature of various therapy tasks and goals early in therapy, and this general procedure needs to again be addressed as goals and tasks change as part of the therapeutic process. This ongoing process can be viewed as a therapeutically preemptive strategy for reducing current and future alliance rupture and repair interactions and activities. This procedure also fosters some level of

"working flexibility" and healthy adaption upon the part of the therapist and patient. Some alliance goals need to remain fixed or relatively unchanged throughout the course of treatment (i.e., drug/alcohol abstinence related to manifesting chronic and severe alcoholic liver disease, transplant patients, etc.) but most therapeutic goals, methods, tasks, and therapeutic structural core interactions change or need to be modified during different stages or junctures in the course of therapy.

3. Addiction therapists need to acknowledge, clarify, and take responsibility for stresses or relational tensions related to their behaviors that adversely impact the therapeutic alliance.

4. Addiction therapists need to generally avoid in-depth transference interpretations, intensive affective work, and confrontational interventions in the early stages of alliance building and therapy.

5. In the event of alliance ruptures resulting in premature termination occurring after a limited number of therapy sessions (3-6), and these ruptures are related to the patient's having experienced an acute relapse episode, the therapist may deter the rupture and be able to repair the alliance by directly contacting the client and exploring the relapse experience triggers, outcome, and his or her ethical and clinical practice interventions pertaining to the therapist's actions related to possibly initiating hospitalization or detox engagement, health and welfare checks, police interventions, and other actions common to the therapy and treatment of addictive disordered persons.

6. Due to the various risk dynamics associated with the addictive disordered patient population in general, addiction therapists need to remain personally vigilant with regard to their internalized emotional reactions to addictive-disordered patients and alliance ruptures as well as the emotional demands of alliance repair work. We need to personally establish and initiate supportive collegial and personal relationships that provide support, nurturing, and therapeutically constructive resources related to our work and general well-being.

7. Commonly in addictions-focused alliance rupture and repair work, it is clear that this work consistently evolves from the patient's repetitive pattern of dysfunctional and self-defecting interpersonal relationship dynamics (repetition-compulsion). Effective therapy with addictive disordered persons involves consistent therapeutic use of strategic, supportive, timely, and non-threatening interpretation and an exploration of the various dynamics related to the patient's addictive disordered repetitive interpersonal behavior. This aspect of therapeutic alliance rupture and repair work process eventually involves therapeutic teaching, education, coaching, and a diversity of therapist cognitive behavioral tools.

8. Finally, addiction therapists need to remain aware of the ever-present propensity for terminating therapy of in other ways precipitating a therapeutic alliance rupture; the therapeutic alliance, as well as alliance rupture and repair work remain byproducts of the therapeutic relationship. Therapists, patients, therapeutic settings, and a matrix of various personal and relational dynamics always contribute to the process of efficacious psychotherapy outcomes as well as the process of constructive alliance rupture and repair work (Forrest, 2016).

Throughout the course of their work, therapists and counselors also need to be continually aware of the paradoxically limited impact of their therapeutic skills and acumen in the face of a full-blown catastrophic relapse. These dynamics also pertain to all mental health and behavioral health therapists and professionals.

PATIENT READINESS AND MOTIVATION FOR CHANGE

As touched upon throughout this chapter and the entire text, a multiplicity of interactive variables or factors continually impact the therapist, patient, therapeutic alliance and psychotherapy relationship, and ultimately the global process and outcome of all psychotherapy relationships. These clinical realities include all therapists, models of therapy and patient populations.

Patient readiness for therapy, motivation for therapeutic involvement, and stages of therapeutic change have long been viewed as important ingredients in the process and outcome of therapy (DiClemente et al., 2001; Miller et al., 2008; Miller and Rose, 2009; Miller and Rollnick, 2012; Bien, Miller and Tonigan, 1993). Motivational interviewing (Miller and Rollnick, 2002) has been defined as "a collaborative conversation style for strengthening a person's motivation and commitment to change." Therapists utilizing this intervention model use empathy, developing discrepancy, rolling with resistance, and supportive client self-efficacy behaviors and cognitions.

In short, addictions counselors and behavioral health counselors and therapists have long used a diversity of therapeutic techniques and strategies to facilitate patient readiness for therapy, motivation for treatment and change, and commitment to the ongoing process of therapy and recovery (DiClemente, 1993, 2006; Hustad et al., 2011; Miller and Rollnick, 2012). In spite of the therapist's attempts to utilize these various therapeutic measures to facilitate patient readiness, motivation for therapy and change, and commitment to the work of therapeutic change and recovery, every practicing clinician learns relatively early in his or her addiction or behavioral health care treatment arena that patients vary considerably with regard to their individual capacities for establishing and maintaining a working and productive therapeutic alliance.

As indicated earlier in this text, addictive disordered patients manifest a diversity of individual differences which impact their capacities for establishing and becoming actively engaged in the working and productive alliance. Patient readiness and motivation for change and recovery at the time of initial treatment engagement may greatly impact the therapist's ability to productively contribute to the development of a working and productive therapeutic alliance. The patient's capacity for alliance development can sometimes be enhanced early within the context of a few therapeutic sessions using motivational interviewing techniques and though therapist facilitation and use of the core therapeutic ingredients. However, these measures plus a variety of other positive relational and external factors must be experienced and internalized by most addictive-disordered patients outside of the therapeutic context or perhaps within the context of several treatment and psychotherapy experiences prior to their ability to develop the essential qualities and level of readiness and motivation for change that constitute the essential prerequisites for forming therapeutic alliances that consistently result in long-term recovery (i.e., commitment to change and generalized adaptive behavioral change).

PATIENT COMMITMENT TO CHANGE AND THE RECOVERY PROCESS

Patients who manifest clinical histories that encompass several years of perhaps decades of florid alcoholism, drug dependence and other severe addictive disorders generally require many months, if not a few years or perhaps a lifelong commitment, to the work of recovery and the recovery process (Forrest, 1975–2020). It has been the author's (Forrest, 1997, 2016) experience that very few of these patients experience one or two extended and intensive treatment episodes of virtually any form (residential or IOP programs, detox, brief or extended intensive psychotherapy engagement, ongoing self-help involvement, pharmacologic treatment, protracted correctional incarceration, or multimodal treatment programs), and subsequently remain drug abstinent or addiction free for many years or a lifetime. In clinical reality, most people who manifest severe addictive disorders are simply unable to sustain extended patterns of substance abstinence or non-problematic substance use in the absence of having actualized patterns of behavior. Brief therapy or very limited therapy is frequently very ineffective with these patients. Moreover, many alcoholics, opioid addicts, eating disordered persons, and other drug addicts including nicotine dependent persons, remain incapable or sustaining relatively short-term abstinence, let alone a period of 20 to 40+ years of abstinence and global recovery.

The addictive disordered patient's ability to initiate an extended commitment to the work of psychotherapy, and the establishment and maintenance of a working and productive therapeutic alliance ultimately enhances the patient's capacity for long-term global recovery. This process simultaneously initiates and facilitates the patient's capacity to sustain his or her commitment to the work of recovery and the ongoing long-term life process of recovery. It is imperative for many, if not most, addictive-disordered patients to be able to sustain their commitments to active ongoing psychotherapy or other efficacious treatment modalities which eventually transform the recovery process into an ongoing lifestyle process!

PATIENT CAPACITY FOR RIGOROUS HONESTY AND BASIC TRUTH TELLING

Addictive brain disease most typically includes a developmental process component which involves a progressive loss of the basic capacities for honesty and basic truth telling. Alcoholics, compulsive gamblers, drug addicts, eating-disordered persons, and sexual addicts are all notorious for their incessant lying, denial, covering up, distorting the truth, defensiveness, and lack of honesty. Family members, loved ones, and friends or colleagues of addictive disordered persons routinely describe addictive disordered persons as being "chronic liars," "not capable of telling the truth," or "unreliable and irresponsible." Addicts tend to be seen as notorious "liars." Many addictive disordered people eventually become incapable of being honest with themselves and everyone else. The addiction process fuels the outcropping of a progressive repertoire of deceptive behaviors, lying and dishonesty. These behaviors and transactions serve the self-defeating and dysfunctional purpose of maintaining the addiction process. The program of Alcoholics Anonymous (AA) very wisely identified these behaviors and character traits some eighty years ago, and also stressed the importance of "rigorous honesty" and honest self-disclosure as being basic precursors to the alcoholic's capacity for recovery and living a sober life.

Efficacious psychotherapy relationships and therapeutic alliances require the establishment of therapist-patient relationships that are rooted in the *mutual* capacity for open and honest communicative interactions and therapeutic dialogue. Many addictive-disordered persons simply manifest a significantly impaired capacity for communicating openly and honestly within the context of the therapeutic alliance. Truth telling has not been a basic ingredient in their communicative and interpersonal style. Addictive-disordered persons, including presidents, politicians, international leaders and individuals from every "walk of life" are especially notorious for their often-compartmentalized lies, dishonesty, and lack of truth telling specific to sexual addiction, drug addiction and various other addictive patterns of behavior.

Very early in the process of therapeutic work with addictive disordered patients, therapists need to explicitly explore with the patient the therapeutic requirement and importance of mutual honesty, disclosure, trust and truth telling within the context of the therapeutic alliance. The work of sustaining a pattern of continued mutual rigorous honesty throughout the course of therapy remains a central component of all effective and productive psychotherapy relationships involving addictive disordered persons. Many addictive patients seem to manifest an almost reflective propensity to deny, minimize, rationalize, distort and simply lie about their continued abuse of substances or addictive patterns of behavior early and even throughout the course of therapy.

Therapists need to consistently explore the origin, history, and dynamics as well as self-defeating nature of these patterns of thinking and behaving. This strategy actively helps patients develop the awareness, motivation and cognitive-affective, and interpersonal skills that are essential to the process of initiating and sustaining truth telling and honesty within the ongoing therapeutic alliance. Therapists need to be able to point out, sympathetically and supportively confront (Forrest, 1992), didactically teach, educate, and continually incentivize and reinforce the open, honest, truth-telling transactions of their addictive disordered patients within the context of the alliance relationship.

With continued abstinence and recovery, most of these patients become progressively more capable of manifesting generalized rigorous honesty within their various interpersonal relationships and other important areas of their lives. Therapists also need to remain cognizant of the ever-present impact of their open, honest, authentic and truth telling modeling influences on addictive disordered patients vis-à-vis the alliance and therapeutic relationship. Patient imitative learning, vicarious learning, and other therapist related verbal behaviors additionally foster honesty and truth telling upon the part of their patients. Conditioning and reinforcement also continually shape and enhance the therapist's alliance capacity for facilitating constructive patient personality and global behavioral change.

COMMON EVERYDAY LIFE ALLIANCE
IMPACTING FACTORS AND DYNAMICS

A diversity of common and often random as well as specific factors and dynamics can significantly impact the therapeutic alliance at any juncture in the therapeutic process.

These common and random specific alliance impacting factors often occur suddenly and many have very little or no prior overt relationship to the therapist-patient therapy relationship or alliance. Yet, these potential alliance impacting factors may impact the alliance profoundly at any juncture in the therapeutic process, and may even result in an immediate and unanticipated termination of the alliance and psychotherapy relationship. These therapeutic transactions most typically are not associated with therapist behaviors or therapeutic alliance process dynamics and variables, but rather take place as a result of unanticipated events that randomly occur in the everyday lives of patients and therapists. In some cases, these alliance terminating events are profoundly devastating for the patient as well as highly emotional and infrequently may be dynamically traumatic for the therapist.

Examples of random and relatively common significant alliance impacting factors or even alliance and therapy terminating events include patient moves and relocations, unexpected job loss or perhaps career changes, loss of insurance coverage pertaining to therapy reimbursement, other acute or chronic financial matters pertaining to the patient's ability to pay for ongoing treatment, relapse, and especially relapse events which result in arrests, perhaps brief or long-term incarceration, significant legal and financial consequences, and the sudden onset of major health problems. Debilitating patient accidents may also precipitate sudden and unexpected significant alliance dynamics including therapy termination. In short, patients always possess the ability and power to either consciously actualize a diversity of very significant alliance behaviors and dynamics including abrupt psychotherapy termination, and as also noted throughout this text, an ever-present myriad of nefarious ongoing causative factors associated with the patient, alliance, and therapeutic relationship matrix dynamics continually impact the therapeutic process from inception to finish.

In reality, the patient's spouse, children or family, employer, friends or even complete strangers and certainly a myriad of circumstantial events can randomly and very significantly impact the alliance. Patients may also infrequently and unexpectedly die or become tragically debilitated during the course of therapy. Obviously, these catastrophic events result in abrupt alliance terminations which can also have a very profoundly impactful influence upon the therapist. However, these events may actualize any number of subsequent outcomes ranging from brief or even eventual long-term therapeutic care of a spouse or family of a deceased patient, to outcomes in cases of patient suicide involving suits and litigation against the therapist by the patient's surviving spouse and family. Patient suicide attempts and threats as well as successful suicide completions tend to be especially prevalent among chemically dependent and addictive disordered patients. Actively alcoholic, methamphetamine dependent, heroin and opioid or sedative dependent, cocaine dependent, inhalant dependent, and polydrug dependent patients manifesting several comorbid psychiatric conditions (antisocial personality disorder, bi-polar disorder, schizoaffective disorder, organic brain impairment, anger control and impulse control disorders, and schizophrenia) are especially prone to suicidal and violent or even homicidal behaviors. As discussed in the following chapter, these patient populations present a plethora of potential and conflictual therapeutic dynamics and difficulties for all therapists treating addictive disordered persons within the context of virtually all therapies and treatment settings.

Many of the common and random or specific factors that significantly impact the alliance related to patients can also pertain to addiction therapists and counselors. Simply put, therapists move, change careers and practices, experience health, marital, family or divorce related difficulties, accidents, and experience financial difficulties as well as any number of other life events which may impact the alliance in a diversity of significant ways. Counselors and therapists also continually age, and eventually die. All therapists who happen to also be in recovery from an addictive disorder and/or perhaps some other co-occurring psychological disorder face the ever-present reality of relapse, and both recovering and previously non-recovery addiction therapists can and infrequently also experience a relapse or regression into active addiction during the course of their psychotherapy practice careers. Obviously, a therapist's relapse into active substance abuse or florid chemical dependence almost always impacts both patient and therapist in a globally and profoundly destructive manner. All of these realities pertaining to the therapist, patient, therapeutic relationship, and alliance again demonstrate the multiplicity of vulnerabilities and common everyday living realities and dynamics that shape the totality of the alliance and the total therapeutic enterprise. Human beings and human relationships encompass all of the vicissitudes of our basic humanness, and thus, the therapeutic alliance, psychotherapy relationship, and process as well as outcome of psychotherapy are all subject to the complex, diverse, and other unpredictable limitations that characterize all human psychotherapy relationships. In these respects, the list of real and potential common everyday life alliance impacting factors and dynamics always remains essentially unlimited.

The ever-present list of common everyday life alliance imparting factors includes a continuum of multicultural, ethnic, racial, gender, religious, age-

related, socioeconomic, geographical and values-experiential and phenomenological dynamics and issues. These factors also continuously and interactively impact and shape the therapeutic alliance in a diversity of ways. This
continuous interactive process includes the essential therapeutic ingredients
in effective psychotherapy relationships that were discussed earlier in the
chapter, as well as the powerfully influential secondary dynamics of therapist-patient transference, countertransference, self-disclosure, relapse, and
other essentially patient-focused readiness, motivation, commitment to the
change and recovery process, capacity for rigorous honesty, and truth telling
factors. In the end, this confluence of psychotherapy relationship, process
factors, and other variables always impact the outcome of psychotherapy in
an every-remaining "for better or for worse" manner.

SUMMARY

Several ancillary therapist-patient alliance dynamics and factors that continuously or sometimes precipitously influence and impact the process and
outcomes of psychotherapy or other treatment relationships were examined
in this chapter.

Transference and countertransference dynamics have been viewed as
primary impactful sources of psychoanalytic and dynamically-oriented psychotherapy process and outcome influence for one hundred years. These
early psychoanalytic and psychodynamic constructs generated very little evidence-based research for many decades. However, the more recent empirical and clinical examinations of these psychotherapy constructs reviewed in
this chapter (Forrest, 2002, 2012, 2017; Gelso and Bhatia, 2012; Horowitz
and Moller, 2009; Maroda, 1994; Orellana and Gelso, 2013) clearly indicate
that both transference and countertransference dynamics continually influence and impact the therapeutic alliance as well as the process and outcome
of virtually all psychotherapy and treatment relationships. In fact, transference and countertransference dynamics continually impact all of our ongoing human relationships. These alliance-impacting therapeutic factors are
examined in depth in the chapter within the context of general psychotherapeutic work as well as within the context of addictions-focused psychotherapy and counseling relationships.

Therapist self-disclosure and transparency within the context of the
alliance and therapeutic relationship is explored in the chapter. Rather
extensive evidence-based literature pertaining to therapist self-disclosure,
alliance development, therapeutic outcomes and the utilization of this somewhat controversial therapist technique or tool are also discussed in this chapter. The clinical uses, definitions and historical literature pertaining to uses

and potential therapeutic as well as potentially harmful impact of therapist self-disclosures in psychotherapy are also touched upon in the chapter. The author's earlier work pertaining to therapist and patient self-disclosure and transparency in psychotherapy and addictions-focused therapeutic work is also briefly examined in the chapter.

Relapse-related alliance dynamics in psychotherapy, treatment and the recovery process remain ever-present, impactful, and not infrequently alliance rupture facilitating realities. A wide variety of relapse realities, consequences and outcomes can be associated with relapse events related to all human illness and disease processes. A plethora of relapse related factors and dynamics including relapse prevention strategies in psychotherapy and treatment interventions that work with addictive disordered persons are elucidated in this chapter. The seminal addiction specific treatment relapse and relapse prevention works of Gorski and Miller (1986), Grinstead (1996, 2014, 2018), and the author (Forrest, 1997, 2015), as well as the more empirically-based and academically developed and focused relapse contributions of Marlatt (1985, 2005) and Miller and colleagues (1991, 2008, 2012) are incorporated in this important chapter pertaining to the alliance and overall process-outcome of therapeutic relationships involving people with addictive disorders. Unfortunately, the relapse alliance dynamics arena involving psychotherapy and treatment process and outcome in addictions work has historically received relatively little research attention. The Gorski and Miller (1986) body of relapse prevention work has perhaps been most impactful in the historic training, supervision, and practice of addictions counselors, therapists, and residential as well as outpatient substance providers in America. This general model is also examined in the chapter.

Contemporary evolving psychotherapy evidence-based alliance literature (Cook et al., 2015; Escudero et al., 2012; Fisher et al., 2016; Friedlander et al., 2014; Safran, Muran and Eubanks-Carter, 2011; Sommers-Flanagan and Kindle Lewis, 2017) is also examined in this chapter. Definitions, dynamics, and descriptions of therapist alliance rupture and repair work in general psychotherapy practice as well as addictions-focused therapy are included in the chapter. The chapter also provides therapist guidance and therapeutic strategies for dealing with alliance stressors and the management of potential alliance rupturing therapeutic interactions and events that may occur between the therapist and patient during the course of psychotherapy or treatment. In particular, therapists and counselors need to be able to openly acknowledge and discuss the facets of communication, interpretation and relational misunderstandings, errors or technical mistakes that they may have made or contributed to during the course of a therapy session. Such transactions can occur at any juncture in the therapeutic process, and therapists frequently need to be able to openly address these potential sources of alliance rupture promptly, honestly, and even apologetically. These dynamics are key components of the ongoing process of efficacious alliance rupture and repair work in psychotherapy.

Therapist alliance rupture and repair work is an essential ingredient in the process of effective psychotherapy, and this particular facet of the alliance may provide a wealth of further research and clinical practice data and information for all therapists in the very near future.

A diversity of patient factors and dynamics continuously impact the therapeutic alliance as well as the outcome of psychotherapy and other treatments. Patient readiness and motivation for change, commitment to change, recovery and the recovery process, and the capacity for rigorous honesty and basic truth-telling comprise some of the important patient alliance ingredients that continually exert very significant influences upon the alliance, process and outcome of therapy. These particular patient alliance related factors are discussed in the context of general psychotherapy and addictions therapy work in this chapter.

Finally, and unending number of common everyday life events and factors can impact and/or affect the alliance and therapeutic process in any number of significant ways. The basic realities of human living associated with such things as death and a variety of serious health problems, job loss or career changes, financial problems, divorce and family matters, geographical moves, war and any number of life changes may suddenly or insidiously change or terminate the alliance and the therapeutic relationship. Such alliance and life changing events can be unanticipated and uncommon, but when they do occur in therapy, they also frequently have a rather profound impact upon the patient-therapist alliance relationship. Many of these alliance related transactions tend to be upsetting and disturbing for the therapist and patient, and therapists and addictions counselors sometimes need to implement special interventions for their patients and themselves in these situations.

Chapter 6

PSYCHOPATHOLOGY, PSYCHODYNAMICS AND ALLIANCE DYNAMICS IN INTEGRATIVE ADDICTIONS-FOCUSED PSYCHOTHERAPY AND COUNSELING RELATIONSHIPS

INTRODUCTION

Substance abusers and patients manifesting severe addictive disorders have long been viewed as being "difficult to treat" (Forrest, 1978; Bratter and Forrest, 1985; Forrest, 1996, 2012, 2019). Historically, clinicians and psychotherapists have avoided treating addictive disordered persons, and likewise, therapists and mental health workers have also generally tended to believe that psychotherapy and other treatments were of little benefit for this clinical subpopulation. However, these general sentiments and beliefs have changed significantly over the course of the past twenty or thirty years, and with the slow but progressive evolution of the addictions treatment field and diverse mental health services throughout the United States as well as the world community it is now recognized that (1) significant numbers of patients manifesting addictive brain disease do, in fact, benefit significantly from a diversity of clinical services and treatment interventions, and (2) the substance use disorders and addictive brain disease frequently involve comorbid psychological, psychiatric, and various other behavioral health problems known to mankind.

It has also become widely recognized that the addictive brain disease process creates, or are related to, a myriad of bio-psychosocial, legal, and economic problems. The addictive diseases have impacted every culture, ethnic and religious group, and society in the world for hundreds, if not thousands, of years. One in every ten adult deaths in America is principally related to alcohol dependence or abuse. Contemporary behavioral health science also indicates that substance abuse and drug dependency are frequently causative factors related to many facets of pathologic and maladaptive human behavior. Furthermore, the addictive diseases can occur and impact virtually any person at any point in the human life span process.

Within the specific context of human relationships, the psychotherapy relationship and more specifically, the therapeutic alliance, is always impacted vis a vis the individual psychopathology and psychodynamics each unique human being manifesting addictive brain disease brings to the alliance. The therapist and patient are continually confronted with the process of dealing with these factors within the alliance throughout the course of psychotherapy. The psychotherapy process also continually encompasses the various alliance related dynamics that the therapist brings to the alliance in the form of his or her experiential life history and personal transference and countertransference relationship with each individual patient.

Many of the thorny, nefarious, complex, and often difficult or destructive alliance related dynamics that therapists and counselors continually encounter in their psychotherapy work with addictive disordered patients are examined in this chapter. Addictive disordered persons are also continuously confronted with the many painful realities associated with their dysfunctional adjustment styles via the alliance and ongoing course of the therapeutic process. The eventual therapeutic modification and resolution of these patient dynamics and pathologic behaviors, beliefs, cognitions, affective regulation and impulse control management difficulties, and interpersonal adjustment style, constitute much of the work of successful therapeutic outcomes and patient recoveries.

The psychopathology and psychodynamics of narcissistic injury, trauma, human attachment, interpersonal dynamics and the psychogenic etiology and development of the addictive brain disease process are initially examined in this chapter. The second and major component of this chapter encompasses an exploration of the structure and process of effective individual psychotherapy work and the alliance in therapy with addictive disordered persons. Therapeutic techniques and strategies that are specifically designed and utilized to help addictive disordered patients resolve and change many of their historic maladaptive and dysfunctional behaviors and dynamics are included in this chapter. Alliance specific therapist relational dynamics, behaviors, strategies, and experiential ways of being with the patient can contribute significantly to the alliance cohesion, patient commitment to the therapy process, and the ongoing work of the therapeutic process, as well as the global change and recovery process that characterizes efficacious therapy outcomes.

A good deal of the clinical concepts, information, and content in this chapter pertaining to the etiology, psychopathology, psychodynamics, and alliance related psychotherapy work with addictive disordered patients reflects the compendium of the author's previous professional publications over the course of some fortyfive years of clinical practice with this patient population (see Forrest references, 1975 to 2019).

This chapter clearly demonstrates the diversity of pathological and psychodynamic factors that may contribute to a myriad of ever-present alliance, therapeutic relationship, and addictions-focused treatment psychotherapy work related to difficulties or potentially therapeutically corrosive therapy dynamics and poor therapy outcomes. The case studies and therapeutic vignettes included in the chapter further demonstrate these various alliance and therapeutic process related realities.

THE PSYCHOPATHOLOGY AND
PSYCHODYNAMICS OF ADDICTIVE DISORDERS

Patients manifesting addictive brain disease manifest a diversity of clinical symptoms that may include many of the DSM-IV-R and DSM-V, ICD10 (20002015) diagnostic classifications ranging from alcoholism or polysubstance dependence to diagnoses involving comorbid PTSD and trauma, major depression, schizophrenia, generalized anxiety disorder, obsessive-compulsive disorder, borderline personality disorder, antisocial personality disorder, ADD/ADHS, sleep disorders, and various other contemporary medical, psychiatric and psychological disorders (Forrest, 2018, 2019; Glidewell, 2015; ICD10, 2015). Addictions-focused clinicians also continue to see addictive-disordered patients who initially appear to be rather well adjusted in most areas of functioning and do not manifest florid comorbid psychopathology. In this regard, it is important to note that both the addictive disorders and various comorbid pathological diagnoses that are frequently cooccurring in either condition exist on a continuum. Thus, alcoholics, eating-disordered persons, opioid addicts, and other persons manifesting an addictive brain disease present with a rather broad spectrum of symptoms, severity and adjustment styles related to their addictive disease; however, they may also present with a broad continuum of symptoms and clinical dynamics related to cooccurring pathological disorders such as bipolar disorder, schizoaffective disorder, anxiety disorder or various other psychiatric disorders. These clinical realities demonstrate the relatively individual nature of human beings in healthy as well as disease states, and also demonstrate the complexities that can be associated with the diagnosis and treatment of all behavioral health conditions.

Few would argue that the essential common denominators of all addictive brain diseases include the patient's inability to control, self-regulate or simply successfully terminate the diversity of thoughts, behaviors, affects and related social dynamics associated with their addictive brain disease process.

Addictive disorders consistently involve clinically descriptive symptoms including (1) an inability to terminate and sustain the termination of a pattern of dysfunctional behaviors related to a particular addiction or spectrum of addictive disorders, (2) engaging in addictive substance use or a pattern of repetitive addictive behavior involving more frequent and progressive use, increased quantities or concentrations, and this dysfunctional pattern of behavior persists for increasingly longer periods of time sometimes, in spite of the addictive disordered person's persistent efforts to terminate or control the addictive disease process, and (3) an inability to control or stop the progressively debilitating and progressively dysfunctional, self-defeating global symptom structure related to the addictive disease process.

Addictive disordered persons also engage in a plethora of progressively dysfunctional time structuring behaviors and activities which are designed to maintain the addiction process. Eventually, every facet of the addict's familial, social, occupational, recreational, health, and psychosocial life becomes progressively and adversely impacted by the addictive brain disease process. Destructive patterns of physical and psychological behavior and dependence develop, resulting in various patterns of social withdrawal and isolation, and the globally pathologic addictive disease progress becomes progressively maladaptive, self-defeating, dysfunctional, and life threatening. These general patterns of addictive behavior pertain to all substance use disorders and include the eating-disorders, gambling disorders, and sexual disorders. The progressive outcropping of a diversity of psychological and psychiatric disorders related to or directly caused by the addictive brain disease process characterize the addictive disorders. While many addictive disordered persons manifest clinical disorders that preexist the development of their addictive brain disease, these individuals also tend to deteriorate earlier, and they also manifest progressively more severe premorbid primary and secondary psychopathology as their addictive brain disease process progresses.

The author's earlier clinical publications (Forrest, 1975-2019) explored many of the historical conceptualizations as well as the interpersonal, developmental, familial, learning and conditioning, genetic, biopsychosocial, and psychodynamic psychopathology facets of alcoholism and other addictive disorders. This multivariate etiological model of alcoholism also provides readers with a wealth of clinical assessment and treatment strategies that are designed to modify the various dysfunctional behaviors, thoughts, and globally pathologic dynamics and adjustment dynamisms that constitute the essential core etiological components of the addictive brain disease process.

This model includes a comprehensive examination of the role of trauma, early-life narcissistic injury, and infantile narcissistic need and entitlement deprivation in the etiology of alcoholism and the addictive disorders. Thus, interpersonal and intrapersonal dynamics and realities constitute significant components in Dr. Forrest's (1999) earlier psychogenic conceptualization of the addictive disorders. The following table provides a schematic representation of the key clinical psychodynamics, psychopathological components, and adjustment dynamisms that are related to the early-life experience of profound narcissistic injury and subsequently constitute much of the core adjustment pathology pertaining to the addictive disorders. Biologic, genetic, and familial factors are included in Dr. Forrest's original model but it has clearly become apparent via the more recent brain science research of the past two decades involving brain faction, brain chemistry, neurotransmitters, and brain circuitry, as well as genetic factors play a crucial role in the developmental etiology and psychopathology of approximately one third or more of addictive disordered persons (Koob and Volkow, 2010; McCauley, 2012; Volkow, 2015, 2015; Weiss, 2015).

In essence, the psycho-genetically determined components of narcissistic injury frequently evolve as a result of dysfunctional parenting skills, parental objects, and significant traumatic experiences occurring during infancy, early childhood, and frequently over the course of the patient's lifespan. Narcissistic injury and trauma related to infancy and childhood parenting behaviors and dynamics can play a major role in the etiology and eventual outcropping of the addictive brain disease process. Profoundly abusive, neglectful, and inadequate parenting dynamics associated with parental alcoholism or drug abuse, divorce, and multiple divorces, psychological difficulties and various psychiatric disorders, poverty, cognitive and various health conditions, learning disorders, impulse control and maturity matters, and other conditions are frequently related to the morass of factors that can contribute to the destructive and pathologic early life parenting realities that addictive disordered persons have experienced.

Extreme narcissistic injury and trauma can and does result in the physical death of infants and children, and narcissistic injury and acute trauma in adult life can also impact human beings in a diversity of very adverse physical and psychologically devastating ways for the entirety of the traumatized person's life.

The interpersonal histories of addictive disordered persons tend to be rife with experiences involving narcissistic need and entitlement deprivation, and the evolving and progressive nature of these faulty life experiences shape and affect the later life development, adjustment style, personality, cognitive functioning, and character styles of addictive disordered patients. Narcissistic injury has been a consistent and chronic experiential reality in the case of persons who develop alcoholism and other addictive disorders (Forrest, 1997).

The author (Forrest, 1985) indicates that,

Narcissistic injury is used, as a construct, interchangeably with the concept of narcissistic need and entitlement deprivation—most fundamentally, narcissistic needs refer to the life-sustaining needs of the human organism. Oxygen, food, appropriate temperature control, physical contact, and the maintenance of excretory functions are narcissistic needs. These needs of the infant and young child must be managed by significant others (mother, father, and family system). These basic needs are selforiented, thus narcissistic and life-sustaining. Should significant others fail to meet the narcissistic needs of the infant, death may occur.

Narcissistic entitlement deprivation refers essentially to the absence of those psychological and interpersonal processes which convey a basic sense of dignity, love, respect, worth, esteem, concern, and trust to the infant and child. As human beings we are generally entitled to feel loved, worthwhile, adequate, valued, and respected within the contexts of our relationships with significant others. Such needs are lifelong.

Narcissistic needs pertain to essentially physiological processes, while entitlement needs refer more to interpersonal and psychological processes. However, narcissistic need and entitlement trauma and deprivation clearly include both physiological and psychological components.

Narcissistic injury occurs when the narcissistic needs and entitlements of the evolving person are inadequately managed by significant others. Narcissistic need and entitlement deprivation most catastrophically affect the growth and healthy development of the person under pervasive and chronic circumstances. Narcissistic need and entitlement deprivation are interpersonal processes that encompass the life process and the evolving self and significant others.

Quite simply, the addictive disordered person has consistently been hurt and traumatized by significant others throughout much of his or her life. Many patients manifesting addictive brain disease can vividly recall in psychotherapy having been physically, emotionally, and sexually abused or neglected very early in life. Parental addiction, mental illness or psychological disturbance, neglect, extreme physical abuse, beatings, abandonment and parental attachment failure, as well as the long-term interpersonal "programming" that accompanies this developmental process constitutes the psychogenic "royal road" to an addictive disordered adjustment style" (pp. 312–313).

The narcissistic injury process or dynamism eventually constitutes a significant facet of the interpersonal modus vivendi pertaining to many addictive disordered individuals. As schematically presented in Table 1, profound early life narcissistic injury precipitates the prototaxic experience of acutely intense infantile and chronic developmental anxiety that addictive disor-

Table 1.
The Psychopathology of Alcoholism

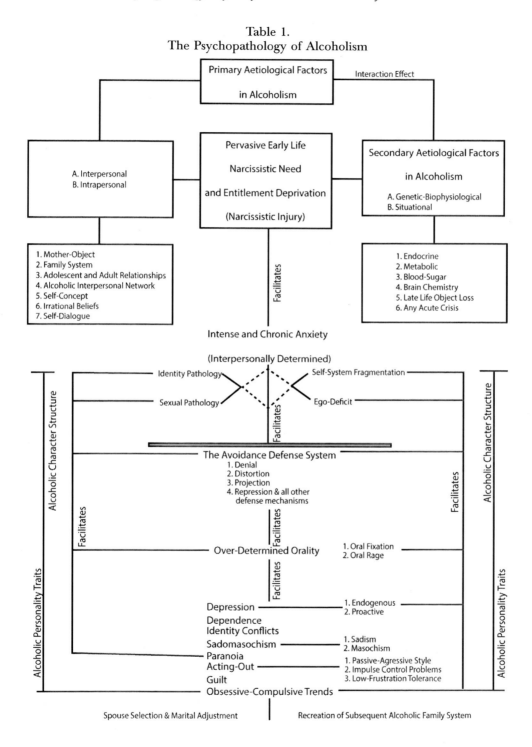

dered persons manifest. Orally addictive patients (alcoholics, compulsive overeaters and eating disordered patients, prescription and other "pill" addicts, and nicotine dependent persons) have experienced intense infantile anxiety within the interpersonal context of their mothering and parenting relationships during the initial weeks and months of life. Juxtaposed to this, the addicted person inconsistently experiences a significant degree of orally-oriented anxiety reduction, relief and oral pleasure during the developmentally-related epoch with the mother object. Feeding and eating experiences result in a significant degree of intermittent anxiety reduction, and these dynamics contribute to the overdetermined orality of addicts. Primitive matters pertaining to rejection, physical pain, abandonment, and annihilation are also related to the early-life anxiety the infant experiences vis à vis the mothering relationship. In essence, addictive disordered patients have experienced intense and chronic early-life anxiety related to prototaxic or organismic fear of destruction, annihilation, and death by significant others.

Pervasive anxiety and terror within the context of the infantile mothering relationship and significant others during this developmental epoch also results in a less than adequately consolidated nuclear sense of self and self-system fragmentation. These factors create the addict's chronic vulnerability, the experience of intense anxiety, a propensity for regressive behavior, problems pertaining to a blurring of the ego boundaries and chronic identity conflicts. These dynamics additionally foster the utilization of over determined oral methods of binding anxiety and stress, and containing the experience of ego-diffusion.

Addictive disordered persons tend to unendingly search for an answer to the question, "Who am I?" This issue remains an ongoing struggle associated with nuclear identity. Self-esteem, gender identity, and matters pertaining to adequacy, body image, masculinity and femininity, and attractiveness, are also central to the addict's unending search for identity. It is within the context of a symbiotically warm, loving, human or mothering physical and emotional context based and essentially anxiety-free early life mothering relationship context that the evolving person is prototaxically able to experience a consistent sense of wellbeing and consensual validation which fosters the development of an adequately consolidated nuclear sense of self. Consistently healthy, nurturing, and loving early-life mothering and parenting relationships facilitate the development of the infant's and child's capabilities for developing an adequately consolidated nuclear sense of self, establish sufficient anxiety management skills, and generally develop enhanced life coping skills. Anxiety associated with early-life narcissistic injury is a primary factor in the development of an addictive disorder, and effective anxiety management tends to remain on an ongoing or life-long relapse risk factor for all addictive disordered persons.

Addictive disordered persons adaptively develop an avoidance defense system (Forrest, 1983) during the initial months and years of their lives in order to cope with and survive the catastrophic anxiety associated with the ongoing experience of profound narcissistic injury. The avoidance defense system is developed during the first three or four years of life and is basic to the lifelong characterological makeup of addictive disordered persons. In essence, this system consists of a tripartite set of core primitive defense mechanisms including denial, distortion and projection. The avoidance defense system "protects" the addictive disordered person from basic human relatedness, contact, and the experience of human intimacy. The human interactive and contact-oriented, intimate infantile experiences of the addict have been anxiety-ridden and traumatizing. Thus, addictive disordered individuals have learned and been prototaxically conditioned via these pathologic early-life experiences that form intimate human relationships and encounters are often viewed by the addicted person as being dangerous, emotionally painful, and potentially even life-threatening. Therefore, the addictive disordered patient reflexively attempts to avoid or control intimate human encounters and relationships during subsequent developmental life stages.

Another function of the avoidance defense system includes an avoidance of self-awareness and self-being. Paradoxically, many addicts and substance abusers are painfully aware of their feelings, experiences, and pathologically self-focused behaviors and thoughts. Thus, the avoidance defense system serves the dual purpose of protecting the patient from anxiety and fear associated with interpersonal intimacy and contact as well as the interpersonal anxiety related to self-awareness, self-focused cognitions, fantasies, and behaviors. The patient's cognitive and affective self-process involving guilt, shame, low self-worth, failure, feelings of inadequacy or worthlessness, anxiety, dread, and depression can be partially contained, denied, repressed, and otherwise "controlled" *vis à vis* the avoidance defense system.

The addictive process, *per se,* eventually becomes a lifestyle of avoidance. Addicts maintain a constant avoidance of self, significant others, and the phenomenal world via the ingestion of chemicals, drugs, addictive substances and their repertoire of addictive behaviors and obsessive thoughts. Addictive disordered persons experience self, others, and the world through the medium of what can be referred to as a "semipermeable membrane" (Forrest, 1978, 1997). This semipermeable membrane can be alcohol, heroin or sedatives, marijuana, food, cigarettes, sex or other addictive substances and behaviors. It is important for clinicians and therapists to always bear in mind that addictive disordered patients employ all of the human defense mechanisms in the service and maintenance of their addictive disorders.

These various early-life narcissistic injury related psychodynamics and developmental realities also contribute to the depressive symptomatology that frequently characterizes the addictive disordered person's adjustment style. Endogenous depression, bipolar disorder and dysthymia diagnoses frequently co-occur with the addictive disorders (Fleming, 2013), and the depressive struggles of addicts and substance abusers are often chronic. The psychogenic and neurobiological impact of ongoing trauma and narcissistic injury facilitate the addictive disordered person's sense of hurt, pain, sadness, shame associated with having been rejected, chronically criticized, belittled, and many times, physically abused or traumatized by significant others. While some addictive disordered patients verbalize that they have "never been depressed," addictions therapists usually discover rather early in the therapeutic process that these individuals manifest clear-cut clinical anxiety and depression that becomes evident with sustained abstinence and active recovery engagement.

Successful psychotherapy work with addictive disordered patients is often contingent upon the therapist's ability to help the patient resolve his or her depressive disorder associated with establishment of the recovery process, and the addictive process can thus be viewed as a neurotic defense against depression.

The dependency-oriented psychopathology and psychodynamics of addictive disorders is closely associated with overdetermined orality and depression. The addictive disordered person's dependency pathology reflects a primitive attempt to resolve or undo the experience of early-life narcissistic injury via attachments to healthy "mother substitutes." The addictive disordered person chronically searches for a "mother" or significant others who can provide the love, warmth, nurturing, and healthy parenting and oral-related-interpersonal supplies which were absent during their infantile and childhood experiential lives. Addicts become addicted to mood altering chemicals, behaviors and substances, and many eventually maintain long-term "love affairs" with their addictive disease object replacement. This pathologic process ultimately represents an attempt to resolve, repair and undo the prototaxic experience of narcissistic injury via the neurotic transference of feelings of impotence, well-being, adequacy, warmth, power, and basic humanness via the use of alcohol, other drugs, food, sex, nicotine, and other addictive mechanisms. Addiction, *per se,* represents an example *par excellence* of dependency, and this reality also defines the adjustment style of counterdependent appearing addictive disordered persons who attempt to neurotically deny or mask their pathologic dependency via the development of overly aggressive, assertive, and seemingly independent adjustment styles. At some juncture in the addictive disease process, the patient's dependency pathology may be most clearly apparent *vis a vis* his or her drug dependency and the disease process, *per se.*

As delineated in Table 1, several personality traits or adjustment styles, behavioral, and cognitive characteristics eventually become clinically manifest as a part of the addictive disease process. Many, if not most, addictive disordered persons who enter therapy or are seen within the context of residential and intensive out-patient addiction treatment, psychiatric hospital settings and mental health centers, or private practice, and are diagnosed by psychiatrists, psychologists, addiction counselors, and other behavioral health specialists, with a wide diversity of cooccurring psychiatric disorders or conditions. These diagnoses include the spectrum of anxiety disorders, mood disorders, personality disorders, learning disorders, major mental illness and various other medical/psychiatric conditions.

The author (Forrest, 1975–2016) has also long indicated that addictive disordered patients frequently manifest comorbid anxiety disorders, depressive disorders, borderline personality disorders, antisocial personality disorders, obsessive compulsive disorders, paranoid personality features, passive-aggressive personality structures, selfdefeating adjustment styles, and other adjustment difficulties related to guilt, anger, impulse control, low frustration tolerance, sexuality, identity, and acting out. These various adjustment dynamisms may co-occur as personality disorders, personality traits, or features and/or also may be viewed as characterologically based adjustment dynamics or styles.

For example, the author (Forrest, 1985) indicates that, "addictive disorders can be viewed as an obsessive-compulsive disorder. Furthermore, the obsessive-compulsive dynamism is both a defense against anxiety and a neurotically maladaptive means of "binding" anxiety. Addictive disordered patients develop an obsessive-compulsive personality style in order to control and bind chronically ego-dystonic levels of early life anxiety, and this facet of the patient's personality style and character structure becomes progressively more apparent as the patient progresses into the middle and later stages of the addictive disease process. These persons tend to be rigid, perfectionistic, orderly, preoccupied with matters pertaining to time, and often manifest very structured lifestyles. An obsessive-compulsive cognitive and behavioral makeup eventually dictates that the addictive disordered person ruminates about alcohol, opioids, sedatives, food and eating behaviors, and other addictive processes. These patients also ingest, use, and engage in highly repetitive, compulsive, ritualistic, and highly predictable patterns of thinking and behaving. People who develop alcoholism, prescription drug dependence, or nicotine dependence may ingest these substances in an extremely obsessive-compulsive manner for several decades.

The recent DSM-V (2014) diagnostic model includes "substance-induced obsessive-compulsive related disorder" which specifically includes obsessions, compulsions, skin picking, hair pulling, and other body-focused repetitive behaviors and symptoms associated with substance abuse obsessive-compulsiveness.

Addictive disordered patients also obsessively and compulsively ruminate about their addictive behaviors and substances throughout the course of the addictive process. Patients learn to ingest mood, cognitive, and behavioral altering substances in order to experience a sense of enhanced freedom from anxiety and the loss of self-control. These patients eventually attempt to control every facet of their lives and the phenomenal world via their addiction. Paradoxically, addictive disordered persons progressively destroy themselves, every facet of self-control, and many eventually experience substance dependence related brief psychoses, psychiatric and "detox" hospitalizations, or incarcerations, as a direct consequence of the malignant nature of the addictive disease process. The obsessive-compulsive "magic" of the addictive disease process frequently fosters a complete collapse of the patient's ego defenses and coping skills.

Addictive disorders almost always involve problems associated with acting-out, impulse control, antisocial features, and passive-aggressive behaviors. Addiction can also be viewed as an impulse control disorder (Forrest and Gordon, 1990; Forrest, 1985, 1996). Many addictive disordered patients experience difficulty internalizing conflicts and mal-adaptively resolve interpersonal and intrapersonal difficulties via a plethora of impulsive, poorly controlled, risky and self-defeating acting-out behaviors. Addictive disordered patients continually demonstrate the clinical manifestations of their impulsiveness *vis a vis* disordered behavior, thoughts, lack of control, global actions, internalized, antisocial traits, self-defeating and risky behaviors. These patients also manifest low frustration tolerance, and all of these faulty adjust mechanisms are further fueled and reinforced via the neurobiological effects of a wide variety of psychoactive substances and chemicals. The specific impulsive or acting-out behaviors of addictive disordered patients may include anxiety, anger and rage, sexuality, manipulation, exploitation, poor judgement and decision making, and generalized irresponsibility. These patients often manifest a rather disinhibited and impulsive adjustment style prior to the outcropping of a florid addictive disorder, but once the addictive disease process begins these individuals tend to evince a progressive and often rapidly more generalized pattern of disinhibited behavior and lack of impulse control.

Impulsive acting-out and the various malignant behaviors and thoughts which accompany the process of poor impulse control again serve the neurotic process of binding the addictive disordered persons' prototaxic early-life experiences of anxiety with profound early-life narcissistic injury as well as chronic trauma over the life span. Many of these patients verbalize a conscious fear of becoming "insane" or "going crazy" related to their internalized sense of loss of control and various acting-out behaviors; however, they also tend to persist in a chronic pattern of pervasive addiction-related impulsive self-defeating behaviors that continues until the patient becomes fully engaged and actively committed to the difficult integrative addictions focused therapeutic work involving psychotherapy and the recovery process. Patients manifesting addictive brain disease also tend to be catastrophically afraid of dying, in spite of their repetitively self-destructive, self-defeating, and sometimes suicidal addictive behaviors. Impulsive, acting-out solutions and dynamics related to internalized feelings of threat, anxiety, and dissonance can also represent neurotic attempts to feel important, worthwhile, adequate, powerful, in control, "normal," and more fully human. The impulsive and acting out behaviors of the addictive disordered patient represent a defense against powerful underlying feelings of inadequacy, inferiority, worthlessness, shame and guilt, and personal impotence. However, clinicians also need to continually realize that the ingestion of various addictive substances and chemicals, at some point, always synergizes the impulsivity and acting-out behaviors of the patient.

Addiction and substance abuse *per se* represent acting-out solutions for the entire human repertoire of difficult and painful realities that are associated with the human life process. Historically, alcoholics and addicted persons were generally characterized as psychopaths or sociopaths (Sutker, 1971), largely as a function of their impulsive, acting-out, manipulative drug facilitated behaviors, and the other antisocial facets of their behavior. In clinical reality, the majority of addictive disordered persons also manifest primary conflicts associated with severe anxiety, affect regulation, guilt, remorse, shame, and other adjustment difficulties that preclude an antisocial personality disorder diagnosis. However, many, if not most, addictive disordered patients do manifest antisocial personality disorder traits or features and these realities are reflected in the more recent clinical research literature indicating that antisocial personality disorder is the most frequent personality disorder diagnosis given to adult male alcoholics and substance abusers receiving treatment and care within psychiatric hospitals, emergency rooms, and acute care in behavioral health settings (Forrest, 1996; Hesselbrock, Meyer, and Kenner, 1985; Nace, 1990).

A small percent (5 to 10 percent in the author's clinical experience) of patients manifesting addictive brain disease do, in fact, manifest florid psychopathy (Forrest, 1996; Hare, 1970) or antisocial personality disorder (Forrest, 1996; AMA, DSM-V, 2014). However, it should be noted that several research studies report "a strong association between personality disorders and substance abuse disorders" (Nace, 1990), and Helzer and Pryzbeck (1988) report that 15 percent of alcoholic males manifest comorbid Antisocial Personality Disorder (ASPD), nonalcoholics have a lifetime ASPD prevalence of 4 percent, and 10 percent of alcoholic women manifested ASPD while less than 1 percent of non-alcoholic women manifested ASPD.

Other researchers have found that diagnosed "Primary" ASPD occurs in 27 percent of opioid addicts and "secondary" ASPD in another 27 percent of addicts (Rounsaville et al., 1983), 65 percent of narcotic addicts manifest a personality disorder including nearly 50 percent with ASPD (Khantzian and Treece, 1985), and "it would seem safe to assume from the clinical studies now available that within the substance-abusing population, the prevalence of personality disorder is at least fifty percent" (Nace, 1990, p. 187). Sex ratio and other demographic data pertaining to these issues clearly indicate that the co-occurrence of substance abuse and other addictive disorders. ASPD indicate that males are significantly and more prone to manifesting most addictive diseases with cooccurring ASPD. In this regard, borderline personality disorder (Forrest, 1996) is the second most common disorder found in substance abusing female patients. Addictions therapists and clinicians are encouraged to explore these clinical factors in more depth within the context of the DSM-V, ICD-10 (2014), and various other professional journals or publications specific to the treatment of all addictive brain diseases.

Evolving historic DSM diagnostic criteria for antisocial personality disorder have indicated (Forrest, 1996) the essential feature of this disorder is a pattern of irresponsible and antisocial behavior beginning in childhood or early adolescence and continuing into adulthood, a history of conduct disorder prior to age 14, and the individual is at least eighteen years of age. DSM-V (2014) requires evidence of conduct disorder with onset before the age of fifteen.

Common or "typical childhood signs" of an adult antisocial personality disorder (Forrest, 1996) include "lying, stealing, truancy, vandalism, initiating fights, running away from home, and physical cruelty to animals and people, forced sexual activity, use of weapons in fights, destroying property and setting fires, forgery, armed robbery and muggings." These general characteristics commonly characterize the diagnosis of childhood or adolescent conduct disorder, and a diagnosis of florid antisocial personality disorder may be accurately made by clinicians pertaining to a small percentage of pre-adolescent children. Substance abuse, dependence, and a plethora of drug related criminal behaviors also characterize the antisocial behavioral style and diagnosis pertaining to the majority of adolescents and adults manifesting this diagnosis. Home invasions and break-ins, robberies in general, assaults and murders, use of weapons, sexual assaults, human trafficking, prostitution, and the entire spectrum of organized crime activities have long been directly related to drugs, drug dependence, and the sales and distribution of a diversity of addictive drugs. Current diagnostic criteria (DSM-V, 2014) for adult antisocial personality disorder include "a pervasive pattern of disregard for and violation of the rights of others, occurring since age fifteen, as indicated by three or more of the following: (1) Failure to conform to social norms with respect to lawful behaviors, as indicated by repeatedly performing acts that are grounds for arrest, (2) deceitfulness, as indicated by repeated lying, use of aliases, or conning others for personal profit or pleasure, (3) impulsivity or failure to plan ahead, (4) irritability and aggressiveness, as indicated by repeated physical fights or assaults, (5) reckless disregard for the safety of self or others, (6) consistent irresponsibility, as indicated by repeated failure to sustain consistent work behavior or honor financial obligations, and (7) lack of remorse, as indicated by being indifferent to or rationalizing having hurt, mistreated, or stolen from others.

Antisocial personality disordered individuals frequently drive while under the influence of alcohol and various other drugs, tend to be promiscuous, experience chronic interpersonal difficulties and legal entanglements, and almost always have a markedly impaired capacity to sustain lasting, close, warm, loving, responsible relationships with family, friends, or sexual partners" (Forrest, 1996).

The author (Forrest, 1996) has also suggested in concert with DSM information (APA, 1987–2014) that the psychoactive substance use disorders are commonly associated with ASPD or psychopathy. This particular personality disorder is often "incapacitating," has an early onset, and premature violent death is associated with this disorder. Antisocial personality disorder is five times more common among first-degree biologic relatives of males with the disorder than among the general population, and the risk to first degree biologic relatives of females with the disorder is nearly ten times that of the general population. This disorder appears to have a strong genetic component. It has been observed that psychopaths and ASPD disordered persons tend to become less antisocial as they enter middle age and progress into their early 50s and older. These individuals often exert a very malignant influence upon the individuals, institutions, and social systems which they become involved with. Politicians, government leaders, military personnel, physicians and health care professionals, attorneys, clergy and corporate executives who manifest this disorder exert a particularly malignant impact on society and the world in a diversity of very destructive ways.

The author (Forrest, 1996, 2012, 2017) has indicated that most chemical dependency counselors and therapists working with the spectrum addictive disorders do not have extensive clinical training and practice experience with antisocial personality disordered patients. In relation to this, a relatively small percent of patients manifesting an addictive brain disease have comorbid antisocial personality. However, it has also been suggested (Forrest, 1996, 2015) that (1) many, if not most, floridly addictive disordered patients eventually manifest ASPD traits or features, (2) ASPD traits or features often evolve as a core component of the addictive disease process, and (3) addictive patients who do not manifest a pre-morbid antisocial personality disorder prior to the onset of their addictive brain disease generally respond quite well to psychotherapies utilized for resolving antisocial personality disorder traits, behaviors and thinking patterns. The author (Forrest, 1996) has indicated that the "vast majority of antisocial personality disordered patients are *consistent* abusers of alcohol, psychoactive substances" and other addictive disordered behavioral patterns.

Methamphetamine dependence, cocaine dependence, opioid and sedative dependencies, alcohol dependence, and polydrug dependence clearly appear to foster and synergize the development of floridly antisocial behaviors and the outcropping of an antisocial personality disordered adjustment style. Criminal behaviors including murder, extortion, sexual assault, human trafficking, and any other form of violent or destructive behavior may be associated with these particular addictive disorders. Experienced correctional therapists, and counselors who work within the mental health, substance abuse, and sex offender programs in prison environments understand the many complexities associated with attempting to treat, manage, and "rehabilitate" these patients. They also generally appreciate the relational dynamics and alliance difficulties that accompany integrative addictions-focused psychotherapeutic work with persons manifesting ASPD, psychopathy, or even antisocial personality features and/or traits. The lies, dishonesty, self-defeating, passive-aggressive, hostile, manipulative, deceitful, impulsive, conniving, acting out, risk taking, and various other relational dynamics associated with the antisocial behaviors involving sex addicts, compulsive gamblers, and nicotine addicts are difficult and unendingly conflictual for families, spouses, friends, employers, and therapists, counselors, and behavioral health treatment providers as well!

Therapists who consistently work with addictive disordered persons manifesting co-occurring ASPD or ASPD traits may want to explore the author's earlier in-depth text dealing with these specific clinical matters (Forrest, 1996).

Many other behavioral characteristics and personality traits can be associated with the experience of profound early life narcissistic injury and lifespan trauma. This adjustment dynamism can be triggered by a wide range of adolescent and adult experiences involving profound trauma and narcissistic injury. The development of Post-Traumatic Stress Disorder (PTSD) can evolve at any juncture in life, and can also be associated with a diversity of human experiences involving extreme acute or prolonged trauma and narcissistic injury.

Addictive disordered persons frequently evince a paranoid personality style, and some of these patients have paranoid personality disorders or experience florid paranoid decompensations that are triggered by the experience of either acute drug binge episodes or acute drug/chemical withdrawal and detoxification as well as protracted alcohol dependence, withdrawal and brain dysfunction. However, addictive disordered patients manifesting a history of severe infantile narcissistic injury and profound trauma manifest structural weakness of the ego, self-system and identity fragmentation, and an inadequately consolidated nuclear sense of self (Forrest, 1985; Kernberg, 1975) which renders them chronically vulnerable to paranoid thinking and the eventual experience of developing a paranoid personality disorder. Paranoid symptomatology can be viewed as an underlying basic component of the progressive addictive brain disease process, and is closely associated with infantile narcissistic injury related sexual role, identity, self-system confusion, and the inadequately consolidated sense of self. Simply put, many addicts tend to be confused and experience paranoid ideation related to their sexuality.

Experienced integrative addictions focused therapists and counselors are very cognizant of the drug or chemical dependence related and facilitated facets of the patient's paranoid thinking, ideation, and frequently bizarre behaviors. Both acute and chronic, alcohol, methamphetamine, cocaine, psychedelic, and various other mood-altering addictive substances can and frequently do precipitate acute paranoid psychoses. Chronically addicted patients often tend to develop a paranoid adjustment style as they enter the middle and late stages of the addiction process, and their movement into an essentially paranoid position may also be fostered via (1) cognitive decline, (2) the core experiences associated with multiple and frequent substance induced "black-outs" over many years that sometimes result in consequences and outcomes that eventually facilitate the development of "logical" paranoid ideation, and (3) the combined impact of the progressive global nature of human decline associated with aging, the addictive brain disease process, including perhaps hundreds of "black-out" experiences related to substance abuse, intoxication, cognitive decline, and basic biopsychosocial deterioration. Clinicians also need to remain cognizant of the infrequent role of the one-time experiences or very limited drug ingestion experiences that can precipitate a brief psychotic episode or paranoid episode involving adolescent and younger drug users. A few of these episodes do eventually become a clinical prelude to the development of paranoid schizophrenia or other forms of major mental illness.

The addictive-disordered life-style can create paranoid thinking and a paranoid world view. Addiction can cause paranoid thinking, and addictive disordered persons frequently engage in a diversity of aberrant and socially deviant behaviors, which synergize paranoid ideation. Many of the social role behaviors of addictive disordered patients also become dysfunctional, and reinforce the patient's feelings of anxiety, depression, paranoia, low self-worth, anger, and eventually foster the outcropping of social deviation and paranoid thinking, behaviors and cognitions that become ego syntonic with the addictive brain disease process.

Therapeutic measures that result in substance abstinence, arrest the addictive disease process, and potentiate global constructive personality change sometimes precipitate a rather abrupt extinction of the floridly paranoid adjustment style that many addictive disordered patients manifest. However, a sizeable segment of the addictive disordered population sustains various levels of the paranoid process following years of abstinence and sustained arrest of the addictive brain disease process. Trust, intimacy issues, suspiciousness, questions of trustworthiness, a sense of threat, carrying grudges, and recurrent pre-occupations pertaining to sexual and relational fidelity of a spouse or significant others commonly describe the residual cognitive-behavioral style of many recovering addictive disordered patients. Again, these paranoid dynamics may also fade significantly with the ongoing evolution of the recovery process in many cases.

Table 1 also includes several additional common personality features which clinically characterize a segment of the addictive disordered patient population that has historically been referred to as impulsive personality disorder, immature personality disorder, passive-aggressive personality disorder, self-defeating personality disorder, anti-social personality disorder, sadistic personality disorder, narcissistic personality disorder, borderline personality disorder, and mixed personality disorder. As depicted in Table 1, the author (1983, 1999) originally indicated that these personality traits characterized the psychopathology of alcoholism. These particular personality features as well as the cognitions, behaviors, and relational dynamics generally describe the spectrum of contemporary addictive disorders (Forrest, 2015).

Alcoholics and addictive-disordered patients have not generally been viewed as being sadistic, masochistic, or sadomasochistic; however as the author noted many years ago (Forrest, 1983), when the historically sexual aspects of these particular clinical constructs are essentially excluded, the behavioral, cognitive, affective and relational dynamics and realities of these constructs are often quite relevant and clinically very descriptive of the overall addictive-disordered patient's adjustment style. These clinical realities become particularly apparent within the context of the therapeutic alliance and ongoing therapeutic relationships in long term integrative addictions focused psychotherapy work with addictive-disordered persons. An essential clinical sine qua non of the addictive disordered person involves sadomasochistically inflicting physical and/or emotional hurt and pain on self and significant others.

This author has also suggested that (Forrest, 1983) sadism and masochism are ego-fused and, thus, the various sadomasochistic facets of physical and emotional pain related to the generalized maladaptive behaviors of addictive-disordered persons including suicides, automobile accidents, physical health problems, divorces, child and family abuse, mental health problems, arrests and incarcerations, economic or legal costs, and other self-defeating patterns of behavior, represent the tragic concrete clinical realities associated with this dynamism. Addicts and addictive-disordered persons continuously hurt themselves and others in a myriad of ways; hangovers, accidents, verbal abuse and neglect, multiple divorces, job losses, and the self-defeating and often sadomasochistic modus vivendi of the addictive disordered family system often involve diffuse and seemingly unending punitive self and other relational dynamics. Physical and emotional survival become paramount issues in the lives of addictive-disordered persons and their families and loved ones.

Sexually abusive and sadomasochistic behaviors and transactions are usually of limited or little relevance in the psychotherapy and treatment of addictive disordered patients. However, these dynamics can be manifest and destructively impact clinical realities associated with extramarital affairs, divorces, sexual performance and desire problems, and episodic acute drug-induced debauchery.

The procrastination, irritability, resentment, obstructiveness, angry, dependency, lying, forgetfulness, and chameleon-like related behaviors of many addictive disordered patients are manifestations of a diagnosis of passive-aggressive personality disorder. These individuals also tend to hide behind a façade of congeniality but their resentments, fear, selfishness or self-centeredness, and passive-aggressive traits become clearly evident and manifest within the context of ongoing therapy relationships and personal relationships. These patients experience chronic difficulties in their relationships with authority figures, and as a direct result of their passive-aggressiveness they are also more difficult for therapists to work with. Addictive disordered patients may express verbal agreement with initially established therapeutic goals and the important therapeutic tasks, but they subsequently and consciously tend to resist, forget, or intentionally fail to do their share of the therapeutic work essential to meeting basic therapeutic goals including sustained drug abstinence. The passive-aggressive personality style (Wetzler, 1993) of the addictive disordered patient represents an attempt to bind anxiety and establish a basic sense of internal cohesion and control within the context of the therapeutic relationship as well as other relational interactions.

In many ways, all addictive disorders represent the clinical example *par excellence* of a self-defeating personality disorder. Addictive disordered patients invariably manifest clinical histories that clearly evince an ongoing pattern of self-defeating behavior. These patients are clearly their own worst enemies. Examples of this adjustment style include making repetitive choices that result in failure, disappointment and bad outcomes, rejection of attempts by others to provide helpful assistance or guidance, inciting angry responses and rejection or painful consequences from others, and failure to accomplish important tasks in spite of having the ability to do so. Alcoholic patients who are arrested for driving under the influence of alcohol and are subsequently arrested again and again end up spending thousands of dollars on attorney fees, and may eventually spend one or two years in a correctional facility or perhaps even commit vehicular homicide. Another common example of the many patterns of self-defeating behavior that characterize addictive disordered persons involves spending thousands or hundreds of dollars for numerous treatments, medical care and hospitalizations, legal counsel, divorces or criminal related offenses. A wide diversity of other self-defeating patterns of behavior accompany the progressive addictive disease process that clearly demonstrate the clinical vicissitudes of a self-defeating personality disorder or adjustment style.

The psychodynamics of narcissism, early life narcissistic injury, and the development of vacillating narcissism-related addictive brain disease related conflicts are explored in depth throughout the author's original alcoholism, narcissism, and psychopathology text (Forrest, 1983). The various maladaptive and pathologic diversions of the extended core early-life experiences involving profound narcissistic injury constitute the paradoxically and neurotically adaptive developmental foundation of the addictive disordered patient's global adjustment style pertaining to basic physical and psychological survival. These paradoxically adaptive adjustment dynamics include the avoidance defense system and every personality trait, disorder, or categorization of maladaptive human behavior discussed in this chapter.

This vacillating narcissism and narcissistic disturbance related to adult and adolescent alcoholic dependent persons prototaxically evolves as a function of the inability of the primary mother object and significant others to provide consistently sufficient mothering, nurturing, and developing loving secure attachments resulting in healthy parenting experiences for the infant and young child. These very destructive early-life relational experiences eventually facilitate the development of the addicted parent's maladaptive, and yet paradoxical, sense of uniqueness, needs for power, sense of entitlement, needs for attention and admiration, lack of empathy, over-sensitivity to criticism, exploitativeness, and the other diagnostic features associated with narcissistic personality disorder. The narcissistic traits of addictive disordered patients are quite simply become manifest via their self-centeredness which was clearly identified some eighty years ago by the authors of the Alcoholics Anonymous "Big Book."

Very often, the addictive disorders and the narcissistic adjustment style are syntaxic, but this reality most basically reflects the addictive disordered person's lifelong compulsive use of overdetermined or neurotically adaptive ability to obtain and replace the narcissistic need and entitlement gratifications that he or she did not experience in infancy and childhood. Grandiosity, megalomania, vanity, self-centeredness, and self will run rampant reflect some of the addict's neurotically adaptive attempts to secure primitive narcissistic supplies. Addicts unconsciously act out a lifelong attempt to convince self and significant others that, in fact, they are worth loving. Very often, this process becomes progressively more malignant, and at some juncture significant others further reject the addict. This process also further reinforces self-encapsulation as well as the outcropping of additional maladaptive social behaviors.

Narcissistic patients manifesting addictive brain disease tend to differ from other narcissistic personality disordered populations in the context of the continually evolving and vacillating nature of the addictive disordered patient's narcissistic disturbance. Addicts periodically and sometimes frequently experience intensely emotional and cognitive self-shifts in their core sense of self-worth, self-esteem, and beliefs. At these times, their pathological narcissism and veneer of special self-worth and grandiosity collapses, and the patient experiences a profound sense of personal inadequacy, worthlessness, failure, depression and non-well-being. This vacillation and pattern of shifting narcissistic behaviors can be associated with severe drinking or drugging binges, eating disordered binges, relapses, detoxification, or engagement in intensive integrative addictions-focused psychotherapy, self-help care, or other treatment modalities. This pattern may also continue to occur for extended periods of time in the absence of many of the above circumstances. The fragile and evolving routine of the addictive disordered patient's avoidance defense system, maturation, education, and random life changing or impacting circumstances and events may also trigger the pattern of vacillating narcissism. Few addictive disordered patients manifest florid narcissistic personality disorders. However, most of these patients do manifest narcissistic personality traits or features which contribute greatly to their self-defeating adjustment style, relational difficulties, and more specifically, prove to be challenging and difficult for their therapists and health care providers.

The author (Forrest, 1983, 1985) has previously noted that the "overt behavior, interpersonal style, and internal world of the alcoholic and borderline are similar." The progressive development of an addictive disorder also entails an all-encompassing narcissistic self-encapsulation. Virtually every facet of the addictive-disordered patient's internal and external world eventually revolves around the pathologic self-focused process of maintaining his or her addictive disease process. The addictive disease process, in effect, becomes an essentially narcissistically adaptive but progressively pathological and destructive adjustment style.

Borderline personality symptomatology also characterizes the adjustment style of many addictive disordered patients. This particular personality disorder has historically been the most frequently diagnosed personality condition given to women manifesting various addictive disorder specific and co-occurring mental health or psychiatric conditions who have been treated in a diversity of health care settings (Forrest, 1996). The author (Forrest, 1983, 1985) has historically identified the borderline personality disorder adjustment style as a common co-occurring condition among female patients entering treatment programs and engaging in integrative addictions focused psychotherapy.

Kernberg (1975) also noted the "technical requirements" required for the analytic psychotherapy of borderline patients include "(1) systematic elaboration of the negative transference in the 'here and now' only, (2) interpretation of the defensive constellation of these patients as they enter the negative transference, (3) limit-setting in order to block acting-out of the transference, with as much structuring of the patient's life outside the treatment hours as necessary to protect the neutrality of the analyst, and (4) non-interpretation of the less primitively determined modulated aspects of the positive transference to foster the gradual development of the therapeutic alliance" (p. 74).

Although the borderline personality is generally viewed as a specific nosology or diagnostic category, these individuals often abuse drugs and are prone to various forms of addictive behavior. Kernberg (1975) identifies the following "presumptive" diagnostic characteristics of borderline personality organization:

> (1) chronic, diffuse, free-flowing anxiety, (2) multiple phobias (phobias relating to body and physical appearance in contrast to phobias involving external objects, phobias involving severe social inhibitions and paranoid trends and obsessive-compulsive symptoms), (3) polymorphously perverse sexual trends, (4) pre-psychotic personality structure (paranoid, schizoid, hypomanic or "cyclothymic" personality organization), (5) impulse neurosis and addiction (including alcoholism), drug addiction, kleptomania, and certain forms of obesity, and (6) "lower level" character disorders. (pp. 64–65)

Many clinicians have also indicated over the past several decades that addictive-disordered patients, borderlines, and narcissists as well as other patient subcategories are particularly recalcitrant and difficult to work with in psychotherapy. As experienced addictions focused therapists and clinicians know all too well, addictive disordered patients generally manifest co-occurring disorders and patients manifesting these particular personality disorders or major mental illnesses usually prove extremely challenging and difficult for therapists and other treatment providers.

As discussed in Chapter 7 of this text, structured treatment models and often structured residential and intensive out-patient treatment settings tend to be conducive to better therapeutic outcomes with addictive-disordered persons manifesting more severe co-morbid psychopathology.

Kernberg's (1975) classic analytic work pertaining to narcissistic patients indicates that the "main problem" with these individuals

> —appears to be the disturbance of their self-regard in connection with disturbances in their object relationships—on the surface, these patients do not appear to be severely regressed; some of them may function very well socially. These patients present with an unusual degree of self-reference in their interactions with other people, and show a great need to be loved and admired by others. Their emotional life is shallow. They experience little empathy for the feelings of others, and they obtain very little enjoyment from life other than that from the tributes they receive from others or from their own grandiose fantasies, and they feel restless and bored when external glitter wears off and no new sources feed their self-regard. They envy others, tend to idealize some people from whom they expect narcissistic supplies, and to deprecate and treat with contempt those from whom they do not expect anything (often their former idols). In general, their relationships with other people are clearly exploitative and sometimes parasitic— Their haughty, grandiose, and controlling behavior is a defense against paranoid traits related to the projection of oral rage, which is central to their psychopathology. (pp. 64–65)

The DSM-V (2014) as well as earlier versions of the DSM include Kernberg's (1975) clinical description of the narcissistic personality disorder and also include the patient's sense of uniqueness and being special, needs for admiration, sense of entitlement, and arrogant attitudes.

DSM-IV-R and DSM-V (2000, 2014) diagnostic criteria for borderline personality diagnosis include chronic interpersonal relationship instability, impulsivity, abandonment issues, identity disturbance and a persistent unstable sense of self, impulsivity related to sex, spending, substance abuse, and binge eating, self-mutilating, suicidal or self-destructive behavior, affective (mood) instability, anger control problems, transient stress, paranoid ideation or dissociative symptoms. These basic diagnostic features and characteristics are included within the context of the Table 1 schematic presented earlier in this chapter (Forrest, 1983, 1997), and these particular diagnostic features are clearly evident within the context of a wide range of addictive-disordered patients. Furthermore, these general adjustment style features or personality disorder diagnostic characteristics can be key components related to the alliance psychotherapy process, and relational difficulties that therapists and health providers experience in their relationships with addictive disordered patients.

These particular personality and adjustment styles (borderline and narcissistic) have no doubt contributed significantly to the long history of therapist and health service provider aversion to treating addictive disordered persons, clinical realities related to poor treatment outcomes, and our general systemic health care system belief set these particular patient populations are untreatable.

Addictive disordered patients far less frequently manifest co-morbid schizoid personality features, schizotypal personality traits and disorders. These patients do present with histrionic personality features and avoidant personality features or disorders, and in the author's clinical experience, most, if not virtually all, addictive disordered patients seen within the context of long-term psychotherapy relationships (12 to 36+ months) manifest "mixed or other specified" personality traits or disorders (DSM-IV, 2014).

It is also very apparent that Table 1 does not include a diversity of adjustment styles and behavioral characteristics that have long been referred to as various forms of major mental illness, depression, sexual dysfunction or aberrations, somatic symptoms, identity or gender, anxiety disorders, and an unending list of other patterns of maladaptive human behavior (DSM-V, ICD10CM, 2014). The addictive brain diseases can, and generally do cooccur, in 40-60+ percent of patients who are initially, or eventually, diagnosed with a schizophrenia spectrum or other psychotic disorder, bipolar disorder and related depressive disorders, anxiety disorders, and the other adjustment diseases included in the different historic mental health diagnostic taxonomies. Moreover, it has long been recognized that a wide spectrum of both mental health disorders and addictive disorders commonly cooccur with virtually all of the other human chronic disease processes, including cancers, cardiovascular disease, gastrointestinal disease, and so forth.

The etiological and pathological model pertaining to alcoholism and all the addictive diseases presented in Table 1 includes the essential theoretical relationships between profound early life narcissistic injury and trauma and the subsequent development of various character structure facets and personality characteristics, traits, disorders and adjustment style that eventually characterizes the general addictive brain disease patient population. These particular relational dynamics and the resultant patient adjustment styles also very significantly affect every facet of the addictive brain disease process. The addictive disordered adjustment style reflects a wide variety of initially neurotic or maladaptive adjustment mechanisms that operate in defense and service of the ego, and ultimately, these same disorders, maladaptive personality characteristics and adjustment dynamisms operate in both the service of the patient's ego and ultimately the destruction of the ego or self. However, in a paradoxical manner, the destructive, maladaptive and painful life consequences associated with the personality traits, behaviors, psychodynamics, and addictive brain disease process pathology discussed in this chapter also eventually operate to propel or motivate a sizeable segment of the spectrum of addictive disordered population into a wide variety of treatment modalities and health care programs. These programs may also arrest the addictive brain disease process, and result in sustained recoveries including global personality change and healthy growth.

Finally, it should be noted that the over-all etiological model, psychodynamics and psychopathological facets of the addictive disease process that the author has elucidated (Forrest, 1978, 2019) includes a lifelong developmental (latency, adolescent, and different adult stages) path involving various dynamics and pathologic processes which continue to reinforce and synergize the active addictive brain disease process.

TRAUMA AND POST-TRAUMATIC STRESS DISORDER

Trauma has long been associated with the development and etiology of a broad spectrum of psychiatric conditions and disorders (Freud, 1912, 1913; Fenichel, 1945; Kernberg, 1975, 1976; Stekel, 1952; Sullivan, 1953). The initial clinical literature pertaining to trauma and narcissistic injury and the subsequent development of depression, anxiety, alcoholism, and various other categories of psychopathology were based almost solely upon the clinical observations and practice experiences of psychiatrists and other behavioral health workers. Patient case histories and the self-reported early-life experiences of persons who were treated in state mental hospitals, Veterans Administration hospitals and programs, mental hygiene, clinics, and eventually mental health centers, as well as psychiatrists and psychologists practicing in private settings and psychiatric hospitals consistently chronicled their observations pertaining to the impact of severely traumatic experiences of patients manifesting many debilitating psychiatric, psychological, and permanent medical conditions.

Addictive disordered and substance abusing persons have also historically been "lumped together" among the many patient populations manifesting trauma-based psychiatric and psychological conditions being treated within the context of the various health care treatment settings. Nonetheless, in spite of the earlier dichotomous categorization of psychiatric illness and the addictions, it has been widely recognized and accepted for many decades within the context of our American health care system that these conditions quite frequently co-occur and are concomitantly precipitated *vis à vis* the psychogenic common denominator of both early-life as well as life-span-related severe traumatic experiences (Cohn et al., 2014; Lehavot et al., 2014; Forrest, 1999; Gregg et al., 2014; Haller and Chassin, 2014).

Addictive-disordered persons tend to become the victims of their own self-defeating addictive behaviors and repetitive self-traumatization over the course of their life-span process. Many of these patients have some conscious realization of their seemingly unending pattern of repetitively engaging in a diversity of self-destructive and traumatic interpersonal transactions but none the less remain entrenched in this process in spite of various half-hearted attempts to change. Addictive disordered persons notoriously and consistently traumatize themselves *vis à vis* their divorces, and various patterns of dysfunctional and relational chemically induced behaviors involving their families, law enforcement, friends, employees, and colleagues, health care providers and complete strangers.

Post-Traumatic Stress Disorder represents a particular diagnostic category of trauma (DSM-IV-R, 2000; DSM-V, 2014) that encompasses a number of clinical criteria for adults, adolescents, and children above the age of 6. These current diagnostic criteria include (DSM-V, 2014:

> Exposure to actual or threatened death, serious injury or sexual violence in one or more ways (including directly experiencing the traumatic event, witnessing in person the event(s) as it occurs to others, learning that the traumatic event(s) occurred to a close family member or close friend, experiencing repeated or extreme exposure to aversive details of the traumatic event(s), i.e., first responders collecting human remains, B. presence of one (or more) of the following intrusive symptoms associated with the traumatic event(s) beginning after the traumatic event(s) occurred including recurrent, involuntary, and intrusive distressing memories of the traumatic event(s), recurrent distressing dreams in which the content and/or effect of the dreams are related to the traumatic event(s), C. Dissociative reactions (i.e., flashbacks), and other. (p. 144)

Additional current PTSD diagnostic criteria include (DSM-V, 2014):

> (C) persistent avoidance of stimuli associated with the traumatic event(s) beginning after the traumatic event(s) occurred, (D) negative alterations in cognitions and mood associated within the traumatic event(s), beginning or worsening after the traumatic event(s) occurred, (E) ongoing alterations in arousal and reactivity associated with the traumatic event(s), beginning or worsening after the traumatic event(s) occurred, and (F) duration of the disturbance (Criteria B, C, D, and E) is more than one month. (pp. 145–146)

Each of these additional DSM-V (2014) PTSD diagnostic categories (B, C, D, E, and F) include several additional two-seven clinical symptoms/descriptive features.

The most recent DSM-V PTSD diagnostic model also includes specific diagnostic criteria and clinical symptom characteristics associated with the following additional PTSD diagnostic sub-types: Posttraumatic Stress Disorder for Children 6 years and younger, Acute Stress Disorder, Adjustment Disorders, Other Specified Traumata and Stressor-Related Disorders, and Unspecified Trauma, and Stressor-Related Disorder.

As touched upon earlier in this chapter, many addictive disordered persons have been repeatedly traumatized via the framework of their earliest parenting and familial developmental interpersonal experiences. These experiential realities are consistently correlated to physical and sexual abuse, caretaker mental illness, abandonment and neglect, health issues, and a myriad of other psychosocial stressors. Addictive disordered patients also tend to be repetitively re-traumatized and self-traumatized throughout latency, adolescence, and the ongoing life span process within the context of their various human relationships, evolving personal adjustment styles and self-defeating addictive brain disease behaviors. They may also experience catastrophic random chance traumatic life changing events at any life stage. Addictive patients frequently recall in therapy their childhood and adolescent or later life involvements and familial experiences involving parental brutality, beatings, spousal abuse, or emotional experiences related to a diversity of drug or alcohol facilitated traumatic events.

Simply put, human beings who experience a wide range of profoundly traumatic life events such a war, severe injuries and chronic health disorders, rape and sexual abuse, infantile abuse or abandonment, and the other forms of trauma delineated in this chapter develop a diversity of trauma based clinical symptoms (Kevorkian et al., 2015). As Khantzian (2003, 2014) so astutely pointed out, addictive disordered persons generally develop patterns of substance abuse and a wide array of addictive behaviors as a method of self-medication and paradoxical adaptation. The author (Forrest, 1983, 1999) also indicated many years ago that alcoholism can be viewed as a paradoxically adaptive human process. The addictive disordered adjustment style almost always involves the dynamics of self-medication and dual-diagnoses including multifactorial trauma.

Haller and Chassin (2014) indicate that exposure to trauma is "surprisingly common," involving approximately sixty-one percent of men and fifty-one percent of women. These authors also report that traumatic events "lead to the development" of PTSD among adults with substance abuse disorders and "range from 14–60%, of studies involving adolescents with substance use disorders indicate PTSD rates ranging up to 20%." (p. 841)

The Haller and Chassin study (2014) is only one of a few

—longitudinal, community-based studies to test the directions of influence among trauma exposure, PTSD and alcohol and drug problems—results demonstrated that PTSD symptoms may have long-lasting effects on substance abuse problems, thereby highlighting PTSD symptomology as an important etiological factor in the development of substance abuse disorders. Findings also indicated that family environments characterized by high levels of conflict, stress, and psychopathology may influence risk for post-trauma substance use problems by increasing the likelihood of developing PTSD symptoms after a traumatic event.

Finally, this study (Haller and Chassin, 2014) also provided support for adolescent substance use problems and binge drinking as "risk factors for assaultive violence exposure, which conveys an especially high risk for PTSD compared with other traumatic events, and may thus increases the likelihood of post-trauma substance use problems" (p. 851).

These findings are highly congruent with the general content of this chapter, and the historic (Forrest, 1983, 1984, 1985, 1999) clinical works of the author pertaining to profound narcissistic injury, alcoholism, and a diversity of addictive disorders. Interestingly, these researchers also note that patients manifesting comorbid PTSD symptomatology and substance use disorders are "especially hard to treat, and do not optimally benefit from standard substance use disorder treatment interventions." The author has also historically and consistently addressed the many clinical realities and use of efficacious treatment interventions specific to this facet of clinical practice involving addictive disordered patients (Forrest, 1975–2019).

ATTACHMENT

Attachment (Bowlby, 1969) generally encompasses the infants' and children's early life experiences with the mother-object and/or primary caregivers. Attachment and the capacity for adequate and healthy attachment-object related behaviors upon the part of the mother-object and primary caregivers remains a primary foundation and the basis for the evolving person's later life capacities for object attachment as well as a basic sense of emotional security, safety, and healthy life long relational skills. Both early-life and the ongoing relational experiences of the evolving person with the primary attachment objects (persons) and significant others shape the evolving internal and interpersonal adjustment of the style person. These human relationship dynamics create the cognitive, emotional and behavioral adjustment style of each person, and also eventually become a cornerstone for the conscious and unconscious expectations pertaining to the availability and responsiveness of not only primary attachment figures but generalize to others. This process significantly impacts the individual's internal world, the self-system including one's sense of self-worth, and global adjustment style. In this regard, the importance of attachment to the primary object across the life span has been clearly demonstrated via several long-term longitudinal studies (Grossman and Waters, 2005), as has the attachment relation to psy-chopathology including substance abuse (Dozier, Stovall-McClough, and Albus, 2008).

Rosario et al. (2014) have suggested that "substances medicate the frus-tration and hopelessness of establishing or maintaining a relationship with, for example, an unsupportive, unavailable, abusive, or rejecting parent, as well as assist in protecting the self against the implications of having such a parent/or family system, etc." (p. 792). Furthermore, Rosario et al. (2014) completed a recent study involving sexual orientation, substance abuse, stress and attachment paradigm and reported that:

—relations between sexual-orientation and substance abuse were moderat-ed by the stress markers as: the mother's discomfort with homosexuality increased, more bisexuals and mostly heterosexuals than completely het-erosexuals used substances. As childhood gender nonconforming behaviors increased, more lesbian and gays than completely heterosexuals used sub-stances. Relations between sexual orientation and substance use were medi-ated by attachment and maternal affection. In addition, sibling comparisons found that sexual minorities reported more substance abuse, more child-hood gender nonconforming behaviors, and less secure attachment than completely heterosexual siblings; mothers reported less affection for their sexual minority than completely heterosexual offspring. (p. 790)

The authors (Rosario et al., 2014) further report that only a few empiri-cal investigations have studied attachment among sexual minorities, and none, as far as we know, with respect to substance abuse.

The general clinical and empirical evidence (Thomas, 2015) clearly implicates early-life attachment dysfunction and dynamics in the etiology of substance use disorders and other types of psychopathology. It is also appar-ent that the theoretical underpinnings of general clinical and research evi-dence as well as literature related to narcissistic injury, trauma, and post-trau-matic stress disorder, as well as attachment constructs includes a multiplici-ty of shared or common etiologic factors.

The narcissistic injury and attachment paradigms focally target infancy and early-childhood parenting experiences involving parental objects, sig-nificant stress, and the evolving person in the development of adjustment pathology including the addictive disorders. Trauma and PTSD paradigms (Weinhold, 2016) also encompass early-life parenting dynamics but general-ly tend to include a wide repertoire of life-span related profoundly traumat-ic events and experiences which many human beings may experience at any juncture in the life process. Certainly, the core common denominators of narcissistic injury, attachment, trauma, and PTSD include profoundly de-structive other-person related experiences such as severe physical or sexual abuse, neglect, deprivation, abandonment, exposure to murder, war, combat, and extreme violence, first responder incidents and experiences, and repeated incidents of bullying.

DSM-V (2014) trauma and stressor related disorder diagnostic categories and classification criteria include reactive attachment disorder, disinhibited social engagement disorder, posttraumatic stress disorder, posttraumatic stress disorder for children six years and younger, acute stress disorder and other specified trauma and stressor related disorder and unspecified trauma and stressor related disorder. PTSD diagnostic criteria apply to adults, adolescents, and children older than 6 years. For children 6 years and younger, see corresponding criteria in this diagnostic category (DSM-V, 2014).

Integrative addictions focused clinicians may frequently diagnose addictive disordered patients with a cooccurring trauma or stressor-related disorder in their clinical work. Relatedly, addictions focused therapists treating families and children in actively addictive disordered or recovering family systems rather commonly may diagnose children in these families with reactive attachment disorder or PTSD, and spouses, siblings, and significant others in these family systems may also qualify for the diagnosis of PTSD or one of the other trauma- and stressor-related disorders.

SUMMARY

Freud (1910) and the early psychoanalysts (Fenichel, 1945; Fromm-Reichmann, 1950, 1959; Menninger, 1938; Reich, 1961; Reik, 1948; Stekel, 1943; Sullivan, 1953) wrote extensively about the role of trauma in the development of neurosis and psychopathology. These clinicians and analysts contributed numerous clinical case studies and therapeutic vignettes which examined the impact as well as various dynamics associated with early-life traumatic experiences and subsequent outcropping of various forms of maladjustment. Freud postulated that the initial human experience of birth represents the most prototaxic or foundational basis for human trauma and subsequent psychopathology. Otto Rank (1929) subsequently developed the "birth trauma" theory or model of adjustment pathology.

Most therapists, clinicians, and behavioral health professionals have continued to view human trauma as a very significant factor which contributes to the etiology of a wide spectrum of human adjustment difficulties in a multiplicity of ways. This generally shared consensus has persisted among clinicians and health professionals for well over one hundred years.

Earlier clinicians as well as contemporary therapists and clinicians and researchers (Haller and Chassin, 2014; Ouimette and Read, 2014) have a diversity of constructs or concepts, meanings, and definitions or descriptions to the various experiences of human trauma. The content of this chapter largely focuses upon (1) the publications and works of the author (Forrest, 1978 through 2019), utilizing the concept of narcissistic injury within the explicit clinical context of the psychopathology of addictive disorders, and the psychodynamics, psychotherapy, and treatment of addictive disordered patients, and (2) contemporary clinical practice and research evidence associated with traumatic stress, posttraumatic stress disorder, and attachment dynamics related to current addiction pathology, assessment, integrative addictions focused psychotherapy, and other treatment models.

It is generally quite apparent to experienced addictions focused therapists and treatment providers that most, if not all, of the core contemporary trauma-based clinical literature and evidence-based research constructs, definitions, etiologic and practice-based findings encompass the information discussed within the parameters of narcissistic injury, traumatic stress, attachment and posttraumatic stress disorder (PTSD) in this chapter. Furthermore, alcohol dependence and other addictive disorders are commonly "associated with psychiatric disorders, second only to major depression in the US" (Kessler et al., 1994), and the majority of men (78.3%) and women (86.0%) with a clinical history of alcohol dependency "meet criteria for at least one other psychiatric disorder" (Kessler et al., 1997). Comorbidity of alcohol use disorders with posttraumatic stress disorder (PTSD) is

> —a condition that may develop as a result of exposure to a traumatic event, is especially prevalent, and has been well documented—for example, data indicate that over 26% of women and over 10% of men with alcohol dependence meet criteria for PTSD—and studies have also found that this co-occurrence is associated with greater clinical inpatient treatment for individuals with either disorder alone. (Lehavot et al., 2014, pp. 42–43)

Haller and Chassin (2014) indicate that:

> —exposure to traumatic events is surprisingly common" and further note that approximately sixty-one percent of men and fifty-one percent of women experience at least one traumatic event during their lifetimes. These authors also report that "traumatic events may lead to the development of not only posttraumatic stress disorder (PTSD) but also alcohol and drug problems. Rates of PTSD among adults with substance use disorders range from fourteen percent to sixty percent, and studies of adolescents with substance use disorders indicate PTSD ranging up to twenty percent. (p. 849)

Haller and Chassin (2014) conclude that these high rates of co-morbidity "suggest that traumatic stress and trauma-related symptomatology may play a role in the etiology of substance use disorders and vice versa."

The Haller and Chassin (2014) study investigating several pathways that may underlie the link between PTSD and the substance use disorders (i.e., the high risk and susceptibility hypotheses, the self-medication hypothesis, and the shared vulnerability hypothesis) represents "one of the few longitudinal, community-based studies testing the directions of influence among trauma exposure, PTSD, and alcohol and drug problems." The results of this investigation demonstrated that:

> (1) PTSD symptoms may have long-lasting effects on substance use problems, thereby highlighting PTSD symptomatology as an important etiological factor in the development of substance use disorders, (2) family environments characterized by high levels of conflict, stress, and psychopathology may influence risk for post trauma substance use problems by increasing the likelihood of developing PTSD symptoms after a traumatic event, and (3) also provided support for adolescent substance use problems and binge drinking as risk factors for assaultive violence exposure, which conveys an especially high risk for PTSD compared with other traumatic events, and may thus increase the likelihood of post trauma substance use problems. Findings are thus consistent with the notion that multiple, non-mutually exclusive pathways may underlie the link between PTSD and SUDS. (p. 850)

The historic integrative clinical literature (Fenichel, 1945; Freud, 1910; Fromm-Richman, 1950, Forrest, 1975-2019; Kernberg, 1976; Menninger, 1938; Reich, 1942, 1961; Reik, 1948; Stekel, 1943, 1952; Sullivan, 1953) as well as contemporary supportive research evidence associated with trauma, PTSD, attachment, traumatic stress, childhood trauma, and the general conceptualization of narcissistic injury relative to both the development and etiology of a diversity of addictive disorders and the psychopathology of these disorders is quite compelling (Blalock et al., 2011; Cohen et al., 2014; Forrest, 2017; Haller and Chassin, 2014; Kaysen et al., 2014; Lehavot et al., 2014; Oshri et al., 2011; Read et al., 2012; Thomas, 2016).

Recent evidence-based trauma and childhood trauma focused research findings (Blalock et al., 2011) clearly demonstrated that trauma contributes to the etiology of the full spectrum of addictive disorders. These authors (Blalock et al., 2011) report that there is increasing evidence that exposure to trauma during childhood is predictive of *smoking initiation and nicotine dependence*. Furthermore, a population-based study of adolescents (Roberts et al., 2008) found that childhood sexual and physical abuse increased risk for lifetime smoking, and among current smokers, childhood sexual and physical abuse was significantly related to the number of cigarettes smoked per day and nicotine dependence. Large population based cohorts further report that childhood sexual abuse significantly increases risk of nicotine dependence—risk of nicotine dependence increased with sexual abuse severity, and the other studies (Jun et al., 2008) have found evidence for "a graded relationship between severity of trauma, current smoking, heavy smoking (20 or more cigarettes per day), and early smoking initiation (onset by 14 years of age)" (p. 653).

Blalock et al., (2011) note that the "most common explanation offered for the association between nicotine dependence and childhood trauma is that nicotine is being used to ameliorate negative affective states, trauma symptoms, and mental health disorders." Several authors (Anda et al., 2006; Widom, DuMont, and Czaja, 2007) also note that "numerous studies provide evidence that early life stress impacts brain structure and function and results in dysregulation of the hypothalamic – pituitary – adrenal axis, the system that is primarily responsible for regulation of stress and emotion, and such affects may lead to increased risk for the development of mood and anxiety disorders" (p. 653).

The authors (Blalock et al., 2011) further suggest that a history of childhood abuse "may be a marker for relapse susceptibility," and that such individuals may require more intensive or more targeted forms of smoking cessation interventions. This author (Forrest, 2015) would suggest that this stance should axiomatically be applied within the context of all therapeutic contexts involving the spectrum of addictive disordered persons.

In summary, narcissistic injury, trauma, PTSD, and attachment dynamics can play very important roles in the development of all addictive disorders. However, a multiplicity of additional biopsychosocial factors and random factors can also contribute to the etiology of addictive disorders. These combined etiologic factors also contribute to the outcropping of often difficult and thorny alliance dynamics and problematic therapeutic relationship issues that are frequently associated with the process and outcome of addiction psychotherapy work. These alliance-related psychotherapeutic issues and the process of effective psychotherapy work with addictive disordered patients are addressed in depth in Chapter 7.

Chapter 6 explores much of the general historic and contemporary clinical and empirical literature pertaining to the spectrum of emotional difficulties and adjustment pathology that can be involved in the developmental evolution of the addictive disorders. The models of addiction that are presented in this chapter will be especially useful for early career addictions therapists and other clinicians who provide direct individual services for addictive disordered persons. Experienced addictions counselors and therapists realize that a diversity of factors are associated with many models of addiction, and these factors can play any number of roles in the development of an addictive disorder. Furthermore, each addictive disordered person manifests many relatively similar, but also rather unique individual patterns associated with their particular addiction brain disease process. Skilled and experienced therapists are able to identify these individual and collective patterns of maladaptive addictive behavior, and subsequently initiate individualized strategies of therapeutic intervention which become relatively patient specific addictive disorder focused recovery plans. Recognizing and providing patient-addictive disorder specific core interventions within the alliance relationship and over-all therapeutic treatment process foster improved outcomes in most, if not all, forms of addictions-focused care.

This chapter will also no doubt enhance the reader's awareness of the many challenges and difficulties that he or she faces in the daily work of assessing, diagnosing, and treating addictive disordered persons. Within this context, the content of the chapter serves as a more global reminder that the addictions do represent a very real human disease process, and as Volkow (2015) reminds us, contemporary science tells us that the addictive disorders represent a brain disease process that can be successfully treated but is also difficult to test, involves relapses, and continues to be poorly understood within the realm of contemporary science models. These core precepts certainly pertain to the psychopathology, psychodynamics, etiology and alliance related issues that are addressed in this chapter. However, it is also very clear that the therapeutic alliance, therapy relationship, and all therapeutic work involving addictive disordered persons remains in a continually relative state of flux *vis a vis* the patient's historic and ever-present underlying addictive brain disease process.

Finally, it is important for clinicians and addictions therapists to remain ever cognizant of the multi-variant or multifactorial nature of all facets of human adjustment and behavior. Early childhood trauma, stress, life-span, trauma, PTSD, and attachment do not represent a univariant path or paths to the development of a singular addictive disorder or the entire spectrum of addictive disorders. A multiplicity of factors or different variables always interactively impact and shape every facet of evolving total adjustment style of individual human beings. As human beings, "we are all simply more alike than otherwise" (Sullivan, 1953). Nonetheless, we also remain relatively unique in a wide diversity of ways, and these relative individual differences permeate both the healthy and pathologic facets of our behaviors and adjustment styles. A diversity of non-specific etiologic individual factors can contribute to the psychopathology as well as the potential recoveries pertaining to patients manifesting addictive brain disease.

Chapter 7

ALLIANCE DYNAMICS AND THE PROCESS OF EFFECTIVE ADDICTIONS-FOCUSED INTEGRATIVE PSYCHOTHERAPY AND COUNSELING WORK

INTRODUCTION

Much of the content in every chapter of this text is devoted to an examination and explanation of a wide spectrum of facets pertaining to the therapeutic alliance in general psychotherapy as well as the process of psychotherapy with addictive disordered patients. However, the heart of this chapter addresses a multiplicity of issues and facets associated with the process and outcome of alliance related efficacious addictive disorder specific psychotherapy relationships.

Chapter 6 provides the reader with a fundamental understanding of the core etiological and psychodynamic process associated with the development of the various addictive disorders. These factors in combination with a mosaic of learning, conditioning, reinforcement, genetic/biophysiological (brain based), social-multicultural and other individual differences contribute to the development of the addictive disorders. These various patient realities in combination with the developmental history of the therapist or counselor also potentially impact every facet of the therapeutic alliance and psychotherapy relationship involving addictive disordered persons. Therapist awareness, understanding, clinical experience, personal sensitivity, and therapeutic skills, or general acumen related to the examination of these various matters will hopefully provide readers with an enhanced framework for utilizing many of the etiologic, diagnostic, and actual counseling and psychotherapeutic conceptualizations, strategies, and interventions in their clinical work with addictive disordered patients.

This chapter includes a wealth of therapeutic alliance related clinical information and clinical practice enhancement skills for chemical dependency and addictions therapists. Therapeutic alliance dynamics associated with the diagnosis and assessment of the addictive disorders as well as "dual-diagnosis," "co-morbid disorders," "complex co-occurring disorders," patient motivation and readiness for change, models of change including structured out-patient intensive psychotherapy, intensive outpatient (IOP) programs, detox programs, residential care, extended care programs, drug maintenance programs (methadone maintenance and suboxone), self-help care, and other treatment modalities are discussed in the chapter. Alliance and stages of addictions focused psychotherapy, relapse and relapse prevention, alliance rupture and repair, recovery, and the dynamics of sustained life-long growth, change and adaptation are elucidated in this section.

Finally, the chapter includes several clinical case studies and psychotherapy vignettes that demonstrate and elucidate many of the dynamics and "real" psychotherapy practice aspects that are associated with the ongoing process of intensive individual psychotherapy engagement with addictive disordered persons. The actual therapy vignettes and case presentations have been taken from the author's earlier publications as well as current and active psychotherapy experiences with addictive disordered patients over the course of a 45-year practice history involving this specific patient population.

Therapists and clinicians who work with a diversity of addictive disordered patients being treated in diverse treatment settings, and employing diverse "treatment" interventions with their patients will find the clinical practice information provided in this chapter to be stimulating and very useful within the context of their contemporary therapeutic work. Indeed, all addictions therapists and counselors will be able to enhance their therapeutic skills and acumen via the global content of this particular chapter.

ALLIANCE DYNAMICS IN EARLY STAGE ADDICTIONS-FOCUSED INTEGRATIVE PSYCHOTHERAPY AND COUNSELING WORK

Persons who engage in counseling and psychotherapy relationships often enter treatment with various levels of ambivalence. People also enter psychotherapy for a diversity of reasons that are related to a broad spectrum of problems and life circumstances. Likewise, the ambivalence that patient's experience associated with both their conscious and unconscious ambivalence associated with entering and being in therapy can be related to a wide range of individual issues, experiences, beliefs and dynamics. Social stigma and continued beliefs pertaining to "mental illness," embarrassment about particular personal struggles and problems, reservations about the value, helpfulness, and efficacy of therapy, pervious failed attempts at treatment, cost factors, and fear are but a few of the sources of reservation and trepidation that can be related to any persons ambivalence about entering counseling or intensive psychotherapy.

Addictive disordered persons generally tend to manifest a great deal of overt and conscious ambivalence associated with entering psychotherapy or engaging in other treatment modalities that are widely recognized and available for persons manifesting a diversity of addictive disorders or addictive brain disease. As noted in Chapter 6, many addictive disordered patients have experienced profound early-life trauma involving parental abuse and addictive brain disease, neglect, abandonment, rejection, mental illness, attachment, relational and emotional dynamics. Furthermore, these destructive interpersonal transactions frequently continue to play out and are repetitively a part of the addictive-disordered persons adjustment style throughout the course of his or her life span. The development of addictive disordered patterns of behavior during adolescence, adulthood and even the later years of life are invariably accompanied by continued and enhanced relational and adjustment pathology. These dynamics further reinforce isolation, interpersonal dysfunction, and a myriad of additional issues related to the matter of ambivalence related to entering and sustaining an involvement in psychotherapy and other treatments specific to the addictive disorders.

These patient population realities dictate that addictions therapists, clinicians, and ancillary treatment program providers utilize supportive, empathic, genuine, warm, disclosing, and generally exude unconditional positive regard in their therapeutic interactions with addictive disordered persons during the early therapy sessions. Early constructive alliance development is generally crucial in therapeutic work with addictive disordered patients. In addition to the thorny, conflictual and dysfunctional interpersonal histories that most of these patients' manifest, their basic adaptive adjustment styles have also been historically constructed vis a vis the maladaptive but ego-syntonic utilization of denial, distortion, projection, repression, manipulation and a diversity of other primitive defense mechanisms. Working and productive therapeutic alliances with addictive-disordered persons become possible, develop, and constructively evolve in large part as a result of the therapist's ability to sustain high level therapeutic conditions throughout the course of the ongoing therapy relationship.

Addictive disordered patients can also be constructively impacted by the initially supportive, nurturing, empathic and helpful interactions they experience and internalize via their interactions with secretaries, office colleagues, and even other patients within the context of private practice psychotherapy settings as well as residential treatment programs, detoxification centers, and various other treatment settings. All treatment programs and care settings for addictive disordered patients also benefit from the skillful, empathic, therapeutic boundary or limit setting, supportive and other healthy psychosocial interactions with therapists and other staff who consistently interact with patients. These therapist-patient-treatment setting interpersonal transactions are especially important to the process of initiating working and productive therapeutic alliances with additive-disordered patients; however, the continued and ongoing work of sustaining the alliance throughout the psychotherapy process requires that therapists and other treatment providers also consistently provide the core therapeutic qualities that are essential to the maintenance of the therapeutic alliance or therapeutic bond.

In the absence of a constructive therapist and treatment setting emotional climate such as has been characterized throughout this text, many patients manifesting severe addictive disorders will quickly disengage or even flee from therapy, relapse, or reactively become anxious, depressive, angry, and oppositional with concordant feelings of guilt, remorse, and shame. These factors also partially explain why so many addictive disordered persons enter psychotherapy and "drop out," complete or partially complete several residential treatment programs, are admitted to "detox" facilities on numerous occasions, or continue to be arrested for DUI or repetitively become engaged in court-ordered programs several times with seemingly very little or no constructive change!

The author (Forrest, 2012, 2016, 2018) has consistently observed that recovering therapists and counselors as well as recovering office staff and ancillary treatment personnel who are appropriately open and disclosing with their patients are often able to form initial therapeutic alliances and therapeutic bonds with addictive patients that are somewhat more resilient and prove to be more conducive to patient sustained therapeutic engagement than early alliance development and relationships that include non-recovering addictions therapists. These sharing experiences related to personal treatment experiences, the recovery process, and therapist early recovery dynamics can reduce the patient's anxiety, trepidation and other sources of distress associated with recovering and engaging in therapy and treatment. These dynamics may have evolved over the past 50-year history of addictions therapy and treatment in America which was largely provided by other recovering therapists and professionals working essentially in self-help oriented residential and other care settings. However, recovering therapists and counselors also tend to experience more difficulties associated with the middle and later stages of alliance work and the psychotherapeutic process with addictive disordered patients. These dynamics are frequently related to therapist projection, transference, and countertransference dynamics associated with relapse matters and control as well as the process of psychotherapy termination.

Psychotherapists and treatment providers in the addictions care industry need to better understand the role of the therapeutic alliance in all forms of addictions work, and to this end, better recognize how important the alliance is within the context of basically being able to provide both the patient and therapist with mutual opportunities for fostering potentially incredible growth, change and long-term recovery pertaining to a wide continuum of patient behaviors, emotions, beliefs and perceptions, and life skills that far transcend the recovering addictive disordered patient's earlier global life adjustment style.

It is also important to note that therapists may also adaptively grow, change and become more fully functioning and effective human beings as a result of their therapeutic relationships and alliances with addictive disordered persons.

EARLY STAGE ALLIANCE DYNAMICS AND DIAGNOSTIC COMPONENTS IN INTEGRATIVE ADDICTIONS-FOCUSED PSYCHOTHERAPY AND COUNSELING WORK

As alluded to earlier, constructive patient alliance building and "shaping" begins within the context of the patient's initial contacts and interactions with secretaries, office staff, and via phone contacts, scheduling, and e-mail dialogues prior to the actual psychotherapy process or assessment sessions with the therapist or counselor. Initially supportive, helpful, and empathic office or treatment program interactions with patients can help reduce or alleviate feelings of apprehension, resistance, and other sources of patient fear and anxiety related to treatment. These interactive social transactions with various office personnel can also help foster patient relational attachment, bonding and a sense of trust associated with the general office and therapeutic emotional climate. Office secretaries and office managers who are experienced and also consistently exude personal therapeutic qualities but also are able to sustain appropriate boundaries and other professional role behaviors can play subtle but very important roles in the development of patient motivation for therapy engagement, change, hope, enhanced relationships, and potential alliance skill-building skills.

Many addictive disordered patients entering therapy and other forms of addictions specific treatment also respond positively, and integratively internalize even the behaviors, dialogue, friendliness, support and humor that other patients openly exude within the context of the therapist's waiting room before and after initial diagnostic or psychotherapy sessions. Even in these early limited transactions, some patients very quickly perceive and respond to the healthy and adaptive social behaviors and global demeanor of other recovering and actively engaged therapy patients.

Recovering patients also always represent potential healthy role models for clients entering or involved in early stage care, and many patients with long-term recovery as well as constructive psychotherapy experiences have active involvement in the self-help community plus (AA) sponsorship work. Recovering persons may also manifest a diversity of other constructive, personal recovery-based skills and strengths that can foster the early-stage patient's understanding, commitment, and motivation related to all facets of the ongoing diagnostic and therapeutic recovery focused process and adaptive change process. In sum, experienced and skilled addictions therapists can actively reinforce, encourage, and potentially facilitate patient involvements in a diversity of new or different and healthy social relationships which foster the development of general relationship skills and potentially enhance therapeutic alliance dynamics within and beyond the specific therapeutic alliance context.

Alliance work begins for the therapist and patient during early psychotherapy sessions usually involving completion of (1) the patient's psychosocial history, and (2) diagnostic assessment. A thorough psychosocial history encompasses an exploration of the (1) patient's presenting "problem(s)," (2) family and developmental background, (3) current and historic medical status including health history, medications, sleep, eating, smoking, and other self-care behaviors, prior diagnoses, cognitive functioning, marital, parenting, and sexual issues, (4) legal history, (5) in-depth substance abuse and addictive disorder specific information including current addiction use status, (6) detailed prior psychotherapy, and other mental health treatment(s) history (i.e., psychiatric hospitalizations, residential care, IOP's, detox, extended care programs, etc.), (7) current and past suicide/self-harm history, (8) anger, and impulse control issues, and other potential self-harm risk factors. Therapist's may also find it useful to (9) provide the patient with opportunities to discuss or share other information and background experiential history material which he or she feels the therapist should be aware of or additionally needs to be addressed in therapy. This author finds it useful to address these alliance related dynamics at the completion of the diagnostic interviewing process which typically can be completed in the context of 1-2 hours. The author also completes the initial diagnostic interviewing process vis á vis face to face interviewing with the patient rather than having patients simply fill out on-line or paper and pen "canned" assessment questionnaires which are subsequently reviewed with the patient by many counselors and therapists.

The therapist-patient diagnostic process inherently provides the therapist and patient an opportunity to explore the patient's history, elaborate upon this information, question, and develop a reciprocally open, honest and genuine relational and communication context which also contributes to the subsequent steps involved in the therapists ability to openly and honestly share his or her diagnostic impressions with the patient, and then begin the process of alliance work and building related to the therapeutic tasks of developing a structured treatment plan involving shared therapy goals, tasks, and strategies for effecting the recovery process.

Addictive disordered patients manifest an overdetermined avoidance defense system which is constructed around the utilization of denial, distortion, projection, defensiveness, rationalization and repression mechanisms which neurotically and destructively operate in the service of the patient's ego. These issues contribute to many of the difficulties associated with alliance formation, assessment and effective therapeutic treatment work with this patient population. Thus, an initially crucial step in the psychotherapy of addictive disordered persons involves accurately diagnosing and assessing the patient's addictive disorder(s) and co-occurring adjustment disorders, and the therapist's ability to openly and constructively discuss these clinical realities together with the patient in a manner which contributes to the development of a working and productive therapeutic alliance between the therapist and the patient. In some situations, it can be helpful to include the patient's spouse, children, family members or employer in the initial diagnostic session or sessions. This strategy tends to work best with patients who have significant others that are clearly supportive and constructively engaged with the patient as well as aware of the patient's difficulties related to his or her addictive disorder and other adjustment difficulties.

The therapist's openness, honesty, empathy, and authenticity associated with discussing his or her diagnostic impression of the patient facilitates several sources of potential constructive alliance building and potential psychotherapeutic gain. This technique does not foster or reinforce maladaptive patterns of deceit, lying, denial and defensiveness or repression. This strategy models the importance of alliance honesty, genuineness, openness, and reality. It also lets the patient know how the therapist perceives the patient's addictive disorder and other conflicts.

The author (Forrest, 1984, 1997, 2012, 2017) has also long used this diagnostic strategy to assess patient readiness and motivation for treatment involving patients who demonstrate great ambivalence associated with simply participating in the initial therapy sessions. These patients often verbalize resistance to engagement in treatment, present in an angry or combative manner, or clearly indicate that they will not enter treatment under any circumstance—even in the face of a court-directed order to engage in therapy. Some patients will not be as open or rejecting relative to treatment engagement but respond to feedback from the therapist which supportively but clearly affects the reality of manifesting an addictive disorder or other disorder by failing to make another appointment, abruptly terminating the session, or perhaps initiating care at a later date. Addictive disordered patients generally experience some anxiety and may be upset about hearing their diagnoses, but most clearly respond very favorably to this strategy and become active participants in the therapeutic process. These individuals also usually manifest the interpersonal relationship skills that are essential to the process of establishing a working and productive therapeutic alliance, and they are also tend to be capable of sustaining long-term productive therapeutic engagement. Many patients eventually and openly experience or verbalize a sense of relief associated with knowing that their therapist basically understands them and is also able to discuss the various dynamics associated with their addictive disorder. These factors synergize active patient and family engagement in the recovery process as well as enhancing constructive alliance development, trust, and confidence related to the therapist's abilities to facilitate patient change and recovery.

Therapists generally know that diagnosis literally means "knowing through," and as Rollo May (1973) noted many years ago, this diagnostic technique incorporates the magic of words and is tantamount to the therapist saying "your problem is known and has causes-we can do something to effect constructive and positive change." This strategy also helps addictive disordered patients begin to accept and deal with the various stigmas and often their personal irrational belief systems associated with having been identified and labeled "alcoholic," "addict," or "worthless, lazy, stupid," and other such pejorative terms. Diagnostic openness with patients who have been in therapy several times and/or unsuccessfully completed (i.e., "chronic relapse patients") several treatment programs can be a catalyst for real therapeutic engagement in the here and now relationship with their current therapist. Indeed, diagnostic sharing and understanding is an integral component of alliance formation and the initiation of the psychotherapy relationship.

It is important for therapists to realize that a patient's diagnosis is never static. Diagnostic work in the context of ongoing individual psychotherapy is always process oriented. Addictive disordered persons may arrive at the therapist's office for their initial consultation or therapy session intoxicated or present in a manipulative, angry, depressed, passive aggressive, narcissistic, confused and agitated, or even threatening manner. However, these patients may also initially present in a pleasant manner, behave appropriately, manifest good communication skills, good cognitive and relational skills, and also indicate to the secretary and/or the therapist that they do not having an "eating disorder," "drinking or drug problem," or any other problems associated with addictive disease or behavioral health problems. Such patients often report that they have "decided" to come in for therapy or "an evaluation" at the request of a spouse or family member. However, a sizeable segment of addictive disordered patients also eventually initiate therapy and treatment on their own, and openly acknowledge a diversity of current and historic severe problems and conflicts that have been associated with their addictive disease. These patients frequently have experienced prior treatments for their addictive disease that have produced little or very limited therapeutic benefits. Some of these patients desperately realize that they are literally dying as a result of their addictions, and concordantly they may present for treatment with high motivation for psychotherapy and another attempt or chance for "recovery." Others who have experienced no earlier treatment or therapy involvement also may present with significant motivation and readiness for change. However, these individuals also tend to have been "pushed" or "nudged" repeatedly by significant others to enter therapy or other care alternatives related to their addictive behaviors. At this juncture in the course of their addictive disease process, these persons manifest the foresight and are simply wise enough, or respond to a combination of factors that foster their ability to seeking out help. Many of these patients respond very well in psychotherapy as well as other treatment contexts.

Pain associated with a wide gamut of issues, experiences, and consequences related to manifesting an addictive brain disease can eventually become a primary catalyst for patient engagement in active, committed and productive psychotherapy relationships as well as other forms of efficacious and constructive treatments.

A diversity of therapist dynamics also impact the process of alliance development associated with the diagnostic and assessment component of addictive disorders focused psychotherapy work. Psychotherapists and counselors manifest rather divergent viewpoints related to the usefulness, relevance, and roles of diagnosis and assessment within the context of psychotherapy relationships with various patient populations. Therapists and clinicians who practice in addictions treatment settings or specialize in the practice of psychotherapy with patients manifesting addictive disease also have different conceptualizations pertaining to the roles and relevance of diagnosis and assessment in therapy.

The role of diagnosis has remained controversial in the treatment of psychiatric and mental health disorders as well as the addictive disorders for several decades (Rogers, 1952; Glasser, 1965; Szasz, 1974, 1976) and many highly respected clinicians have historically indicated that psychiatric diagnoses contribute to the stigmatization, alienation, labeling and even persecution of patients. Szasz (1974, 1976) wrote extensively about the alienating, stigmatizing, and labeling aspects of psychiatric diagnoses. He essentially suggested that diagnostic labels can have a very destructive, damaging, and are medically iatrogenic.

During the past two or three decades, modern psychiatry, clinical psychology, social work, professional counselors, chemical dependency and addictions therapists, and general mental health therapists and behavioral health clinicians have all become progressively more engaged in the medically-orientated models of treatment and general health care. Diagnosis has remained a fundamental cornerstone of modern medicine, and increasingly sophisticated medical technologies have continued to be developed throughout the world that are used to diagnose and treat a vast number of diseases involving everything from cardiac disease to brain pathology, gastrointestinal problems, eating disorders, emphysema, liver disease, mental illness, sexual problems and virtually every other facet of the various human health subsystem. Indeed, these diagnostic technologies have continued to greatly improved and enhance the global efficacy of modern medicine, and contributed to the improved longevity, health and well-being of hundreds of millions of people around the world.

In accord with these realities, contemporary medical, psychiatric, behavioral health and addiction treatment providers view both psychiatric disorders and addictive disorders as disease oriented or brain disease-based adjustment dynamisms. This viewpoint has changed rather radically over the past six or seven decades, and while psychogenetic models and etiological explanations associated with psychopathology remain real and relevant, most clinicians currently view many forms (diagnostic categories) of psychopathology as diseases that are caused by multiple biopsychosocial factors. However, as noted earlier in the chapter, therapists and clinicians certainly manifest individual and sometimes very different beliefs pertaining to the dynamics of diagnosis, etiology and treatments pertaining to mental illness, severe addictive disorders, and mental health "problems" in general.

While Rogerian (person centered), existential and humanistic therapists remain less focused upon diagnostic issues pertaining to counseling and therapy, (Ellis, 1979; Forrest, 1997, 2012; Glasser, 1965; May, 1973) and different "schools of therapy" including reality therapy, rational emotive therapy, and family therapy also generally do not emphasize the relevance of diagnosis in therapy relationships. Medically trained clinicians and psychotherapists have certainly become more impacted by the importance and relevance of diagnosis, differential diagnosis, and the complex diagnostics issues related to a diversity of human mental health and adjustment problems. All therapists and behavioral health workers are continually confronted with a diversity of realities that are routinely associated with making diagnoses, and being versed in the current diagnostic nomenclature in order to be reimbursed by the health insurance industry for their professional services including psychotherapy and most other health services. The alliance and therapeutic relationship is also continually impacted and shaped by a diversity of dynamics associated with a multiplicity of relational dynamics pertaining to the patient's diagnosis.

Addictions therapists and other behavioral health professionals have historically utilized a rather broad diversity of methods, models and tools to diagnose and assess people manifesting the full spectrum of addictive disorders. An accurate patient diagnosis is essential to (1) the development of appropriate individualized treatment plans and goals, (2) implementing alliance related treatment interventions and goals associated with the patient's specific addiction disorder and global symptom structure, and (3) receiving reimbursement for treatment and professional health care services that are insurance related.

All of these diagnostic related transactions involving the therapist and patient require mutual collaboration, and this process which usually encompasses the initial one or two consultation and therapy sessions in addictions therapy work also involves crucially important foundational alliance development work. Recent research evidence suggests that (Campbell et al., 2015; Wiprovnick, Kuerbis and Morgenstern, 2015) early positive alliance formation is essential to effective and successful therapeutic outcomes with this general patient population. Early constructive alliance development has been particularly associated with treatment engagement and retention (Brorson et al., 2013; Meier et al., 2006), and this robust evidence also supports focusing retention research on several treatment variables. A diversity of therapeutic "bond" studies provide supportive but somewhat inconsistent findings related to early alliance or bond relationships, and therapeutic outcomes with alcoholic as well as other addictive disordered populations, but these early works also have utilized a rather wide spectrum of research designs, models and methods. Recently (Wiprovnick et al., 2015), report that the "quality of the relationship between a therapist and his or her client can make a significant contribution to recovery from substance abuse disorders—high levels of therapeutic bond and empathic resonance predicted decreased alcohol use at the end of treatment for participants in both conditions—we found a linear relationship between therapeutic bond and outcomes" (pp. 129, 133).

This body of alliance related psychotherapy process and outcome evidence reinforces the clinical relevance of therapist-patient face to face interaction in the establishment of an alliance building therapeutic relationship with the client during the assessment phase of the therapy process. The therapist's diagnostic acumen, thought out, planned, skilled and strategic utilization of support, non-judgmental acuity, openness, and honesty involving the combination of high-level therapeutic conditions discussed throughout this text form the essential ingredients which are necessary for the establishment of an ongoing working and productive therapeutic alliance with the patient.

Needless to say, some addictive disordered patients manifest defense systems, temporal states or recalcitrant adjustment styles that form relational dynamics and obstacles to the establishment of healthy alliance attachment. A segment of the addictive disordered patient population appears to remain chronically refractory to any form of professional treatment, and in this author's clinical experience these individuals frequently manifest clinical histories including profound and chronic severe interpersonal dysfunction, and co-morbid psychopathology associated with their prior and current diagnostic status.

The following brief therapy vignette illustrates how therapists can actively initiate and begin the process of efficacious alliance development within the context of completing the initial patient biopsychosocial history and diagnostic assessment process. This vignette also elucidates how fluid and initially therapeutic the process of constructive alliance work can be with persons who manifest internalized motivation for change, recovery, therapy involvement, and do not manifest major co-occurring psychopathology in combination with an addictive disorder. This vignette was taken from the patient's second consultation and therapy session with the therapist.

Case 1

DOCTOR F.: Well, we completed most of your history last week Kay, and I know that it was difficult to share some of the painful stuff about your childhood and adolescence, but I hope it was helpful for *both* of us—the drug and substance use information that you shared— those experiences were painful, too, but you sure seem to be aware of how you've been you own worst enemy in some ways, but I do sense your determination and commitment to make some real changes in your life.

KAY: Yeah, it was difficult and upsetting to talk about growing up and my family stuff—I've just about ruined my marriage, and the kids need a sober mother—it was upsetting to tell you a lot of the stuff from the past and what's been going on the last few years, but I did feel better about all of it after I left. My husband actually wanted to know what we talked about, and then he and I stayed up late talking about a lot of things—that was emotionally upsetting too, but most of it was a civilized conversation—He didn't think I would actually come in for therapy, and he's definitely not convinced it will help but we both agreed it was a start—at least I'm going to try and make some changes—and I was actually looking forward to coming in today—But I'm still nervous about it.

DOCTOR F.: Coming in and talking to a therapist—a stranger that you meet for the first time in your life is understandably difficult for all of us—plus talking about personal life issues and problems—we all have to start somewhere, and that's a part of what it takes to change our lives—and it's a one day at a time process—especially just getting started in therapy and recovery.

KAY: After I left your office, I sure understood what you said last week about taking our time putting together my history, but there is a part of me that really wants to get it all out and deal with it—I've kept a lot of stuff secret for nearly forty years—stuff I've never shared with my husband or family—I do feel safe discussing other stuff with you, and actually your receptionist was also really easy to talk to—that helped, and just knowing that what we talked about is private—confidential.

DOCTOR F.: Last week we talked some about putting together a therapy or treatment plan and some of your goals related to being in therapy—let's focus on what we can do or how both of us can work together to help you get out of the drinking and Xanax abuse today, and we'll work together on some of the other problem areas as we progress—so you basically felt positive about continuing in therapy, and that's definitely a good starter—I sensed that you were honest with me during our first session, and you also seem to be motivated to make some big changes in your life, and I will sure do my best to help you make those changes—getting on with your life—it's a team effort, and there are a lot of ways or tools that help people get better—we need to figure out what tools will work best for you, and then begin to use them consistently as you move down the road to recovery life.

KAY: You know, I also realized after our session that I was able to be totally honest with you last week—God, did that feel good—I've lied to myself and my family—others too for so long—I think I've gotten sick with myself—I really can't live with myself anymore, and my family and friends can't live with me the way I've been—all the drinking, drugs, and crazy shit the last few years—I felt like I had some hope this week—and maybe I can get better—you know, like you said it's not too late—what we discussed helped, and I think I can trust you—that's saying a lot—I've gotten so bad that I lie to myself, don't trust myself or my family, and lord knows, they don't trust me when it comes to a lot of things now—you were right about my being addicted, and those test results hit the nail on the head about being depressed and anxious—plus the impulsiveness—it kinda scares me to face all of these problems.

Clinicians and therapists who work with addictive disordered patients utilize a diversity of diagnostic and assessment instruments or tools. However, the clinical interviewing process represents the potentially most useful tool in therapist's armamentarium for early therapeutic alliance development.

Initial diagnostic interviewing as well as initial therapy sessions provide both the therapist and patient with a wide range of intensive, intimate and personal encounters. By contrast, the utilization of structured topical psychosocial histories and clinical assessments that are limited to brief interviews or perhaps no clinical interviewing between the patient and therapist provide comparatively little opportunity for alliance work and development and early therapist-patient relational learning experiences.

Psychometric assessments with instruments such as the MMPI-II, MMPI-II-RF, MCMI-IV, MAST, MAC, AUI, SASSI-II, CAGE, audit and various other diagnostic tools can provide very helpful ancillary diagnostic information which can eventually be used in treatment planning. However, these tools again limit the opportunities for early therapist establishment and focus on alliance formation dynamics. Even the matter of openly discussing psychometric results with addictive disordered patients early in the therapeutic process and in the absence of preliminary opportunities for basic alliance and relationship building between the patient and therapist can be somewhat iatrogenic for patients. Psychotherapy patients who simply complete standardized and structured psychosocial histories, limited or even extensive psychological testing, and subsequently are scheduled by an office secretary for an appointment to discuss the results of the testing information that has been collected in the course of one or two such sessions sometimes fail to engage in treatment. For some individuals who choose to initiate therapy, the therapist and patient may face additional early therapy alliance tasks that are associated with the upsetting and perhaps traumatic facets of dealing with the patient's psychological test results. These situations also tend to facilitate very early stage therapeutic interactions which are highly emotionally changed and very upsetting for the patient in the absence of substantial therapeutic alliance formation. These dynamics can foster premature patient terminations in addictions-focused psychotherapy and counseling.

The therapist's specific diagnostic formulations and clinical nosology pertaining to the addictive disorders and all behavioral health disorders have historically evolved and changed greatly over the past one hundred and twenty years. The diagnostic categories and "labels" that contemporary clinicians have generally utilized for diagnosing the spectrum of addictive disorders and psychiatric disorders between the late 1930s and the contemporary DSM-V and ICD-10 or 11 (2013, 2014) have changed considerably, but none the less encompass many of the same essential diagnostic constructs within the context of several diagnostic classes of psychopathology.

Clinicians have also historically utilized a rather broad spectrum of diagnostic classifications, categories, labels and models to describe and categorize people manifesting the spectrum of addiction disorders. For example, Knight (1937) delineated three diagnostic alcoholic subtype categories or types (primary, secondary, and reactive) with relatively specific diagnostic features and characteristics for each category. The pioneer of empirical research pertaining to alcohol use disorders assessment (Jellinek, 1945, 1960, 1962) delineated specific developmental stages of alcoholism as well as several different categories of alcohol use disorders including alpha, beta, gamma, delta and epsilon alcoholism. These diagnostic categories also include different diagnostic characteristics and features. For example, gamma alcoholism focused on loss of control over drinking, and was chronic with very high prevalence in the United States, and was also associated with the disease concept of alcoholism including severe physical, psychological, social and spiritual deterioration. Epsilon alcoholism was conceptualized as episodic or periodic "binge drinking." The American Medical Association first classified alcoholism as a disease in 1956, and also delineated a comprehensive list of clinical and medical symptoms associated with the diagnosis of alcoholism.

Virtually all of the clinicians, researchers, and professional health care organizations who have been involved in the work of identifying, diagnosing and treating persons manifesting addictive disorders over the past twelve decades have also advocated for the treatment of addictive disordered individuals, and also stressed in a variety of ways the importance of the physician, therapist, or treatment provider relationship and alliance dynamics that can potentiate change or recovery from addictive disorders.

It should also be noted that beginning with the DSM-I and DSM-II (1968) through the current DSM-V (2014) and including the recent history of the ICD- (10 and 11) (2016) World Health Organization behavioral health diagnostic taxonomies, the importance of professional human treatments involving therapeutic relationships involving the therapist, physician or clinician have continued to remain at the heart of treatment alternatives for this diverse patient population. Inferentially if not by recommended directives, the therapeutic alliance and psychotherapy relationship also remain essential to effective care within the context of assessment and diagnosis as well as the actual psychotherapy process and ongoing treatment and recovery process. As noted earlier, working and productive therapeutic alliances in large measure are initially constructed via the therapist's empathy, genuineness, warmth and sensitive positive support during the history completing and diagnostic work very early in the treatment process.

EARLY STAGE ALLIANCE DYNAMICS AND COMPONENTS IN INTEGRATIVE ADDICTIONS-FOCUSED AND COUNSELING WORK

The initial treatment plan that therapist and patient jointly construct following completion of the patient's thorough biopsychosocial history including diagnostic assessment from a structural framework for continued constructive relational and alliance development between the therapist and patient. Treatment planning between the patient and therapist involves mutual discussion, agreement, and clarity pertaining to the basic essential goals, tasks and structural components of the psychotherapy process. These initial therapeutic tasks are directed and facilitated by the therapist, but mutual agreement on initial therapy goals, tasks, structure and process work dynamics require both patient and therapist commitment to the therapeutic process, therapeutic relationship, and become the ongoing mutual therapist bond or alliance which forms the structural framework in which constructive growth, change and recovery can take place.

Patients as well as therapists need to consciously understand and accept that the therapeutic relationship mirrors all intimate human relationships which encompass differing beliefs, struggles, and varying levels of relational conflict associated with a myriad of human issues and dynamics. As noted earlier in the text, a working and productive therapeutic alliance also requires mutual capacity for resolving, acknowledging, discussing and working through different levels and types of therapy stressors in order to accomplish significant change and growth upon the part of the patient.

With the initiation of managed care treatment some twenty years ago, and the advent of various "brief therapy" treatment models, the length of time parameters, insurance dynamics, and even accessibility to psychotherapeutic care have changed very significantly. Some patients who have insurance coverage have very limited "mental health" or addiction specific care benefits, or perhaps no benefits. In general, many patients are eligible for a limited number of psychotherapy sessions in the course of a year (15-30), and other coverage benefits for the addictive disorders may or may not be covered by different policies. To the contrary, some patients "self-pay" for therapy and do not wish to use their insurance for therapy. These various factors are also generally applicable to all forms of medical and behavioral health care for addictive-disordered persons. These issues also need to be openly addressed between the patient and therapist as well as included in the initial treatment plan and throughout the treatment process.

Most actively addictive disordered patients will need to be seen weekly or perhaps two or three times a week during the initial stage of psychotherapy, and many actively addicted persons require some level of brief or extended "detox" care, possible hospitalization, intensive out-patient care, or out-patient medically assisted care as a prerequisite to engagement in effective intensive addictions-focused psychotherapy. Therapist alliance skills can also synergize these pre-psychotherapy activities with the patient, and contribute to patient motivation for change as well as subsequent active ongoing psychotherapy engagement.

It is currently realistic to view the initial 8–15 psychotherapy sessions with the patient as "early stage" psychotherapy. During these early stage therapy and counseling sessions, the essential therapist-patients tasks include (1) completion of the biopsychosocial history, (2) diagnostic assessment, (3) development of a patient specific treatment plan, (4) establishment of a working and productive alliance, (5) developing a recovery care plan, and 6) initiating and essentially completing the genetic reconstruction phase of therapy (Forrest, 1994, 2010, 2017).

ALLIANCE DYNAMICS AND THE STRUCTURAL COMPONENTS OF EARLY STAGE INTEGRATIVE ADDICTIONS-FOCUSED PSYCHOTHERAPY AND COUNSELING WORK

Alliance development is fostered vis á vis the therapist's sensitive and open discussion of his or her initial diagnostic impression of the patient as well as a discussion of the patient's responses to the therapist's diagnostic impressions, and discussion of various relatively specific recovery, treatment and psychotherapy alternatives. At this therapeutic juncture, therapists sometimes become clearly aware of the patient's extreme resistance to therapy engagement, other forms of potential treatment, or complete denial and extreme resistance to involvement in any form of treatment. In these situations, the therapist needs to wisely and appropriately share these perceptions related to "readiness" for care and motivation for change. It may be appropriate to refer such individuals to another therapist, treatment program or other care facility. Therapists need to help these patients actively and openly explore their global readiness to enter psychotherapy very early in the treatment process. A good therapist-patient "fit" is an essential prerequisite for effective alliance development and the capacities for establishing and sustaining an ongoing alliance attachment as well as potentiating efficacious psychotherapy outcomes.

It is also important for the therapist to explain and openly discuss the reality that effective psychotherapy usually requires several months of active therapeutic work and patient commitment to change and recovery. It is highly unrealistic to expect addictive disordered patients to establish long-term recovery or change within the context of 3–6 therapy sessions, and many addictive disordered patients will, in fact, experience 5–10 or more treatment experiences involving a diversity of therapies and treatments prior to establishing sustained recovery. The working and productive therapeutic alliance always represents a potentially profound source of hope for addictive disordered persons who have in essence failed within the context of multiple prior treatment episodes. In accord with this, therapists and the therapeutic relationship always represent a very real and viable vehicle for constructive patient personality growth, change and recovery. The following vignette demonstrates the clinical realties associated with patient motivation and readiness for change, and the sometimes profoundly therapeutic and unrecognized nature of the therapeutic alliance.

Case 2

Jim was referred for individual therapy within the context of a military substance abuse program some 45 years ago. The client was 41 years old at the time, married and the father of three sons, and one year away from military retirement. His company commander accompanied him to his initial treatment appointment and indicated that he "never wanted to see the patient again in his unit." Jim had been ordered into the "Rehab Center," and his captain would see him "on the parade field at 01300 for his official retirement" in one year. The patient was an e-1 at that time after having attained an early rank of E-8 (Master Sergeant). The patient was somewhat intoxicated when originally seen for consultation and provided a brief history involving some 13 years of chronic intoxication.

In short, this patient was seen in therapy on a weekly basis for some 13 months prior to his military discharge. The client was acutely intoxicated at each of his weekly therapy sessions over the initial nine months of his "therapy," and each session lasted no more than 10–15 minutes as the author supportively and repeatedly attempted to explain to the patient the requirement of coming to sessions sober. Jim was also referred to attend group therapy and participate in various recommended adjunctive treatment activities. Some nine months later, the patient arrived for his first sober therapy session, began attending weekly group therapy, was seen in marital therapy, and he sustained alcohol abstinence until the time of his retirement and for the duration of his life which encompassed twelve years. He graduated from college during that time, remained married, became employed as an addictions counselor in the VA hospital system, and the author continued to receive Christmas cards with a lengthy "family" letter every year until the patient passed away. Each correspondence credited the author and "our sessions" with "saving" his life. At the time, and as I write this case study, Jim remains one of the "least likely to succeed" patients that I ever treated within the context of nearly 50 years of addictions specific practice; nonetheless, the memories of our extremely difficult and unusual therapy experience over the course of some 13 months still evokes significant personal emotions-ultimately very positive emotions for myself as well as his family. An obviously positive but unusual alliance eventually did evolve within the rather bizarre dynamics associated with this case.

The core structural components of effective individual psychotherapy work with addictive disordered patients include (1) the individual psychotherapy process, (2) active and ongoing addiction focused education and recovery self-help support group engagement and/or active AA involvement with sponsorship, SMART STOP group/ other community based recovery support services, (3) possible appropriate ongoing addiction specific medication assisted treatment, if medically and therapeutically indicated, (4) medically appropriate active and ongoing physical exercise regimen, (5) enhanced nutrition and therapist-patient focused awareness related to basic health habits, (6) possible residential, brief "detox," intensive out-patient care, or extended residential care as a component of the ongoing psychotherapy process, and contingent upon patient treatment progress and care needs, (7) possible patient specific establishment or re-engagement of a spiritual or religious/church based recovery program, and/or (8) other integrative care modalities such as mindfulness, relaxation training, meditation, yoga, acupuncture, and patient specific adjunctive treatments. Many patients also benefit significantly from involvement in concurrent therapies such as conjoint marital therapy, family therapy, EMDR and various other forms of therapy while being engaged in addictions-focused intensive psychotherapy. These core structural components of efficacious addictions focused alliance and integrative psychotherapy and counseling work may be perceived as adjuncts to the process of ongoing intensive psychotherapy by some addiction therapists and counselors.

The therapeutic alliance can be enhanced via the patient and therapist relational work that is involved in the process of developing the patient's individualized treatment and recovery program, and each patient manifests various individual ongoing goals, tasks, and needs that must be continually re-addressed throughout the course of psychotherapy. Therapists and patients need to consistently realize that there are common sets of behaviors, cognitive and interpersonal styles, and sources of biopsychosocial dysfunction that generally characterize each category or form of addictive disorder; however, all patients manifesting severe addictive disorders demonstrate a diversity of individual differences. Simply put, all opioid addicted, alcohol dependent or eating disordered patients are not the same, and likewise all patients do not respond to the same therapeutic models in a like manner. Individualized treatment plans and psychotherapy formats or models are essential to successful outcomes. It can certainly be argued that perhaps the only core characteristic that addictive disordered patients share in common as a group is the particular addictive disorder which they share with a particular cohort of similar addictive disordered persons. Personality factors, gender, cognitive skills, various co-morbid conditions, education, multi-cultural differences, age, socioeconomic status, and a myriad of other factors permeate each and every addictive disorder category.

The structural components of each patient's individualized treatment program constitute a therapeutic holding environment in which the alliance can develop into a potent vehicle for change that also incorporates the utilization of several external-real world sources of reinforcement and social learning experiences that also frequently and significantly synergize the recovery process. Support and self-help engagement experiences also provide valuable and potential support as well as enhancing social skill development experiences for addictive disordered patients. Active and ongoing self-help and group therapy involvement provide tools for over-coming social anxiety, feelings and beliefs associated with stigma, guilt and shame, and furthermore include the social experience of being consistently engaged with many people who become healthy "real-world" ego introjects who also consistently model a plethora of adaptive behaviors that represent overtly constructive adjustment dynamics for patients in early stage psychotherapy.

These relational processes provide ongoing grist for the therapist and patient within the therapeutic alliance context. With many patients, this facet of the alliance contributes to the patient's capacities for healthy attachment and trust involving not only the therapist but significant others as well as other people in general. These experiences help resolve chronic interpersonal conflicts associated with narcissistic injury, trauma, low self-esteem, self-defeating behavior, and awaken the patient's basic awareness that he or she not only has the capacity to resolve or overcome his or her addictive disorder, but also constructively grow and change many facets of their previously globally dysfunctional lifestyle. Hope and internalized motivation for change evolve as a result of this process, and again, these various conscious dynamics contribute to the patient's capacities for continued alliance work and commitment to the therapeutic process.

An active and medically appropriate physical exercise regimen, self-help, therapy and support groups, possible medication assisted therapy, enhanced nutrition and generally enhanced health self-care, spiritual or religious activities, meditation, mindfulness and other structural components of the patient's treatment plan likewise provide a diversity of sources of gain for addictive disordered persons. Patient self-help group related sponsorship relationships can also significantly enhance treatment and therapy outcomes. However, infrequently sponsorship relationships can be disruptive to alliance formation and the ongoing therapeutic process. Patient commitment and consistency with these adjunctive therapeutic activities is essential in early stage psychotherapy and this reality remains an ongoing source of alliance focus between the therapist and patient. It is important within the alliance context that therapists initially identify and incorporate individual patient differences with regard to a diversity of issues related to the structural components of therapy.

For example, some addictive disordered patients initially refuse to participate in programs such as weight watchers, alcoholics anonymous, narcotics anonymous, a therapy group, gamblers anonymous or any form of spiritually based groups. Therapists and patients need to address such sources of potential alliance dissonance early in therapy. However, therapist-patient alliance dissonance early in therapy, therapist-patient flexibility, and evolving constructive alliance work usually becomes a vehicle for resolving these therapy process issues.

The following brief therapy vignette demonstrates an example of how therapists and patients can resolve issues associated with patient refusal, marked resistance or ambivalence related to engagement in potentially beneficial structural components of the therapeutic process.

Case 3

JACK: The stuff we were talking about last week—our plan and goals to help me change. I've thought about it, and like I've said, I've known that I was addicted to those pain pills for over two years, and the alcohol has been a problem for at least fifteen years, plus the cigarettes since I was fourteen years old—it's been one or two packs a day too—at least I've been able to stop smoking a few times over the years—and I've thought about it—I've decided to start going to AA again, and I'm open to getting a sponsor—

DR. F.: So you've recognized your addiction issues for quite some time, and have had some success with being able to "cut back" or stop at times—you mentioned that when we did your history and you were able to quit on your own for a while—no therapy, or any kind of help or treatment—it sounds like you're feeling kinda overwhelmed just thinking about and discussing get beyond all of your past addictions—maybe even a bit scary?

JACK : Yeah, you've got it right Doc—and it's not just coming in for therapy—but the other things we're discussing, like starting to go to NA or AA—the smoke cessation program, and the time it's all going to take—plus my wife keeps telling me I need to quit, but then she sometimes tells me I'll never quit—I know this shit is killing me, and I really want to get out of it.

DR. F.: I sense that you definitely want to get out of it too, Jack—and I think it will be a bit easier for you to accept the time demands related to really working on yourself if you begin taking all of it one day at a time—you mentioned last week that you really didn't want to go to NA—but it sounds like AA and a sponsor are a starting point—why don't we begin with the open AA meetings each week, try to get a sponsor in a few weeks, plus start getting out for a 10-20 minute walk four or five times a week or try the gym once or twice a week for starters—we can schedule one therapy session a week, or twice a week if you feel you need it?

JACK : The day at a time approach helps—I've been to a few AA meetings in the past, I've heard it—and I feel better about going to AA—I really don't like being a "drug addict," but I can do the stuff—the plan the way you spelled it out—I think I told you last week, my wife started going to Al-Anon again. That helps her but I've been the problem in the past—I want to do it for myself this time, and these last five weeks with no pills or drinking sure as hell have helped me feel better—physically and mentally I can sure tell the difference, plus my wife has even noticed—at least that's a start, and our sessions have helped.

DR. F.: It all takes time and work Jack—probably helps to just see it as a process—a daily thing, and you're not trying to do it yourself this time—we all need help—different kinds of help related to different things, at different times in our lives, Jack—we're both getting on board with our plan and goals, and that can change during therapy too.

The structural components as well as the alliance relationship in addictions focused psychotherapy provide patient support, and reinforce abstinence and recovery in a myriad of ways. Prosocial learning, adaptive time structuring, and various other alliance related dynamics discussed in this section of the chapter facilitate constructive patient change.

Key therapist ingredients within the context of the structural components of the psychotherapy process and the development as well as ongoing maintenance of a working and productive therapeutic alliance with addictive disordered patients include non-possessive warmth, empathy, effective communication skills, and genuineness (Forrest, 1999, 2002, 2012, 2016; Truax and Carkhuff, 1967). These ingredients are discussed and described throughout the course of this text. Therapists who do intensive and extended psy-

chotherapy work with addictive disordered patients will also find it efficacious to utilize a structured model of therapy which encompasses a focused
exploration of select patient specific related topics and dynamics that are
also sequentially explored throughout the course of therapy. As indicated
earlier, therapist high level therapeutic conditions are prerequisite to successful therapeutic alliance work throughout this process. The therapist's
ability to (1) accept the addictive-disordered patient unconditionally, (2)
remain affectively, cognitively and relationally attuned to the patient's feelings, experiences, and behaviors, (3) effectively communicate to and with
the patient and a conscious understanding of this awareness and relational
dynamics, and (4) remain open to his or her own experience within the
alliance context and psychotherapeutic encounter. These therapist related
factors remain at the heart of efficacious psychotherapy relationships and
outcomes. Therapists need to remain open, honest, and genuine in their
relationships with patients. These factors and dynamics begin to significantly impact the patient during the early stage of addictions-focused alliance
work associated with genetic reconstruction exploration. The process of
genetic reconstruction work also tends to stir significant patient and therapist
awareness of evolving and sometimes powerful transference and countertransference dynamics within the alliance relationship. These dynamics also
contribute significantly to the development of the "real therapeutic relationship" (Gelso et al., 2005).

EARLY STAGE ALLIANCE DYNAMICS AND GENETIC RECONSTRUCTION IN INTEGRATIVE ADDICTIONS-FOCUSED PSYCHOTHERAPY AND COUNSELING WORK

"Genetic reconstruction" work within the context of intensive psychodynamically oriented alliance-focused psychotherapy refers to the "therapist's
structuring of the treatment process and alliance relationship in a manner
which focuses upon the patient's early life experiences, behaviors, feelings,
cognitions and personal family dynamics. The global experiential past of the
patient remains grist for therapeutic exploration and focus during the early
stage phase of psychotherapy involving addictive disordered patients. Addictive
disordered patients tend to be pathologically fixated upon the past and their
future unrealistic illusions, and their addictive disorders largely represent a
neurotic solution to the many painful, traumatic, and self-defeating realities
which characterize their developmental-relational histories. Addictive disordered persons attempt to deny and avoid the various realities associated with
their experiential histories via the addictive disease process. The therapeutic
alliance and psychotherapy process in concert with other recovery focused

measures during the initial recovery process can provide therapists with the paradoxical opportunity and task of helping addictive patients fully and honestly explore their pasts in the absence of chemical intoxication and their prior floridly active addiction brain disease process. The patient's beliefs, goals, and perceptions related to his or her current and future lives can also more realistically be impacted within the context of the real therapeutic relationship as a result of genetic reconstruction work.

The basic therapeutic tasks of the therapist during the course of genetic reconstruction work involve 1) sustaining and maintaining a working and productive therapeutic alliance with the patient while 2) helping the patient openly explore his or her past in the absence of active addiction or relapse during this phase of therapy. Successful completion of this process and phase of therapy frequently fosters very significant positive alliance enhancement and strengthening, as virtually all addictive disordered patients are initially ambivalent and sometimes highly defensive about sharing or disclosing (Forrest, 2012, 2015) their conflicted and traumatic early-life as well as adolescent and adult experiential histories with the therapist or significant others. Genetic reconstruction work also fosters patient self-awareness, promotes honesty, self-acceptance, and begins to erode the patient's prior propensity for lying, distorting and denying the many realities of his or her life.

The process of successful genetic reconstruction work in psychotherapy with addictive disordered patients is basic to the development and maintenance of a working therapeutic alliance. Therapists need to understand and remain sensitively aware of patient fears, anxieties and ambivalence relative to personal disclosures, and during early therapy sessions the therapist supportively begins to uncover and help the patient begin to explore and more realistically understand as well as self-initiate the process of resolving or letting go of the painful and traumatic developmental realities associated with his or her past. This component of therapy eventually enables many persons to resolve or relationally "come to grips with the pain of the past."

Historically, it was perhaps most efficacious for the therapist to focus the initial weeks (6–8 weeks) of therapy exploring the patient's childhood through adolescence and early adult history. Anxiety and a plethora of uncomfortable affects and memories usually accompany this process. Patients also manifest conscious and preconscious fears, guilt, shame and embarrassment associated with the process of uncovering and personal disclosures that take place at this time. However, this phase of therapy not only fosters alliance development but usually results in a tremendous patient sense of release and catharsis. Many addictive disordered patients have never before discussed their personal historicity in an open, honest, extensive manner with another human being. These patients have also never openly and honestly discussed their addiction histories with others prior to active therapeutic engagement. The psychotherapeutic relationship becomes more intense and depth-oriented with this process, and the patient-therapist trust bond can also be enhanced by the genetic reconstruction work that is completed during this stage of therapy.

Effective genetic reconstruction work continues during the middle and later stages of addictions therapy; however, the core relational and alliance-based information and adjustment style dynamics that are gleaned by the therapist often form the nexus of therapeutic work that takes place much later in the therapeutic process. While the focus on genetic reconstruction work is less intense later in therapy, and the alliance based therapeutic strategies and interventions become temporarily focused on more here and now issues and dynamics later in therapy, the therapist nonetheless continues to make associations and dynamic interpretations which link the patient's past and present experiences, feelings, patterns of behaviors, and cognitions.

As the genetic reconstruction phase of addiction therapy unfolds, many patients begin to discover that they no longer experience the compulsion to escape the past or attempt to cope with present or anticipated future realities vis a via their addictive brain disease process. Chronic feelings of anxiety, depression, avoidance and intimacy difficulties, rage or anger, guilt, identity diffusion and low self-esteem, and relational dysfunction that have been associated with the patient's experiential past become less intense and debilitating or are resolved. These patients may become capable of resolving the more global conflicts and other sources of dysfunctional bondage associated with their lifelong developmental histories.

Genetic reconstruction work eventually reveals the Procrustean bedrock of the patient's addictive disease process as well as general psychopathology and character structure. This facet of alliance building within the therapeutic process is initiated following the patient's commitment to the process of ongoing psychotherapy and recovery. When treating adult individual psychotherapy patients manifesting severe co-morbid addictive disorders, this therapeutic strategy (Forrest, 1985, 1992, 2014) tends to be most efficaciously initiated by initially "focusing upon the patient's high school and late adolescent years." As the therapeutic process unfolds, the therapist progressively shifts the therapeutic focus to include an exploration of preadolescent, grade school and early childhood experiences, relationships, behaviors, affects and familial dynamics. This therapeutic procedure becomes progressively more regressive in a developmental sense; however, by beginning the genetic reconstruction phase of addictions psychotherapy by focusing upon the patient's late adolescence usually results in (1) less intensive affective conflict for the patient, (2) a reduced incidence of premature treatment terminations and anxiety triggered patient episodes of "fleeing" from treatment, and (3) this therapeutic approach provides the additional time and relational strengthening for continued therapeutic alliance development, and enhances the development of a therapeutic relational structure that can endure both the therapeutic work and tasks of childhood reconstruction as well as the ongoing therapeutic process.

Addictive disordered patients are notoriously resistive to engaging in psychotherapy or other forms of personal health care and treatment (Bratter and Forrest, 1985). These patients also tend to terminate treatment prematurely, deny their addictions, and flee from affective focused therapies and the intimacy of therapeutic relationships (Forrest, 2012, 2015). Self-exploration, honest and open disclosures and the intimacy of therapeutic genetic reconstruction work can be painful, very emotional and also potentially traumatic for addictive disordered persons. These realities create a multiplicity of ongoing alliance dynamics that can result in the outcropping of therapeutic relational struggles. For these reasons, therapists need to be especially sensitive to the patient's global functioning as well as therapist-patient alliance dynamics during this stage of therapy. The therapy process at this juncture generally proceeds in a rather superficial, nonthreatening content-oriented manner to a more intense, in-depth and often affectively charged ego-dystonic state upon the part of the patient and also some therapists. Therapist timing, sensitivity, awareness and personal self-care are essential ingredients throughout the process of effective genetic and constructive reconstruction work.

In the absence of a working and productive alliance relationship that includes the therapist's continued abilities to provide supportive, timely, concrete high levels of active therapeutic engagement with the patient over the course of reconstruction work, patients may become more prone to the experience of acute anxiety and feelings of panic or decompensation that can precipitate iatrogenic treatment outcomes and terminations. As noted earlier, the patient's active and continued engagement in self-help or support groups, sponsorship relationships, an active exercise regimen, and various other therapeutic modalities that have been central to his or her alliance-based treatment plan greatly reduce the anxiety and other difficulties that patients and therapists encounter during this phase of the therapeutic process.

Effective reconstruction work initiates and opens the door for further therapeutic work and patient self-repair or healing via the patient's alliance facilitated enhanced capacities to openly explore, understand and change a diversity of historic maladaptive behaviors, beliefs, feelings and thoughts related to early life parenting and relational experiences, anxiety and depression, the avoidance defense system, intimacy, identity and self-esteem, impulsivity and antisocial traits, marital and parenting, impulse control, anger, shame, relationship difficulties, and a diversity of other addictive brain disease related emotional and pathological adjustment dynamisms discussed throughout this text.

As touched upon earlier, genetic reconstruction work continues to be an integral component of the ongoing process of successful dynamically-oriented alliance-focused psychotherapy involving addictive disordered patient populations. As a part of the evolving therapeutic shift into the middle and later stages of therapy, therapists continue to make associations and dynamic interpretations which link, examine and help patients more clearly understand as well as modify or resolve past and present patterns of maladaptive behaviors, feelings, cognitions and beliefs, and relational styles.

The following brief therapy vignette demonstrates how patient's frequently respond to the ongoing process of genetic reconstruction work in therapy, and also provides insight for therapists regarding patient stage of therapy related integrative reflections on the reconstruction focused component of therapy. This therapeutic segment took place after some eighteen months of every other week individual therapy work with the patient. She had also completed a residential treatment program during this time frame, and was actively engaged in a structured treatment program involving a number of other ancillary therapeutic adjuncts including limited self-help involvement, weekly women's support group, exercise regimen and medication related infrequent psychiatric consultations (three monthly 15–20 minutes medication management consultations.)

Case 4

SUSAN: Even discussing those things we talked about when I started the evaluation, and therapy—just thinking about it is painful—looking back, I was so into the denial and cover-up—lying to my husband and the kids, and those test results—plus the report to the board—I knew I was depressed and had been abusing the pain meds, but getting arrested, forging the prescriptions and stealing my doctors pad—and he was a friend, all of it black and white, having to get a lawyer and the embarrassment with my colleagues—

DR. F.: Coming to grips or facing all of those issues at one time was really stressful and difficult—it must have felt like your whole world fell apart at once—but like we discussed, it really took two or three years to play out—it's a progressive process—any addiction, and the lying and denial stuff are progressive too.

SUSAN: You know, the embarrassment and shame I had back then, plus the fear of losing my license to practice—and, I sure didn't want to be in therapy and the monitoring program—plus the inpatient treatment was the only way I could keep my license—looking back though, it's really hard to believe the changes—I've been feeling like I did ten years ago these last few months, and I really look forward to the groups—my parents, especially my father and family are behind me 100% . . . and you've helped me so much. God, just being able to start talking about all of it was difficult. Facing it—and I had been keeping so much of it to myself.

DR. F.: I'm not sure you even trusted your lawyer in the beginning, and the evaluation—testing results were the last thing you wanted to hear, but you hung in there—and it's worked out—do you remember us putting together your treatment plan, and my constant message that things would get better—you could get your life back on track, if you did the work—you've made your appointments and worked in here, but you've also really participated in all of your recovery activities—and you kept your license, and your life has turned around—that's all a part of staying better, continuing to work your own recovery plan and like we've been focusing on recently, avoiding the risks associated with relapse—plus the opioid, depression, and eating disorder aspects of your addiction make it all the more important for you to continue to maintain your own ongoing recovery—treatment program.

SUSAN: I'm on board with all of that now, Dr. F—and the eating disorder was really a thing I've been aware of since I was in high school—always needing to be perfect, and obsessed with how I looked and achievement—that's stuff that you've really helped with, but the eating-disorder treatment program was really helpful—I'm just so happy about today—where I'm at now, and not two or three years ago—I don't think I could ever go through all of that again—and I don't want to put our family through it ever again either.

As touched upon earlier in this chapter, therapists actually begin the most basic and formative phase of genetic reconstruction work during the initial psychosocial history taking and assessment process, and varying levels and facets of genetic reconstruction focused dynamics permeate the course of alliance work and the ongoing psychotherapeutic process.

EARLY STAGE ALLIANCE DYNAMICS INVOLVING INSIGHT AND SELF-AWARENESS IN INTEGRATIVE ADDICTIONS-FOCUSED PSYCHOTHERAPY AND COUNSELING WORK

Therapeutic work involving virtually all patients, therapeutic models, and treatment approaches include some level of therapeutic emphasis upon the goal of fostering patient insight and self-awareness. Indeed, learning related to these and many other therapeutic matters is germane to virtually all therapeutic relationships. A major goal in dynamically oriented alliance-focused psychotherapy work with addictive disordered persons is that of directly enhancing patient insight and self-awareness. The therapeutic alliance quickly becomes a potential patient vehicle for new learning experiences and growth pertaining to the total self. This facet of the therapeutic relationship and working alliance represents another paradoxical aspect of the process of psychotherapy with addicts. Addictive disordered persons frequently tend to be consciously or pre-consciously aware of many of their historic pathological experiences and emotional difficulties as well as the various pathologic vicissitudes of their present addictive disease process. Prior to involvement in more intensive psychotherapy, these patients have also attempted to deny, avoid, minimize and repress personal insight and self-awareness related to these very personal matters. These patients have historically tried to block out and suppress personal self-awareness, sensitivity and conscious insights via their addictive brain disease process. Addictive disordered patients also tend to experience generalized anxiety and uncomfortableness internally and in their relationships with others. These dynamics reinforce fears and further trepidation relative to patient insight and awareness, and eventually synergize the addiction process.

Addictions therapists actively structure the alliance and therapeutic relationship in a manner which enhances the patient's capacity for conscious insight and self-awareness development which can be expressed more directly, openly, and honestly explored between the therapist and patient. The alliance provides a relationship context and medium which actively facilitates patient self-exploration, authenticity, self-disclosure and enhanced openness (Farber, 2006; Forrest, 2012, 2016; Jourard, 1964). Therapist qualities including high levels of non-possessive warmth, empathy, genuineness, concreteness, support, openness and appropriate and timely disclosures foster the patient's evolving and growing capacities for heightened self-awareness and insight. These alliance-based dynamics also facilitate motivation for change, constructive social learning, enhanced self-esteem and improved social skills, and a myriad of other potential healthy global adjustment behaviors that constructively impact the recovery process. These strategies also help resolve the patient's addictive brain disease process as well as other comorbid dysfunctional adjustment dynamisms.

The therapist's consistent use of clinical interpretation techniques in a consistently supportive, empathic, learning and clarification-based manner within the alliance context of the therapeutic process helps to elevate the patient's unconscious and pre-conscious self-oriented beliefs, feelings, self-dialogue, perceptions and other processes to the conscious level of personal experience. This facet of the therapeutic process contributes greatly to the therapist and patient's abilities to explain and potentially resolve or modify a wide diversity of dysfunctional, self-defeating, and chronic patterns of dys-regulated behavior and being.

It should also be noted that these alliance-based therapeutic strategies clearly prove most efficacious when patients are committed to drug abstinence and their ongoing process of recovery from an addictive disorder. Continued drinking or drugging, active eating disordered behaviors, continued smoking or gambling, and frequent sexual acting out during the ongoing course of therapy not only result in poor therapeutic outcomes, but frequently precipitate therapeutic terminations related to alliance ruptures and other more severe deleterious patient outcomes. Paradoxically, addictive disordered patients not infrequently experience relapse episodes while in therapy. However, a brief relapse in the process of therapy can eventually produce paradoxically positive treatment related patient growth and gains, and provide positive reinforcement for continued therapeutic engagement. Nonetheless, all relapse episodes can prove to be catastrophic within the context of psychotherapy work and other treatments involving severely addictive disordered patients.

Kernberg (1975, 1993) noted that interpretation is the core technique in the psychodynamically oriented therapist's armamentarium for potentiating patient insight and self-awareness, but patient insight, self-awareness, and global growth and change are also facilitated via a diversity of other alliance-related therapeutic strategies. These strategies include reflection, listening, clarification, didactic and experiential learning, suggestion, support, imitative learning, homework and rehearsal, humor and active therapist engagement as well as constructive feedback.

An initial therapeutic task for addictions therapists and counselors involves fostering patient insight and awareness related to the explicit realm of the patient's addictive disorder. Addictive disordered patients scotomize their relationships with addictive substances, behaviors and the "drug-addictive disordered-person" relationship which remains grist for the therapeutic process during the early, middle and later stages of therapy. Indeed, addictive disordered persons usually manifest a diversity of distorted, irrational, and neurotic or intensely conflicted insights, self-conceptualizations and distorted self-perceptions early in therapy. The patient's insight, awareness, beliefs, perceptions of significant others, and the external world also tend to be distorted and generally parataxic. The alliance framework and the therapeutic process contribute to the patient's enhanced capacities for reality-oriented and globally more rational self, other, reality-oriented and more rational self-other perceptions, beliefs, insight and personal awareness.

Recovery is contingent upon the patient's ability to integratively learn and practice a broad spectrum of new and more adaptive behaviors involving insight pertaining to self, significant others, and the phenomenal world.

Significantly improved insight and self-awareness are central ingredients in the recovery process. The patient's insight and awareness pertaining to feelings, emotions, and affect in general are also distorted and extremely conflicted in early therapy and recovery. Patient insight and awareness related to the internal and external management, and even the labeling of different affective states is frequently very limited or poorly conceptualized during the early stage of therapy. Alliance work in this particular domain becomes a major point of focus during the middle and later stages of addictions-focused psychotherapy. A premature and intensive focus on affective work in early therapy tends to stir patient feelings of intense anxiety, and as noted earlier, may trigger premature patient terminations, relapse, or a "flight from therapy."

From an analytic-dynamic perspective, the working and productive therapeutic alliance becomes an intimate human relationship framework whereby the patient progressively internalizes many of the adaptive healing and therapeutic qualities of both the therapist and the therapeutic relationship. In short, a diversity of alliance facilitated qualities related to the psychotherapy process become patient ego interjects which synergize the patient's capacities for growth and adaptive change. The following brief therapy vignette demonstrates how therapists utilize the alliance context to foster enhanced patient insight and awareness related to the various pathological facets of his or her addictive disorder.

Case 5

JACK H.: I always kept stuff to myself—but I did start to tell my wife about growing up, and how my parents left us when we were so young—hell, we were married for ten or fifteen years before I even told her anything about that—you kept stuff to yourself in those days, and in the military—but after being drunk for so many years, it all started to come out—God, it hurt—my wife helped me, but since we've been meeting, and I know it's only five or six weeks—I really feel less stressed—starting to talk to you every week about it has helped—and I'm sober now—I always got into this stuff—crying and nasty as hell with my wife, when I was drunk in the past—it's different talking with you—I mean talking about all that pain and all the shit that's happened in my life—sober, just being as honest as I can and trying to remember what actually happened—see, I'm startin' to tear up again—

DOCTOR F.: Yeah, being sober is a big part of being able to deal with all of it, Jack—dealing with all of the things that all of us struggle with at times, but you also seem to be saying that you're see-

ing how a lot of it all fits together—you're handling it a lot more rationally now—drinking to cope with your past, having it all come out at
times when you were drunk, and even the way you treated your wife
through it all—and we've been able to get this far without you having
to drink over it—you're making some real changes Jack, and Ilsa tells
me that you seem different—things are better between you, and your
feeling physically better—plus you all and us—we can talk about the
all those issues without the overwhelming feeling you've had in the
past.

JACK H.: She's taken care of me for so long—and put up with a
lot, I know I've been a mess—but I'm working on it, and when I'm
ready, I've got to make it up to her—the amends thing in AA—making amends to the people you've hurt—I've been hurting myself for
twenty-five years, and that includes her and a lot of other people—I
sure as hell don't want Ilsa to leave me, like my folks did—just wake
up one day—maybe even sober, and she's gone.

DOCTOR F.: Maybe you've been driving her away by the drinking—and the destructive behavior that goes with alcoholism—like testing her over the years—as long as she put up with the abuse, she loved
you, and at the same time maybe you were somehow trying to get
even with your mom and dad, for abandoning you?? But it's time to
change, and you're realizing that now—driving her away is like being
your own worst enemy, but that's also different from having your parents abandon you at eight years of age—those two situations are similar, but also really different—and the drinking was sure as hell a way
to punish yourself and your wife—you can chose to do what you need
to do to improve your relationship—change things with Ilsa, but *the
past is the past,* and you sure as hell had no choice about your parents
devastating decision to leave you—and you eventually were out of
control with the drinking and your life until you got sober—

JACK H.: I did a lot to drive my wife away for many years—I've
kinda known that, but I really didn't know why—I did it over and
over, but I never connected what happened with my folks over all
those years ago—plus, the drinking sure made all of it worse and hell,
I'd be lost again if Ilsa left me—under any circumstances—we've been
married over 25 years, and she's kept me alive all this time—one way
or another—I'd probably be dead a lot of times if it weren't for her—
I've lied to her, promised her I'd never drink again a thousand times,
all of it, I just want to keep getting better, you know Doc, I really got
crazy at the end of my drinking.

DOCTOR F.: It's difficult to start dealing with the wreckage and
pain of the past, Jack—but again, we're beginning to make some sense

out of all of it—and I think we both realize that putting this together is a first step, and then beginning to understand and see or understand what you need to do, to stay in recovery and make the changes you need to—not just with Ilsa, but with other things too—again, it takes time and work but you're on your way.

EARLY STAGE ALLIANCE DYNAMICS AND ADDICTION FOCUS IN EARLY STAGE INTEGRATIVE ADDICTIONS-FOCUSED PSYCHOTHERAPY AND COUNSELING WORK

Historic psychiatric and psychological models associated with the addictive disorders (Bratter and Forrest, 1985; Forrest, 1996; Forrest and Gordon, 1990) viewed underlying and more serious psychopathology as the core causative factors associated with these disorders. Thus, counselors, psychiatrists, psychologists and other clinicians who provided care for addictive disordered patients were primarily concerned about treating the patient's underlying problems related to depression, impulse control, anxiety, schizophrenia or other adjustment disorders. While the patient's addictive disorder may have been recognized by early clinicians, the focus of psychotherapy and other professional treatments generally tended to be directed at the "underlying" and more severe psychopathology that was thought to be "causing" the patient's addictive behavior. These clinicians were far less concerned about the actual psychotherapeutic treatment of the addictive disordered patient's addictive disease process.

With the development and evolution of the addictions and chemical dependency treatment profession over the course of the past twenty-five years, contemporary addictions therapists, counselors and treatment providers generally establish a priMaryddiction focus during their initial treatment sessions involving completion of the patient's biopsychosocial history and clinical assessment. Addictive disordered persons initially present in a diversity of ways, but as indicated earlier a sizeable segment of these individuals clearly attempt to minimize, deny, rationalize, and in a multiplicity of other pathological ways, attempt to convince the therapist that they do not manifest a severe addictive disorder or other co-existing difficulties. Not infrequently, patients may initially report that they "do not know" why they are being seen for therapy or report that they "came in because my husband, wife, or parents wanted me to." Most of these patients attempt to present themselves in a favorable light, deny experiencing significant difficulties related to drinking, drug use, eating behaviors or such, and often attempt to assure the therapist that they are not in need of therapy. To the contrary, a sizeable segment of addictive disordered persons entering psychotherapy and other treatment programs or models of care initially acknowledge through their initial and ongoing work with the therapist that they clearly manifest a severe addictive disorder, and often these individuals are able to sustain an active and ongoing focus upon the various dynamics associated with their addictive brain disease throughout the therapeutic process.

The alliance-based focus component of additions therapy work is initiated during the early therapeutic and interviewing contacts with patients, and must be maintained throughout the ongoing process of intensive addictions psychotherapy. Addictions therapists and counselors need to actively maintain an ever-present addiction focus in their therapeutic work with addictive disordered patients. This process involves an evolving exploration of the patient's historic developmental pattern of addictive behavior, and more recent or present and ongoing dynamics associated with his or her addictive disease process. An active and ongoing therapeutic exploration of the patient's various feelings, emotions, behaviors, and cognitions related to his or her addictive disorder remains essential to the addictions focus component of the therapeutic process. This work also fosters the ongoing process of constructive alliance development, enhancement, and the patient's awareness and insight into the various mechanisms and sources of conflict that have facilitated as well as maintained his or her addictive disorder and other maladaptive behaviors.

The therapeutic alliance-based addiction focus shifts during the later stages of psychotherapy to a more intense exploration and examination of the patient's thoughts, beliefs, feelings and plans about future behaviors and dynamics associated with enhancing, maintaining and sustaining the ongoing recovery process. Patient specific triggers, cognitions, emotions and relational dynamics related to possible future drug-taking behaviors and relapse prevention skills are focally related to the course of therapy and especially the early and middle stages of addictions psychotherapy. Therapists also need to actively reinforce patient commitment to the recovery process and the patient's ability to sustain an addiction free life style during and after completion of the psychotherapy treatment process.

A working and productive therapeutic alliance framework enables the therapist and patient to uncover, identify, explore, consciously understand, and actively modify the various factors and dynamics which have contributed to the patient's pattern of addictive disease. This alliance-based work eventually helps the therapist and patient develop a wide range of adaptive patient coping skills, behaviors, self-regulation strengths, cognitive skills and interpersonal skills which simultaneously reinforce constructive change and the recovery process. Patient fears, anxiety, feelings of depression and social anxiety, trauma, prototaxic fears associated with loss of control, self-defeating behavior, low self-esteem, guilt, extinguishing avoidance defense mechanisms, and a myriad of other conflicts associated with the addictive disease process can be therapeutically modified or resolved via the process of efficacious alliance work.

Therapists and patients rather naturally tend to remain focused on clinical matters that pertain directly to the addiction focus early in therapy. However, addictions therapists and counselors as well as patients are also prone to significantly reducing or sometimes failing to maintain a consistent addiction focus during the middle or later course of their treatment relationships. The failure to sustain an active and ongoing addiction focus throughout the course of psychotherapy with addictive disordered patients may occur more frequently with patients who establish significant early treatment gains, do not experience early or middle stage therapy relapses, actively maintain and sustain a working and productive therapeutic alliance, and in other ways are simply "good" patients.

A significant loss of addiction focus during the middle or later stages of therapy may represent an unconscious collusion between the therapist and patient which is also reflective of unresolved issues pertaining to mutual denial, minimization, suppression or repression and a host of other dynamics related to the addictive disease process as well as the therapeutic relationship.

Therapist's need to remind themselves that relapse and regression in psychotherapy can be associated with acute situational stressors and various other chronic life or therapist-patient alliance relationship factors. A reduced or lack of addiction focus in therapy can clearly be a therapist-patient alliance precursor to the process of relapse, and a subsequent patient regression into a floridly active disease state. Addictive disordered patients may consciously or preconsciously interpret the therapist's reduction or discontinuance of the addiction focus as "permission" to re-engage in the addictive brain disease process. Experienced addictions therapists generally recognize that many addicts manifest an uncanny ability to utilize any therapist or nontherapy relational, behavioral, communication, or life circumstance related self-ideation in the direct service of their active addictive disease process. For these reasons, therapists need to maintain a keen sense of self-awareness relative to the messages which they communicate to their addictive disordered patients. Unresolved transference and countertransference dynamics are also frequent salient therapist-patient alliance related factors which eventually contribute to an inadequate or parataxic hypervigilant addiction focus in addictions psychotherapy. Indeed, alliance-based transference and countertransference dynamics can become the "royal road to relapse" in addictions therapy work.

As I have alluded to earlier (Forrest, 1985, 2002, 2010, 2018), experienced addictions therapists and clinicians are sometimes able to sense when patients are setting themselves up for relapse or a regressive return to the active addictive state. At these therapeutic junctures, therapists need to (1) actively explore and supportively interpret the patient's regressive thoughts, affects, and self-defeating behaviors, (2) actively reinforcing patient enhancement of his or her early recovery plan, (3) enhance and intensifying the frequency of therapy sessions and the alliance specific addictions focus, and (4) initiate appropriate relapse prevention alternatives. When relapses or "slips" do occur in addictions psychotherapy, it is imperative that the therapist and patient explore the various dynamics and "triggers" associated with the relapse episode, and also strategically identify and discuss patient specific relapse prevention alternatives that can be implemented to deter potential future relapse episodes.

Therapists generally need to spend ten to fifteen minutes of each early stage therapy session establishing and discussing addiction focused therapeutic content including (1) the patient's addictive disorder history and various present and historic facets of his or her addictive disorder, (2) obsessive and compulsive mechanisms and behaviors associated with the patient's addictive disorder, (3) current "cravings," cognitions and substance use related obsessive-compulsive thoughts, regressive behaviors and addressing current interpersonal dimensions of the addictive process, and (4) begin the process of educating and exploring the various processes which the patient can utilize in order to enhance his or her individualized treatment plan for modifying, extinguishing and eventually establishing extended recovery.

During the middle and later stages of addictions therapy, the therapist and patient may significantly reduce the scope of the addiction focus to five or ten minutes per session contingent upon the patient's evolving treatment status.

The following two brief therapy vignettes provide examples of sustaining an active addiction-focus stance in psychotherapy. The initial therapy vignette was taken from a segment of the third therapy session with Susan, and the second vignette comes from the patient's twenty-sixth therapy session.

Case 6 (Early stage vignette, session 3)

DOCTOR F.: It's been over a month since you've used any opioid medication—you must feel good about that, and you mentioned last week that you felt physically better—a lot less anxious—more energy.

SUSAN: I do feel a lot better—at least I know I can do it—stop the pills, but I still think about using again—at times, it seems like it's all the time—I was at my mother's yesterday and I had to check in the bathroom cabinet to see if she still had any Vicodin—the pills sure took away the anxiety, but I know where it leads to—I wasn't able to stop, and now I've got legal problems and ARC to deal with—but using again isn't the answer to any of it—including the depression.

DOCTOR F.: You see all of those issues more clearly now, Susan—but the addiction has ruled your life the last few years, and the obsessive thoughts about using don't go away in a few days or weeks—what all have you been doing to deal with the obsessive thoughts about using between our sessions?

SUSAN: I have been going to the gym a lot, plus going to a few meetings every week—still haven't gotten an NA sponsor, but going to the women's group—that stuff has helped get my mind off a lot of it—at least while I'm working out or in a meeting—I know I don't ever want to use again, and I sure don't want to lose my kids and family—plus it's all still so embarrassing—I'm afraid to even see my colleagues, or go to the office.

DOCTOR F.: Can you see how your addiction eventually took over your life? It was literally controlling almost every facet of your life—in a lot of incredibly destructive ways—do you ever feel grateful to be out of the process at times? . . . I mean the self-destructive parts of the old addictive behaviors—

SUSAN: I knew I was an addict, deep down, but that was at the end—before, I told myself I could control it, or I would stop the next day—all that stuff, but now I'm realizing that I've got a long-way to go to get over this—and it's not easy, but at times I start crying just thinking about what I've done to myself—and I do feel better—I'm sure grateful to be getting better, but I wish it was all behind me—I've got to keep the bad stuff in the front of my head—it helps to remember what I am, and how I got to this point—plus like you've said, it takes work to get better and it's not easy—but in the end, it's got to be easier than staying screwed up and in trouble—I don't ever want all of that again.

DOCTOR F.: Yeah, and you're right—that's why we need to stay focused on the different aspects of your addiction and what we can do together—you're doing the lion's share of the work, I can't do it for you and nobody else can either, but support and help from others always helps—that's all a part of getting better and the ongoing recovery process.

(Middle-Later Stage Therapy Vignette, session 26)

SUSAN: It's been almost nine months now since I've used—really, coming up on a year—it's hard to believe, actually coming up on a year before we know it—one day at a time, as they say—you know, and I've said it before, it has gotten easier—God, at first it was so hard—just facing all of it, and going to therapy, doing the rehab program, getting to meetings, the court stuff, plus dealing with Bob and the kids—plus telling my parents—it was overwhelming at the time—when I look back on it now—

DOCTOR F.: It's never easy getting started—with recovery, and treatment—or all of it, and even the way you started out was traumatic—getting arrested, the drug charges, your family and career—you *should feel better* about all of it now, the way you've really worked in therapy—the progress you've made over the months, and you did the work—you've followed through on all of your court requirements—and you're still focused on your recovery process.

SUSAN: I'm getting better with all of it—looking back, I was so afraid and embarrassed about getting caught—arrested, and my family knowing—they have all accepted me, and really been supportive—you know, I think that's a big part of why I'm not nearly as depressed and anxious—it felt like I was going crazy those first couple of months—like you've told me—and I've heard it from the group and others, it will get better—if you keep working on your program—and I'm sure the meds, and my therapy, the group, all of it has helped—you know, it's kinda strange—but good, I look forward to seeing you, and God was I ever anxious about coming in and going to group when I first started—it was hard to just be here or involved in all the other treatment stuff a few months ago—now I'm able to be open, and really engaged in my recovery—being out of all the pills has got to be a big part of it too.

DOCTOR F.: Being actively committed to your recovery program and basically "showing up" are definitely components to getting better—staying focused on your addictions and what you and I need to do to help you get better, grow and change, and stay drug free are important parts of how therapy helps people change—and you're the major person in that process, and that's also why you need to consciously recognize and acknowledge to yourself the positive changes you have initiated and sustained in your recovery life from time to time—plus the positive feedback you periodically get from others in your life. It's okay to give yourself some credit—ha-ha—that's reality—but never forgetting what got you into this process is also a part of maintaining and enhancing your recovery.

The therapeutic alliance context remains the major relational framework for addiction focused work as well as the utilization of all other therapeutic components of effective addictions therapy work. The addiction focused aspects of the therapeutic relationship are also continually modified and strengthened throughout the course of therapy.

EARLY STAGE ALLIANCE DYNAMICS AND IN INTEGRATIVE ADDICTIONS-FOCUSED AND COUNSELING WORK

Many years ago, the author (Forrest, 1982, 1992) indicated that confrontation can be a useful ingredient in successful psychotherapy work with alcoholics. Furthermore, this author has indicated that the absence of the therapist's use of timely, supportive, strategic and empathic confrontations may result in diminished therapeutic outcomes. These rather bold positions were based upon the author's clinical impressions and initial fifteen years of clinical practice experience. It should be noted that the author (Forrest, 1982, 1984, 1992) also pointed out that therapists have generally been reluctant to use confrontations techniques in therapy. Furthermore, confrontation can precipitate iatrogenic therapeutic outcomes. It needs to be recognized that the many conceptualizations, definitions, perceptions, meanings, and interpretations pertaining to what constitutes a strategy of confrontation in psychotherapy vary considerably among diverse therapist and patient populations. Forrest (1984) initially defined confrontation techniques in psychotherapy work with alcoholics as therapeutic interventions that (1) imply force, activity and focus the patient's attention on self and the addiction process, (2) heighten self-awareness, (3) provide the patient with direct interpersonal feedback relative to the therapist's global or specific perceptions pertaining to a wide range of the patient behaviors and dynamics, (4) teach the patient to attend to self and the therapist, and (5) provide the patient with supportive and constructive reality-oriented feedback from the therapist which potentially fosters constructive social learning experiences involving a wide variety of patient behaviors, affects, and internalized beliefs. Supportive, empathic, and appropriate timely confrontation interventions may also strengthen the therapeutic alliance framework.

These early works (Forrest, 1984, 1992) also suggested that "facilitative confrontation interventions are employed by the psychotherapist through the medium of a working and productive alliance—rational and effective confrontation interventions in intensive addictions psychotherapy must *always* incorporate high levels of therapist non-possessive warmth, empathy, genuineness, concreteness and support—it is important for the therapist to confront the patient in a relational and affective manner which conveys his or her profound sense of concern, love, empathy, and compassion for the patient" (pp. 64–65).

This author has noted that psychonoxious confrontations generally occur in therapy when the therapist is (1) frequently not genuinely concerned about the over-all well-being of the patient, (2) insensitive to the patient's overall clinical history and adjustment style, or (3) responding to the patient in a pathological therapeutic relational manner as a result of countertransference and/or transference dynamics (Forrest, 1994, 1999). Psychonoxious confrontations additionally tend to be devoid of empathy, warmth, support and compassion; anger, insensitivity, frustration, and the out-cropping of a wealth of countertransference dynamics also synergize pathological confrontations.

Therapeutically facilitated confrontation techniques and interventions contribute to the development of a working and productive therapeutic alliance by fostering the process of recall/and genetic reconstruction work, modify the patient's avoidance defense system, enhancing patient personal awareness and insight associated with a wide repertoire of maladaptive addictive disordered patterns of behavior and thinking, reinforcement, and meaningfully stimulate patient commitment to the structural components of the treatment process as well as the ever present addiction focus. Finally, these actions provide an ongoing therapeutic alliance relational framework which remains conducive to global patient learning experiences related to social skills development, rational thinking and problem solving, and in-depth affective work.

In concert with earlier chapters in this text, it is important for addictions psychotherapists to remain aware of the personal historic destructive roles that confrontation has played in the lives of many, if not most or all, addictive disordered persons. These patients have frequently been severely abused in a multiplicity of ways throughout the course of their lives by parents, significant others and themselves. Addictive disordered patients also tend to confront others in a diversity of maladaptive and parataxic ways. These confrontation-related therapeutic alliance dynamics contribute to the thorny and many difficult therapist-patient relationship issues that can arise vis á vis therapist inappropriate, insensitive, and non-supportive, non-empathic confrontation interventions during early stage alliance development.

Juxtaposed to these patient specific sources of potential dissonance and conflict associated with confrontation interventions in addictions psychotherapy work, many therapists personally experience relational and therapeutic difficulties and significant ambivalence related to this particular therapy technique. Therapists generally tend to be warm, nurturing, supportive and sometimes rather passive individuals who have also been trained to utilize a myriad of non-confrontational-oriented treatment interventions. In sum, there are a plethora of intrinsic therapist and patient factors which contribute to problems, risks and conflicts related to the use of confrontation techniques in intensive addictions psychotherapy and other treatment models that are used to treat people who manifest various severe addictive disorders.

Experienced, skilled, and well trained and supervised addictions therapists and counselors are also usually very sensitive, empathic and skilled in their uses of confrontation interventions early and throughout the process of ongoing addictions psychotherapy. These clinicians avoid utilizing premature, highly affective, high impact confrontations in all stages of therapeutic work with addictive disordered persons. Most therapists quickly discover that their addictive patients flee from the psychotherapy relationship, alliance ruptures occur, and premature patient terminations tend to be associated with very personal, affectively changed, and premature therapist confrontations. Controlled, affectively low impact, supportive, empathic, educational and constructive teaching-oriented early stage therapy interventions in addictions therapy work provide the patient with (1) various sources of reality-oriented feedback that convey a point of emphasis, and (2) usually are related to a matter of specific behaviors, feelings, or perceptions upon the part of the therapist which are somewhat dissonant with the self-perceptions or beliefs of the patient.

These forms of low impact confrontation do not threaten the patient, reinforce denial, defensiveness, distortion or projection upon the part of the patient, and most importantly, these therapeutic transactions do not threaten the alliance or psychotherapy relationship. To the contrary, controlled and supportive therapist confrontation-oriented interventions and feedback can facilitate constructive alliance development via communicating to the patient a deeper understanding and sense of the therapist's honesty, authenticity, concern, empathy, professional acumen, and a willingness to actively work toward the goal of helping the patient change and resolve his or her addictive disorder.

While many contemporary clinicians, therapists and a body of empirical research evidence (Norcross and Wampold, 2011) clearly indicate that confrontation interventions or strategies frequently can and do contribute to alliance dysregulation, ruptures, and treatment terminations as well as poor therapy outcomes, this author nonetheless (Forrest, 2016) suggests that when used properly by sensitive, empathic, and experienced addictions therapists who consistently form strong working and productive therapeutic alliances with their patient's via the medium of consistently providing high level therapeutic conditions, confrontation-oriented treatment measures can indeed become a catalyst for constructive patient change, growth and recovery. However, addictions therapists also need to exercise skill, insight, sensitivity, and a consistently vigilant awareness of the potential "for better or worse" dynamics associated with the use of confrontation strategies in psychotherapy work with addictive disordered persons.

Therapists need to remain cognizant that most, if not all of their transactions with patients involve various dynamics associated with a plethora of confrontation related issues and relational transactions. Physicians, dentists and other health service providers also continually deal with a diversity of care issues associated with confrontation related dynamics. These realities continually involve all forms of individual as well as collective human interactions. The simple act of making an appointment with a psychotherapist involves various levels and forms of patient self-confrontation, and the initial experience of actually entering the therapist's office and beginning a therapeutic relationship stirs conscious feelings of anxiety, trepidation, and fear in many patients. Entering a physician's office or a dentist's office may evoke intense feelings of fear and anxiety, and many people avoid health care for years. When people are confronted by their health providers with the clinical realities of having severe depression, an addictive disorder, mental illness, cancer, diabetes, cardiovascular disease, melanoma and a wide range of other illnesses and diseases both the patient and doctor are confronted by a broad spectrum of issues and relational dynamics which can also nefariously involve confrontation.

The author (Forrest, 2017) has recently seen a few patients manifesting chronic alcohol dependence related to liver disease who for various reasons have refused to be involved in psychotherapy or any forms of addiction-focused "treatment" as one of the pre-cursors for receiving a liver transplant which would in all probability have saved their lives. A diagnosis, decisions regarding treatment options and engaging in personal health care involving payment for services or court-ordered care, care associated with divorce and custody or criminal matters such as DUI, drug abuse or incarceration, and a myriad of other psychosocial real-life matters that place therapists, clinicians, and all parties involved in such transactions related to the complex realities of confrontation.

The following brief case vignettes demonstrate the uses of appropriate, supportive and alliance-enhancing therapist confrontation interventions in the process of early stage alliance development and alliance work.

Case 7

DOCTOR F.: You really felt that you were an "alcoholic" when we first got started in therapy—when you came in to see me with your wife, and we were doing your history—the first few sessions,—you said you had finally "accepted" your alcoholism, and the amount you were drinking those eight months before you came in—a fifth of Jack a day, or more—plus the arrest, the DUI, and all the issues with work and the family—even the 5,000 dollar attorney retainer fee was a big issue—but it sounds like you're not sure about the addiction part of it *now*—I picked up on your "problem drinking" self-reference last week, and then again a bit ago you referred to your "drinking problem"—where do you think you are now with these issues?

BOBBY: I really don't like that word—"alcoholic," and you know, I've never wanted to be called an alcoholic—but you're right, Doc—deep down, I've known I was an alcoholic for ten years—maybe longer, and I was sure as hell was out of control when I came in to see you—plus my wife and kids, and all the trouble—and, the drinking caused all of it and I know that, but it seems to creep back in every time—after I'm sober for a few weeks or months, I start to think maybe I can control my drinking. You know, there was a time when I could control it—drink without any problems—you know, have a few and quit—without getting screwed up, but really that ended three years ago—about the time that Barb and the kids called the cops, and all of that—you know, I don't want to go down that road again.

DOCTOR F.: So, it's kind of okay to refer to yourself as an "alcoholic." You basically realize that you don't like the label, but it does fit—you seem to clearly realize that for whatever reasons, drinking no longer "works" for you—accepting is the hard part of it for you.

BOBBY: Yeah, you got it—and I don't want to hear it . . . not from you, or my wife—not the cops, the kids or anyone—not even from myself—maybe I need to start reminding myself I'm an alcoholic—maybe that is also why I've been struggling with going to AA, I just don't want to hear it—or somehow accept it—you know, who really wants to be an alcoholic?

DOCTOR F.: For sure, none of us want to be sick or have problems—think about all of the people trying to live within any or all of the different diseases—cancer, diabetes, heart—let alone alcoholism or liver disease—all of it.

BOBBY: But I've got to tell you, I'm still not really sure about the "disease" thing and my drinking, or that alcoholism is really a disease—that's part of the problem with AA, and my sponsor—probably therapy too, but it's sure as hell gotten worse over the last four or five years—the drinking—really, I do know that I can't seem to stop once I get started, and it sure as hell has gotten worse—we both know I need to stop, and we agree on that, plus all the trouble I've gotten into—I just need to really start letting myself—and believing it, believe that I can't drink—like you said, it doesn't "work" for me—whether or not it's a disease, and all of that stuff.

DOCTOR F.: We sure agree on one thing, your life has gotten totally unmanageable as a result of your drinking, and it's definitely time for us to do all we can to help you get out of it and stay out of it—like we talked about a few weeks ago about the goals, and recovery plan.

Case 8

CAROL: Things sure have gotten better these last five months—I can't begin to tell you how good it feels now—just to be "straight"—all the trouble I was in, and waking up every morning to all that stress and worry—not knowing what was going to happen next with my practice, and all the embarrassment, guilt, legal stuff with the board—and my family—I know it's all one day at a time now—this recovery stuff, but I never want to go back to all that nightmare again—I've lost so much these last four or five years, and I did it to myself—but I'm not beating up on myself about all of that stuff anymore—before I got into therapy—and, I didn't really trust you or anyone else before—it's taken a while, and like you said, it would get better with time and work—and really working a recovery program—I didn't understand it all then, and to tell the truth, I just didn't think I could do it all—so much work—and I didn't want to do it.

DOCTOR F.: You sure have made a lot of really positive changes over the months, but I can also remember all that stuff you were dealing with at the time—it's not easy, and I definitely sensed your distrust—remember a few of those sessions going over your evaluation results? . . . your lawyer even indicated that the "eval" results would not help your case, plus you were really angry, anxious and agitated about all of it—and you really had very little, if any, motivation or readiness to deal with so many issues at the time—it must have felt like somebody, or somehow, you dropped a ton of bricks on yourself—overwhelming.

CAROL: God, I really don't want to think about all of that—it even makes me nervous—or anxious, and sad to talk about it now—five months and it's all a lot better, but I still really don't like to think about or talk about all of that stuff—like it never happened, but—it did, and I've got to keep focused on dealing with it all—one way or another—different issues on different days, but I sure know how different it all feels today—definitely better, but I still don't understand how I became so out of control in so many ways—I wasn't the same person I used to be, but I feel like I'm getting the "real" me back.

DOCTOR F.: I understand where you're coming from, but like we've discussed a few times over the months, it's important to keep a lot of that old painful stuff from the past in the front of your head—even making a conscious effort to recall many of those painful realities associated with taking the "pain pills," drinking—even the arrest and going to jail, the pain associated with all of it—it also helps to consciously remind yourself that none of these painful realities and experiences basically ever took place in your life before you began taking, abusing or becoming drug dependent—think about it, you never went to jail, you never had significant parenting or marital issues, and hell—you've never even been sued, arrested or in professional trouble before—that's just some of the cognitive or thinking stuff you can realistically use when you're feeling sorry for yourself or starting to think about using again—relapse prevention tools.

CAROL: You know, when I think about these things, I also realize that I lost control of my entire life—almost most all of my life, when I started down that path—and it's scary to face it, but I know it's reality now—it's still painful, but I guess you're right—I need to remind myself—keep some of it in—like you said, in "the front of my head," and also it's real—and we have talked about not being able to change the past, but how things have gotten a lot better now—how I can work on changing today, and that's what I can control—today, and that's what I've learned to do—without the drugs, and all the drama—

DOCTOR F.: A lot of recovery is really about learning from the past and our mistakes—sometimes it's painful for all of us, but real learning also involves the work of changing the old patterns of behavior and thinking, and it sure isn't easy most of the time—working at changing or just trying to be a better person.

Alliance development and work during the initial stage of psychotherapy with addictive disordered persons encompasses the essential therapist-patient tasks and arenas of focus that have been discussed thus far in this chapter. However, a diversity of additional brief therapeutic intervention strategies and techniques can be implemented to facilitate both alliance development and patient motivation for therapy in the early (12–15+ weeks) therapy sessions. Successful therapeutic alliances and therapy relationships require therapist flexibility and the ability to provide skillful and timely multimodal treatment interventions. These early alliance development focused therapist-patient transactions can include didactic and direct teaching or therapist explanation transactions, direct therapist interpretations, exploration of therapist-patient belief system issues, referral for detoxification or possible medically assisted care, and a myriad of other clinically appropriate and patient specific care directed needs.

MIDDLE STAGE ALLIANCE DYNAMICS IN ADDICTIONS FOCUSED PSYCHOTHERAPY AND COUNSELING WORK

As noted earlier in the chapter, a diversity of patient-therapist as well as "real world" factors contribute to the most fundamental issue of patient duration in therapeutic care. Patient related matters pertaining to readiness and motivation for therapy, insurance coverage limits and fees, possible career demands or legal mandates, psychopathology driven dynamics and health are but a few issues which can impact or determine the course, duration and outcome of psychotherapy relationships. Likewise, a multiplicity of therapist and therapist-patient relationship specific factors and variables can shape, determine, and impact every facet of the course of all therapy alliances and relationships.

From a conceptual and clinical perspective, the middle stage of intensive addictions psychotherapy work generally encompasses the third or fourth through sixth months of therapy. Many patients are ready to begin a therapeutic regimen involving every ten days to every other week psychotherapy sessions at this time. Patients manifesting more chronic, severe, and recalcitrant co-morbid psychopathology may need to be encouraged to remain actively engaged in weekly or periodically more frequent therapy sessions during the middle stage of addictions psychotherapy.

Early stage alliance therapeutic work with addictive disordered patients provides much of the basic framework and therapeutic grist for middle stage alliance development and the therapeutic process. Major therapeutic tasks that therapists need to successfully orchestrate and actively implement with addictive disordered persons include (1) sustaining consistently high level therapeutic alliance ingredients, (2) shifting the treatment format and therapeutic focus to a more here-and-now temporal orientation, (3) initiating a therapeutic style that is generally more cognitive behavioral, eclectic or multimodal in scope, and (4) initiating, utilizing, and maintaining therapeutic interventions that address a diversity of patient-specific conflicts and dynamics related to the patient's addictive disorder as well as his or her specific co-morbid adjustment conflicts and pathology.

As discussed throughout this text, addictions clinicians and therapists who consistently provide high level therapeutic alliance and relationship qualities within the context of their work with patients also produce more efficacious therapy outcome. However, as Eubanks-Carter, Muran and Safran (2015) point out, the alliance is an important predictor of outcome, but psychotherapy outcome research evidence indicates that "therapists vary in their abilities to maintain strong alliances." These authors (Eubanks-Carter, Muran and Safran, 2015) emphasize the importance of several therapist skills that facilitate the maintenance of strong alliances: "therapist self-awareness, affect regulation and interpersonal sensitivity, therapist ability to detect and repair alliance ruptures, capacity for self-awareness related to immediate therapeutic experiences, capacity for tolerating "difficult" emotions, good communication skills, curiosity, exploration and collaboration with patients, increasing patient self-awareness , therapist accurate empathy, and therapist acceptance of responsibility related to their alliance rupture contributions." The authors employ these ingredients in their attempts to facilitate the maintenance of strong alliances via alliance-focused training" (pp. 169, 172).

Middle stage psychotherapy work with addictive disordered patients who are highly motivated, exude readiness for change, and also establish and maintain very significant therapeutic gains during the early stage of therapy may paradoxically lend to the therapist's diminished attention to various therapeutic facets associated with providing diminished high-level therapeutic conditions. Therapists may also consciously or pre-consciously assume that these patient's will simply continue on their path of continued growth and recovery, and both the patient and therapist may unconsciously collude in an extended therapeutic "honeymoon" phase in the middle stage of therapy which eventually precipitates or contributes to patient relapse.

The middle stage of addictions psychotherapy also encompasses a diversity of intensified emotional alliance and relational dynamics between the therapist and the patient. These intensified emotional alliance and relational dynamics may also extend to the patient's spouse or family system, and these realities can impact the patient, therapist alliance and therapeutic relationship in a diversity of ways—for better or worse. Patient relapses at this therapeutic juncture and the relational intensification of the alliance may additionally foster the outcropping of potentially disruptive therapeutic process dynamics related to resistance, transference and countertransference. For example, patients may begin to feel that they essentially have "*recovered*" from their addictive disorder and no longer "need" to be in therapy, attempt to self-initiate less frequent therapy sessions, become more resistant to treatment involvement or terminate self-help engagement, resist continued medication management and engagement in other therapy and recovery intervention modalities that have fostered their ongoing recovery process. Patient transference dynamics that impact the therapist and therapeutic alliance in these situations can include thorny and unresolved patient conflicts related to control, anger, authority issues, dependency and self-regulation. These alliance, relational and therapeutic process realities always remain components of the transference-countertransference matrix which continually impact the therapeutic alliance in a diversity of often unpredictable ways (Forrest, 2002).

Middle stage alliance dynamics may also stimulate therapist counter-transference conflicts associated with a wide range of potentially disruptive therapist reactions and issues including frustration and anxiety, self-doubt, control, sense of professional competency, abandonment or a sense of personal rejection, and feelings of anger or even fear. However, it must be realized that the transference-countertransference matrix also continually provides relational-alliance context opportunities for potentiating constructive growth and change upon the part of the therapist, patient and therapeutic relationship. Patients and therapists learn more about themselves and their alliance relationships, and potentially become more constructively sensitive and self-aware as a function of their therapeutic relationship transference and countertransference dynamics. Effective therapist alliance work related to these ongoing therapeutic process dynamics during the middle stage of therapy provide a multifaceted relational learning environment for both patient and therapist which can facilitate constructive patient, therapist and constructive alliance changes. For these reasons, it is of paramount importance that addictions therapists and counselors (Forrest, 2002) consciously understand, identify and be able to consistently manage transference and countertransference material within the psychotherapy alliance relationship context. However, therapist salience (Forrest, 2002, 2012) always limits the parameters of his or her ability to globally manage the various realities and vicissitudes of countertransference and transference within the ongoing context of the therapeutic alliance.

MIDDLE STAGE ALLIANCE DYNAMICS AND HERE-AND-NOW DYNAMICS IN INTEGRATIVE ADDICTIONS-FOCUSED PSYCHOTHERAPY AND COUNSELING WORK

As noted earlier, the focus of early stage addictions therapy work encompasses completing the patient's clinical history, diagnosis and assessment, establishing a patient specific treatment plan and therapeutic goals, development of the over-all treatment structure and format including in-depth genetic reconstruction work, initiating and building the therapist-patient alliance and actively fostering the relationship development process. While a here and now temporal focus is also a very real and important component of all early diagnostic, clinical interviewing, history taking and other essential therapeutic tasks of early stage psychotherapy work with addictive disordered persons, the therapist needs to actively initiate a shift in context involving a primary focus on therapist-patient alliance interactions in the here and now. This middle stage therapeutic strategy and focus on the here and now is therapist directed and orchestrated, and gradually becomes a consistent psychotherapy process dynamic involving the alliance-based tasks, goals and activities of both therapist and patient.

During this phase of addictions psychotherapy, the basic alliance grist of the treatment process remains centered in the here and now facets of the patient's life. Middle stage therapist-patient alliance work is focused on the patient's present behaviors, relationships, beliefs and cognitions, and affects as well as the various facets of everyday living, global adjustment dynamics, and recovery. Therapeutic alliance and the interactive relational specific dynamics between the therapist and patient essentially center on present oriented psychotherapy process interactions. This therapeutic stance helps the patient develop an expanded repertoire of strengths and social skills that can be used beyond the confines of the therapeutic relationship. This process enhances the patient's abilities to deal more effectively with a diversity of present-oriented realities including the struggles and demands of everyday life as well as the challenges of recovery. Patients need to unlearn and re-learn how to live in the present, and solve, resolve and overcome a plethora of problems in the here and now. Ultimately, the patient's addictive brain disease and dysfunctional pathologic past is overcome in large measure through the development of healthy, nurturing and globally constructive relationships as well as interpersonal and intrapersonal realities that constitute the patient's present internal and external worlds.

Psychotherapy cannot change the patient's past, but therapy can help most patients revisit their difficult and dysfunctional histories, and vis a vis the working and productive therapeutic alliance and other adjunctive treatments overcome many of the painful realities of their pasts. This process reinforces and synergizes the patient's various skills and capacities for changing their addictive disease process as well as utilizing a much more adaptive and functional set of social skills, behaviors and interpersonal strengths that are associated with living more productively and constructively in the present.

The therapist's consistent integration, exploration and synthesis of prior early stage therapeutic material related to the patient's past oriented experiences, behavior, feelings, relationships, and internal self-dialogue form an integral component of the shift into the present "here and now" therapeutic focus in middle stage psychotherapy. Within the context of this therapeutic approach, the addictions therapist also helps patients consciously understand, accept, identify, integrate and synthesize this prior therapeutic material relating to many facets of their current lives. The alliance framework provides a therapeutic holding environment in which addictive disordered patients can stop repressing, denying and minimizing the many painful and often traumatic realities of their developmental pasts. This facet of the therapeutic process further reduces the patient's feelings of anxiety, depression, self-system fragmentation, low self-worth, guilt, and other maladaptive adjustment dynamics associated with living life in a far less threatening here and now fashion. These therapeutic strategies and interventions also frequently contribute greatly to the patient's resolve and commitment to the recovery process, and can significantly reduce the life crippling dynamics associated with his or her addictive disease process. These therapeutic interventions simply impact the patient's life in a more rational, reality-oriented and healthy present-centered manner.

Therapists need to supportively and consistently help addictive disordered patients face their past traumas, narcissistic injuries, and dysfunctional experiences. These patients also need to be reminded that they had very little or no control whatsoever over the general and specific circumstances surrounding their parenting experiences and general development during the initial decade of life. At the same time, the therapist maintains an alliance based therapeutic stance that clearly communicates to the patient that he or she has a great deal of control over present behaviors, feelings, relationships, and cognitions associated with sustaining drug, alcohol, and/or the other significant spectrum of pathologic symptoms related to the addictive disorders. Addictive disordered persons eventually exercise healthy control over the course of their recovery lives by consistently actualizing more rational choices, behaviors, decisions and therapeutic recovery facilitated new learning experiences pertaining to virtually every facet of their lives.

Addictions therapists need to consistently and actively explore the addictive disordered patient's thoughts, feelings, impulses and behaviors related to the patient's specific addictive disorder throughout the course of middle stage therapy work. Alliance focus on therapeutic gains, plateaus and regressions, shifting goals or the patient's ongoing structured program for recovery, transference-countertransference dynamics, and the use of relapse prevention counseling strategies (Grinstead, 2014, 2016). Alliance enhancement issues and possible alliance rupture repair work are also key therapist ingredients that characterize the process of effective middle stage therapy work. Alliance facilitated therapeutic work additionally involves an exploration of the patient's preconscious, past and present "triggers," or "set ups" for relapse related to the potential re-engagement in their earlier active addictive disease process. This facet of alliance based therapeutic work frequently becomes a deterrent to full-blown patient relapses, premature therapy terminations, protracted and conflicted or extended alliance rupture repair work involving infrequent catastrophic patient-therapist treatment outcomes.

It is also important at this juncture in therapy for therapists to orchestrate the avoidance of lengthy segments of therapy that are focused around past eating "binges," "drunk-a-logs," gambling wins or great losses, extended cocaine or methamphetamine "runs," and other facets of the spectrum of addictive disorders. Recovering addictions counselors and therapists need to remain vigilant against engaging in extended segments of therapy with their patients that are devoted primarily to personal self-disclosures related to *their* addictive disease, and the specifics of *their* treatment and recovery process. The following brief vignette demonstrates the therapist's role in maintaining a middle stage therapy here-and-now alliance focus with addictive disordered patients.

Case 9

JACK: I did have a lot of good times drinking—hell, I drank hard for fifteen or twenty years, and really didn't have any big problems—no DUI's or jail, and I've got the same wife too—she's stuck with me.

DOCTOR F.: Alcoholism doesn't usually develop overnight—you probably did have positive drinking experiences in the past—but that was a long time ago, and you've sure told me that your life has gone to hell over the past three or four years of drinking—it sure created a lot of problems recently.

JACK: Yeah, it got hard—real bad, like I've said, I stayed drunk for two years before they took me to the hospital for detox—drunk all day, every day—and nights too—it's a wonder I'm still alive, and I don't ever want to go back to the bottle again.

DOCTOR F.: And that's a part of why you came in for therapy three months ago. Let's switch gears—you mentioned last week that you had some recent thoughts about drinking—wondering if you could control your drinking now that you've been sober for a few months, how good "a couple of beers" would taste, that stuff—plus cutting back on therapy, and the AA meetings—when you really *think* about drinking again, or changing your recovery program—doing it on your own—how has that worked out in the past?

JACK: Deep down, I know that it would never work—hell, I've tried to quit a thousand times over the last twenty years—and, I did it once for several months—but that was fourteen years ago—dying scares me, but all of it—going back, makes me nervous just talking about it—to tell you the truth—we've had old friends over to the house a lot this month, and my wife makes sure to stock up the refrigerator with plenty of beer—and they sure drink it up—did I tell you that a couple of weeks ago or so?

DOCTOR F.: So let's get back to the recovery program we put together F.: No, you haven't brought the beer in the refrigerator up at all—and that's probably helped trigger your thoughts about drinking—relapse again recently?

JACK: You know, it kinda pisses me off—I mean that I can't drink and control it, and my wife can but most of my friends can't handle it either—they're drunks too

DOCTOR F.: So let's get back to the recovery program we put together F.: So, what have you been doing to deal with all of these triggers—the things you've been aware of the past couple of weeks that have been upsetting you recently? It sounds like you are definitely upset about the others drinking at your house—you said, you've started thinking about drinking, and thinking or maybe even planning to cut back on your treatment plan. Do you see these changes as triggers, or possible "set ups" for relapse?

JACK: Yeah, I've started realizing that I'm more tense and upset recently, and angry too—so has my wife—she keeps telling me that she feels like she's "walking on egg shells" when she's around me—it could be a "set up." Like you said, and all hell would break loose if I started hittin' it again—Katie bar the door!

DOCTOR F.: So let's get back to the recovery program we put together a few months ago; what can you—or what do we need to do *now*, to get you back on track—so to speak—perhaps we need to meet twice a week for a few weeks, and we've discussed short term Antabuse or naltrexone maintenance in the past—how about some of the other treatment alternatives we touched on over the months?

The here-and-now focus in middle stage addictions therapy work encompasses the use of many cognitive-behavioral and eclectic therapies and interventions. Furthermore, the evolving psychotherapy, counseling and behavioral health professions continue to develop new and ever-changing techniques, models of therapy, and intervention strategies specific to the additive disorders as well as all other forms of dysfunctional human behavior.

MIDDLE STAGE ALLIANCE DYNAMICS IN COGNITIVE BEHAVIORAL THERAPY AND ECLECTIC THERAPY IN INTEGRATIVE ADDICTIONS-FOCUSED PSYCHOTHERAPY AND COUNSELING WORK

During the middle stage of addictions focused psychotherapy, therapists utilize various specific cognitive-behavioral treatment techniques and various other therapeutic modalities and strategies in order to help their patients resolve or modify a diversity of maladaptive behaviors and human problems. Cognitive-behavioral and integrative therapy interventions can be highly effective and widely utilized tools that are currently used to treat the spectrum of addictive disorders. These therapy interventions have provided a 65-year evidence-based efficacious approach to the treatment of addictive disorders as well as a broad spectrum of psychological disorders and adjustment problems (Berger, Boettcher, and Caspar, 2014; Berggraf et al., 2014; Ellis and Harper, 1961; Lazarus, 1981; Forrest, 2012, 2017; Vittengl et al., 2015).

Cognitive-behavior therapy techniques need to be integratively used to enhance and supplement the therapeutic efficacy of alliance-focused psychodynamic, person centered, reality therapy and various other psychotherapeutic approaches. Indeed, contemporary addictions therapists and treatment providers generally employ individual patient based integrative therapies and modalities which also frequently incorporate a diversity of self-help (Alcoholics Anonymous, Al-Anon, Smart-Stop, OA, GA, etc.) interventions as well as non-traditional, alternative, therapeutic or medically based forms of care. Enhanced CBT therapeutic interventions for addictive disordered patients can actively address and provide a therapeutic basis for constructive patient growth and change associated with a wide range of dysfunctional and maladaptive patient cognitions, behaviors, affects, self-regulation, and various other biopsychosocial health and adjustment dynamisms.

CBT therapy interventions are generally based upon the principles of learning theory and applied learning therapy (Forrest, 1984, 1997) which generally incorporate three priMaryssumptions regarding maladaptive patterns of behavior: (1) all voluntary behavior is learned, (2) since behavior is learned, it can be "unlearned" or extinguished, and (3) the "problem" area is the maladaptive behavior per se. Maladaptive or ineffective patterns of human behavior including self-talk, beliefs and cognitions, relational patterns and social dynamics, affective expressions, and self-regulation. These facets of human behavior are essentially produced by learning, conditioning, learned responses and nothing more. Most simply put, CBT treatments may be seen as attempts to modify or extinguish maladaptive or inefficient patterns of thinking, behaving and emoting. From this perspective, addictions therapists focus upon the therapeutic tasks and strategies that can be implemented to change and extinguish many facets of the addictive disordered patient's maladaptive patterns of thinking, behaving and emoting.

It is important for addictions therapists to be able to both diagnose and apply CBT and other treatment interventions accurately, appropriately, and in accord with the individual needs of each patient. For example, most alcohol dependent, opioid dependent and sedative dependent patients manifest co-morbid generalized anxiety disorder and/or other anxiety driven disorders including social anxiety disorders and related OCD personality disorder features. In accord with the Khantzian and Albanese (2008) self-medication model or theory of addiction, these patient populations are biopsychosocially prone to the development of these particular additive disorders because these additive substances and chemical agents also directly affect the peripheral and central nervous systems in a manner which temporally acts to greatly reduce and/or extinguish the human experience of anxiety. These agents pharmacologically and psychologically dampen and extinguish the patient's feelings of tension, stress, fear and acute anxiety in a dose related manner which persists for protracted intervals of time with the eventual establishment of sustained use, dependence, sustained tolerance and the development of the addictive disease process.

The addictive disordered patient's initially neurotic and maladaptive repertoire of substance-related and sustaining addictive behaviors eventually become progressively habitual or chronic, dysfunctional, and maladaptive. Eventually, this aspect of the developmental addictive brain disease process breaks down completely and frequently results in the outcropping of extreme patient experiences of anxiety, terror, tremors ("shakes"), possible brief psychosis, and the various clinical features of acute withdrawal. This sequence of clinical events also frequently facilitates the need for patient medical hospitalization, brief or extended detox episodes involving controlled and tapered withdrawal from the particular addictive substances. However, eventual substance abstinence with efficacious therapeutic care may also result in patient recoveries as a faction of this process.

CBT therapy interventions in therapeutic work with addictive disordered clinical populations often includes specific therapist interventions involving the use of relaxation training, mindfulness, thought stopping, hypnosis, imagery training, role playing and rehearsal, biofeedback, EMDR, emotive expression, assertion training, behavioral contracting, chemical or verbal aversion therapy, DBT, yoga, sensitization and desensitization, stress management techniques, meditation, energy or bioenergetic work and other modalities.

Contingent upon the therapist's level of practice skills and training, many of these eclectic therapeutic modalities can be effectively utilized within the context of the therapeutic alliance relationship and the ongoing psychotherapeutic process. Effective early stage alliance work can enhance the development of an ongoing alliance environment which is conducive to alliance-based uses of rather specific CBT interventions during the middle stage therapy process. These interventions can be directed at patient addiction related or driven maladaptive patterns of adjustment associated with anxiety, depression, low self-esteem, impulse control and self-regulation, anger control, PTSD, social skills including parenting skills, fear and phobic behavior, perfectionism, sexual issues and the gamut of human problems. Therapist's need to didactically teach and assist patients with learning and practicing the various skill sets which are associated with many of these CBT interventions. In essence, the therapeutic alliance provides an ongoing relational framework in which addictive disordered patients have the opportunity to learn, try out, and practice a wide spectrum of new and more adaptive skills, behaviors, patterns of thinking, emoting, and interpersonal relatedness. Significant constructive changes in these domains of human living also enhance constructive patient growth and change in the realm of recovery from the addictive disease process as well as the patient's global functioning.

Addictions therapists may also choose to refer patients who evince various specific therapeutic intervention needs to professional colleagues that have been trained and specialized in the use of interventions related to their patient's particular needs. These situations often involve rather brief (less than 10 sessions) therapy work with a colleague. More protracted ancillary therapeutic work with a colleague can become somewhat disruptive to the ongoing process of therapy with the primary therapist, but these situations can be ethically dictated and quite frequently patients and therapists are benefitted by such transactions. It is imperative for all addictions therapists to remain consciously aware of the parameters of their personal therapeutic armamentarium, and to practice with the scope of their practice skill sets.

The therapeutic alliance also represents a consistent real world "training experience" for the patient. The working and productive therapeutic alliance fosters patient identification with the therapist, and the vicarious patient learning experiences involving the therapist in this context often include emulation, modeling and the incorporation or internalization of many of the therapist's prosocial behaviors, values and adjustment dynamics. In this context, patients and therapists must continually experience and deal with the many facets of transference and countertransference on a regular basis. This facet of the alliance relationship often facilitates significant changes and positive therapeutic gains associated with the patient's general set of social skills and interpersonal adjustment style. As Bandura (1969) noted many years ago, most learning phenomena resulting from direct experiences can occur on a vicarious basis as a result of the observation of other individuals' behaviors, and the consequences of their behaviors. Addictive disordered persons have frequently spent thousands of hours learning, modeling, emulating and practicing a myriad of socially inappropriate, unacceptable, dysfunctional and often socially "bizarre" behaviors within the context of their familial interactions, self-experiential world, and their addictive interpersonal life. These patient realities and dynamics are therapeutically germane to the consistent therapeutic identification, exploration, interpretation and resolution of many patient addictive disease related maladaptive social behaviors.

Focused and intensive affect-specific work also constitutes an important facet of middle stage psychotherapy with addictive disordered patients. This therapeutic work takes place within the alliance framework and again, a working and productive alliance relationship involving the therapist's and patient's capacities for effecting mutually reparative alliance work and activities results in successful therapy outcomes. Helping addictive patients appropriately express, recognize and identify or label various affective states and emotions during early stage therapy is an important arena of therapy. This general process is intensified within the context of the transference-countertransference matrix (Forrest, 2002) during the middle stage of psychotherapy

Integrative cognitive-behavioral and more dynamically-focused therapeutic strategies and interventions consistently help addictive disordered patients openly discuss and modify or resolve a diversity of issues associated with a wide range of feelings and emotions. Premature intensive affective work with addicts can precipitate intense patient emotional reactions that contaminate and/or significantly erode the therapeutic alliance equilibrium, and may ultimately contribute to alliance rupture, and therapy related relapses or terminations. This therapist (Forrest, 2018) has indicated that addictions therapists need to remain vigilant about matters pertaining to patient emotional sensitivity, affect regulation, and cathartic expression during this stage of therapy. Effective therapists also consistently attempt to titrate the depth, length of time, and content of emotionally upsetting and expressive therapeutic exploration work with these patients. The therapeutic exploration, interpretative and over all process associated with reducing and resolving patient maladaptive behaviors, cognitions and affect regulation or management often stems from relational conflicts associated with (1) early life narcissistic injury trauma and subsequent chronic interpersonal and intrapersonal dysfunction, (2) chronic affect regulation disturbance involving anxiety, depression, anger, and low self-worth, (3) characterological rigidity and the patient's addictive brain disease related avoidance defense system, (4) identity and sexual conflicts, and sometimes includes (5) a self-defeating and ultimately sadomasochistic character style. Needless to say, these various biopsychosocial realities can be associated with very difficult life-realities that have long remained profound sources of internal and external conflict for the patient.

Addictions therapists need to supportively and very sensitively help their patients explore these issues, and they also need to consistently interpret and explain to the patient how and why these processes originated, and how they have continued to adversely impact and maintain the patient's current addictive disordered adjustment style. These essential therapeutic tasks and goals frequently cannot be actualized in the absence of a sustained working and productive therapeutic alliance involving a focus on affect regulation and emotional stabilization.

MIDDLE STAGE ALLIANCE DYNAMICS, INSIGHT, INTERPRETATION AND SELF-AWARENESS IN INTEGRATIVE ADDICTIONS-FOCUSED PSYCHOTHERAPY AND COUNSELING WORK

Facilitating enhanced patient insight and self-awareness are basic goals and ingredients that have long been associated with the process of most effective psychotherapies. The actual development of patient insight and self-awareness begins in the process of early therapy, and these goals and processes are enhanced and most saliently accomplished during the middle and later stages of addictions therapy work. During middle stage therapy, the working and productive alliance relationship continues to be a vehicle for the therapist's active in-depth and greatly enhanced use of interpretation techniques. Patients are generally much more self-aware, insightful and receptive to the emotional alliance-based work that is involved in the process of exploring and constructively responding to the therapist's interpretations. The earlier stage therapeutic foundational work involving collaboratively examining and "making sense" of the patient's global history and dysfunctional addictive disordered adjustment style greatly improves the patient's capacities and strengths which are prerequisite to the process of internalizing, exploring and therapeutically examining and responding to the therapist's active interpretations.

The therapist's use of interpretation, insight and self-awareness techniques and strategies during this juncture in the therapeutic process also need to be timely, supportive and sustained in an alliance context that involves consistently providing high level therapeutic conditions. These alliance ingredients provide the basis for the patient's ability to use interpretative material in a constructive, controlled, and rationally internalized manner which operates in the service of the patient's growth and recovery process. Healthy growth and behavioral change take place, in part, as a result of the patient's abilities to internalize insight and expand reality-oriented self-awareness associated with the therapist's various interpretations that are related to a wide range of past and present patient experiences, thoughts and beliefs, emotions, behaviors and adjustment dynamisms. Patient resistance, anxiety, denial, distortions or projections, and fears that may be associated with the therapist's interpretations related to insight and self-awareness facilitating interventions in early therapy tend to be greatly dissipated during the middle stage of therapy vis á via the establishment of a consistent working and productive therapeutic alliance context. The patient's preconscious and unconscious levels of personal experience also become more accessible to therapeutic exploration during this stage of therapy. This heightened level of patient personal awareness fosters or further synergizes the patient's general level of self-awareness and insight.

The patient's middle stage therapy transference reactions and dynamics additionally become grist for active and non-threatening therapeutic exploration. This facet of the alliance and therapeutic process also may contribute very significantly to the patient's capacity to use interpretation-based self-awareness, insight and strength dynamics for personal growth and recovery. Likewise, the protracted stability of a working and productive middle stage alliance relationship actively synergizes the therapist's abilities to more openly, actively, intensively and selectively share countertransference material and dynamics directly with the patient in a manner which (1) does not threaten the integrity of the alliance, and (2) further enhances the patient's level of self-exploration, ability to internalize insight, and incorporate a greater reality-oriented sense of self, and (3) function more effectively and adaptively in a global manner within the context of his or her "real-world" relational interactions.

Addictions-focused counselors and psychotherapists will find it very useful to review the three-stage helping skills training model (exploration, insight, action, self-disclosure) publications of (C.E. Hill and others C. Hill, C.E., 2004, 2005, 2014; XULI, Kivlighan, D.M., Jr., Hill, C.E. et al., 2018) related to this chapter.

The following case study and brief psychotherapy vignette demonstrate the importance uses of early stage patient case history material, and the subsequent middle stage implementation and alliance related therapeutic uses in CBT, eclectic, and insight, interpretation and self-awareness in addictions psychotherapy.

Case 10

Barb, was a 67-year-old woman who entered out-patient psychotherapy with the author following completion of a brief psychiatric hospitalization for "brief detox," and completion of a subsequent 28-day residential chemical dependency treatment program. These earlier treatment episodes were associated with a prior 30-year clinical history of physician prescribed sedative (valium) abuse and florid dependency. Barb had originally been prescribed a 10mg dose of valium for social anxiety by her family physician. The patient's family physician continued to prescribe her valium until the time of his retirement some twenty years later; he then referred her to a colleague for continued care. The patient reportedly "always took her valium the way it was prescribed." When her husband passed away five years later, the patient experienced heightened feelings of anxiety, began having rather frequent panic attacks, became progressively isolated and home bound, depressed and repeatedly verbalized that she had "lost her mind." During this time frame, her family physician had boosted her daily valium prescription to a 30mg regimen. Barb eventually experienced an apparent complete collapse of the ego which resulted in her psychiatric and chemical dependency related residential care experiences. The patient reported during the completion of her biopsychosocial history and in her early therapy work that she recalled very little of her initial ten day in-patient psychiatric "detox" care, but indicated that following the first couple of weeks of residential chemical dependency treatment she became somewhat more lucid, less agitated, anxious and confused, but also began experiencing frightening feelings of detachment and depersonalization. Her counselor and other staff at the residential program provided support, and reassurance that she would eventually feel "like her old self;" however, she was also repeatedly told that the program staff had "never before treated" a sedative dependent person who had remained drug (sedative) dependent for thirty years, and thus they did not know how long it would take for her to "get better."

Barb's brief biopsychosocial clinical history encompassed growing up in a small rural farming community as an only child, being raised by seemingly nurturing and functional parents, being a good student including her eventual graduation from high school and college, and a successful 27-year career involving teaching high school. She also reported that her marital relationship had always been "good," her only child (son) had experienced "some difficulties" during adolescence but eventually became a successful professional man with a "great wife and family," and her general family history reportedly included one paternal "alcoholic" uncle. The client also had no prior history of psychiatric or substance abuse treatment, individual, marital or family therapy or self-help involvement, and she also had no significant prior legal, medical other major adjustment difficulties.

This patient was motivated for therapy when initially seen, and she remained actively engaged in weekly and bi-weekly individual psychotherapy with the author for nearly three years. She was an active and constructive participant in the alliance development and maintenance component of therapy, and she remained totally sedative and other drug abstinent through the course of her therapy. Barb also participated on a near weekly basis in the author's weekly education and recovery support group during the course of psychotherapy. The client had long manifested a social anxiety disorder prior to entering therapy and initiating her detox and residential treatment; however, the loss of her husband had also significantly exacerbated her anxiety disorder, resulted in depression associated with profound feelings of loss, and synergized a number of other issues related to dependence, co-dependency, and feelings of grief, inadequacy, loneliness, as well as a sense of "being lost and confused." Barb repeatedly verbalized in early stage therapy "I don't know who I am anymore," and continually asked for the therapist's reassurance that she would "be my old self again." She also repetitively inquired about "how long" it would take for her to "recover her former self," and manifested real concerns about getting old and her emotional and physical decline.

The following therapy vignette was taken from a therapy session with the patient during her fourth month of individual psychotherapy with the author.

BARB: I do remember when we talked about how easy it can be to get hooked or—addicted to the valium, and how my doctor never explained it to me, and I didn't know—and I always took it like he told me to for all those years, and it sure helped for a long time—it helped when you had me read that short medical article about those drugs, and the risks—the information about getting addicted, and withdrawal—the risks—that really helped to understand, and stop blaming myself—plus those Narcotics Anonymous meetings you finally got me to attend—some of them were scary at first, and you always pointed out my denial about a lot of it, and kinda made me mad at you back then—but that helped too—at least I got out of it, and a lot of those people were really having problems—a lot worse than me.

DOCTOR F.: You've been able to see what happened more clearly—a better understand of your addiction, and accepting the realities of where it led to—and the process more clearly over the months—by being out of it, and making a lot of really constructive changes—and I also hear you saying—that in retrospect, the early goals and therapy tasks or homework assignments we put together helped too . . . I know it's difficult at first, just the nature of accepting the realities of where you're at in life—seeing yourself as an addict, or beginning to dig out of it—being motivated for recovery.

BARB: I don't even know how long I was in complete denial, about all of it, but I sure felt different and knew I didn't feel okay that last year or so—before I ended up in the hospital, but when I started to get better the last week or so in rehab, and after we began meeting plus the support group—I started to really feel like I could make it without the valium—and the resentments started to go away too—I could really sense you here helping me—now I really didn't have anxiety about coming to see you or being in group—really, I look forward to our meetings, and you know, I feel like I've made the first real friend in ten years at group—Sally has really helped me too—she's been in recovery for over twenty-five years, and when she told me—and she brings that up in group too at times, all of it has helped me have hope—whatever lies ahead in the future, and I'm not nervous about all that stuff now. I can face it all now, but I sure don't want to dwell on it now.

DOCTOR F.: All of that has helped, and you've been the major catalyst in your therapy and recovery—and it all shows, like I've said to you over the past few weeks, and you've heard it in the group from a number of people too, you look so different—maybe ten years younger, you're laughing and really involved, and think of all you've accomplished—you've become really computer—high tech savvy, and optimistic about the future—all of it—we have really worked together on a lot of issues, but you've really worked hard to make your life better.

BARB: A lot has changed, you're right—and it's all been for the good—I feel so much better about myself, and less anxious—it's really hard to believe when I think about it and I'm not worrying about the future all the time—going to the Apple store and getting the help with my computer and I-phone has helped so much—I don't feel like I'm old and lost in this high-tech world anymore—like I'm able to understand a lot of things better—just more aware, and I don't want to go back to what I had become—ever, and I know it's early—one day at a time, but I feel like I can keep going—be a better or stronger person.

MIDDLE STAGE ALLIANCE DYNAMICS AND RESISTANCE, TRANSFERENCE AND COUNTERTRANSFERENCE IN INTEGRATIVE ADDITIONS-FOCUSED PSYCHOTHERAPY AND COUNSELING WORK

Resistance is a concept that can be used to describe the addictive disordered patient's various behaviors, thoughts, emotions and interpersonal movements away from treatment engagement, and involving the psychotherapy alliance and relationship, recovery process, and various other ancillary recovery-based care modalities. Most experienced addictions therapists clearly recognize that addictive patients are generally quite ambivalent about initiating psychotherapy or other treatment modalities. It is also very difficult for some patients to remain committed to the ongoing work of the therapy process as well as the process of attempting to change a spectrum of ancillary maladaptive and dysfunctional behaviors. Simply put, addicts manifest differing types and varieties of treatment resistance throughout the various stages of therapy and the recovery process. These alliance dynamics and therapist-patient relationship realities likewise impact the therapeutic alliance in a diversity of ways.

As noted earlier (Forrest, 1997), addictive disordered patients who are not motivated for therapy and do not manifest sufficient readiness for change frequently terminate treatment during the early stage of therapy. As a group, these patients also frequently lack the interpersonal skills and relational readiness set that are prerequisite to the capacity for efficacious alliance formation. The patient's current addictive brain disease state forms the nexus of symptoms associated with these patients severely restricted capacities for establishing working and productive therapeutic alliances.

The middle stage of addictions therapy also encompasses various alliance and therapeutic relationship dynamics that can erode and eventually result in alliance discord or alliance ruptures. Relapse or multiple brief relapses constitute a very salient dynamic that can be profoundly damaging to the alliance and therapeutic process. Relapse and repetitive patterns of relapse also constitute a major source of ongoing alliance threat and alliance rupture throughout the course of ongoing therapeutic work involving addictive disordered persons.

During the middle stage of therapy patients are often challenged by the process of beginning to consciously recognize, understand and actively struggle with their various sources of psychotherapy treatment resistance. This struggle can reactivate intense feelings of anxiety, resentment and other upsetting patient affects and cognitions. A full-blown relapse into the patient's prior active disease state is perhaps the best and worst clinical example of resistance. Cancelling therapy sessions, missing or forgetting sessions, consistently being late for therapy sessions, missing or refusing to attend self-help meetings, discontinuing an exercise regimen, and "forgetting" to take prescribed medications can also be viewed as classic forms of patient treatment resistance. Failure to pay for therapy or consistently late payments may be additional indications of the patient's resistance. These patient patterns of resistance-based behavior impede the therapeutic and recovery process, further undermine the patient's motivation and commitment to therapy, and actively and directly jeopardize the therapeutic alliance. These dynamics frequently result in patient relapses.

These various facets of patient middle stage therapy resistance clearly encompass transference-based conflicts and dynamics. Patient transference conflicts often become overtly and acutely manifest within the alliance context during the middle stages of addictions psychotherapy work. As Freud (1953) indicated, transference generally refers to the patient's distorted or neurotic responses to the therapist and the psychotherapy relationship. More specifically, transference impacts and takes place within the alliance context. In essence, transference encompasses the patient's distorted or parataxic early-life experiences and emotions that stem largely from prior early-life parental and familial-interpersonal interactions. The emotional intensity, relational closeness and intimacy, enhanced self-awareness, and insights that addictive disordered patients may experience in the alliance framework can result in regressive patterns of behaviors involving such things as relating to the therapist as a bad father or authority figure, mother figure, or incorporating significant others that foster historically conflictual personal experiences. The patient's authority conflicts, impulse control difficulties, need for independence, obstinance, affective conflicts, intimacy issues, cognitive distortions, and generalized neurotic behaviors as well as addiction specific struggles can be exacerbated as a result of transference phenomenon in the therapeutic alliance.

The addictive disordered patient's transference distortions tend to be repressed and relatively well-controlled during the initial weeks of therapy; however, following a few months of early stage recovery and ongoing active psychotherapeutic engagement, more frequent and potentially more acute alliance threatening dynamics often evolve. Interestingly, the early psychoanalysts and therapists (Fenichel, 1945; Freud, 1953; Kernberg, 1975) indicate that the therapeutic resolution of the transference neurosis constitutes the essence of effective treatment. Fenichel (1945) went so far as to indicate that a therapeutic "cure" can only be affected through the successful therapeutic resolution of the transference neurosis.

Within the context of contemporary addictions therapy work, the ability of the therapist and patient to constructively manage and resolve a diversity of transference issues via the working and productive middle stage therapy alliance is certainly a core facet of highly effective treatment and successful recovery outcomes. It is also important for addictions counselors and therapists to remember that (1) the psychotherapy alliance relationship spontaneously contributes to the development of transference, and (2) therapists need to allow transference dynamics and the transference related alliance relationship dynamics to develop. Transference and a related myriad of alliance dynamics help reveal many of the patient's most basic conflicts and the sources of many relational as well as addiction related problems. Therapists should not avoid or attempt to suppress the patient's transference reactions. Rather, the therapist needs to (1) experience the patient's alliance based transference reactions, (2) maintain a consistently supportive and explorative therapeutic stance of technical neutrality in this realm, (3) consistently point out and therapeutically interpret, explore, and supportively help the patient consciously recognize and understand how his and her transference reactions are manifestations of prior relational and real world realities the patient has experienced in the past. These reactions may be related or totally unrelated to what is occurring within the context of the current psychotherapy alliance and therapeutic relationship. The therapist also needs to differentiate self from the patient's ongoing transference imagoes, and help the patient more clearly recognize and identify personal transference dynamics related to the past which may have contributed to his or her addictive brain disease and generalized patterns of dysfunctional behavior. These therapeutic techniques and strategies set the stage for the therapist to initiate the use of a number of CBT, didactic, psychoeducational, and other therapeutic modalities which can significantly improve and enhance the patient's global level of functioning.

Middle stage therapy patient transference reactions and dynamics stimulate and may spontaneously synergize the outcropping of therapist countertransference reactions. Countertransference in psychotherapy (Fenichel, 1945; Forrest, 1982, 2002; Maroda, 1994; Reik, 1948; Searles, 1987) refers to the therapist's inappropriate and neurotic reactions to the patient within the context of the therapeutic relationship and the evolving alliance process. Countertransference reactions can result in psychonoxious alliance shifts, alliance ruptures, and poor treatment outcomes. The therapist's unresolved personal conflicts associated with a diversity of issues can result in countertransference problems in the alliance and therapy relationship at any juncture in the therapeutic process. Some addictions therapists remain unaware or insensitive relative to their personal countertransference issues. This therapist scotomization response also can systemically contribute to consistent poor therapeutic outcomes. Therapist training and education as well as experience and supervision are essential to the effective management of countertransference issues in addictions therapy.

Countertransference difficulties can be associated with such factors as therapist denial, anxiety, insensitivity, emotional over-reactiveness, depression, personal early life trauma and narcissistic injury, perfectionism, personal recovery dynamics, abandonment, anger, dependence, "rescuing" behaviors, avoidance and intimacy conflicts, and difficulties related to providing sufficient warmth, empathy, genuineness, and other therapeutic ingredients that are essential to successful patient treatment outcomes. For example, patient relapses following a few months of recovery and productive therapeutic work may trigger the therapist's role shift from being a supportive and therapeutically nurturing alliance object to a disappointed and covertly angry patient persecutor. These transactions tend to threaten the therapist's sense of competence, and sometimes further erode patient confidence in the therapist, psychotherapy alliance and treatment process. This process may further synergize the active relapse disease process. Countertransference matters can be closely tied to the therapist's self-esteem, narcissism, sense of self-worth, professional sense of competence, and more global experiential life history. Needless to say, repetitive patterns of alliance behaviors associated with active patient disagreements with the therapist, anger, acting-out, treatment non-compliance, and a pattern of repeated patient failures in prior therapy work can precipitate severe countertransference reactions.

Controlled countertransference feelings, thoughts, and reactions can often become useful and constructive therapeutic ingredients in middle stage addictions therapy alliance work and throughout the course of addictions therapy. As Searles (1987) noted, the therapist's keen awareness and controlled management of personal countertransference reactions during the very early stages of therapy can be especially informative in the realm of diagnostic work. Forrest (2002) and Maroda (1994) have also indicated that the experienced therapist's skillful, timely, and sensitive sharing of countertransference material can also strengthen the therapeutic alliance and enhance the patient's ability to change vis a via the direct feedback and interpersonal learning experiences that can be gleaned through the use of this technique. Addictions therapists may find the author's text Countertransference in Chemical Dependency Counseling (Forrest, 2002), to be a very useful resource that deals with a wide range of issues related specifically to the psychotherapy, alliance relationship, and treatment of the addictive disorders.

The following therapy vignette demonstrates middle stage addictions psychotherapy resistance, transference and countertransference alliance related dynamics as well as therapist strategies that can be implemented to constructively manage or resolve these facets of the psychotherapeutic process.

Case 11

DOCTOR F.: Mary, I'm glad to see you today—you had missed our last three scheduled sessions, and that's why I called—plus you hadn't missed a session in three months, and during our last session we really had focused on your apprehension about your brother coming and the family reunion—you seemed anxious about all of it, and we talked about being pro-active, setting boundaries, and relapse risk associated with the sexual abuse.

MARY: You told me that I really needed to ask myself if I was ready to be around my brother—that it would be okay to exclude him, but I felt I could handle all of them—but I couldn't, and I ended up being drunk for two weeks—at least I didn't have to go to detox again, but I think I've learned my lesson—I just can't be around him—it brings back all those issues and feelings, and I've always had problems setting boundaries and believing or trusting others. Both of my parents were always messing around, and like I told you, I caught my mom having sex with one of my dad's best friends in our house when I was fourteen years old.

DOCTOR F.: There was no way that I knew you *would* relapse, but you said your brother sexually abused you for ten years—and you had only been sober for three months, and you're also possibly looking at trying to get a liver transplant if you keep drinking—a lot of issues on the line, and we have been talking about how you have had a long history of doing things your way, difficulties with trusting males in particular, and the addictive sexual risks you've been taking for years. Those family of origin issues have continued to play out in a lot of the trauma of your life, but we need to really work on your commitment to healthy self-care—plus in spite of the men you've been involved with over the years, we're not all in the same basket. These issues tend to continue to play themselves out over and over again, but at this point it simply might be helpful for you to remind yourself from time to time that I'm not your father, all families are different, and *we* know that you are certainly capable of being sober and out of the addictive sexual stuff—plus all of the other strengths you have—you had a sponsor, did you call your sponsor before or after the relapse? I've also encouraged you to call the office if you're in crisis—part of that is trusting or believing that I can help you get better—but it takes both of us.

MARY: I know I have trouble asking for help, and really I don't trust men or women—and I was really stressed about the whole family coming to stay with me—I get along with all of them except Bob, but I didn't feel right about excluding him. And I do trust you—a lot more than I did when I first came in, and you even remind me a little bit of my favorite uncle—ha, ha. Staying at my sister's house was really fun and—it was a safe place—the drinking and sex stuff began at our home—it involved all of us, one way or another, and I sure don't want to destroy myself over all of that—and I look forward to seeing you. I really felt like I screwed up—and let you down when I relapsed this time, but it wasn't that bad and sure didn't last three or four months—or five years—and I want to stay in therapy—I'm not going to give up this time.

DOCTOR F.: I was concerned about you. When patient's all of a sudden stop coming in and don't let us know what's going on, it can definitely be a bit anxiety producing—most of us understand all too well where relapses can take people. Do you think we need to begin meeting once or twice a week again for a while, and how do you feel about briefly revisiting some of the goals and different aspects of the recovery plan we developed a few months ago?

MIDDLE STAGE ALLIANCE DYNAMICS AND MAINTENANCE OF THE ADDICTION FOCUS IN INTEGRATIVE ADDICTIONS-FOCUSED PSYCHOTHERAPY AND COUNSELING WORK

As noted earlier, it is essential for addictions therapists to maintain an addictions-focus throughout the course of psychotherapy. Most addictive disordered persons are initially seen for treatment as a result of their particular addictive disorder. Thus, both therapist and patient tend to be spontaneously focused on a spectrum of patient specific addictive disease issues during the early stage of addictions psychotherapy.

Sometimes it becomes all too easy for the therapist and patient to fail to sustain an addiction focus as the psychotherapeutic process moves into the middle and late stages of treatment. The author (Forrest, 1985, 1994, 1997, 2010) has observed that the failure to maintain an ever-present addiction focus during the middle and later stages of therapy tends to occur most frequently in cases where the patient has evidenced very significant gains in early therapy, and the therapeutic alliance has also directly contributed to the patient's global recovery focus earlier in the therapeutic process. When addictive disordered patient's establish and sustain early stage alcohol or drug abstinence, smoke cessation and nicotine abstinence, lose significant weight or gain much needed weight, and successfully extinguish a variety of malignant patterns of addictive sexual behavior or terminate a long standing destructive gambling pattern, it may be surprisingly easy for both therapist and patient to unconsciously collude, "forget," "lose sight," repress, and/or deny the fundamental primary overt reason the patient initially engaged in therapy. In this respect, it can be helpful for therapists and patients to continue to periodically explore and discuss the old AA based adage "alcoholics and addicts are always only one drink or "slip" away from a "drunk" or drug relapse. While this reference is clearly not always an ever-present reality, it clearly bears credence relative to the relapse dynamics that can be associated with the spectrum of addictive disorders at any juncture in the treatment or recovery process.

Simply put, after several months of recovery and global constructive adjustment change, the therapeutic alliance can be very negatively impacted or even ruptured during the middle stage of addiction psychotherapy due to therapist and patient unconscious collusion and collective dyadic denial of the patient's addictive disease process vis a via a failure to maintain an addiction-based focus during this stage of treatment. This general process (Forrest, 1984, 1997, 2016) has also been referred to as an "unconscious therapeutic conspiracy" involving the therapist, patient and therapeutic alliance associated with the therapist's fundamental inability to recognize and effectively manage the "therapeutic honeymoon" facets of the early stage of addictions-focused psychotherapy work.

In juxtaposition to the loss of an appropriate addiction focus in middle stage addiction psychotherapy work, clinicians also need to remain sensitive to the issue of avoiding the utilization of an over-determined addictions focus during the middle stage of therapy. Paradoxically and historically, psychotherapy and various other treatment modalities specific to the addictive disorders have been focally limited to an all too frequent addiction focus only! Many addictions counselors and therapists historically fail to address the many and diverse primary or secondary factors that are associated with their patient's addictive disorders. Effective therapeutic work with these patients transcends the addiction focus, and involves active and efficacious therapeutic modification of a wide range of behaviors, affects, cognitions and interpersonal as well as intrapersonal dynamics specific to the addictive brain disease process.

A balanced, systematic, consistent, and ongoing addiction focus is always central to successful therapeutic work with addictive-disordered patients. Helping patients understand and constructively change or resolve dysfunctional life-style patterns that are secondary or tertiary to the patient's addictive disease process is another facet of the working and productive alliance relationship which fosters successful therapy outcomes and ongoing recovery process. Therapists need to actively explore and interpret the patient's alliance related maneuvers, and foster patient skill sets that are designed to either 1) enhance the therapeutic process of sustaining a healthy ongoing therapeutic alliance, and 2) sustain a balanced and appropriate addiction focus throughout the ongoing course of therapy. Therapists also need to avoid becoming fixated upon the constricted and very limited realm of addiction focus.

The following therapy vignette provides an example of late middle stage addiction focused therapeutic work with a recovering alcoholic patient who previously manifested a severe long-term clinical history of active and chronic alcohol dependence.

Case 12

> JACK: Yeah, I guess it still bothers me a bit when we get back into the "old stuff," about my drinking in the past—it's still kinda

upsetting to talk about all the crazy shit I did—and especially how I used to hurt my wife, and kids—but it doesn't bother me that much anymore, I mean now that I'm not drinking—plus I know I can't drink—I think I've really accepted that part of it.

DOCTOR F.: But it still bothers you some when I bring up the past drinking episodes, or we get back to some of those painful drinking related experiences you went through—remember a couple of sessions ago when you were "wondering if," you could have a drink or two now that you've been sober for so long, and how we ended up dealing with that topic for half the session?

JACK: Yes I do—and when it comes up in here, it also reminds me of how many hundreds of times I've tried to control my drinking over the years, and all those failures—even if it took two or three months to be really out of control, and the DUI's and all the shit I put myself and everybody through—I've paid the lawyers thousands of dollars over the years, and all of it—I've damned near killed myself, and probably a lot of others other the years—plus all the trips to hospitals, the treatment centers and my family stuff. No, I don't need any of it again, and I don't ever want to be like I was before I started seeing you—it all just really makes me sick about myself to think about it—but I guess I'll always need to keep some of the painful stuff in my head—remind myself of it all from time to time, and like you've always said, it helps to share—disclose this stuff to your sponsor or therapist at times.

DOCTOR F.: That's part of not getting back into the denial piece of it, Jack—not continually beating yourself up about the past—sure can't go back and change any of your past, but by keeping most of the destructive realities associated with those experiences in the front of your head, and working at getting a little bit better and stronger today and tomorrow sure helps you feel better about yourself and keeps the active addiction part of your life behind you.

JACK: I try to do that, one day at a time—like they say in the program, ad I know that you've helped me a lot—the painful sessions about my past, and being out of all of that and actually feeling like I understand what I've been doing to myself now—it's all helped, and I sure feel better about myself and life—it's hell to be drunk, and depressed or scared all the time—just sleeping better, not shaking— being able to face my family—I just couldn't face all of that before when I was drunk—I think that I'm finally beginning to feel like a real human being now.

MIDDLE STAGE ALLIANCE DYNAMICS IN INTENSIVE AFFECT-FOCUSED INTEGRATIVE ADDICTIONS-FOCUSED PSYCHOTHERAPY AND COUNSELING WORK

The addictive disordered patient's initial engagement in psychotherapy or other forms of treatment, therapy or even self-help care are frequently characterized by spontaneously cathartic emotional reactions, marked affective dysregulation, periods of active addiction (relapse), synergized and poorly controlled acting out related to a wide range of earlier life experiences, and continued severe global dysfunctional feelings and poorly controlled emotions. Many of these patients manifest current severe struggles, global dysfunction, acute deterioration, and they have also struggled with ongoing internalized intrapersonal and interpersonal attempts to deny, repress, suppress, minimize, and defensively avoid the many painful realities that have been associated with the various vicissitudes of their lives. These patient dynamics also partially explain the great sense of relief that many addictive disordered patients experience associated with the decision to simply enter therapy, and the concomitant profound feelings of emotional release and a global sense of well-being that can accompany the emotional catharsis that frequently characterizes the early stage therapy recovery process. A successful five or ten day "detox" experience for patients who have remained chronically alcohol or opioid dependent for several years understandably can also result in the patient's sense of experiencing a profoundly enhanced state of physical and psychological well-being.

Early stage therapy alliance interventions in the realm of affective work need to supportively and actively encompass helping patients better understand, accept, partially resolve, and deal with the various facets of the intense or dysregulated emotions they are currently experiencing within the framework of their chaotic internal world. Realizing how the addictive disease process has also directly contributed to their long history of self-medicating related problems, emotional difficulties, dysregulation and self-regulation problems, and the neurotic facets as well as the paradoxically adaptive nature of these facets of the additive disease process. Finally, the eventual complete break-down of the patient's ability to self-regulate feelings and maintain emotional control may paradoxically help the patient experience a sense of hope, relief, personal control and begin to establish a more rational sense of the emotional chaos and affective turmoil and pain he or she has historically endured as a function of the addictive brain disease process. This process frequently fosters the patient's ability to accept, surrender, and clearly become fully committed to the therapy and recovery process.

During early stage therapy alliance work, therapists also focus on helping addicted disordered patients develop an enhanced awareness and the ability to identify "triggers" that tend to provoke or reinforce their strong dysfunctional emotional reactions. At this juncture, patients need to develop a skill set associated with the ability to label these internalized and externalized historic dysregulated affects, and then begin to practice and learn how to overtly verbalize and change their personal internal self-talk dialogue process. Learning to utilize other behavioral-relational modalities that facilitate improved patient affective expression and more global self-regulation can also be initiated during this time frame.

The author (Forrest, 1997, 2012, 2014, 2018) has consistently suggested that addictions therapists need to actively initiate more in-depth and intensive therapeutic affective work and emotionally expressive focused interventions during the middle stage of psychotherapy. Patient's need to be able to cathartically express and share feelings and affects with their therapists early in therapy, but more intense, in-depth and protracted affective work during the middle stage therapy alliance of the therapeutic process can also quickly become overwhelming for some patients. Thus, this process may result in the outcropping of severe alliance disturbances, ruptures, or contribute directly to premature and iatrogenic early treatment terminations and poor outcomes. However, middle stage intensive therapy affective focused alliance-based therapeutic interventions generally facilitate very positive patient gains, and consistently enhance outcomes involving improved and more effective therapist-patient management of the ongoing therapeutic alliance relationship.

The middle stage working and productive alliance relationship includes a relational context involving therapist-patient bond, and historic resilience that fosters and helps sustain the patient's capacities for in-depth exploration of many of his or her most conflictual feelings, affects, and personally disturbing thoughts, experiences and beliefs. Anger, rage, profound feelings of abandonment, and a diversity of emotions associated with trauma, narcissistic injury, identity, self-esteem, guilt, self-defecting behavior, abuse, and shame can be openly expressed and therapeutically addressed at this time. Prior suicide attempts, hospitalizations, prior addiction/ substance abuse treatment episodes, criminal behaviors, and the patient's former abusive, destructive, and dysfunctional patterns of behavior involving family members and significant others may become grist for intensive affective work at this juncture in the therapeutic process.

Therapists need to foster this component of middle stage therapeutic work with addictive disordered persons in a consistently supportive, sensitive and nurturing manner. Patient motivation and readiness for more intensive affective focused middle stage therapeutic work is always a key alliance ingredient that can contribute to the process of successfully changing or resolving many of the patient's conflict's associated with affect regulation.

Therapists also need to remain open to the clinical reality that some, if not many, of their addictive disordered patient's may benefit significantly from the use of short-term or longer-term medication assisted interventions specifically directed at various issues associated with affect dysregulation. For example, as therapists widely recognize today, addictive disordered patients can and do present with co-morbid bi-polar disorder, depression, anxiety, and a spectrum of other problems that may also include a wide range of dysfunctional patterns of emoting. In addition to psychotropic medications, a diversity of other historically non-traditional therapeutic interventions including EMDR, acupuncture, yoga, equine therapy, mindfulness, chiropractic care, relaxation, hypnosis and other modalities may be utilized by the therapist or another health care specialist to help patient's deal more effectively and constructively with affective dysregulation. Patients can be actively encouraged or directly referred to other appropriate health providers for these ancillary services.

The following case study and therapy vignette provide examples of middle stage therapy work with an addictive disordered military patient who had completed several tours of combat duty over seven years in the Middle East war. This patient manifested co-morbid alcohol dependence, PTSD, and severe depression in combination with multiple significant medical problems and affect regulation difficulties related to an earlier divorce, continued child custody conflicts, and the transition to civilian life. This case study also elucidates the constructive role that active self-help care can play in therapy and the over-all patient recovery process.

Case 13

Ben was a 34-year-old US Marine Corp Captain who was seen in weekly and every other week individual psychotherapy by the author for some two years. Ben completed five combat tours over the course of eleven years. Captain C. was born and raised in the Southeastern part of the US. His biological parents had been married for many years, and he had one sister. The patient was a high school and college graduate who also successfully completed a college ROTC program. He subsequently became a career military officer. His marriage of nearly ten years had ended in a bitter divorce as well as an extended and contested custody dispute involving his former wife and two children.

The patient reported that both he and his former wife were "alcoholics." However, the patient had successfully completed a military alcohol and drug rehabilitation program and intensive outpatient treatment program relatively early in his military career. He had been totally abstinent from alcohol for over four years prior to therapeutic engagement, and he had also attended Alcoholics Anonymous with active sponsorship for several years prior to entering therapy with the author. When initially seen, Ben was completing a two-year process of transitioning out of the military which had also previously involved intensive and multifaceted PTSD treatment, multiple knee, shoulder, and wrist surgeries as well as treatment for major depression and spinal surgery. The patient had been exposed to a multiplicity of psychological and psychiatric treatment modalities over the course of his two-and-a-half-year military and VA treatment. During this extended time frame, Ben also continued to attend several self-help recovery meetings (AA) on a weekly basis, and he had also sustained an active sponsorship relationship within the self-help community for many years.

Ben continued in active and ongoing out-patient psychotherapy with the author for over four years, completed a graduate degree and quickly became a 4.0 student. He subsequently entered the behavioral health profession working with PTSD patients and addictive disordered persons. He gained full custody of his children, and has maintained a stable significant other relationship for over two years. His depression, PTSD, alcohol dependence and global health status has remained greatly improved, but he also continues to be seen in therapy sporadically and supportively, takes antidepressant medications, remains active in the self-help care community, and has engaged in a few relationship counseling sessions with his significant other. His children are reportedly doing very well in school and their over-all adjustment has continued to be good. Ben's affect, self-regulation, internal control, self-esteem and global functioning have remained consistently stable and greatly improved over the past few years. He remains internally committed to the ongoing self-care and recovery process. His anger control issues, road rage, and *persistent resentments also remain in remission.*

BEN L.: That last rotation really was hell—I know we talked about it before, but it's still on my mind a lot of the time—we lost a lot of guys, and it was IEDs, recons, and ambushes almost every day or night—really, you never knew what it was next—and you felt sorry for all the little kids, or old people in those villages too—it seemed like they were getting killed like flies at times too, and they had nothing—illiterate,—just tryin' to keep alive. It was all insane.

DOCTOR F.: I'm sure the last go-around was tough—to say the least, but going back for more each time had to take a progressive toll on all of you—you've been able to stay sober through all of it, and you realize that the AA foundation for recovery plus the counseling you got several years ago helped you get through all of it, but the never ending issues with your "X," and the surgeries and physical pain over the last year and a half or so have been hell to deal with—no energy, the depression and sleep problems, and just not knowing when it's going to end or even when you're going to get out of the service—in here you sure seem to be able to see and accept that all of these things are a part of what you're struggling with, but it's a different deal trying to manage all of it on a daily real-world basis—and we sure don't know when all or most of it will end—even that's a real piece of what you are trying to make sense of.

BEN: I try to deal with what I can each day—if I just had more energy it would be easier, but your in-put to my psychiatrist about considering changing my antidepressant medication—the switch to Wellbutrin, seems to be helping—at least I've been able to get over to the University Campus this week, and begin to talk with the admissions folks about getting back in school—plus the VA—yeah, the new medication seems to be working—after taking all those other ones, and the other medication cocktails for the last two or three years—and I can tell that I'm not as angry or pissed at my "x"—it's all a start, and—my girlfriend even mentioned that I seem happier last night—hell, I laughed at her—I can't remember when I've really felt happy?

DOCTOR F.: How about sleep? It's only been what—two or three weeks since your psychiatrist switched you to the Wellbutrin, but have you been sleeping better?

BEN: Guess I left that out, I have slept better the last couple of nights, but that could have been because I'm doing a lot more, and even back in the gym this week—I'm tired when I go to bed, but I'm sure not up half the night—the other thing is—thinking about it, I've been able to get back to sleep if I do wake up.

DOCTOR F.: Backing up, it sounds like you've definitely been feeling better and hopefully the depression you've been struggling with has started to improve significantly—also, I wanted to ask if you started looking into graduate school when you got out to the campus?

BEN: I forgot that piece, I did get the grad school info and I need to schedule an appointment with someone in the graduate school to find out what I need to do to get started—it looks like I might have to do three or four undergraduate classes before I can get accepted , but I can do that with VA and Voc. Rehab help—you know, for the first time in a long time I'm not really afraid or nervous about getting out of the service—after all these years, plus my finances are really good now. I need to keep working on the road rage, but my biggest pain is dealing with my "x"—she's in "contempt" of court again, and my lawyer is taking her back to court—the kids don't even want to see her anymore, so all the shit isn't over by any stretch of the imagination—but the therapy has helped, and I'm also working on getting off the pain meds with Dr. Z at the VA.

DOCTOR F.: So you can see yourself slowly improving on a number of fronts, and you also seem to realize you can have a better future in spite of the issues you're still working on, and struggling with at times—hope, energy, positive motivation and continued self-care are sure part of the mix—plus you've only got two more surgeries to go in that area, and if it all works out you'll be out of the service in a few months and into the challenges of graduate school and a new life style—it's all a plate full, but I'm excited for you—and all those military experiences, and what you've been through can somehow—in one way or another potentially contribute to a very new and successful life for you in the future.

BEN: Doc, you're kinda an eternal optimist, but you know things are generally getting better, and I can see light at the end of the tunnel now—after two years.

DOCTOR F.: Life as a process is never easy, Ben—ups and downs, and all of its relatively unpredictable—but you're on the path to recovery and there's no guarantee with that, like all things—you've kept doing the work that it takes to get better—and we need to stay with the process.

BEN: And I used to even question how any of my military experiences as a company commander, combat veteran, or special ops officer would ever carry over to the civilian world—and I believed that until we began therapy four or five months ago. Now, I'm even considering a mental health career working for the VA—almost unbelievable! Ha-ha.

MIDDLE STAGE ALLIANCE DYNAMICS, SEXUAL COUNSELING AND SEX THERAPY IN ADDICTIONS-FOCUSED INTEGRATIVE PSYCHOTHERAPY AND COUNSELING WORK

Many, if not most, addictive disordered patients manifest clinical histories involving sexual abuse, sexual problems and sexually related conflicts. These sexually-focused conflicts stem from a diversity of causal factors: early-life trauma related to sexual abuse and incest, childhood, adolescent and adult experiences associated with sexual abuse or assault, sexual addiction, and infrequently, the various dynamics associated with human trafficking and involvement in the sex industry realm, faulty parenting, aberrant sexually focused learning experiences, beliefs, or partner sexual problems. Comorbid psychopathology associated with a spectrum of related sexual dysfunctions and paraphilias may also be related to the patient's sexual problems.

It is also paramount for addictions therapists to clearly understand and recognize that the additive disease process constitutes a core etiological component in the development of many, if not most of the various symptoms associated with a wide spectrum of sexual problems, dysfunctions and disorders that patients manifest. Drug facilitated patterns of sexual behavior tend to become progressively dysfunctional and conflictual as the addiction process unfolds, and impulsive, risk-taking and impaired judgement factors may also insidiously precipitate a wealth of ever-increasing sexual problems. The addictive disease process can contribute very directly to the development of a wide range of sexual dysfunctions, problems and sexual-relational conflicts among additive disordered patient populations. These realities can also reinforce and synergize the addictive disordered patient's underlying identity and self-esteem issues, foster self-system fragmentation, impulse control and anger control difficulties, synergize trauma-based conflicts, and even impact basic decision-making skills. Ultimately, the untreated addictive brain disease process may lead to brief episodes of ego-diffusion, psychosis and extremely aberrant, bizarre or potentially destructive patterns of sexual behavior.

As noted earlier by the author (Forrest, 1984, 1997), alcohol dependence can be associated with the direct physiological and psychological consequences of chronic or acute intoxication, and these consequences may include erectile dysfunction or impotence, retarded ejaculation, orgasmic inhibition and frigidity. The historic sexual deviations including incest, rape, child molesting, exhibitionism and other forms of "deviant" sexual behavior frequently occur as a function of acute chronic alcohol dependence and drug abuse or dependence. Problems with desire and arousal, sexually aversive patterns of behavior, avoidance of intimacy and intimacy conflicts, overdetermined sexual acting out, and various other patterns of sexually related dysfunctional behavior are often causally associated with alcohol dependence and various other addictive brain diseases.

Understandably, some addictive disordered patients who enter psychotherapy and other treatment modalities related to their various individual disorders are also motivated and well aware of the need to address and resolve their personal and relational sexual problems and difficulties. These patients often tend to openly discuss and spontaneously explore their sexual histories and problems with their therapist very early in the therapeutic process. Likewise, these patients may express a desire to "work" on their various sexual issues and sexually-focused conflicts at this early juncture. Other addictive disordered patients may deny, repress, and minimize their historic or current sexual difficulties and experience. Obviously, many patients have fear and anxiety associated with discussing sexual issues and sexual disclosures early in the treatment process or within the context of initial stage clinical assessment.

At any rate, it is generally clinically inappropriate for addictions therapists to initiate intense and focused sex counseling and/or sex therapy interventions during the early stage of psychotherapy. This therapeutic stance does not apply to patient's who manifest active sexual addictions and are seeking immediate treatment and care associated with their sexual disorders. Simply put, most addictive disordered patients are usually not psychologically or physically stabilized and ready to begin the process of intensive sexually focused therapy related to severe sexual trauma associated with a wide spectrum of etiological factors associated with sexual problems, dysfunctions, identity, gender and other dysfunctional behaviors. Perhaps more importantly, the early stage therapeutic alliance development and relational bonding process involving the therapist and patient is (1) often fragile and subject to rupture in early therapy work, and (2) the therapeutic holding environment dimensions of the alliance are often insufficient to sustain the patient's ability for successful resolution of a multiplicity of long-term and more severe sexual dysfunctions in concert with the presence of a severe comorbid addictive brain disease.

Recent empirical research evidence indicates that (Farver-Smith, 2015), conflicts associated with early life trauma are almost always (97% of the time) associated with chronic pain. This research also indicates that "all people who abuse alcohol or other drugs experience chronic emotional pain," and Sharp Potter (2010) has noted that chronic physical pain affects "approximately 60 percent of those struggling with alcoholism or addiction." Farver-Smith (2015) further report that emotional or physical trauma prior to chronic pain on-set is associated with sexual abuse 26.7 percent of the time, physical abuse 29.7 percent of the time, childhood accidents 32.6 percent of the time, family drug abuse 36.8 percent of the time, emotional abuse 48.2 percent of the time, and loss of a loved one 75.2 percent of the time. Interestingly, these general findings are quite concordant with the clinical findings and observations that were originally reported over three decades ago (Forrest, 1975, 1983, 1984).

In general, addictive disordered patients are not good candidates for intensive psychotherapeutic work dealing specifically with severe and protracted sexual disorders until they have (1) established and sustained a working and productive therapeutic alliance for three or four consecutive months,

(2) sustained a significant commitment to the recovery process and also have sustained abstinence over the course of their therapeutic work, (3) actively maintained the structural components of their individual multifaceted recovery program for this same-period of time, and (4) evidenced significant global clinical progress in the resolution of their basic underlying symptom structure which has helped precipitate and maintain their various sexual dysfunctions, behaviors and aberrant patterns of sexual responding.

These sexually focused middle stage clinical realities and therapist strategies can enhance and strengthen the working and productive therapeutic alliance, and enhance both the probability for resolution of many of the patient's sexual difficulties as well as continued patient growth, change and recovery related to the patient's addictive disorder and global life-style adjustment.

This particular facet of therapeutic work related to the alliance mirrors many of the dynamics associated with more intensive affective treatment interventions and strategies associated with the ongoing process of treating addictive disordered persons.

Addictive disordered patients almost invariably benefit from some level of basic sex education and the opportunity to openly discuss a variety of issues pertaining to human sexuality in the course of therapy. However, more focused and intensive work in this area often contributes to the process of successful middle stage therapy with this clinical population. Many substance abusers and addicts experience guilt, confusion, and are poorly educated in the arena of human sexual behavior. Irrational beliefs, faulty learning experiences, and even a floridly pathological history of sexual abuse and trauma are generally best addressed relatively early in the middle stage therapy process and over the course of the therapeutic relationship vis a via therapist support, general sex education counseling, and with limit setting relative to the intensity and depth of alliance focused sexual content exploration. Depending upon patient sophistication, education, general awareness, and clinical history related to sexual matters, therapists may be able to supportively help sexually conflicted patients better understand and deal with their conflictual sexual histories via didactic sex education measures pertaining to such issues as masturbation, vaginal, oral, anal, or other forms of sexual behaviors also involving matters pertaining to infidelity, group sex, gender, identity, bi and transgender issues and the sexual dysfunctions during early middle stage therapy.

In sum, addictions clinicians may need to essentially be able to address the patient's sexual conflicts and to some extent, function as sex educators and counselors who often teach patients the basics of human sexual behavior. Therapists also may need to challenge or dispute the patient's irrational sexual beliefs, values, and attitudes in therapy. Clinicians may discover that basic sex education and counseling interventions can result in the resolution or significant modification of some, or even many of their patient's sexual problems and dysfunctional patterns of sexual responding. However, this level of basic sex education frequently serves as an early stage psychotherapy precursor to the process of initiating more intensive middle stage sexual counseling, or perhaps a therapist referral of the patient for specialized intensive sexual trauma focused treatment in the case of counselors or therapists that have little or no prior sexual training and education background.

Basic sexual counseling and sex therapy can be essential ingredients of successful addictions psychotherapy work. Unfortunately, many if not most, addictions counselors and therapists continue to have rather limited clinical and didactic educational training, supervision and focused professional experience in the explicit realm of sex therapy. For clinicians and therapists with significant training, expertise and experience in this realm of care, sex therapy interventions can be an important integrative component of the alliance and the ongoing process of intensive addictions psychotherapy. Again, therapists may need to refer some of their patients to a physician for specific physical examinations or care related to the various sexual dysfunctions or problems patients manifest prior to the initiation of focused sexual counseling or sex therapy.

Addictions counselors and therapists with limited clinical experience, training, and skills related to sexual counseling and sex therapy, or therapists who are simply not comfortable with these particular components of sexually focused addictions therapy work will want to consider referring these patients to other appropriate trained clinicians in their communities who are able to provide specific professional sexual education, counseling and therapy services.

It is also sometimes important for addictions therapists to consider such matters as referring spouses or patient significant others for appropriate sexual education, counseling or therapy services during the course of their treatment relationships. Therapists may additionally realize that it is simply inadvisable to attempt sex therapy interventions when patients or their spouses and significant others are severely sexually conflicted, and extended conjoint therapy or family therapy may be indicated prior to beginning focused sex therapy with these couples. Referrals to therapists specializing in conjoint marital relationship counseling and family therapy are also viable alternatives in some cases, and referrals to intensive residential and out-patient treatment centers providing a wide range of specialized sexual therapy treatments can also enhance successful treatment outcomes and recoveries.

Some addictive disordered patients rather spontaneously terminate their patterns of dysfunctional and destructive sexual behavior, and impulsive or compulsive sexual acting out behaviors following an intensive addictions psychotherapy treatment experience. Spontaneous remissions usually occur within the context of patient ongoing commitment to long term recovery. The addictive disease process may have been a central etiological ingredient driving many of these patient's affect driven patterns of prior dysfunctional sexual behavior and responding.

The psychotherapeutic relationship and therapeutic alliance context always remain a vehicle for helping addictive disordered patients disclose, explore, and resolve or modify a diversity of sexual conflicts, problems, relational difficulties, and dysfunctions. Identity issues and relationship-oriented dynamics associated with sexual issues can also be effectively addressed within both conjoint relationship therapy and individual therapy alliance work. The middle stage of ongoing psychotherapy with these patients usually constitutes the primary temporal framework for effective, intensive alliance related sexually-focused therapeutic work. Alliance stability, flexibility and durability contribute significantly to patient's ability to focus upon a diversity of personal sexual issues at this juncture in the therapeutic process.

As noted earlier in the chapter, middle stage alliance psychotherapy work with addictive disordered patients who have been consistently sustained via a working and productive alliance context develop a relational and emotional framework for less-threatening, more open, honest and in-depth therapist-patient interactions and therapeutic transactions to take place. These middle stage alliance dynamics potentially initiate a wide range of globally significant patient behavioral and over-all adaptive life style changes that remain at the heart of the recovery and ongoing change process.

The following therapy vignette was taken from the eighteenth session with a male patient manifesting complex co morbid gambling disorder, alcohol dependence, and chronic sexual difficulties associated with premature ejaculation, episodic erectile dysfunction and an obsessive-compulsive pornography addiction.

Case 14

JIM: I've always realized that I had a "drinking problem," and the gambling—like we've talked about before, it really wasn't a problem until a couple of years ago when I got into it real bad—my wife was pissed, and we both did a lot of cryin' when it all came out—it still makes me sick to think about all that money down the drain—a quarter of a million dollars, and I'm still working to pay it all off—and the other problems—it's no damned wonder I was drinking so much at the end.

DOCTOR F.: Drinking was one way to cope with it—the self-medicating bit we've discussed related to the gambling and drinking, plus the sexual stuff—the sexual problems you had as a teen, and then all the acting out—the addictive patterns of behavior—your obsession with porn sure didn't help your marriage.

JIM: I can make sense of most of it now, and it sure helps to be sober—but I've learned that it's too overwhelming and upsetting to think about a lot of the past stuff—to dwell and obsess about it too much—that was sure a part of that "little binge" I went on a couple of months ago, and those talks we had then sure helped—I'm able to talk about all of it with you, and working with my sponsor has helped me deal with all of it better too . . . we're working on the steps now, and I know doing that fourth step and then—the amends bit down the road—I've got to do it—the porno stuff, and the other women stuff— you know, I really went nuts at the end, and ending up in rehab and then the psych unit—and all the sexual problems I've had over the years.

DOCTOR F.: Yeah, it was disturbing stuff, and you never want to put yourself or your family through all of that again, Jim—and the one day at a time—and time with therapy, and a real program of recovery has been the road to how you've changed so far—you've made some real changes Jim, and we need to stay on the recovery track.

JIM: You know, my wife even my oldest daughter have started talking to me again—we discussed that a couple of weeks ago—they're still all on eggshells, and they don't trust me about the sexual stuff— and I don't blame them, but they know I'm seeing you and doin' the AA program, plus GA, and I know it takes time—I really feel better when I leave those meetings—I've put off going to SA, but I've made a commitment to go with another guy next week—we both go to the same GA meeting, and he's been open in meetings about being a sex addict—and says he's been out of all of it for over four years—even that gives me a sense of hope—he was into the porn, and had problems getting it up too—I guess he had drinking problems too, for a time—

DOCTOR F.: Getting the trust back really takes time, and you know—before you started therapy and got involved in the recovery community—and really started to show up, everybody in the family had a lot of reasons not to trust you—remember when we were working on learning how to trust yourself when we started, and you were angry as hell at yourself and everybody—it took a couple of months— I think, for us to really reach the point where you could really understand and realize the pain your wife and kids had experienced over all those years—plus getting to the point of working on changing yourself—yeah, it's going to take time and work for all of us that—kind of healing involves all of us.

JIM: I still need to hear a lot of this stuff—and think about it all, just to realize how it really was four or five months ago, or ten years ago—I've really been one self-centered son of a bitch—and stupid about a lot of things over all these years—and a lot of the time I couldn't even get it up with those other women, or else I got off in five or ten seconds—no wonder my wife was ready for divorce, and you know, I would have probably divorced her if I ever caught her messing around one time—and how many times she caught me jacking-off—it's all pretty damn embarrassing too—

DOCTOR F.: You've changed a lot Jim—and things are changing in a positive direction with your family and work—but like we've discussed today, we've got a lot of work to do—and keep the positive change and recovery process going.

The following case study includes a clinical history involving complex sexual pathology and problems with co-morbid alcohol dependence as well as severe marital and familial dysfunction.

Case 15

Dick was seen in outpatient psychotherapy by the author within the context of a military substance abuse treatment program in the southeast many years ago. Sergeant C. initially entered therapy as a result of "severe marital problems," the threat of divorce, and "drinking too much." The patient acknowledged that he "sometimes drank too much," and had "a lot of sex problems," during the initial session. He further discussed these issues including his wife's recent discovery that he was "peeping" in the bathroom window of a 14-year-old girl who lived next door. His wife was very angry about this incident, and his wife had threatened to leave him many times as a result of his drinking behavior. The patient did acknowledge that he had been "drunk" at the time of the window-peeping episode.

During completion of the patient's biopsychosocial history, he reported that his biological father was an alcoholic who had committed suicide when that patient was eight years old. His biological mother had turned the patient and his sister over to her parents to raise shortly after the suicide, and she only returned to see her children every "two or three years." The client had also experienced many interpersonal and academic problems throughout school, and had "burned down" his grandparent's garage at age 11. He continued to experience enuretic episodes until around the age of nineteen and noted that he had started "window peeping" around age thirteen or fourteen. The patient openly acknowledged masturbating "three or four" times a day during adolescence, and had engaged in group masturbation activities ("circle jerks") with peers and engaged in homosexual behavior at this time.

Dick graduated from a rural North Carolina high school, joined the US Army shortly thereafter, and was eventually sent to Germany where he maintained a gay relationship with his first sergeant for nearly one year. Upon returning to the United States he was re-assigned to a base in the south, met his wife who had been previously married and had a young daughter, and following a two-month courtship they were married. His wife was Turkish. The patient completed his military service a year later and his family returned to a small community in North Carolina where he became a member of the local police department. Several months after taking this position, Dick was terminated from his job as a result of an exhibitionistic episode involving exposing his genitals to a woman while on duty in his police patrol car. The patient subsequently rejoined the Army some sixty days later.

Early in therapy the patient openly revealed that he had, in fact, been window peeping on his neighbor several nights of the week, and he subsequently indicated that he also spent a good deal of time driving around the post commissary and PX "shooting beaver," which referred to attempting to look under the skirts of women who had been shopping in order to view their genitals. He often sat in his car in parking lots on the base and used his binoculars for this purpose while masturbating. He reported masturbating to orgasm several times on some days, but also noted that he and his wife also engaged in sexual intercourse and other sexual activities "several" times a week, or "four or five times a night," on frequent occasions. His wife reportedly was an active participant in their various sexual activities including his cross-dressing behavior, but in spite of her willingness to "try everything" in order for Dick to reach orgasm, he had been rarely able to achieve orgasm while engaging in a diversity of these sexual activities with his wife.

The patient reported drinking "several" beers each night early in therapy, and also indicated that every "two or three weeks," he would "throw a good one." On these occasions, Dick would consume over a case of beer on the weekend. During the middle stage of therapy, the patient revealed that he had experienced several alcoholic "black outs" during these binge drinking episodes, he frequently sexually abused and forced his wife to have sex, and verbally abused her as well when intoxicated. He was able to sustain the therapeutic process and eventually developed a very limited alliance bond with the author which also involved the capacity to experience and emotionally express feelings of guilt, remorse, shame and depression as well as fear and anxiety related to his severely conflicted sexual behaviors. He expressed anxiety and fear related to the possible legal ramifications associated with his alcohol dependence fueled dysfunction and pathologic sexual behaviors, and he also worried about these matters related to his marriage and military career.

Dick was seen in individual therapy some fifteen times over the course of four-and-a-half months of treatment. He did reduce the frequency and level of his alcohol use while in therapy, self-reported that his "window peeping" and other voyeuristic behaviors were greatly reduced but not extinguished, and the marital relationship and family adjustment remained severely dysfunctional. His wife reportedly did attend Ala-non a few times and also saw a counselor for three sessions but reportedly terminated these treatment modalities because she felt they were "a waste of time."

Unfortunately, no follow-up data is available in this case as the patient was transferred for an unaccompanied tour of duty to South Korea some six months later.

The following case study is taken from a recent article in the New York Times Magazine entitled "Confessions of a Seduction Addict" (Gilbert, 2015). This article provides readers with a very lucid, real, emotional, and exceptionally well written example of the underlying dynamics of sexual addiction as a human addictive disease process.

Case 16

MISS "X": It started with a boy I met at summer camp and ended up with the man for whom I left my first husband. In between, I careened from one intimate entanglement to the next—dozens of them—without so much as a day off between romances. You might have called me a serial monogamist, except that I was never exactly monogamous. Relationships overlapped, and those overlaps were always marked by exhausting theatricality, sobbing arguments, shaming confrontations, and broken hearts. Still, I kept doing it. I couldn't not do it.

I can't say that I was always looking for a better man. I often traded good men for bad ones; character didn't matter much to me.

I wasn't exactly seeking love, either, regardless of what I might have claimed. I can't even say it was the sex. Sex was just the gateway drug for me, a portal to the much higher high I was really after, which was seduction.

Seduction is the art of coercing somebody to desire you, or orchestrating somebody else's longings to suit your own hungry agenda. Seduction was never a casual sport to me; it was more like a heist, adrenalizing and urgent. I would plan the heist for months, scouting out the target, looking for unguarded entries. Then I would break into his deepest vault, steal all of his emotional currency and spend it on myself–" (p. 47).

Truncated snippets from this complete article include the following: " If the man was already involved in a committed relationship, I knew I didn't need to be prettier or better than his existing girl-friend—the trick was to study the other woman and to become her opposite, thereby positioning myself to this man as a sparkling alter-native to his regular life."

"Soon enough, and sure enough, I might begin to see that man's gaze toward me change from indifference, to friendship, to open desire. That's what I was after: the telekinesis-like sensation of steadi-ly dragging somebody's fullest attention toward me and only me. My guilt about the other woman was no match for the intoxicating knowledge that-somewhere on the other side of town—somebody couldn't sleep that night because he was thinking about me. If he needed to sneak out of his house after midnight in order to call, bet-ter still. That was power, but it was also affirmation. I was someone's irresistible treasure. I loved that sensation, and I needed it, not some-times, not even often, but always" (p. 48).

Gilbert (2015) further notes "I might indeed win the man even-tually, but over time (and it wouldn't take long), his unquenchable infatuation for me would fade, as his attention returned to everyday matters. This always left me feeling abandoned and invisible; love that could be quenched was not nearly enough love for me. As soon as I could, then, I would start seducing somebody else—These epi-sodes of shape-shifting cost me dearly. I would lose weight, sleep, dig-nity, clarity—I could endure these painful episodes only by assuring myselF.: This is the last time. This guy is the one" (p. 48).

"In my mid-twenties, I married, but not even matrimony slowed me down. Predictably, I grew restless and lonely. Soon enough I seduced someone new; the marriage collapsed—before the divorce agreement was even signed, I was already breaking up with the guy I had broken up my marriage for" (p. 48). The woman in this case further acknowledges "you know you've got intimacy issues when, in the space of a few short months, you find yourself visiting two completely different couple's counselors, with two completely different men on your arm, in order to talk about two completely different emotional firestorms" (p. 48). She also acknowledges that "trying to keep all my various story lines straight" made "my hand shake and my mind splinter."

The author (Gilbert, 2015) goes on to describe how this client finally responded to a very distressing phone message from her lawyer by asking herself, "what are you doing with your life?" The client further elaborates, "for the first time, I forced myself to admit that I had a problem-indeed, that I was the problem. Tinkering with other people's most vulnerable emotions didn't make me a romantic; it just made me a swindler. Lying and cheating didn't make me brazen; it just made me a needy coward. Stealing other women's boyfriends (and husbands) didn't make me a revolutionary feminist; it just made me a menace. I hated that it took me almost 20 years to realize this: I felt shameful. But once I got it, I really got it. There is no way to stop a destructive behavior, except to stop" (p. 49).

"I spent the next six months celibate and serious, working with a good therapist, trying to learn if I even existed at all when I wasn't blazing in the heat of somebody's longing gaze. Then one afternoon I ran into a guy I liked. We went for a long walk in the park, flirted. Laughed. It was sweet. Eventually he said, "would you like to come back to my apartment with me?" Yes! "My God, how I wanted to unwrap this man like a Christmas present!" (p. 49).

"But I also didn't want to: I was only beginning to pull myself together, and I feared unraveling. Uncertain, I tried something radically new. I said, "do you mind if I take a moment to think about this?" "Sure," he said" (p. 49)."We sat down on a park bench, and I got very quiet, picturing all the imaginable outcomes of this decision. The man took a magazine from his backpack and started reading, just to pass the time. This helped, actually. It proved the absence of intoxicating desperation. This was not seduction; this was merely two sober adults, deciding whether they should get more involved with each other.I said: "You know what, my friend? I don't think I'm ready for this." He replied: "No problem. Let's get Italian ices, instead."We spent a few more pleasant hours together, then said our goodbyes. I walked about alone, but calm. And that's when I realized that the better part of my life had already begun" (p. 49).

MIDDLE STAGE ALLIANCE DYNAMICS, CONFRONTATION, RELAPSE, TIME STRUCTURING AND ANCILLARY DIMENSIONS IN INTEGRATIVE ADDICTIONS-FOCUSED PSYCHOTHERAPY AND COUNSELING WORK

As noted earlier in this chapter, a variety of confrontation-oriented dynamics and transactions are inherently associated with every facet and stage of the psychotherapy process and other forms of treatment associated with all forms of human health care.

The thoughtful, consciously orchestrated confrontation-focused transactions and techniques that addictions therapists may choose to utilize during the middle stage of the intensive addictions psychotherapy process tend to differ from those used early in therapy. Therapists need to consistently utilize supportive, controlled and non-emotionally charged, patient enhancing and alliance building confrontation focused interventions during early stage therapy work.

Movement into the middle stage of therapy generally may involve the therapist's ability to therapeutically use more direct, more affectively charged and in-depth interpretations and various other constructive interventions that are clearly perceived as confrontational in nature by both patient and therapist. At this juncture in therapy, the working and productive therapeutic alliance provides the relationship framework for enhancing significant constructive and focused in-depth confrontation work with many addictive disordered patients. Experienced therapist's use timely, empathic, sensitive, supportive, and frequently high impact, affectively charged confrontations which are much less likely to precipitate brief episodes of alliance dissonance or precipitate an alliance rupture at this stage in treatment. Patients are committed to the psychotherapy process at this time and they also experientially and rationally understand that the psychotherapist has remained a stable agent of constructive change throughout the treatment process. Patient's rarely flee from therapy, become angry, extremely agitated, enraged or relapse as a function of the therapist's appropriate and thought out uses of confrontation at this time.

A consistently working and productive therapeutic alliance rather spontaneously leads to the development of a fluid, nurturing and mutually open communitive relational bond between the therapist and patient which provides the essential relationship "cement" for continued patient growth and adaptive change over the course of therapy. The therapist's sense of concern, support, compassion, continued encouragement, and in many respects, love for the patient, underlies his or her use of confrontation and the various other strategies and tools related to the bi-lateral work of efficacious psychotherapy. Bi-lateral therapist and patient qualities of trust, openness, respect, commitment, motivation for growth and change, and sufficient levels of *mutual* non-possessive warmth, empathy, genuineness, and concreteness also become key ingredients in most, if not all, facets of effective alliances in addictions psychotherapy work.

These mutual therapist-patient relational qualities and characteristics become realities that are usually developed and contribute to the therapeutic elasticity or malleability that characterize the middle and later stages of the psychotherapy process. Unlike early stage therapy confrontation-oriented therapist interventions related to denial, defensiveness, projection, and rationalization, "real relationship" (Gelso, 2010) based alliances provide an emotionally and relationally stabilized and strengthened relationship context for constructive therapeutic work. This relational context can also incorporate various uses and levels or styles of confrontation. In this regard, it should also be noted that most, if not all, addictive disordered persons do not require and/or do not benefit from the use of protracted intensive, in-depth, high-impact confrontation work *during any stage in the process of effective addictions psychotherapy.* The author's earlier work (Forrest, 1982, 1991) examined many of the provocative, psychonoxious and nefarious and inappropriate parameters associated with the use of confrontation in psychotherapy work with addictive disordered patients.

Relapses or acute therapist awareness and concerns associated with patient "set ups" related to preconscious planning behaviors may precipitate appropriate therapist actions and exceptions related to the generalized guidelines pertaining to the uses and abuses of confrontation in the addictions psychotherapy literature discussed thus far in the chapter. In these potential acute or incipient relapse-based situations, the therapist may need to actively or more forcefully and directly confront the patient relative to (1) his or her "red flag" perceptions, concerns, and prior clinical experiences related to recent patient specific patterns of behavior, thinking, verbiage, and relational or possible acute situational stressors that are frequently precursors to relapse, (2) the irrational and often transient nature of the dynamics associated with this process, (3) further exploration of the potential consequences of a relapse episode, and most importantly, (4) supportively but firmly exploring the active initiation of immediate intensified treatment strategies, and engagement in a relatively specific and perhaps time limited and highly structured relapse prevention program.

As noted earlier in the chapter and touched upon in earlier chapters in this text, relapse episodes at any juncture in the ongoing psychotherapy and treatment process may precipitate any number of potentially very destructive outcomes. Middle stage psychotherapy related relapse episodes do contribute to alliance ruptures, brief or extended breaks in the therapeutic relationship, and infrequently may be associated with a broad spectrum of very devastating patient outcomes including death, incarceration, job loss, hospitalizations, divorce and family relationship problems, and generalized health consequences. Addiction therapist's need to actively utilize a variety of patient-specific relapse prevention focused therapeutic interventions in their efforts to help patients "head off" the active relapse process. Successful management, curtailment, and recovery from a relapse episode always remains a core function of effective alliance work in the process of effective addictions psychotherapy.

A plethora of time structuring dynamics and concrete realities are associated with the development, maintenance, treatment and recovery facets of all addictive disorders. The maturity and strength of the therapeutic alliance as well as the "real person" dynamics of the alliance relationship (Forrest, 1997, 2016; Gelso and Hayes, 1998; Orellana and Gelso, 2013) contribute to the middle stage therapeutic zeitgeist facilitated via an in-depth exploration of the patient's addictive disordered time structuring dynamics, rituals, and obsessive-compulsive or neurotic and self-defeating patterns of behavior. These particular facets of the addictive brain disease process can also be viewed as a rather classic example of the Freudian (Freud, 1910) repetition-compulsion construct. The therapist's timely and focused middle stage therapy exploration of these patient behaviors and dynamics need to include a good deal of didactic teaching that involves identifying and examining the origins, development, rational and dysfunctional purposes, maintenance, emotions and beliefs, adaptive and maladaptive dimensions, and interpersonal facets of the patient's addictive disorder related repetition compulsion. Therapist and patient alliance-based identification and exploration of each patient's relatively unique patterns of ritualistic, obsessive-compulsive, and repetition-compulsive driven addictive brain disease-based behaviors must also encompass elucidating direct and concrete examples of these maladaptive adjustment dynamisms.

For example, severely alcohol dependent patients frequently attempt to hide their drinking, deny drinking or report drinking "1 or 2" drinks, hide bottles and drink in isolation. Many of these individuals tragically begin to establish a pattern of daily obsessive-compulsive, ritualistic maintenance drinking. A number of these individuals eventually end up homeless, and are hospitalized and/or "detoxed" on hundreds of occasions prior to dying. These persons develop a lifestyle or life career, in effect, that revolves almost solely around the process of obtaining and maintaining a state of chronic intoxication. Compulsive eaters and other eating disordered patients may develop obsessive-compulsive, ritualistic, dysfunctional and other destructive eating behavior patterns involving hiding, storing, and buying food. They may continuously eat around the clock, eat in their cars or bed, purge, or frequently ingest laxatives, binge eat, and deny these behaviors as well as divert family monies to purchase supplies of food. Again, these patterns of ritualistic and repetition-based behaviors eventually control virtually every facet of the patient's life. The particular eating-disorder becomes the patient—a potential life career or occupation, an unending addictive brain disease process that controls and negatively impacts every facet of the patient's waking and sleeping life as well as his or her interpersonal and intrapersonal worlds. In short, the patient becomes the repetition-compulsion, and this facet of the eating-disordered spectrum of addictive brain disease tragically takes the lives of many patients (Isserlin and Couturier, 2012; Maxwell et al., 2014, Folke et al., 2017).

These core dynamics and maladaptive addiction-based realities also apply to nicotine dependent patients, gambling disordered patients, sexually addicted individuals, patients manifesting opioid or sedative dependence, marijuana dependence, and every other form of addictive brain disease. These patients become progressively trapped within the context of their globally maladaptive addictive brain disease process, and this process is fundamentally driven and maintained vis a via a destructive matrix of progressively obsessive-compulsive, ritualistic, and repetition-compulsive based maladaptive patterns of behavior. Brain-based neurochemistry, circuitry, genetics, and pre-frontal cortex factors including learning, conditioning, reinforcement and the anticipatory reward system also contribute to the development of the addictive brain disease process (Volkow and Koob, 2015).

The alliance based therapeutic process of making these historic patient patterns of maladaptive behavior consciously known, recognized, and understood by the patient provides an opportunity for the patient and therapist to begin the very important therapeutic task of changing and resolving these globally destructive and self-defeating patterns of thinking, behaving and relating. This process is difficult to resolve but also can eventually become incredibly liberating for many addictive disordered patients. Patients usually begin to experience an incredible sense of "freedom," serenity and emotional relief as they begin to significantly modify these long-standing patterns of self-defeating behavior during the middle and later stages of therapy.

This therapeutic work constitutes a core facet of efficacious addictions therapy. As patients begin to clearly understand and become more cognizant of the "economics" of their addictive disease process and conversely the "economics" surrounding early stage and middle stage therapeutically induced positive global life style change, the recovery process can become synergized and certainly self-reinforcing. Therapists need to actively point out to patients the increased time gains that they are beginning to experience in the here-and-now, monetary savings, relational improvements, emotional economics, and the "economics" of daily living and life-style gains that are associated with the resolution of their addictions. Terminating long standing self-defeating patterns of repetitive behavior involving paying attorneys thousands of dollars related to multiple arrests associated with DUI's, divorces, child custody payments, drug possession, domestic violence, and public intoxication expenses, or perhaps thousands of dollars for physician and hospital expenses related to several unsuccessful addiction treatment experiences make up some of the significant benefits that occur via the recovery process.

All of these sources of potential therapeutic gain, in effect, can be related to the time structuring dynamics that are inherently and destructively associated with every facet of the patient's active addictive brain disease process. Patient's, therapist's and the alliance collectively become "ready" for the arduous middle stage therapeutic work that is associated with the core process of facilitating patient growth and change related to chronic patterns of repetitive, ritualized and obsessive-compulsive addiction-specific behaviors.

Addiction therapists frequently find that the use of humor related to the patient's historic and current addiction specific time structuring struggles in therapy and life prove very beneficial for patients. Addictive disordered patients really begin to understand the costly and globally self-defeating parameters of their addictive disease process during the middle stage of therapy, and like all people, it simply helps patients to be able to laugh and see some humor and folly in their lives. Within the context of hindsight associated with having transcended or terminated their addictive brain disease process, many of these prior problems involving patterns of dysfunctional self-defeating behavior contribute to a sense of therapeutic humor that can contribute to a sense of personal hope for today and the future!

Finally, the middle stage of addictions psychotherapy generally affords addiction therapists with an opportunity to effectively utilize a number of ancillary alliance-based psychotherapy intervention strategies and tools. Addictions therapists who are trained and clinically experienced in the uses of hypnosis, EMDR, DBT, mindfulness, relaxation training, bio-feedback and the ever developing and evolving repertoire of other therapeutic models or intervention strategies may employ these specific modalities to help modify or resolve any number of relatively patient-specific dysfunctional patterns of behavior. As touched upon earlier in the chapter, addictions therapists may also need to refer their patients for any number of possible professional services to other therapists, physicians, or health care providers at any juncture in the process of psychotherapy work with addictive disordered patients.

Many of these patients benefit from sleep study work-ups, and brief-therapy associated with chronic sleep disorders (Glidewell, 2016). It is not uncommon for addictions therapists to discover very early in the assessment stage of therapeutic work that a significant percent of their patients have not completed a basic physical/medical examination in several years. Addictive disordered patients who have not completed a basic medical examination in the past year, and certainly patients who initially present manifesting significant medical complications or problems, need to be immediately referred for appropriate medical assessment and care.

Clinician experience and training in the realm of residential addictions care settings, hospital or psychiatric units, detoxification centers, and mental health or extended behavioral health care programs can provide addictions therapists with a much keener awareness and understanding of the spectrum of patient care and ethical issues that are associated with the matter of initiating appropriate professional referrals for specialized patient care needs.

The following brief therapy vignette demonstrates alliance-based uses of confrontation, relapse intervention and prevention dynamics, and time structuring focused interventions in the process of middle stage addictions psychotherapy. This vignette was taken from a therapy session-some five months into treatment and following the patient's relapse and brief hospitalization.

Case 17

TONY: Hell, Doc—I don't even remember talkin' to you on the phone—I can't even remember the cops coming to my apartment,—I just know I felt real bad when I woke up—came to, in the hospital, and I definitely knew I was in trouble—plus sick as hell—and I was real paranoid at first about being in trouble with the cops again—but I had no idea how I got there.

DOCTOR F.: Remember us talking about relapse a number of times—the two or maybe three sessions before your relapse—we sure focused on "setting yourself up" again by going back to the bar—the VFW, you were going there two or three times a week, even though you hadn't been drinking—that "testing yourself," and having a "couple of tonic waters with lime," and watching "the others" get drunk—you sure didn't think that process was risky business at the time, and all that "stuff" about not drinking, and the piece about not making sense—relapsing after everything had been going so well—does all that feel like denial or maybe just making it a lot easier to get back into your alcoholism at this point??

TONY: Sure, I've got 20--20 hindsight about all of it now, but it's still kinda hard to believe—it's also hard to believe I'm startin' all over again, damn, how many times am I going to have to go through this to really get it—you know Doc, it's been that way for ten years or so now—we've talked about that too. How many times have I quit for a while, and then I start drinking and it always ends up the same—I'm on a drunk, and I get in trouble—the wife and kids are pissed, and don't talk to me for a month, or so—or it's the job or cops. Sometimes I wonder if I'll ever get it, but one thing I've learned for sure from you is that I've got to get back up and put it all behind me—deal with today, and get back to my recovery program.

DOCTOR F.: You've been in the pattern of punishing yourself and everybody around you for a long time—you've made it part of your lifestyle, and your family too—it's all a part of the self-defeating behavior we've talked about as well—and do you remember being kinda pissed off at me for bringing that part of it up when we were talking about relapse triggers before this last relapse?? You sure did-n't want to hear it, and you let me know in no uncertain terms that it would never happen again—maybe there's something to be learned from all of that, this time, as you're getting back into sobriety and *really* starting to take care of yourself . . . there's definitely some things to learn from all of this that can be a part of making it—long term recovery.

TONY: My ego keeps getting in the way, and that's a part of why it's always kinda hard talking about some of these things with you—I know I don't want to hear some of it, and I was a little pissed at you at the time—I really believed it was all behind me—in the rear view mirror, so to speak, and now I think I'm beginning to realize it's never in the rear view mirror—maybe I'll always be dealing with being an alcoholic—or "recovering" alcoholic as you say—for the rest of my life, but really—even that's kinda hard, and I know that I still really have a hard time accepting that too—reality can hurt. You know—when I really look at it, I've always done things my way—we talked about how my wife's always said I was self-centered, and I really get angry when she calls me a narcissist, and it kinda hurt—but you know she's right, I guess—that's probably part of not listening to anybody else, and screwing things up a lot—not being able to see some of the relapse stuff coming, wanting to do it my way—even not listening or hearing, and even the self-defeating behavior thing we have talked about.

DOCTOR F.: Tony, you're touching on a lot of real issues—all of those things are a part of what we're working on from my perspec-tive—and from the outside, but also after getting to know you and the "other side" of you sober, it's even painful for me to see you put your-self through the wringer again—and you've got to see that in your wife and kids too, plus yourself—in spite of yourself, you've still got a lot of folks in your corner—.that includes me too, and I sure as hell haven't given up on you—this episode can be a new start to some extent for all of us—and the ball is really in your court and our court as I see it.

TONY: Yeah, I feel like we've made some real progress over the last few months, Doc—but I realize I've got a long ways to go—we've all got some stuff we need to work on, but, you know, most of it is up to me—and I've got to get my mind right again, at this point. It's kinda like startin' over for all of us—come to think of it, you may have even saved my life by callin' the cops and gettin' the ambulance out to the house—and I was even angry about that when I finally woke up in the hospital—god, I'm ashamed about it, Doc—I didn't even know that you were the one who called 911 and the cops, and I was angry about that at first—when Mary told me the next day—I don't feel that way now, Doc—I just let everybody down again, and I feel real bad about it.

LATE STAGE ALLIANCE DYNAMICS AND THE PROCESS OF EFFICACIOUS ADDICTIONS-FOCUSED INTEGRATIVE PSYCHOTHERAPY AND COUNSELING WORK

This author (Forrest, 1984, 1997) previously viewed the later stages of intensive alcoholism psychotherapy as the eleventh through eighteen months of treatment. With the advent of contemporary "managed care" some twenty years ago, and the evolving restricted health care insurance benefits related to behavioral health, mental health, and addictive disordered patient populations, in addition to the evolution of the brief therapies and other psychosocial, economic and cultural shifts in western culture, the majority of patients engaging in various forms of behavioral health care and treatment models remain in treatment for significantly shorter periods of time. Practicing additions-focused therapists, treatment providers and other behavioral health clinicians currently conceptualize the later stage of addictions psychotherapy work as generally encompassing continued active psychotherapy relationships that extend beyond one year.

However, a small number of experienced addictions therapists and counselors may continue to sustain working and productive therapeutic alliances and relationships with some of their patients that encompass well over twenty or thirty years, and these therapeutic alliances and relationships also may involve intermit and various other levels of care. The author (Forrest, 2016, 2017) has continued to see some addictive disordered persons in ongoing psychotherapy for over forty years. None of these individuals have been seen on a weekly or even monthly basis, but several have been seen at least on a yearly basis and others perhaps were seen situationally or seen during the course of periodic life-span crisis episodes involving such issues as divorce, family dynamics including substance abuse, depression, anxiety, aging, substance abuse, children, financial crisis, job loss, brief relapse, health and death. Almost all of these patients have sustained total abstinence and full recoveries over the course of ten to over forty years, and this clinical population has encompassed mostly alcohol dependent individuals but also includes patients manifesting polydrug abuse and/or dependence as well as the spectrum of addictive disorders. Several of these patients were also able to sustain ongoing recovery in the face of very difficult and sometimes protracted personal death process experiences.

Later stage addictive disordered patients do not generally require ongoing weekly psychotherapy engagement. Many of these patients can be treated very effectively within the context of one or two sessions per month, and therapist-patient alliance facilitated therapeutic examination of ongoing patient status, expectations, goals and needs may result in mutual patient-therapist agreement that continued therapy on an "as needed" basis or some other frequency based regimen may be appropriate at this juncture in the therapy process. Abstinence and over-all recovery status, global behavioral change and personality growth, vocational, marital and family as well as relational stability, affective and cognitive factors, and general impulse control stability are some of the important alliance-related dynamics that therapists and patients need to examine and explore in the later middle stage and early late stage of addictions therapy work. These alliance focused factors and therapist-patient transactions form the relational basis for effective establishment of the late stage therapy structure, goals and tasks. Recovering addictive disordered patients need to be *actively* involved in this phase of the therapeutic decision-making process. Alliance established and mutually developed frequency and structure of treatment plans during the later stages of psychotherapy generally enhance the fluidity and continued success of the later stage therapy process, but also contribute to the patient's internal sense of independence and self-sufficiency while providing an extended relapse prevention net.

As noted earlier, patient or therapist specific factors related to insurance benefits, health, career, motivation for care, financial status, and a wealth of personal, situational or unpredictable factors can always impact or determine the duration, frequency, intensity or even outcome of therapy at any juncture in the therapeutic process. Therapists are well advised to remain cognizant of these ever-present concrete realities associated with the process of therapy including late stage therapy work.

LATE STAGE ALLIANCE DYNAMICS INCLDING IDENTITY CONSOLIDATION, SYNTHESIS, AND WORKING THROUGH IN ADDICTIONS-FOCUSED PSYCHOTHERAPY AND COUNSELING WORK

The later stage of addictions psychotherapy work generally involves a consistent working through and reworking or enhancing therapy material and content that was elicited, partially resolved or remains unresolved during the early and middle stages of therapy. Patients also tend to be able to recall, consciously recognize, and tolerate the exploration and change process associated with a broad range of previously unconscious and highly repressed personal conflictual issues during the later stages in therapy. Not uncommonly, addictions therapists find that crucial long-term recovery facilitating work occurs during this stage of therapy. Patients continue to be confronted with the difficult realities and life tasks associated with making decisions, coping with personal and family traumas, crisis situations, loss, and other significant life stressors. In this context, the process of daily living becomes an increasingly important source of grist for therapy later in the psychotherapy process. Therapeutic alliance-based corrective emotional experiences occur as the patient develops a diversity of more effective coping skills associated with the resolution of various daily living problems. Effective real-world coping skills reduce or eliminate the neurotic and addictive brain disease driven need to utilize alcohol, drugs, food, nicotine, sex and other dysfunctional addictive disordered patterns of behavior. Patients become progressively more adapt at practicing, utilizing, and choosing more rational patterns of thinking, emoting, behaving and living as a result of effective therapy experiences and the ongoing late-stage therapy recovery process.

The alliance-based therapeutic process involving late stage addictions psychotherapy work essentially involves revisiting, reworking, reframing, and synthesizing the material and content that has been partially resolved via earlier therapeutic work. These residual and dysfunctional facets of the patient's previously addictive disordered adjustment style have frequently continued to contribute to the ongoing relational and intrapersonal difficulties that patients experience in the "here and now" process of therapy. The late stage therapeutic alliance focus and synthesis of the patient's dysfunctional repetition-compulsion based patterns of behavior including fragmented or irrational thoughts, beliefs, self-perceptions, feelings, and other intrapersonal and interpersonal processes that foster the patient's ability to integrate many formerly repressed, denied, and ego-dystonic or ego-alien pathologic issues. Therapeutic synthesis occurs when thoughts, affective, and behavioral processes that were once repressed, denied, distorted and ego-alien become conscious, ego-syntonic, and integratively and significantly modified vis a via here-and-now behaviors and through the patient's evolving global adjustment style. These alliance-based tasks are accomplished via the therapist's use of (1) active middle stage and late stage interpretations, (2) consistent and supportive association and elucidation of the patient's past and present dysfunctional addictive disordered related behaviors and neurotic conflicts, (3) continued reinforcement of rational and behavioral alternatives and choices to these dysfunctional patterns of adjustment in the here-and-now, (4) practicing new behaviors and interpersonal skill sets, challenging or disputing self-defeating and irrational pattern of self-talk, and (5) consistently associating and relating the patient's addictive symptom structure to the therapeutic material that has been explored and partially resolved or modified earlier in the psychotherapy process.

Addictions therapists need to consistently point out and reinforce the various adaptive changes and global sources of gain that patients have actualized throughout the course of treatment while continuing to focus upon areas where the patient and therapist clearly need to do more concentrated and intensive work. Frequently, it is relatively easy for the therapist to point out and remind the patient how he or she previously thought, behaved, and emoted relative to rather specific dysfunctional patterns of behavior and issues associated with everyday life situations. Late stage therapy patients are usually able to see and identify the distortions and cognitive errors associated with their earlier patterns of addictive disordered thinking, perceiving, self-talk, and behaving.

At this juncture in therapy, patients may experience some sense of anxiety and threat; however, the resilience and malleability that is associated with later stage alliance development, therapist sensitivity, and the understanding of patient specific adjustment dynamics support, actively encourage, and foster the use of humor within these late stage alliance interactions. These dynamics can also greatly reduce patient anxiety as well as significantly strengthen the patient's sense of self-discovery, confidence, sense of self-worth, personal awareness, and synthesize the patient's fragmented and ego-dystonic self-system adjustment dynamics.

A continued therapist focus on the patient's historic narcissistic injuries, early life trauma, and developmental struggles and dynamics are played out in the patient's daily here-and-now relational living struggles. These therapeutic dynamics can also be revisited in late stage therapy work. Patients are also better able to recognize and modify destructive patterns of self-related narcissistic injury at this time. They may also become more astute at recognizing the narcissistically pathologic dimensions of their object relationships. These alliance-based late stage therapy dynamics potentially help patients develop a more synthesized, consistent, and integrated self-concept. This process also fosters the patient's ability to develop an adequately consolidated nuclear sense of self. Patterns of maladaptive and extreme narcissistic shifts in self-esteem may be extinguished and neutralized by these therapeutic interventions.

Therapist support and encouragement continue to be important facets of late stage therapy work, and therapists need to help their addictive disordered patients realize and move well beyond the core basics of their addictive disease process. Ongoing recovery is based upon the patient's continued commitment to progressive adaptive growth, change, integration and learning. The recovery process is never static in nature, but rather remains a challenging and at times difficult and exciting life journey.

Many addictive disordered persons vicariously learn a diversity of self-care and healthy self-therapy techniques via the alliance and therapeutic process. In effect, the therapist teaches and models many strategies and techniques that can be used to adaptively cope with a diversity of problems and trauma-based difficulties that the patient may encounter in life long after therapy has been terminated. These self-care techniques may involve enhanced communication skills, stress management, relaxation, and dealing with life and life's issues on a "one day at a time" basis. Improved social awareness and social skills, being able to say "no," setting boundaries or being assertive, overcoming anger, resentment and impulsiveness, and even recognizing when it is time to re-engage in psychotherapy or another appropriate care model or program to enhance patient self-esteem and interpersonal skills.

LATE STAGE ALLIANCE DYNAMICS INVOLVING IDENTITY CONSOLIDATION AND RESOLUTION OF PROJECTIVE IDENTIFICATION IN ADDICTIONS-FOCUSED PSYCHOTHERAPY AND COUNSELING WORK

Addictive disordered patients present with a diversity of personal backgrounds, clinical diagnoses, adjustment difficulties and various addictive disease related symptoms. These patients seek out treatment as a result of diverse reasons and many have been seen for addictions-focused treatments and behavioral health care treatment during middle-late adolescence and early-middle adulthood. In recent years, more substance abusers and addictive disordered patients are entering various treatment programs as well as various forms of psychotherapy during the later decades of their lives. Indeed, the addictive brain disease spectrum encompasses the human life span, and contemporary society includes an ever growing and progressively more addictive disordered senior patient population.

Many addictive disordered persons (Forrest, 1983, 2018) have experienced profound early life trauma or narcissistic injury which very quickly becomes a catalyst for life-long attachment dysfunction. These harsh relational and developmental realities often result in patient self-system fragmentation, structural weakness of the ego, identity and gender issues. Many addictive disordered patients also manifest an inadequately consolidated nuclear sense of self. Simply put, many if not most, addictive disordered persons have suffered an experiential infancy and childhood which contributes to profound ongoing identity fragmentation, and some patients eventually appear to lose their core identities via the addiction process per se. These patients may spontaneously tell their therapists that they are confused, no longer know who they are, and some become disoriented or experience infrequent and brief drug or alcohol induced psychotic episodes. These patients become increasingly capable of being more in touch with themselves as they initiate and sustain treatment engagement and become actively involved in the recovery process. Basic substance abstinence, sustained healthy eating patterns, and the cessation of various patterns of destructive addictive behavior, including thoughts, beliefs, and obsessive-compulsive addiction driven behaviors foster the patient's potential capacity for healthy identity consolidation.

The relational working and productive alliance framework that contributes to the patient's early stage therapy capacity for initiating and sustaining the recovery process also become a potent vehicle for constructive identity consolidation, the capacity for healthy relational attachments, an enhanced sense of nuclear self, and radically improved patient self-esteem and personal sense of self-worth during the late middle stage and later stages of addictions therapy.

Not uncommonly, addictive disordered patients manifest a diversity of co-morbid psychiatric disorders. These patients may also have experienced psychiatric hospitalizations, multiple "detox" experiences, and addiction and/or substance dependence induced brief treatment episodes. Some of these patients have been perceived by others as being "strange" or perhaps even insane, and many have internalized self-defeating fears, beliefs and thoughts about being mentally disturbed. Addictive disordered patients typically experience conflicts related to anxiety, bipolar disorder, panic and depression. These experiences and affective states may trigger periods of disorganized behavior and confused thinking. Effective middle stage and late stage alliance work involving the therapist's use of ongoing supportive interpretation, in-depth exploration, sensitive and timely strategic confrontations, experiential learning, modeling, mindfulness and other therapeutic strategies can foster significant patient growth and change in the realm of identity consolidation. Patient issues associated with paranoid thinking and trust, avoidance defenses, self-defeating and sadomasochistic behavior, impulsiveness and rage or anger control issues also become more amenable to change later in the psychotherapy process.

The process of identity consolidation sometimes includes the explicit realm of gender identity and issues related to sexual-orientation confusion. Unlike twenty or fifty years ago, contemporary American culture and society no longer stigmatizes homosexual, lesbian, transgendered, bi-sexual and many other forms of previously viewed "deviant" or aberrant sexual behavior. Addictive disordered patients manifesting various co-morbid sexual problems generally tend to feel less reluctant to reveal or openly discuss these sexual matters with their therapists, and specialized clinical services related to a diversity of sexual problems including sexual addictions and dysfunctional patterns of sexual behavior now exist within the American residential and out-patient treatment facility communities. Many clinics, psychotherapists and counselors also provide services for persons manifesting the spectrum of sexuality-related problems and issues.

In concert with these recent general cultural and social changes, a segment of the addictive disordered population continues to struggle with a plethora of sexually-focused conflicts. Issues related to internalized feelings and perceptions of inadequate masculinity, femininity, intrusive homosexual or bisexual thoughts and fantasies, obsessive-compulsive and addictive patterns of sexual behavior, acting-out, cross-dressing, pornography and exhibitionism as well as common questions, self-doubts, irrational beliefs, faulty prior learning experiences, and perceptions associated with a diversity of sexual matters can be important facets of the identity consolidation psychotherapy work that provides grist for significant exploration, resolution or modification during the late stage of addictions psychotherapy.

Needless to say, a wide range of identity-related conflicts can also be functionally driven by the addictive disordered patient's issues related to premature or delayed ejaculation problems, concerns about penis or breast size, weight, anorgasmia, painful colitis, low desire or arousal issues, and other common sexual dysfunctions and problems.

Many addictive disordered patients simply fail to realize the devastating impact that their addictive disease process eventually has upon every facet of their identities including sexual identity, responding, and biopsychosocial related sexual behaviors. The addictive disease process can eventually precipitate a wide range of medical and identity based debilitating psychological, relational and physical changes. Likewise, the addictive disease process can also cause or contribute significantly to the development of a wide range of psychiatric and psychological disorders including depression and anxiety, cognitive impairment, and premature brain aging, psychotic episodes, paranoid thinking, impulsive control deficits, floridly antisocial behavior, and various other personality disorder traits and forms of psychopathology.

Healthy identity consolidation often begins with alliance-based resolution of the patient's historic specific intrapersonal and interpersonally determined anxiety. Intense and chronic anxiety creates self-system fragmentation, ego-deficits including continued structural weakness of the ego, basic identity de-fusion very early in life, and not only does this maladaptive adjustment dynamism persist well into adulthood, but this process may ultimately and later in life become partially or neurotically controlled and adaptively regulated vis a via the addiction process. However, this process also synergizes the evolution of the addictive disease process, sometimes resulting in the eventual complete collapse of the patient's ego via acute panic states and brief psychotic episodes. Intrapersonal and interpersonally triggered severe and chronic anxiety states remain deterrents to healthy ego development, and healthy identity consolidation; consensual relational validation cannot consistently take place when one or multiple people involved in intimate human encounters, including psychotherapy, remain profoundly, chronically, and acutely anxious.

Essential components of later stage alliance based therapeutic work with these patients always includes (1) successful termination of the patients active addictive disease process, and (2) helping patients resolve, extinguish and modify the various sources of chronic interpersonal and intrapersonal anxiety which has precipitated identity diffusion, self-system fragmentation, and blocks or greatly inhibits the patient's capacity to develop an adequately consolidated nuclear sense of self. These therapeutic tasks and goals are also not limited to the realm of anxiety regulation, but generally include a diversity of other patient specific addictive disease process factors which contribute to and synergize the patient's identity consolidation related conflicts.

Finally, the later stage of addictions therapy and alliance work needs to encompass a focus on the recovering patient's ability to integratively incorporate a very personalized identity consolidation involving his or her sense of simply being a "recovering person." Experienced and recovering addictions clinicians are generally very aware of this particular facet of the later stages of successful therapeutic work with their patients. Successful later stage psychotherapy patients also tend to spontaneously self-initiate the process of openly referring to themselves as a "recovering person" within an ever-increasing variety of social contexts. Addictions therapists can actively begin to shape this facet of the patient's identity consolidation process within the therapeutic alliance framework during middle and late stage therapy, but patients who develop the spontaneous capacity to integratively express this core self-identity construct in a much wider range of social arenas often appear to be able to internally embrace and sustain long-term or even life-long recoveries.

Being able to consciously accept and internalize the reality of one's personhood as a "*recovering person*," and also clearly realizing that this is one very important facet of one's life also makes it somewhat easier for the addictive disordered patient to sustain various new recovery-based behaviors, thoughts, and necessary ongoing recovery-focused ingredients needed for long-term recovery. Self-acceptance and ongoing focused appropriate self-care as a person with a chronic debilitating health condition, illness or disease generally fosters improved health care outcomes. Addictive disordered patients who overtly and consistently resist or deny acceptance of their addictive disorders within the alliance context during the later stages of therapy generally have not developed the adequately consolidated nuclear sense of self which can be a core facet of the long-term recovery process. These patients tend to consistently question their capacity for returning to "controlled drinking," continued "social" or recreational use of marijuana, opioids, sedatives and other addictive behaviors including altered diets on weekends, "controlled gambling," and other forms of previously and chronically destructive addictive disordered behavior. These late stage therapy dynamics are obviously "red flags" for addictions therapists. Thus, therapist strategies, alliance dynamics, structure, goal modification and other measures may need to be utilized during the later stage of therapy in order to continue the process of enhancing continued patient growth and recovery work in this arena involving identity consolidation as well as initiating relapse prevention measures for long term recovery success.

Continued late stage alliance work focusing on a diversity of dynamics associated with the patient's historic sources of narcissistic injury, trauma and ongoing sources of conflict additionally help foster the process of healthy identity consolidation. As patients improve their ability to recognize and modify chronically dysfunctional patterns of self-involving and significant other induced relational sources of emotional pain, trauma, loss and narcissistic injury, they also become progressively better able to synthesize, consolidate and regulate a more balanced sense of self. These therapeutic processes synergize and reinforce the patient's healthy and appropriate sense of self-esteem and positive self-worth.

Extended effective long-term therapeutic alliance relationships generate the potential for continued patient self-work (Forrest, 1997, 2014) associated with a multitude of identity-based issues and conflicts that have evolved as a direct result of the patient's ongoing addictions therapy experiences; however, these adjustment conflicts can also be associated with many life span realities that may re-occur during the remainder of the patient's life span. In essence, therapists often teach patients a plethora of self-therapy and potentially lifelong techniques or tools that can be effectively used to both sustain the long-term recovery process as well as the core process of coping with various ongoing life traumas, and the spectrum of human experiences that characterize the process of aging.

LATE STAGE ALLIANCE DYNAMICS, PROJECTIVE IDENTIFICATION, INTENSIVE AFFECTIVE WORK, AND ANCILLARY STRATEGIES IN ADDICTIONS-FOCUSED PSYCHOTHERAPY AND COUNSELING WORK

The author (Forrest, 1984, 1997) has previously indicated that projective identification is "perhaps the most adaptive, and yet a potentially pathological component" associated with the addictive disordered patient's avoidance defense system. The avoidance defense system was also discussed earlier in this text, and principally is associated with the paradoxically adaptive and maladaptive development of the additive disordered patient's denial, distortion and projective identification defenses. While all of the addictive disordered patient's defense mechanisms eventually begin to operate in the service of the patient's ego, these particular defense mechanisms operate to keep patients "out of touch with self-perceptions, feelings and emotions, and rational self-dialogue; the avoidance defense system becomes a defense against the painful realities of the world as well as the internal world of the self, and additionally reinforces continued patient isolation, interpersonal attachment-detachment anxiety, and the development of poor social skills.

Projective identification allows the patient to initially blame others and the external world for a morass of personally threatening feelings, difficult life circumstances, relational difficulties or repetitive failures, and conscious or pre-conscious uncomfortable or disturbing thoughts associated with the patient's addictive disease and general life station. However, during the course of early stage psychotherapy and the course of early-middle stage process of recovery, continued over-determined use of the projective identification mechanism can become an "ultimate barrier" to the patient's development of healthy, fully functioning human relationships. This malignant facet of the projective identification process refers to the patient's projection of self or fragments of the self (compartmentalized beliefs, patterns of behavior, feelings, etc.) upon significant others in order to facilitate attachments and identification with significant others. In other words, the projective identification mechanism continues to be a dysfunctional component of the patient's ongoing interpersonal and intrapersonal real-world experiences involving the establishment and maintenance of healthy interpersonal relationships. Thus, many addictive disordered persons continue to essentially identify, accept, interact and establish relationships with people or "objects" that they perceive as internalized extensions of self.

Projective identification dynamics can be played out vis á via a multiplicity of contexts within the addiction psychotherapy process. For example, a segment of addictions counselors and treatment professionals as well as patients continue to believe that "non-addictive disordered" clinicians and therapists are less than able or perhaps should not or cannot successfully work with this clinical population. Vestiges of this aspect of the projective identification mechanism continue to be evident within the Alcoholics Anonymous community and other self-help care alternative programs. This irrational belief system supporting the long-held adage that "only an alcoholic or addict can help other alcoholics and addicts" is steeped in projective identification.

Effective late stage alliance-based addictions psychotherapy work involving the modification and resolution of projective identification related issues encompassing an active and in-depth exploration of the patient's beliefs, patterns of interpersonal behavior, and affects associated with rigid thinking, compartmentalization, ego-splitting, and a "black or white" world view. The projective identification mechanism can also contribute to the addictive disordered patient's underlying paranoid ideation which also reinforces the patient's suspiciousness, as well as defensiveness and the avoidance defense system. This guarded interpersonal style, and "world view," ultimately becomes a core symptom of the patient's addictive disease process.

Thus, the projective identification mechanism interferes with healthy identity consolidation on several levels. This mechanism reinforces the early life trauma and attachment disorder related conflicts that many addictive disordered patients have struggled with throughout the course of most of their active disease process. This defense mechanism facilitates the development of a regressive and static interpersonal adjustment style that limits the patient's object attachments to the realm of self-significant others who rigidly maintain the same or similar dysfunctional beliefs, attitudes, values, behaviors and general life-style adjustments. These issues can further contribute to problems related to healthy self-other differentiation, detachment, internal feelings of inadequacy, selflessness, dependence, low self-worth, chronic anxiety, and depression.

Experienced clinicians and addictions therapists generally realize that the projective identification mechanism can be paradoxically adaptive, and can also contribute to the patient's over-all recovery process early in treatment. This mechanism can help foster constructive relational attachments within the self-help community, with therapists, self-help sponsors, and others early in therapy. These dynamics can also facilitate early stage patient attachments to therapists, and particularly so with recovering clinicians that may contribute to the "therapeutic honeymoon" phase of therapy. However, the projective identification mechanism may provide a measure of healthy attachment that contributes to the patient's ability to form an initial empathic alliance bond with the therapist. Indeed, the patient's conscious and preconscious perceptions and attachment dynamics related to the therapist as a self-extension can synergize the patient's initial motivation, commitment and early bond within the therapeutic alliance context.

Therapist's need to develop (1) a general understanding of the addictive disordered patient's projective identification defense dynamics, and (2) consciously and systematically attempt to help patient's change and modify this process throughout the course of therapy. Early in therapy, the therapist allows the transference relationship to develop and supportively explores, examines, identifies and supportively interprets and explains various parameters of these issues as they are related to the patient's addictive brain disease process as well as more global historic patterns of behavior. The therapist also allows and may encourage some facets of the projective identification process to develop within the therapist-patient alliance context. The therapeutic relationship building and constructive alliance-based work that takes place early in therapy provides the therapist and patient with an in-depth alliance foundation which will strengthen the patient's identity, and constructively contribute to the patient's abilities to complete the therapeutic work associated with identity consolidation. The resolution of the patient's over-determined projective identification mechanism spans the course of the middle and later stages of addictions psychotherapy work.

Later stage therapist alliance intervention strategies which can be used to resolve and modify the patient's identity consolidation related conflicts can foster resolution of the projective identification dynamism, effect significant ego-synthesis, and facilitate healthy identity consolidation including: (1) a consistently and more intensely focusing upon the *patient's* feelings, behaviors, beliefs, attitudes, and cognitions associated with the self-process as well as previous and current external interpersonal behaviors, (2) consistently and supportively differentiating between the patient, therapist and significant others (in the patient's interpersonal world) global self-process in relation to the various facets listed in number one; (3) didactically, actively and experientially explaining , teaching, exploring, interpreting, and focusing in-depth upon the patient's particular uses and style of unhealthy projective identification associated with these identity consolidation matters, and (4) actively clarifying the core interactive relationships that are associated with these constructs (i.e., identity consolidation, projective identification, and self-other differentiation).

Therapists often need to redundantly explore and focus on these later stage therapy issues; however, enhanced therapist-patient alliance work and focusing on these dynamics at this juncture in the treatment process can potentially foster significantly improved interpersonal functioning, enhance general social skills, more efficacious relational decision making, improved boundary setting awareness and skills, improved self-esteem, improved affect regulation and impulse control, and a consolidated nuclear sense of self as well as improved recovery outcomes.

Late stage psychotherapy with addictive disordered patients may also involve the use of any number of ancillary integrative therapeutic intervention modalities or treatment techniques and strategies. These facets of late stage therapy are generally associated with patient specific needs and dynamics, and various evolving therapist-patient alliance matters may also be the result of a wide range of unpredictable circumstances related to the therapist, patient, alliance developments and situational real-world life events. However, rather commonly addictions counselors and their patients find themselves dealing with much more intensive, in-depth, and potentially emotionally threatening or emotionally complex facets of the patient's current and past experiential world at this juncture within the therapeutic alliance relationship. Therapists not infrequently find themselves experiencing or re-experiencing similar or related intense feelings and emotions associated with their own real personal life struggles and life journey during this phase in therapy.

In short, intensified and in-depth therapeutic work that takes place later in the addictions psychotherapy process tends to result in a myriad of relatively new transference and countertransference dynamics between the patient and therapist, and these dynamics also may obviously and significantly impact the integrity of the working alliance as well as the outcome of treatment.

Throughout the course of therapy, addictions therapists and clinicians need to keep in mind that their patients generally tend to fear their emotions and feelings. Patients avoid and repress a wide range of intense personal emotions, and some experience difficulties with simply labeling and identifying their emotions. Early in therapy and prototaxically, addictive disordered patients who have experienced profound early life trauma and narcissistic injury, experience intense emotional expressions as potentially chaotic, catastrophic, anxiety-producing and sometimes even life-threatening events. The therapist's consistent, supportive, sensitive and openly expressed understanding of these various realities related to these patient dynamics is essential to the continued uses of appropriately timed and focused affective work throughout the course of therapy. Often it is important for the therapist to simply affirm to the patient that it is appropriate, "ok" or normal to express a wide range of emotions and feelings in therapy as well as in the context of all relationships.

Male addictive disordered patients in particular tend to believe that any open display of intense emotions can be indicative of weakness, loss of control, instability, inadequacy or femininity. In such cases, the therapist may need to explore or actively challenge these irrational beliefs, and supportively confront, interpret, and dispute the patient's cognitive belief system related to his or her repressed or conflicted management of feelings and emotions. With some patients it can also be very helpful for the therapist to focally address the potential benefits of catharsis in psychotherapy. Untreated and unresolved affective disturbance and affect regulation difficulties contribute significantly to the development and maintenance of all addictive disorders, and these realities also need to be clearly recognized and explored by the therapist and patient. Furthermore, therapists and patients also need to perceive their alliance based affective work as an important ingredient in the ongoing recovery process.

Verbal dialogue and exploration of the patient's various difficulties related to the expression of affect, emotional control, and more global self-regulation can facilitate the process of practicing and re-learning new and more adaptive patterns for expressing and maintaining the patient's affective parameters of behavior within the alliance framework and other relational contexts during late stage therapy work. The therapist and patient can also rehearse the triggers and situations that have historically been associated with maladaptive patterns of affect regulation. This therapeutic alliance procedure also includes practicing a repertoire of new and more effective methods for affect regulation and internalized self-control. In this context, patients can develop enhanced skill recognition related to the various intense emotions that have historically been associated with personal feelings of hurt, rejection, anger and rage, anxiety, guilt, loss of control, and the wider range of human emotional experience. The alliance framework also becomes a relational basis for patient unlearning, new-learning, re-learning and "corrective emotional experiences" to occur.

Most addictive disordered patients develop the capacity to be increasingly more open to their own internal experiences during the late-middle and late stages in therapy. These patients also become progressively more able to express feelings, more disclosing and rigorously honest, experience and spontaneously express humor and laughter, and simply become more fully functioning human beings. Individual therapy sessions, group therapy sessions, and open or closed self-help meetings involving addictive disordered persons who have sustained long term recovery histories are frequently filled with expressions of humor, laughter, smiles, healthy, and spontaneously warm human emotions. These individuals become progressively less defensive, armored, suspicious, interpersonally guarded, conflicted, avoidant and dysfunctional over the course of middle stage and later stage therapy work.

Addictions therapists will find it useful to encourage and actively support the patient's continued engagement in some form of personally directed, internalized, and structured ongoing recovery regimen later in the therapy process, and the therapist can help facilitate this process by simply inquiring about the patient's level of continuing care engagement at various junctures later in the treatment process (Forrest, 2012, 2014, 2019). Reinforcing the importance of maintaining an ongoing pattern of healthy self-care certainly fosters the recovery process, and the therapist's modeling and active therapeutic roles related to educating, reinforcing and encouraging patient patterns of improved health care involving nutrition, exercise, sleep, appropriate medical care, stress management and the various other parameters of basic health maintenance can synergize the addiction recovery process throughout the entire process of therapy as well as actively synergizing a lifelong recovery process.

Therapists may need to re-visit and utilize or implement a wide range of previously used therapeutic strategies or interventions during later stage therapy work with addictive disordered persons. Patient relapses in late stage therapy can always be alliance debilitating, and while these events tend to be infrequent and short in duration, they can also be potentially catastrophic. Therapists need to be able to implement any number of possible clinically appropriate relapse prevention or deterrent actions in these situations. Brief hospitalizations, medical measures including medication assisted care, residential or IOP program re-engagement, or extended and intensive late stage therapy engagement may also be indicated.

Contingent upon the therapist's training, experience and skill repertoire, and the patient's individual care needs and personal dynamics, some level of therapeutic exploration of the patient's dream life (Forrest, 1997), the use of clinical hypnosis (Zeig, 2017) or mindfulness training and relaxation exercises, and actively encouraging patient completion of a college degree or additional education, career counseling and any number of other appropriate therapy related or directed therapeutic interventions and activities may need to be initiated. These therapist interventions can be utilized in order to facilitate the patient's ongoing recovery process, personal growth and development, and general well-being throughout the course of the addiction psychotherapy process.

The following therapy vignette was taken from a late stage therapy session (fifty-fourth session) with a recovering chronic alcoholic patient. This patient had also been diagnosed with a co-morbid depressive disorder, paranoid personality features, generalized anxiety, and chronic marital dysfunction. This vignette encompasses identity consolidation late stage therapy work related to projective identification, affect, social interaction dynamics, and other alliance-based therapist actions.

Case 18

JACK: I guess I still have trouble being around the "normies." Those social situations we have talked about over the months—I'm a lot better—just not as nervous, but it seemed to all come back at that barbeque last weekend—it's still difficult being around people who are drinking, even if they really can handle it—after being there for a while, I even started to feel sorry for myself again—it would be nice to be able to handle it again—drinking, but I've accepted that it doesn't work for me—and I wasn't craving it either, but Shirley sure as hell let me know that I wasn't any fun to be with—what's wrong with you, and why don't you just relax and have fun stuff? She was glad to leave early, and we left early—but, by that time I couldn't wait to get the hell out of there—it sure as hell isn't any fun to be around a lot of drunk people—I sure realize that now, and that was me a year or so ago—and I'm sure glad to be out of all that, and I'm not worrying about what I did or said talking to you about it this morning—ha–ha.

DOCTOR F.: Going back into those social situations—the drinking people and drinking environments are difficult, and can sure be a relapse trigger for a lot of recovering people—you have realized this for a good while, but this experience sure brought all of that back into focus—and the good news is, you're sober and you handled it pretty well—the stuff we've talked about related to limiting your exposure to these social situations, developing new relationships and social activities involving recovery folks and people who clearly aren't heavy drinkers—the real world transition process—sure, it's still difficult for you, but it does get better—that's why your recovery program or regimen is still so important—Jack.

JACK: The fact that my wife and I were able to discuss this party before we went, and even make a plan—like we discussed in therapy a few months ago—about office parties and social stuff with our neighbors and old friends—most of them drink, and some of them drink a lot—having that plan, and Shirley agreed to get the hell out—just leave if I felt anxious or all stirred up really helped—no arguing, we just said we had to go, and we left—but I could tell that Shirley kinda resented it. We kinda talked about it the next day before I went to the office, and she sure realized that some of the people were getting pretty drunk, so both of us felt better about leaving in the end—it did work out.

DOCTOR F.: Seeing yourself more clearly now as you really are, but also seeing yourself like you were in the past can be a good thing—it seems pretty clear that you don't want to be another drunk at the next social situation you all go to—then it also seems that you realize that you can't build your new life around social situations that are always limited to recovering persons or "normies." It is good to wake up with a clear head, and the ability to remember what you did the night or afternoon before at a "party"—plus you no longer act like you've got eyes in the back of your head related to what you did when you were drunk in those past social episodes—

JACK: What do you mean?

DOCTOR F.: You're not paranoid and suspicious all the time anymore—the self-trust thing too, plus being in control—you were in control of yourself at this party, even though you may have felt anxious as hell, and hopefully, you have more trust in yourself about not drinking in those situations. Does that make sense when you think about it? And even the social anxiety you were experiencing was controlled. You responded rationally—you left, and both of you felt better about all of it. That's one step in the process of beginning to successfully take more control of your life. It sure sounds like you didn't panic—or freak out like you did before—how about Shirley's response to all of this?

JACK: Yeah, I see what you're saying—but you know, I think the plan thing really helped—and maybe that's why my wife didn't get pissed at me, and freak out about leaving—but I'm still working on trusting myself too—I've come to realize in here, how I've lied to myself and convinced myself of a lot of BS for too long—and that's why Shirley still doesn't trust me and you know *me*, Doc—I've been a drunk for a long time, and it's still strange being sober—sometimes I need to look at myself in the mirror in the morning, just to realize that I even look different—and I am different, a lot of people tell me, but it's still kinda unreal at times—uh, don't get me wrong—I like it— the new me, but I guess I'm still working on all that.

DOCTOR F.: With all you've said, you're not nearly as depressed as you were six or eight months ago, and with the party thing too— think about all that. You're not depressed as hell and physically ill, or back in the hospital because you went on a binge to deal with the social anxiety and stuff related to the triggers associated with the party—all of it—you didn't get back into the self-punishment stuff, and you're not in the "dog-house" at home either—think about this whole experience—you're not paying lawyer fees again—and upset as hell about that either. And we—need to revisit the whole issue of being in "party" situations too.

JACK: Doc, talking with you always helps me feel better, and some of it is just telling me these things—it's positive, and you're right about the positive stuff—I know I've been sober, and made a lot of progress—but I seem to still focus on the negativity too much, and that makes me feel really sad at times—it's still hard to see myself in a really positive light, and it's hell that I still don't even trust myself Like I should—you know, at times I still cry about all the shit I've said to my wife, and—I keep working at being a better father too—that's one area that helps me feel better about myself now; the kids are a lot closer to me, and they've both said they love me a lot now—and, Bobby says he's still workin' on forgiving me about the stuff I did on that last drunk—God, I was a real piece of work when I was drunk.

DOCTOR F.: It's a journey, Jack—a process, and you sure have made some changes, but we've got more work to do, and it can be a lot better—we're getting there—at times it seems slow, and really like life, it can be two steps forward and three backwards at times—just hang in there—and that applies to all of this Jack—in different ways and situations.

JACK: Uh, hu—and I still have a way to go with just knowing who I am—I'm glad to be sober, and I know I'm an alcoholic but mainly I need more time to know who I am sober—a recovering person—you know, I think I'm starting to get to really know myself for the first time ever.

DOCTOR F.: Remember us discussing how you're known yourself as a "drunk," and your family and friends have probably viewed you as an alcoholic for fifteen or twenty years and now you've been sober, but it took all those years to get where you're at now—it takes time for you and everybody you've really been involved with to get beyond thinking or believing that you're not the same person—even you—plus, we've never really talked about how most people are drinkers in this world—drinking problems, or not—it's normative to be a drinker, and a lot of people—including you in the past, don't trust or somehow wonder about people who don't drink at all—think about it, you have gone from being a socially stigmatized "alcoholic," to a person who might be criticized or looked at strangely because you no longer drink—a lot of who I am issues and other dynamics associated with your new life Jack—

JACK: You've got me thinking, Doc—I guess it's not much wonder that I'm still confused or struggling with a lot of these things— and it took me twenty years to get where I ended up, and it makes sense—I'm sure as hell not going to get where I want to be in 6 or 8 months.

LATE STAGE ALLIANCE DYNAMICS AND TERMINATION IN ADDICTIONS-FOCUSED INTEGRATIVE PSYCHOTHERAPY AND COUNSELING WORK

As noted throughout the course of this text, psychotherapy and counseling terminations can occur at any stage or juncture in the therapy process, and terminations may also take place as a result an almost endless number of factors and situational-relational dynamics and reasons. Freud (1953) addressed the issue of when to terminate psychoanalysis and analytic therapy over one hundred years ago. The progressive evolution of an ever-growing number of psychotherapy and counseling "schools" or approaches and models of psychotherapy has been accompanied by a diversity of recommendations, models and practice-based guidelines and beliefs related to such issues as the optimal length of therapy, frequency of sessions, and timing as well as therapist-patient strategies related to the process of terminating counseling and psychotherapy relationships.

Suffice it to say, over the course of the past three or four decades most psychotherapy treatment models, and the actual course of therapeutic treatment involving the therapeutic alliance context have become (1) less intensive, (2) much shorter in duration, (3) more cognitive-behavioral (CBT) or "brief-therapy" oriented, multimodal or eclectic in scope, (4) integrative, (5) evidence-based, and importantly (6) increasingly determined and shaped by the over-all government directed American Health Insurance related care system. Factors including the insurance industry, patient specific variables such as ability to pay for professional services, internal motivation for change, or often legal and/or occupational matters as well as other externally mandated or forced therapeutic engagements. All of these "real-world" factors and dynamics have continued to interactively impact the various facets associated with the professional practice of counseling and psychotherapy involving the therapeutic alliance (Bhatia and Gelso, 2017; Forrest, 2014, 2016; Hill et al., 2018).

ALLIANCE DYNAMICS AND THE TERMINATION PROCESS IN INTEGRATIVE ADDICTIONS-FOCUSED COUNSELING AND PSYCHOTHERAPY WORK

Historic and contemporary textbooks and professional literature specific to the theory and practice of counseling and psychotherapy have generally continued to inadequately and infrequently address the matter of psychotherapy termination (Hilsenroth, 2017). Therapist alliance management skills as well as patient related alliance dynamics are almost always crucial ingredients in the process of therapy termination, and the therapist-patient alliance relationship provides a context for the initiation of the therapy termination process (Goode et al., 2017; Marmarosh, 2017) during the later stages of psychotherapy (Forrest, 1997, 2014). However, a diversity of alliance related dynamics and factors also impact treatment terminations at any or every juncture in the psychotherapy process. These matters pertaining to alliance work have historically been touched upon in both the limited research and clinical literature pertaining to psychotherapy terminations, and also within the context of termination within the explicit domain of alliance ruptures and repair work (Escudero et al., 2012; Forrest, 1997; Friedlander, 2015; Safran et al., 2011), therapeutic bond and outcome (Bhatia and Gelso, 2017; Friedlander, 2015; Lo Coco et al., 2011; Ulvenes et al., 2012), transference and countertransference (Anderson and Przybylinski, 2012; Bhatia and Gelso, 2017; Forrest, 2012; Gelso and Bhatia, 2012; Hayes et al., 2011; Ulberg et al., 2014), and recent client perspectives on early-stage alliance formation (Eubanks-Carter et al., 2015; Knox et al., 2011; MacFarlane et al., 2015). It is also significant to note that the topic of psychotherapy termination has infrequently been addressed in the clinical and research publications. However, addictions-focused therapists and other therapists and counselors are encouraged to read the extensive therapy termination research and clinical information published in the recent American Psychological Association Psychotherapy Journal. This journal publication examines a wide variety of therapy termination specific articles and studies that have been conducted by exceptional clinicians and researchers (Hilsenroth, 2017).

Therapists and patients generally need to initiate an alliance-based process focusing on the development of a *jointly constructed flexible* (Goode, J., Park, J., Parkin, S. et al., 2017) psychotherapy termination plan during the early part of late stage addictions therapy work. Within the context of early or middle stage psychotherapy termination work that occurs in cases involving highly premature and unilateral patient-initiated alliance ruptures that occur as a result of patient relapses, psychopathology, or acute situational life circumstances impacting the patient, therapists and patients need to jointly utilize whatever limited number of sessions or therapy time they have remaining to develop a short-term patient recovery plan. Such alliance-based transactions may help the patient sustain his or her recovery process, and eventually foster continued therapeutic engagement with another therapist and or patient reengagement in therapy with another appropriate ongoing treatment program, i.e., residential treatment, intensive out-patient care, or extended care program.

The working and productive therapeutic alliance relational framework always plays a very important role in patient recovery and the ongoing care process at every stage in therapy via the therapist's active assistance with such matters as (1) referral for continuing treatment, and (2) ancillary clinical services which can include in-patient, IOP, "detox," possibly no fee or limited fee community resources, self-help care alternatives, division of vocational rehabilitation evaluations and services, and other patient-therapist community specific services.

Unilateral psychotherapy terminations upon the part of the addiction therapist are very uncommon (Xiao, H., Hayes, J.A., Castonguay, L.G., et al.,

2017), but these actions can also be appropriate and ethically indicated transactions in the care of a small segment of addictive disordered patients. These therapist-initiated unilateral terminations may involve a difficult decision-making process for the therapist, and these transactions generally prove to be quite thorny in nature. Clinicians and addictions counselors sometimes discover very quickly in addictions psychotherapy work that a patient needs significant medical care, psychiatric consultation or hospitalization, structured residential care, or other forms of immediate care which he or she cannot provide. These transactions and clinical realities can occur at any juncture in the therapeutic process. Therapists also may realize as the therapeutic process extends and intensifies that they are professionally ill-equipped to work with some patients. Therapists also may experience acute countertransference conflicts associated with the patient's extremely antisocial behaviors, severe depression or active psychosis, values, boundary issues, trust, or a sense of self-endangerment, and a wide range of other dynamics including matters such as sexuality and multicultural issues. Some addictive disordered patients repetitively miss scheduled appointments, fail to pay or eventually refuse to pay for their professional services, and repetitively attempt to seduce or initiate sexual relationships with their therapists.

In short, any number of rather uncommon but very real patient-therapist specific circumstances and dynamics can necessitate appropriate therapist-initiated actions to terminate his or her therapeutic work with an addictive disordered patient. As noted earlier, these therapist-initiated transactions are frequently conflicted and tend to take place in the early or middle stages of addictions psychotherapy work. In the clinical experience of the author (Forrest, 2016), therapist initiated unilateral addictions therapy terminations almost always take place earlier in therapy, and occur within the context of therapeutic alliances which were initially weak or tenuous in nature. These psychotherapy relationships have continued to remain unstable over the course of therapy preceding termination. Indeed, these alliances routinely never develop into working and productive therapeutic alliances, and severe and chronic patient relationship disturbance appears to play a key factor in cases of therapist-initiated termination.

In all of these situations, it is imperative for the therapist to initiate and utilize or attempt to use an ethically and clinically appropriate termination methodology with their patients including discussion and explanation related to the termination, continued patient support with this process, and referral for appropriate services or other patient centered constructive actions. Addictions counselors, therapists and other clinicians are well advised to consult with their attorney, experienced and well-trained professional colleagues, or perhaps their local or regional professional practice board prior to or during the process of initiating an anticipated acrimonious and thorny patient termination (Swift et al., 2017). Premature terminations upon the part of the patient or therapist can trigger a host of regressive behaviors including relapse. Relapse and generally poor treatment outcome results are also usually associated with highly conflictual therapy terminations.

LATE STAGE TERMINATION AND ALLIANCE BASED DYNAMICS IN INTEGRATIVE ADDICTIONS-FOCUSED PSYCHOTHERAPY AND COUNSELING WORK

This author (Forrest, 1997) has suggested that it is "usually" inappropriate for the therapist and patient to initiate psychotherapy termination prior to the patient's establishment of six to eight months of ongoing recovery including substance abstinence and personal commitment to active involvement in a continuing care regimen. This model is based primarily upon psychotherapy alliances involving alcoholics and psychoactive substance abusers who have been able to consistently sustain working and productive alliances throughout the course of therapy. These patients have also actively sustained the various therapeutic goals, tasks and recovery activities that were established within the alliance relationship framework during the earlier stages of therapy. Furthermore, this patient population responds very favorably to a psychotherapy termination format or structure which involves a therapist-patient based progressive and systematically increased time framework between scheduled psychotherapy sessions (Goode et al., 2017). While some addictive disordered patients are ready to begin the termination phase of therapy following a few (2-4) months of active ongoing treatment, it is not uncommon in the author's clinical experience (Forrest, 2014, 2017) to have some patient's continue in various levels of psychotherapy for as long as 40 years.

It is important for the therapist to help initiate the patient's focus upon feelings and thoughts associated with the process of beginning the termination stage of therapy during several sessions prior to reaching a mutually constructed therapist-patient alliance decision to terminate the therapy relationship. Furthermore, the late stage therapy termination process generally encompasses therapist-patient development of a relatively patient specific and relatively structured treatment termination plan. This alliance strategy can enhance therapist-patient level of conscious awareness dynamics relative to the patient's readiness for termination of the therapy process. Within the alliance framework, the psychotherapist also needs to openly share his or her thoughts, feelings, and perceptions with the patient relative to the patient's over-all progress during the course of therapy, readiness and, motivation for continued change involving long-term recovery, and other personal sentiments related to the termination process and beginning this phase of treatment. These matters can often be adequately addressed within the context of four or five therapy sessions with patients who have sustained several months of ongoing recovery and global improvement-based therapy.

Once the therapist and patient mutually agree that it is appropriate to begin the termination stage of the therapeutic relationship, it becomes important for the therapeutic dyad to further explore and develop an alliance-based, structured short-term termination plan including (1) ongoing psychotherapy process and outcome goals, (2) a modified and long-term ongoing recovery program which specifically addresses therapeutic tasks, activities, frequency of continued psychotherapy sessions, and anticipated length of the treatment termination process, and (3) mutual construction of a patient specific relapse and ongoing recovery prevention plan.

Obviously, common and basic goals of the ongoing process and outcome of the termination phase of addictions psychotherapy encompass the therapeutic process, enhancing long-term patient recoveries and successful therapy outcomes. As basic or "simple" as this matter may seem to be relative to most experienced addictions clinicians, most recovering addictive disordered patients continue to benefit from a therapeutic focus involving continued reinforcement and exploration of the various realities associated with the patient's abilities and capabilities related to sustaining a life process of addiction free living. Non-recovering and neophyte addictions counselors and therapists may find this matter to be somewhat trite as their internal experiential world has never included the realities of living with a protracted or previously severe addictive disorder.

Modified and long-term patient-specific recovery program facets of the termination stage of therapy (Forrest, 1997, 2016) generally begin with reducing the frequency of the patient's psychotherapy sessions. This process may have been successfully initiated during the middle or late stage of therapy with some patients, and in these cases the patient's therapy sessions can be scheduled with extended time intervals between sessions. Changing the frequency of the patient's sessions from a weekly to an every-other-week regimen based upon alliance formulated and mutually agreed upon intervals of time during the early termination stage of therapy can subsequently be utilized to plan and arrange therapy sessions that are scheduled on a monthly basis. Quarterly and semi-annual or annual "check-up" therapy sessions may also be central to the process of final termination with many addictive-disordered patients.

Thus, the alliance determined and formulated decision to reduce the frequency of patient psychotherapy sessions to every other week or once every ten days or three or four weeks initiates the process for successful relatively long-term psychotherapy termination. Addictions therapists need to continually explore their patient's readiness, emotional, and alliance specific relational dynamics associated with the evolving treatment termination format process. At this juncture, therapist's will also want to actively reassure and openly express to their patient's that they are (1) confident that the patient manifests the ability to sustain the recovery process and cope well with possible changes that can occur in the process of treatment and termination, and (2) the patient can always simply call, email, or contact the therapist for additional and/or "crisis" related sessions if this becomes necessary. It is important for addictions therapists to make themselves readily available to their patients during the initial weeks of the termination process, but in the experience of the author (Forrest, 2014, 2016, 2017) relatively few patients experience the need to re-engage in an extended regimen of intensified therapy sessions during the ongoing process of psychotherapy termination. However, it is also important for the patient to know throughout this process that he or she can return to weekly therapy or engage the therapist immediately in the event of any form of crisis-oriented situation including active or incipient relapse. Patients manifesting co-morbid psychiatric and psychological disorders and severe forms of psychopathology generally require more therapist vigilance and care interventions during the therapy termination process. These individuals also tend to contact their therapist more frequently for additional therapy sessions, and may require other integrative services or care during the initial two or three months of the therapy termination process. These alliance-based transactions and dynamics need to be openly explored and resolved as a function of successful termination outcomes. Addictions therapists can be confronted with the realities associated with patient lack of readiness for termination of care during this process, and may also be confronted with the need to refer patients for continued long-term or other forms of ongoing treatment and care.

Following the successful establishment of a therapy regimen format involving every-other-week or every-ten-day sessions for a period of six to ten weeks, the author (Forrest, 1997, 2016) has historically initiated a regimen involving seeing the patient on a monthly or every six weeks basis for three or four months. This final stage of successful alliance developed therapy termination work generally encompasses seeing patients in three subsequent follow-up sessions at six-month intervals, again involving therapeutic interventions aimed at reinforcing, supporting, and consistently encouraging the client to schedule additional therapy sessions if a crisis situation arises or other life circumstances result in the need to address additional treatment interventions relative to the termination process. Some patients may interpret the choice or decision to return to more frequently scheduled therapy sessions as a personal weakness, failure, or regressive turn; however, therapists need to supportively but actively dispute and pre-emptively discuss

(Nof, Leibovich, and Zilcha-Mano, 2017) these issues early and consistently throughout the termination process. Exploration of such perceptions and the feelings and beliefs associated with these issues becomes incorporated into the therapeutic work of termination.

Therapists also find it helpful to remind themselves during the termination phase of therapy that few patients will experience a major life crisis or trauma at this time, but such events do occur and these cases can usually be ameliorated via brief or more extended intensive therapy work with the patient. Patients and therapists often simply need to remain open-minded about the alternative of returning to more active therapeutic work if this is indicated over the course of the termination process. In this context, therapists can appropriately remind their patients that their "door is always open" (Norcross et al., 2017). As indicated elsewhere (Forrest, 1997, 2012), all human beings need or would certainly benefit from some form of counseling or psychotherapy from time to time during their lifespan, and it is highly unrealistic for psychotherapy patients to believe that they will never again struggle with their addictive brain disease related historic behaviors. Psychotherapy and integrative treatment reengagement for several weeks, months, or even years following a successful termination often represents an adaptive and healthy self-care choice deterrent to reengagement in a prior pattern of progressively destructive addictive disordered irrational living involving multifaceted biopsychosocial dysfunction.

Psychotherapy terminations involving eventually scheduling patients for follow-up sessions at more extended time intervals (six, twelve or even eighteen month intervals) following a successful termination can potentially serve several therapeutic purposes: (1) these brief contracts represent a form of therapeutic "booster sessions" for patients who sustain some level of motivation or clinical need for continued contact with the therapist and therapeutic process, (2) therapists are able to actively explore and reinforce earlier therapeutic gains, and provide further encouragement for continued recovery, (3) such contacts continue to be viable relapse prevention interventions, (4) all follow-up contacts provide the therapist with important longitudinal clinical and research data about patients, self, the psychotherapy alliance and relationship, and various facets of patient growth and recovery following extended psychotherapeutic treatment, and in some cases (5) the scope and dynamics of patient relapses. These follow-up sessions also importantly provide the patient and therapist with the opportunity to mutually re-experience their "real relationship" (Bhatia and Gelso, 2017) based sense of ongoing human relatedness, contact, purpose, and meaning in life.

Therapists may also find it useful to consistently and actively reinforce the patient's continued use of integrative care resources throughout the course of the termination process in addictions therapy work. Many, if not most, addictive disordered persons who sustain continued recovery during the course of an extended psychotherapy experience will rather spontaneously and internally decide to sustain their active involvement in various other recovery specific ongoing care or self-help modalities such as OA (Over-Eaters Anonymous) or Weight-Watchers, Alcoholics Anonymous (AA), Smart-Stop, GA (Gamblers Anonymous), or active health club memberships and physical exercise activities. Walking, jogging, tennis, swimming, golf, weight lifting, church-based support groups or perhaps singles groups as well as continued medical or psychiatric care involving medication assisted therapy can also foster long-term recovery. These various recovery-fostered lifestyle and time structuring activities certainly facilitate and can synergize the patient's ongoing recovery process in a myriad of ways. Active social engagement, continued vicarious learning and growth experiences, cognitive stimulation, continued relapse prevention reinforcement and generalized life skill development can all foster the ongoing recovery process.

Longer-term terminations in psychotherapy can be somewhat emotionally stressful as well as rewarding and rather joyous, happy events for both the patient and therapist. While therapists and patients can be ambivalent about terminating therapy, and the emotional and relational alliance bond they have formed over the course of several months or perhaps years of successful ongoing addictions-focused psychotherapy work, the termination process can also become a core catalyst for the resolution of therapist-patient ambivalence related termination issues. This process can further enhance the recovering patients sense of independence, personal mastery and control, self-confidence and global sense of self-worth in the context of recovery.

Therapists sometimes experience conflicted and rather neurotic feelings about "letting go" of their patients. Therapists also sometimes tend to "forget" that their patients (Forrest, 1997) have never or very rarely experienced consistent nurturing, intimate, supportive, loving, stable, globally healthy, and sustained human attachments and relationships. Protracted working and productive therapeutic alliances contribute very significantly to the patient's abilities to initiate and sustain the recovery process, and in this context the therapist becomes a potentially significant patient internalized life-long ego-introject that continues to constructively influence the patient's long-term patterns of adaptive living. Thus, the patient's earlier preconscious, unconscious and sometimes very conscious and quite rational internal experience of anxiety and fear about "letting go" of the therapist and the psychotherapy relationship becomes more clearly understood and more resolvable or manageable upon the part of both patient and therapist (Olivera et al., 2017). The corrective emotional experience (Alexander, 1950) dynamics of effective psychotherapy work also occur within the alliance context, but in contemporary successful psychotherapy work "corrective emotional experience work" also encompasses the relational, interpersonal, biopsychosocial and global changes that are facilitated vis a via the psychotherapeutic process.

In sum, a diversity of patient-therapist specific alliance focused realities and psychodynamic components (Forrest, 1997; Bhatia and Gelso, 2017) are associated with the process of terminating psychotherapy relationships involving addictive disordered patients. As indicated earlier, these various issues need to be continuously and mutually explored, focused upon, and resolved within the therapeutic alliance context during this final stage of addictions therapy work. The process of therapy termination can be abrupt, easy, or quickly initiated as a result of many patient or therapist-related factors, but therapy terminations with productive and successful treatment outcomes can also border on being as recondite and involved as those involved in terminating a parenting or marital relationship. Thus, patients and therapists generally benefit from taking the time and completing the therapeutic work that is necessary to face and essentially resolve these complexities whenever possible.

The termination stage of addictions psychotherapy also needs to involve an alliance based exploration of (1) patient and therapist joint perceptions, experiences, meanings and relevance of the psychotherapy relationship, (2) feelings and emotions that are associated with the therapeutic relationship, (3) possibly revisiting prior patient therapeutic experiences, (4) articulating and discussing mutual grief and loss feelings associated with the process of therapy disengagement and termination, and (5) restructuring of the present and planned future therapist-patient relationship parameters. Intense feelings of grief, loss, and separation anxiety may be associated with some patient therapy terminations. Therapists need to be able to recognize, accept and work through their own feelings of grief and loss that can be related to patient terminations, and in this context, it may be helpful for some therapists and patients to focus on the core issues related to basic termination dynamics associated with many facets of human living and life itself. Termination always paradoxically represents another beginning, and all human beings are continually confronted with the process of learning how to accept and manage the various realities that can be associated with life changes, and the unending number of "terminations" human beings experience throughout the course of their lives (Olivera et al. 2017).

Finally, the process of long-term therapy terminations that, in effect, may continue over the course of an extended period of time associated with ten to more than forty years of ongoing therapy with the same therapist certainly represents an uncommon or infrequent alliance relational process in psychotherapy work involving addictive disordered patients. Psychotherapy alliances and therapist-patient relationships can encompass much of the therapist's professional practice life and much of the patient's life. Perhaps these extended "doctor-patient" relationships mirror many of the characteristics of American physician-patient care relationships that commonly occurred some fifty to more than one hundred years ago. In the author's clinical practice experience involving ongoing individual and/or group therapy work as well as support group therapy with addictive disordered patient's over the course of some forty-five years (Forrest, 2018), these therapeutic relationships consistently become very powerful, and often profoundly positive and influential and meaningful as well as mutually life changing long term human encounters. These therapeutic relationships do become "real-relationships" (Gelso, 2011) over the course of several months of early and middle stage therapy, and subsequently continue to become more human and "real" via the process of continued therapy and productive alliance work spanning the entirety of the ongoing treatment process. Some of these patients may never experience another active addiction relapse over the course of their lives, while others may experience a relapse or multiple relapses which also tend to be of short duration. Other patients may sustain the recovery process for five, ten or perhaps more than twenty or thirty years of recovery with any number of life specific outcomes.

The final brief therapy vignette in this chapter demonstrates late stage addictions psychotherapy termination work involving a recovering polysubstance dependent health professional. This vignette focuses upon some of the relational, emotional and personal attachment related alliance dynamics that can take place between the patient and therapist during this juncture in the psychotherapy process.

Case 19

MARYANN: I guess I'm getting used to coming in every month, or six weeks—but it's different at times if I have a few bad days—

DOCTOR F.: It does seem like a long time between our last couple of sessions, and it's been closer to two months this time—looking at my notes.

MARYANN: Has it been that long? You know, looking back a year or so ago, I would have never believed that I would ever "miss" coming to my therapy sessions—but I can also remember back when I started to look forward to coming—when I was really afraid—frightened about losing my license to practice, and all that legal stuff— God, I needed to come in here then and there were days and weeks when I couldn't wait to talk—when we met once or twice a week— sometimes I just cried, but you kept telling me it would get better—it seemed like my life and practice almost stopped, when I had to do all the UA's and the treatment contract stipulations—but you were eventually right—I'm better—you know, really a different person—and I still look forward to coming in here, and doing the meetings—with no fear—almost none, about the board now—ha-ha—and I'm not depressed and so anxious all the time—

DOCTOR F.: These past couple of years have really gone by in retrospect—I know it seemed like molasses to you for that first year, or so—the process of getting better, and all the board stipulations and treatment related stuff—all of it, but you did the work—you "showed up" one day, one week—one month at a time, and you sure have changed—it's just been great—really a blessing to be a part of your recovery—from my perspective, but you showed up, and you're different—people do change, and therapy helps—and you can see it all now—and I hope you realize your changes, and see this as a very constructive experience.

MARYANN: I sure feel better about myself, now—I feel like my self-esteem—and confidence, plus my sense of integrity is coming back—and it's kinda been a long time since I woke up crying and so stressed—every morning, and God, a lot of those nights I didn't sleep—it's hard to believe how out of control I got at the end with the pills, and the booze—you know, those damned benzo's and the opioids—plus the board stuff about killed me—and I was even angry with you when you put me in the hospital with the "health and well-fare" thing, but looking back on it all—that probably saved my life, in the end—and I'm grateful for all of it—I sure couldn't stop on my own, or stay out of all the trouble—God knows, how many hundreds of times it didn't work—it's all crazy in retrospect—but sure as hell "real."

DOCTOR F.: With all of that, how are you feeling now about seeing the end of therapy coming? Uh, the termination plan and schedule we started putting together at our last session—and we've talked about it since, and made some changes—it's still flexible and we'll change things again if we need to—your thoughts and feelings about where you're at, and how often we continue to meet—all of it.

MARYANN: I think our schedule is still good—like we've discussed, if I'm in a crisis or need to come back more often, I can call Paula and make an appointment—but the feeling is different—ending therapy is still kinda a different thing, I mean I think I'm ready and I'll be happy about it—because it means that I've gotten better, but I guess I'm still kinda apprehensive about stopping therapy completely—er, what I'm saying, I guess, that the feeling bit—it's still not easy—

DOCTOR F.: You've still got mixed feelings about terminating, but you also feel that you're pretty much ready—it sounds like to me.

How about the ongoing recovery program we put together several months ago—are you still consistent with that over the last couple of months?

MARYANN: I sure have—and it's a big part of my life too—the meetings, and I still look forward to going, and I'm golfing two or three times a week, and still goin' to the gym at least two times a week—and I forgot to tell you! I got a big bonus at the office last month—plus, it's official—I'm a partner now, so a lot of good things are happening, but the answer to your question is I'm working on it, and at this point—I don't want to change any of that—and Don,—our relationship just keeps getting' better.

DOCTOR F.: And how about the kids?

MARYANN: The kids are pretty much back on track—Bobby's grades are up, and we don't get the calls from the school anymore— or the anger stuff, and Katie—she's almost all A's, and no issues. Really, all of our lives are better, and like I told you last time I was in, Don doesn't drink two drinks a month—you know, he pretty much cut it off by himself—after I went to the hospital—I guess it took all of that for him to see where it was taking all of us—and we still see Dr. Hill once a month or so—she helped too, and nothing has changed with her—it's a make an appointment when you need to—or want to, with her too—thinking about all of that, I do feel good about terminating and even though it's down the road, it's all of a part of the therapy—that's some of the angst about ending therapy—and I also know I'm, beyond my dependency on you and therapy, but just talking about it now—I know how much I'll miss these hours—it's a lot easier to tell you now Dr. Gary, but I really appreciate all you've done for me—I mean you really helped me get to this point—and it sure wasn't easy a lot of times—I respect you, and it's been a tough journey—maybe for both of us, but you never gave up on me—and— ha—ha, God only knows, but somehow you've always motivated me to get better—I'm starting to ramble—but with all the pain and strug- gle I feel like I've become a better person.

DOCTOR F.: You're sure not alone in all you've said—and again, you did the lion's share of the work all the way through—and I'll miss seeing you too Maryann, when the process ends. And it's around the corner. We've sure developed a positive relationship—with mutual respect, and I've told you, I admire you—and really, your family too for all you've accomplished—we've all been through a lot of tough stuff over the past year or so, and yeah—I'll miss you—we've discussed it before, and it's real—we both have feelings about terminating ther- apy. I suspect Don and the family also have their feelings and thoughts about ending therapy—but for us, like we've discussed—the feelings and emotional attachments or therapeutic bond is a part of what makes terminating successful therapy relationships more emotional, and sometimes difficult for therapists too, . . . as well as patient's—we've been working on this process together for nearly two years, and both of us have put a lot of time and energy to get where we are. How do you feel about scheduling our next appointment for three or four weeks out?

MARYANN: You know, I think I'm ready for that—but I still can call and come in if I feel I need to, or something comes up in the interim that I'm struggling with—that's how we'll still do this?

DOCTOR F.: Absolutely—let me know or just call the office— we'll keep that part of the protocol—do we need to change any other pieces of our recovery termination plan?

The following brief case study involves an alcoholic patient who was seen by the author over a course of some forty years. This rather unusual psychotherapy case involves a very long and complex psychotherapy relationship process as well as an extended termination process. After four years of active individual psychotherapy engagement, the patient continued to be seen at infrequent intervals and his ongoing therapy work with the author eventually encompassed different therapeutic alliance-based modalities that included other family members for varying intervals of time. He eventually participated in the author's weekly recovery support group for some thirty years. When last seen with his spouse, the patient had sustained over forty-one years of ongoing alcohol abstinence and recovery including a globally improved adjustment style.

Case 20

Robert was initially seen within the context of individual psychotherapy on a weekly or every other week basis for approximately four years. He was subsequently seen in monthly, quarterly, semi-annual, and eventually annual individual therapy as well as infrequent and intermittent frequent conjoint marital and family therapy sessions for thirty-six years. The patient eventually participated in the author's weekly education and recovery support group on a near-weekly basis for over 30 years. Robert was last seen with his wife in 2015.

Some ten years after initiating individual therapy with the author related to a very serious automobile accident, DUI arrest and related hospitalization, the patient began attending the author's weekly

1.5 education and recovery support group. The patient continued to be an active participant in this group for approximately thirty years. Robert had refused to participate in AA meetings early in therapy, and throughout his therapeutic work with the author. However, Robert was very open and disclosing in therapy, and he established a working and productive alliance with the author quite early in the therapeutic process. He also actively participated in the development of his initial treatment plan encompassing several therapeutic tasks and goals. Robert proactively advised his physician about his alcohol dependence early in therapy and he remained open and engaged with his family physician relative to the use of Antabuse, antidepressant, and anti-anxiety agents during the early years of his therapy. The patient also quickly initiated and subsequently sustained a very intensive exercise regimen involving almost daily tennis, and eventually daily swimming. At age 82, he continued to swim at least one hour daily, seven days a week.

Robert's biologic father was a professional health care provider who was also an alcoholic. His mother had experienced "problems with prescription medications," and his paternal grandfather reportedly experienced "drinking problems." His paternal and maternal uncles were described as "heavy drinkers" or "alcoholics." All four of his children experienced substance abuse related difficulties during middle and late adolescence and his youngest daughter eventually developed polysubstance dependence. All of the patient's children were engaged in some level of individual and family therapy with the author at various junctures, and all of the children also terminated their various addictive disorders and have lived successful and productive lives including years of sustained alcohol and drug abstinence.

In essence, this patient played a very active role in the ongoing and extended therapy termination process. The trauma, social and legal stigma, and personal embarrassment that accompanied and stimulated (forced) the patient's initial psychotherapy engagement also continued to reinforce his ongoing commitment to the recovery process. He had "known" and consciously realized that he manifested a "serious drinking problem" or was "perhaps an alcoholic" since the time of his undergraduate years at a major university, and he expressed very early in therapy that he was determined to "never turn out like my father." The patient consistently characterized his father as a "mean, abusive, detached and angry man."

The client's family also very actively and consistently encouraged him to remain engaged in some form of therapy and recovery, and they were also amenable to therapeutic engagement related to their personal addictive disorders as they developed after their father had remained in therapy and recovery for several years.

The patient had consistently experienced various levels of ongoing relational conflict throughout his life, and all of his family members were also quite aware of these realities in their own relatively personal relationships and interactions with him. His wife often characterized him as "a difficult person." This facet of the patient's relational style changed somewhat over the years of therapy, but he continued to emphasize to the author the importance of his being able to re-engage in intensified therapy sessions "if he needed to" over the course of therapy. Over the past eight or ten years of therapy, these therapeutic contracts were limited to either one annual individual therapy session and/or one recovery support session during the Christmas holidays. According to the patient's wife, Robert often referred to the author as "one of my real friends," "the only person I can really talk to," and similar positive contexts over the course of his treatment. He also continually referred to himself in the context of being a person who experienced difficulties in the realm of "making friends," and was relatively open about being in therapy and recognized that he needed to persist in some form of treatment related to his historic inability to "stay sober on my own."

When last seen conjointly with his wife, it was clinically apparent to the author and his wife as he openly discussed that the reality they were currently facing were related to his late life cognitive decline and some level of dementia. These realities and a wide range of relational and alliance related experiences associated with our shared 40-year psychotherapy-based relationship experiences involving Robert and his family culminated in a two-hour final therapy termination session which encompassed a wide spectrum of intense emotions, memories, reflections, joy, sadness and ambivalence upon the part of both of us.

Needless to say, the author's personal feelings, emotions and alliance-based relationship dynamics associated with the extended psychotherapy process with "Bob" and eventually his family encompassed an ever changing, unending and wide-ranging mixture of reactions. The client was generally rather difficult to work with early in therapy, and in spite of his initial high level of motivation for change and ability to both initiate and sustain abstinence, he established a working and productive alliance, and basically followed through with our jointly developed treatment plan goals, tasks and structure. He continued to be relationally demanding. Robert manifested underlying resentment and anger, was rather passive-aggressive, and also related to people in an "all or none" or "black and white" manner, in the context of being either "good or bad" ego-introjects. He also demanded a great deal of therapeutic time, attention, and focused energy. The patient did things "his way," and his anxiety and depressive features associated with childhood trauma involving his relationship with his father was a continuing source of therapeutic work during the first two years of our psychotherapy relationship.

Robert's course of therapy following over two years of weekly and every two- or three-week scheduled psychotherapy sessions evolved into an "as needed" format for nearly ten years. During the first several years of this session scheduling format essentially involved patient-initiated therapeutic follow-up contacts. Robert was generally seen in therapy on four to as many as ten individual therapy sessions, and possibly two or three additional conjoint marital sessions. Sometime around the tenth year of this termination related process, the patient experienced an acute panic attack while on an extended vacation in the Caribbean, and was briefly (three days) hospitalized in a psychiatric unit. Immediately upon return from this trip, the patient re-engaged in weekly and every other week therapy for a period of three months. During the first or second therapy session with the author after this episode, Robert indicated to the author that he had not relapsed while on vacation, but the panic attack experience and subsequent hospitalization outside of the United States made him "really" realize how anxious he had been all of his life, and as we had discussed and explored in therapy over the course of his care, his alcohol dependence had always been a self-medication driven dynamism specific to his comorbid anxiety disorder. This process also eventually facilitated and synergized his recurrent depressive episodes, anger, and morass of additional recurrent relational and real-life conflicts. Finally, during this time frame in therapy, he shared that while being in the psychiatric unit and after he was stabilized on anti-anxiety medication he "came to the realization" that he had stubbornly refused to participate in Alcoholics Anonymous and the author's recovery support group because he had "social anxiety," and even the thought of participating in these settings initiated intense feelings of anxiety. This therapeutic dialogue lead to a reinitiated focus on the patient's control-related issues, impulse control, and his long history involving extreme anxiety and difficulties with group situations in his work life and career as well as basic family interactions. His counselor in the hospital had also stressed that he "needed to start attending AA meetings," and/or "your doctor's group," suggesting that these were viable methods for overcoming his anxiety disorder. Furthermore, these clinical recommendations were a part of his hospital discharge plan and his wife had also been involved in his discharge session. In this context, Robert also acknowledged that she had repeatedly encouraged him to "try" AA or group for years, and these matters facilitated further work associated with anxiety and control dynamics related to the marriage, parenting and familial relationships, career, and other various life issues.

The core constructive therapeutic alliance related outcome dynamics associated with this extended therapy and long-term treatment termination process included Robert's active participation in the author's weekly 1.5 recovery support group during the above time frame. However, he continued to resist any form of Alcoholics Anonymous or other self-help group involvement, but attended the education and recovery support group on a near weekly basis until the point of final termination. His final active therapy and support group termination occurred in concert with his professional health care career retirement. As noted earlier, the patient sustained alcohol abstinence over the course of his active psychotherapy and eventual support group involvement with the author which encompassed some thirty-five years. He has continued to attend an "annual check-up" group session during the Christmas season over the past seven or eight years in addition to scheduling three or four individual consultations with the author related to addictions care referral issues related to one of his children who continues to struggle with other mid-life adjustment difficulties.

In sum, patients and therapists are often ambivalent about terminating extended and efficacious psychotherapy relationships. Therapist's need to actively explore and help resolve their patient's feelings, emotions, and beliefs associated with ending therapy. Therapists also need to be able to openly express their personal feelings, thoughts and perceptions related to the patient, psychotherapy relationship, therapeutic process, and the termination process. A patient-specific structured treatment termination format and plan works well with addictive disordered persons, and as noted earlier, the termination process can serve as a very viable relapse prevention tool based upon the therapist's continued encouragement for patients to re-engage in active therapy and other recovery related care modalities, if needed, subsequent to alliance–based pre-planning therapy termination dates, and patient-specific clinical status or life circumstances.

SUMMARY

This chapter includes a thorough and extensive discussion of the therapeutic alliance in addictions-focused psychotherapy and counseling therapy work. Alliance dynamics associated with early stage psychotherapy work involving addictive disordered patients including the initial diagnostic and assessment facets of the treatment process including contemporary clinical models and methods, involving the DSM-V and ICD-10 diagnostic models, early stage addictions psychotherapy goals, tasks, structural components of treatment, genetic reconstruction work in therapy, establishing and sustaining the addiction focus in therapy, confrontation, and the uses of appropriate supportive empathic interventions, are discussed in section one of this chapter. These early stage alliance-based integrative therapy strategies are elucidated and examined in the initial section of the chapter. Several clinical case studies and therapy vignettes demonstrating these particular vicissitudes of alliance-focused psychotherapy work with addictive disordered patients are also included in this section of the chapter.

Alliance dynamics related to the middle stage of addictions psychotherapy work are examined and discussed in the second section of this chapter. Following a general discussion of evolving dynamics associated with middle-stage therapeutic work, the uses of cognitive-behavioral therapy, integrative, and eclectic therapy interventions in addictions therapy are examined in addition to alliance-based insight, interpretation, and self-awareness dynamics related to this stage of therapy. Middle stage addictions psychotherapy alliance focused resistance, transference and countertransference dynamics are subsequently examined in depth in this chapter, and subsequent middle stage therapy dynamics related to (1) maintaining the addiction focus, (2) initiating and using more intensive affect focused therapeutic interventions, (3) alliance based sexual counseling, sex therapy and etiologic sexual-trauma based interventions, and (4) confrontation, relapse, time structuring, and ancillary middle stage alliance focused strategies and tasks are addressed. This segment of Chapter 7 also includes a number of clinical studies and therapy vignettes which illuminate many facets of middle stage addictions work associated with the various therapist-patient-alliance related issues and dynamics.

The final section of this chapter includes a general discussion of alliance related later stage addictions psychotherapy dynamics, treatment interventions and therapist-patient relational processes. A multiplicity of interactive "real-world" as well as therapist-patient relational (Bhatia and Gelso, 2017; Forrest, 1997; Olivera et al., 2017) factors impact and shape the course of late stage therapy work. Several of these impactful realities are also discussed in the initial segment of the chapter. Alliance, identity consolidation and synthesis, working through, resolution of projective identification issues, intensive affective work, and a rather extensive examination of the late stage therapy termination process are discussed and explored in-depth in the last section of the chapter. This section of the book also includes several therapy vignettes and clinical case studies which will enhance the readers understanding, awareness, and professional therapeutic skill-set within the addiction/psychotherapy practice arena.

These therapy vignettes and case studies have been constructed from the author's clinical practice-based publications and works spanning over four decades of private practice psychotherapy work. These vignettes also encompass roughly five years of experience as the clinical director of two military alcohol and drug rehabilitation programs, consultation work in intensive out-patient mental health settings, EAP consulting work for over thirty years, and within the context of mental health center related staff, supervision, graduate level psychology faculty involvement (masters and doctoral level programs) for forty-five years. The author's clinical practice history has also involved extensive legal-criminal clinical evaluations, assessments and consulting work involving addictive-disordered persons and addictive-disordered professional groups including physicians, dentists, lawyers and judges, commercial airline pilots, nurses and other health care professionals including psychologists, social workers, counselors and psychiatrists.

During each stage of therapy, a myriad of alliance related dynamics and factors continually impact and shape the psychotherapeutic process involving addictive disordered patients. As addictive disordered patients progress into early stage recovery, therapists develop an ever-increasing awareness and understanding of the patient's global adjustment difficulties, co-morbid conditions, and related treatment needs. Patients also develop a more conscious understanding and awareness of their various emotional, relational and biopsychosocial difficulties as well as their relatively specific addictive brain disease focused conflicts during early stage recovery. These evolving alliance related patient-therapist relational dynamics continually evolve, impact and potentially enhance constructive patient growth and change during every stage of the psychotherapy process. As the patient's "real person" adjustment conflicts, strengths and basic "being" within the therapeutic relationship progressively becomes understood and experientially known to the therapist, he or she is often able to help the patient initiate a diversity of integrative treatment and care modalities that significantly synergize the recovery process. Patient referrals for nutritional counseling, mindfulness or yoga training, chiropractic interventions, medication assisted care, intensive or extended residential care, EMDR therapy and further education are but a few of the potential constructive avenues that therapists and patients can begin to utilize at any juncture in the process of intensive addictions-focused integrative psychotherapy. Patients also tend to become progressively more open, receptive and pro-active about engaging in alternative integrative care modalities during the middle and later stages of therapy.

In this context, therapists need to continually remind themselves that there are many ways to help patients change their addictions and their life styles. Likewise, there are many "royal roads to recovery." Building upon the patient's core strengths, maintaining and enhancing a working and productive therapeutic alliance, and continuing to help patient's grow and change via multimodal therapeutic interventions, integrative services, and care specific to the patient's specific personal needs leads to successful therapy outcomes and long-term patient recoveries. Effective psychotherapy and recovery outcomes are always ultimately the result of multifaceted factors.

This chapter provides addiction therapists with a compendium of integrative alliance-based interventions, therapeutic strategies, and facilitative care alternatives which foster and enhance patient change, growth, successful psychotherapy outcomes and recovery. The over-all integrative addiction-focused psychotherapy and counseling model presented throughout this text will greatly enhance the therapeutic armamentarium of all addiction treatment providers and professional substance abuse providers.

RECENT PSYCHOTHERAPY AND COUNSELING TERMINATION RESEARCH EVIDENCE

It will be helpful for addictions-focused therapists and counselors to know that recent psychotherapy termination research evidence (Bhatia and Gelso, 2017) indicates that "(1) part of the complexity in studying termination in psychotherapy pertains to the different reasons for ending treatment, (2) therapists perceiving a stronger working alliance and real relationship during the termination phase are also likely to view the termination phase as effective and overall treatment as successful, (3) therapists perceiving greater negative transference during the termination phase are likely to report poorer overall treatment outcomes, (4) no statistically significant relationship was found between negative transference during the termination phase of therapy, (5) therapists perceiving greater sensitivity loss in clients are more likely to identify stronger positive transference and negative transference during the termination phase and, (6)the working alliance, real relationship, and negative transference during the termination phase are associated with successful termination work, and an effective termination phase, in turn, appears to be associated with better overall treatment outcomes—the role of the working alliance during the termination phase seems especially significant in relating to overall treatment outcome. Furthermore, it should be noted that post hoc analyses revealed only the working alliance during the termination phase uniquely predicted overall treatment outcome" (pp. 76–86). An implication of these findings is that therapists and counselors should continue to work on maintaining and strengthening the alliance relationship during the termination phase of therapy.

It should be also noted that other researchers investigating the termination stage(s) of psychotherapy have reported that (1) clients acknowledged grieving the loss of their therapists in cases where termination was described in a positive and affirming terms (Knox et al., 2011), (2) therapist's own experiences of loss significantly predict therapist anxiety and depression at the end of therapy, and therapists perceptions of client sensitivity to loss predicted therapist anxiety during the process of termination, and Fortune (1987) found that more than half of the therapists (social workers) alluded to feelings of sadness and loss during termination in half or more their cases. Half or more of counseling center clients also report positive feelings about ending therapy (Marx and Gelso, 1987).

Bhatia and Gelso (2017) also report that "(1) research on the unfolding of the 'real relationship' in treatment and the strength of the real relationship early versus later in treatment suggests that therapist and client ratings of the 'real relationship' strengthens over the course of treatment, and this strengthening relates to treatment outcomes, (2) in relation to transference and outcome, the evidence is mixed: in two studies, therapists rated negative transference was not found to relate to session outcome or treatment outcome; instead the presence of insight in therapy moderated the relationship between negative transference and treatment outcome." Additional studies (Bhatia and Gelso, 2013, Markin, McCarthy, and Barber, 2013) indicated that "therapist ratings of negative transference were found to relate negatively to indices of process and outcome. Taken together, these findings seem to suggest that in therapies of diverse orientation, negative transference in the later stages of therapy hinders successful treatment" (p. 78).

This body of therapy termination research (Bhatia and Gelso, 2017) conveys a central message involving "the importance for therapists to consider how clients are experiencing the termination phase of therapy, related to the working alliance, real relationship, and negative transference during the termination phase are associated with successful termination work, and an effective termination phase in turn, appears to be associated with better overall treatment outcomes. The role of working alliance during the termination phase seems especially significant in relating to overall treatment outcomes. An implication of this finding is that therapists should continue to work on maintaining and strengthening the alliance during the termination phase of therapy" (p. 86).

Olivera et al. (2017) report that "nearly all (95%) of therapist-initiated termination clients agreed on termination, client-initiated termination cases could be sorted in agreed (49%) and disagreed (51%) terminations. Both therapist-initiated terminations and agreed upon terminations presented more categories of positive termination motives, better therapeutic bonds and higher overall satisfactions with treatment" (p. 89).

Therapists, counselors and addictions-focused clinicians generally recognize that premature termination is a common occurrence. Premature termination has been associated with different variables including client characteristics such as gender, minority status, level of education, diagnostic status, personality traits as well as external variables such as insurance and financial issues, prior therapy experiences or alliance ruptures. Some of the most common reasons for termination also include therapeutic improvement, patient dissatisfaction or discomfort with therapy services or the therapist, and the lack of agreement found between patient's and therapist's motives for termination.

Studies (Hunsley et al., 1999; Westmacott et al., 2010) indicate that "little concordance between both sources regarding improvement due to treatment and dissatisfaction with provided services, and in fact, they found that although dissatisfaction with the therapy and therapist was reported by many clients as an important factor in their decision to terminate, it was rarely cited by the therapists" (Olivera et al., 2017, p. 89).

In juxtaposition to these findings, studies exploring the clients feelings have found that the majority of clients express mostly positive feelings during termination of psychotherapy, such as pride, calmness, and a sense of well-being and accomplishment; clients also highly value the chance to talk openly and share their feelings about termination with their therapists (Hardy and Woodhouse, 2008; Roe et al., 2006, p. 86).

"Negative feelings such as loneliness, abandonment, and anger have been associated with the client's perception of therapists not genuinely accepting or respecting the clients decision to terminate; not having the opportunity to process their dissatisfaction contributed to the client's feelings that their treatment has not been completes, leaving them with a sense of frustration and failure" (Roe et al., 2006, 89).

Once again, it should be noted that this body of research work examines a diversity of psychotherapy termination specific studies and variables, and does not examine these findings within the specific framework of addictions-focused psychotherapy and counseling termination work. However, in this context, it is the author's opinion that the over-all implications of the research data pertaining to these studies and finding will have widespread application within the arena of additions specific psychotherapy, counseling, and treatment work.

Chapter 8

A REVIEW OF THE NORCROSS-WAMPOLD CLINICAL PRACTICE GUIDELINES AND CONCLUSIONS PERTAINING TO EVIDENCE-BASED PSYCHOTHERAPY RELATIONSHIPS

INTRODUCTION

This chapter presents the verbatim conclusions and recommendations of the interdivisional (APA, Division, 29) task force on evidence-based therapy relationships (Norcross and Wampold, 2011). The authors report that "the work in this chapter was based on a series of meta-analyses conducted on the effectiveness of various relationship elements and methods of treatment adaptation. A panel of experts concluded that several relationship elements were demonstrably effective (alliance in individual psychotherapy, alliance in youth psychotherapy, alliance in family therapy, cohesion in group therapy, empathy, (collecting client feedback) while others were probably effective (goal consensus, collaboration, positive regard). Three other relationship elements (congruence/genuineness, repairing alliance reputes, and managing countertransference) were deemed promising but had insufficient evidence to conclude that they were effective. Multiple recommendations for practice, training, research, and policy are advanced" (Norcross and Wampold 2011, pp. 98–102).

CONCLUSIONS OF THE TASK FORCE

1. "The Therapy relationship makes substantial and consistent contributions to psychotherapy outcome independent of the specific type of treatment.
2. The therapy relationship accounts for why clients improve (or fail to improve) at least as much as particular treatment method.

3. Practice and treatment guidelines should explicitly address therapist behaviors and qualities that promotes a facilitative therapy relationship.
4. Efforts to promulgate best practices or evidence-based practices (EBP's) without including the relationship are seriously incomplete and potentially misleading.
5. Adapting or tailoring the therapy relationship to specific patient characteristics (in addition to diagnosis) enhances the effectiveness of treatment.
6. The therapy relationship acts in concert with treatment methods, patient characteristics, and practitioner qualities in determining effectiveness; a comprehensive understanding of effective (and ineffective) psychotherapy will consider all of these determinates and their optimal combinations.
7. These conclusions do not by themselves constitute a set of practice standards but represent current scientific knowledge to be understood and applied in the context of all clinical evidence available on each case" (p. 98).

GENERAL RECOMMENDATIONS

1. "We recommend that the results and conclusion of this second task force be widely disseminated in order to enhance awareness and use of what "works" in the therapy relationship.
2. Readers are encouraged to interpret these findings in the context of the acknowledged limitations of the task force's work.
3. We recommend that future task forces be established periodically to review these findings, including new elements of the relationship, incorporate the results of non-English language publications (where practical), and update these conclusions" (pp. 98–99).

Practical Recommendations

4. "Practitioners are encouraged to make the certain and cultivation of a therapy relationship characterized by the elements found to be demonstrably and probably effective a primary aim in the treatment of patients.
5. Practitioners are encouraged to adapt or tailor psychotherapy to those specific patient characteristics in ways found to be demonstrably and probably effective.
6. Practitioners are encouraged to routinely monitor patient's response to the therapy relationship and ongoing treatment. Such monitoring

leads to increased opportunities to reestablish collaboration, improve the relationship, modify technical strategies, and avoid premature termination.

7. Concurrent use of evidence-based therapy relationships and evidence-based treatments adapted to the patient is likely to generate the best outcomes" (p. 99).

Training Recommendations

8. "Training and continuing education in programs are encouraged to provide competency- based training in the demonstrably and probably effective elements of the therapy relationship.

9. Training and continuing education programs are encouraged to provide competency-based training in adapting psychotherapy to the individual patient in ways that demonstrably and probably enhance treatment success.

10. Accreditation and certification bodies for mental health training programs she develops criteria for assessing the adequacy of training in evidence-based therapy relationships" (p. 99).

Research Recommendations

11. "Researchers are encouraged to progress beyond correlational designs that associate the frequency of relationship behaviors with patient outcomes to methodologies capable of examining the complex associations among patient qualities, clinical behaviors, and treatment outcomes. Of particular importance is disentangling the patient contributions and the therapist contributions to relationship element and, ultimately, outcome.

12. Researchers are encouraged to address the observational perspective (i.e., therapist, patient, or external rater) in future studies and reviews of "what works" in the therapy relationship. Agreement among observational perspectives provides a solid sense of established fact; divergence among perspectives hold important implications for practice" (p. 99).

Policy Recommendations

14. "APA Division of Psychotherapy, Division of Clinical Psychology, and other practice divisions and encouraged to educate its members in the benefits of evidence of evidence-based relationships.

15. Mental Health Organizations as a whole are encouraged to educate their members about their improved outcomes associated with using

evidence-based therapy relationships, as they frequently now do about evidence-based treatments.

16. We recommend that the American Psychological Association and other mental health organizations advocate for the research-substantiated benefits of a nurturing and responsive human relationship in psychotherapy.

17. Finally, administrators of mental health services are encouraged to attend to the relational features of those services. Attempts to improve the quality of care should account for treatment relationships and adaptations" (p. 98–100).

WHAT WORKS IN PSYCHOTHERAPY

The authors of this article (Norcross and Wampold, 2011) continue the "what works" segment of this publication by stating "the process by which the preceding conclusions on which relationship elements are demonstrably and probably effective require some elaboration, as these tend to be the most cited and controversial findings of the task force. These conclusions represent the consensus of expert panels composed of five judges who independently reviewed and rated the empirical evidence. They evaluated, for each relationship element, the previous research summary and the new meta-analysis according to the following criteria: number of empirical studies; consistency of empirical results; independence of supportive studies; magnitude of Association between relationship element and outcome; and the ecological or external validity of research. Their respective ratings of demonstrably effective, probably effective, or promising but insufficient research to judge were then combined to render consensus. In this way, we added a modicum of rigor and consensus to the process, which was admittedly less so in the first task force (earlier studies)" (p. 100).

"The consensus deemed six of the relationship elements as demonstrably effective, three as probably effective, and three as promising but insufficient research to judge" (Norcross and Wampold, 2011, p. 100). The authors go on to provide a rather extensive explanation and examination of a multiplicity of research, statistical and methodological limitations as well as, strengths and scientific design matters pertaining to this study" (p. 100).

DEMONSTRABLY EFFECTIVE ELEMENTS OF THE PSYCHOTHERAPY RELATIONSHIP

1. Alliance in Individual Psychotherapy
2. Alliance in Youth Psychotherapy
3. Alliance in Family Therapy
4. Cohesion in Group Therapy
5. Empathy
6. Collecting Client Feedback

PROBABLY EFFECTIVE ELEMENTS IN PSYCHOTHERAPY RELATIONSHIP

1. Goal Consensus
2. Collaboration
3. Positive Regard

PROMISING BUT INSUFFICIENT RESEARCH TO JUDGE ELEMENTS OF THE PSYCHOTHERAPY RELATIONSHIP

1. Congruence/Genuineness
2. Repairing Alliance Ruptures
3. Managing Countertransference" (Norcross and Wampold, 2011, p. 99).

WHAT DOES NOT WORK

Norcross and Wampold indicate that translational research is both prescriptive and proscriptive. It tells us what works and what does not. In the following section, we highlight those therapist relational behaviors that are ineffective, perhaps even hurtful in psychotherapy.

One means of identifying ineffective qualities of the therapeutic relationship is to simply reverse the effective behaviors. Thus, what does not work includes low quality alliance in individual psychotherapy, lack of cohesion in group therapy, and discordance in couple and family therapy. Paucity of empathy, collaboration, consensus, and positive regard predict treatment drop out and failure. The ineffective practitioners will resist feedback, ignore alliance ruptures, and discount his or her countertransference.

Another means of identifying ineffective qualities of the relationship is to scour research literature and conduct polls of experts. Here are six behaviors to avoid according to that research (Duncan et al., 2010) and Delphi poll (Norcross, Koocher, and Garofalo, 2006):

1. Computations: Controlled research trails, particularly in the addictions field, consistently find a computational style to be ineffective. In one review (Miller, Wilbourne and Hettema, 2003), computation was ineffective in all 12 identified trials. By contrast, expressing empathy, rolling with resistance, developing discrepancy, and supporting self-efficacy, characteristic of motivational interviewing, have demonstrated large effects with a small number of sessions (Lundahl and Burke, 2009). See Forrest (1992, 1997, 2016).

2. Negative processes: Client reports and research studies converge in warning therapists to avoid comments or behaviors that are hostile, pejorative, critical, rejecting, or beaming (Binder and Strupp, 1997; Lambert and Barley, 2002). Therapists who attack a client's dysfunctional thoughts or relationship patterns need, repeatedly, to distinguish between attacking the person versus her behavior.

3. Assumptions: Psychotherapists who assume or intuit their client's perceptions of relationship satisfaction and treatment success are frequently inaccurate. By contrast, therapists who specifically and respectively inquire about their client's perceptions frequently enhance the alliance and prevent premature termination (Lambert and Shimokawa, 2011).

4. Therapist-centricity: A recurrent lesson from process-outcome research is that the client observational perspective on the therapy relationship best predicts the outcome (Orlinsky, Ronnestad and Willutzki, 2004). Psychotherapy practice that relies on the therapist's observational perspective, while valuable, does not predict the outcome as well. Therefore, privileging the client's experiences is central.

5. Rigidity: By inflexibly and excessively structuring treatment, the therapist risks empathetic failures and inattentiveness to client's experiences. Such a therapist is likely to overlook a breach in the relationship and mistakenly assume she has not contributed to that breach. Dogmatic reliance on particular relational or therapy methods, incompatible with the client, imperials treatment (Ackerman and Hilsenroth, 2001).

6. Procrustean bed: As the field of psychology has matures, using an identical therapy relationship (and treatment method) for all clients is now recognized as inappropriate and, in select cases, even unethical. The efficacy and applicability of psychotherapy will be enhanced by tailoring it to the unique needs of the client, not by imposing a procrustean bed onto unwilling consumers of psychological services. We

should all avoid the crimes of Procrustes; the legendary Greek giant would cut the long limbs of clients or stretch short limbs to fit his one sized bed.

We can optimize therapy relationships by simultaneously using what works and studiously avoiding what does not work" (pp. 100–101).

CONCLUDING THOUGHTS

The authors (Norcross and Wampold, 2011) conclude this article by indicating that "in the culture wars of psychotherapy that pit the therapy relationship against the treatment method (Norcross and Lambert, 2011), let us conclude like T.S. Elliot, by "arriving where we started "and underscoring three incontrovertible but often-neglected truths about psychotherapy relationships (p. 101).

"First, this interdivisional task force was commissioned in order to augment patient benefit. We continue to explore what works in the therapy relationship and what works when we adapt that relationship to (nondiagnostic) patient characteristics. That remains our collective aim: improving patient success, however measured and manifested in a given case.

Second, psychotherapy is at root a human relationship. Even when "delivered" via distance or on a computer, psychotherapy is an irreducibly human encounter. Both parties being themselves- their origins, culture, personalities, psychopathology, expectations, biases, defenses, and strengths- to the human relationship. Some will judge that relationship a precondition of change and others a process of change, but all agree that it is a relational enterprise.

Third, how we create and cultivate that powerful human relationship can be guides by the fruits of research. As Carl Rogers (1980) compellingly demonstrated, there is no inherent tension between relational approach and a scientific one. Science can, and should, inform us about what works in psychology, be it a treatment method, an assessment measure, a patient behavior, or yes, a therapy relationship" (p. 101).

The following chapter addresses many of the clinical practice guidelines pertaining to evidence-based psychotherapy and treatment relationships that have been addressed in Chapter 8. However, its content and focus of Chapter 9 encompasses clinical practice guidelines pertaining to evidence-based counseling psychotherapy, and treatment relationships involving the specific practice of addictions–focused psychotherapy and treatment work. Thus, Chapter 9 represents the author's attempt to foster the awareness and utilization of much of the evidence-based clinical practice and research data, guidelines and suggestions related to Norcross and Wampold study (2011), within the global arena of professional addictions treatment and health care. The scope of evidence-based clinical practice addictions specific care matter is also alluded to in the forward chapter of this text which addresses alliance universality as a core construct or ingredient in most, if not all, forms of efficacious or successful human health care and relationships.

Chapter 9

CLINICAL PRACTICE SUGGESTIONS AND RECOMMENDATIONS FOR ADDICTIONS-FOCUSED THERAPISTS, COUNSELORS AND TREATMENT PROVIDERS

INTRODUCTION

Within the over-all context of the Norcross-Wampold (2011) clinical practice guidelines and conclusions related to evidence-based psychotherapy relationships presented in Chapter 8, this chapter addresses and outlines several clinical practice guidelines and recommendations for all contemporary addiction therapists, clinicians and treatment providers. Many of these addictions psychotherapy and treatment provider focused guidelines and recommendations mirror the content of Chapter 8, and as was indicated in the Policy Recommendations segment of the earlier chapter, Norcross and Wampold (2011) indicate that "often practice divisions, mental-health organizations as a whole, administrators of mental health services are encouraged to attend to the relational features of those services, and researchers are also encouraged to examine various facets of the therapeutic relationship and treatment outcomes" (pp. 98–100).

Although Norcross and Wampold (2011) do not directly indicate that their clinical practice guidelines and recommendations be applied within the specific realm of the addictions psychotherapy, counseling and treatment profession, in the context of this author's training, education, supervision and extended clinical practice experience, virtually every facet of Norcross and Wampold review needs to be widely recognized ,examined, addressed and integratively utilized within various domains of clinical psychotherapy practice and treatment relationships involving addictive disordered persons. As noted earlier in this text the addictions treatment field has long struggled for relevance and recognition as a specialty profession within the general behavioral health and mental health practitioner realm. However, also in earlier chapters of the text, psychotherapy research studies and a wide diversity of other behavioral health research and evidence-based studies have increasingly included a significant number of investigations focusing a wide diversity of addiction and addictive disorder specific issues are associated with a wide variety of therapies and treatment modalities. The results and empirical evidence related to several of those addictions are substance abuse specific studies and findings were also addressed in earlier chapters of this text. These various realities pertaining to the addiction treatment profession and additions psychotherapy practice reflect the distinctive and progressive impact that the addictions and substance abuse disorders have influenced on the American and Worldwide population over the course of the past one hundred years.

Finally, addictions therapists and treatment providers share the common over-riding task of helping their patients improve, grow, change and recover. All behavioral health professionals work to benefit their patients and clients, and ultimately psychotherapy is always at root "a human relationship—in psychotherapy and counseling relationships the over-all empirical therapy outcome evidence pertaining to "what works" indicates that the therapist-patience alliance is a consistently crucial relationship component in successful psychotherapy outcomes and treatment.

GENERAL SUGGESTIONS AND RECOMMENDATIONS FOR ADDICTIONS THERAPISTS, COUNSELORS AND TREATMENT PROGRAMS

1. Education: The addictions treatment profession has evinced a slow but steady professional developmental process throughout the United States over the past forty years. This process has also included the didactic and experimental educational components of addictions and substance abuse related to psychotherapy, counseling, assessment, relapse prevention, expertise and outcomes (Hill et al., 2017), and a myriad of other facets associated with the full spectrum of therapies and counseling related to the treatment of addictive disorders. More recently, co-occurring or co-morbid behavioral health and mental health conditions as well as the emergence of integrative care (Chandiramani, 2015; Genovese, 2016) within the addictions and overall American Healthcare system reflects the evolutionary nature of education in the addictions and substance abuse health care industry. The evolution of didactic addictions education related to the practice of chemical dependency counseling and addictions specific to psychotherapy between the 1970s and 2016 has generally encompassed state and mandated requirements pertaining to completion of substantive academic coursework in an ever ex-

panding realm of clinical practice means including causative factors, or etiology, assessment, and diagnosis, treatment and therapeutic work or models including, self-help care, detoxification, ethics, infectious diseases, basic health matters including HIV and STD's and relapse. Addictions counselors, therapists and treatment providers and "professionals" have evolved from the ranks of recovering individuals with very little addiction- specific to education other than their own personal recovery-based experiences, to a broad spectrum of both recovering and non-recovering. Therapists and clinicians who have now generally learn required to complete a nurse of educational and academic certifications including bachelor's and master's degrees as well as doctoral degrees and other addiction specific certifications. Furthermore, these individuals are required to engage in continuing education programs over the course of their professional addictions careers in order to continue active clinical practice.

2. Alliance and relationship focused education should be encouraged and emphasized in the didactic, experimental, and undergraduate and graduate level educational preparation of addiction therapists, counselors and treatment providers. The recent establishment of under- graduate and graduate level addictions specific counselor education programs within University Counseling Psychology programs and other Counselor Education programs need to provide and consistently encourage extensive examination as well as a thorough understanding of alliance and relationships related to evidence-based research pertaining to addictions therapy and treatment.

Indeed, evidence-based alliance and relationship informed practices should be an actively encourages care ingredient in all addiction counselor and behavioral health education programs. Thus, clinical psychologists, social workers, addictions counselors and therapist, corrections counselors, psychiatrists, licensed professional counselors, couple and family therapists, adolescent counselors, and marriage and family therapists need to be educated and quite knowledgeable and skilled in the realm of alliance awareness, information and encouraged to utilize alliance specific practice skills within the context of their therapeutic relationships in addictive disordered programs.

3. All too frequently in the addiction treatment profession, the author has encountered clinicians, therapists, program administrators and other primary care specialists who have very little and sometimes no pain awareness, educational or treatment familiarly with the concept of "alliance". Needless to say, these individuals also manifest little if any understanding of the global evidence-based alliance implications that are associated with alliance factors and "what works" or outcome in addictions therapy and treatment outcomes. Such clinicians need to be encouraged to complete additional education and training specific to the relationship and alliance parameters specific to their clinical practice and professional development.

4. Finally, all contemporary addictions therapists and clinicians should be encouraged and/or required to complete undergraduate (BAIBS) and graduate level (MARMS) behavioral science/ behavioral health curriculums in fully-accredited University or College academic settings. These programs also need to include focused and extensive addiction psychotherapy course context and clinical practice education. Moreover, these educational programs and faculty should involve faculty and supervisors who have extensive personal and professional practice experience with the addictions therapy and treatment profession as well as extensive alliance-based training and education.

TRAINING AND SUPERVISION

1. Addictions training and supervision programs involving student and trainee agency fieldwork placements, internships and practicums are encouraged to select trainee clinical placement sites written clinical environments which provide alliance-relationships based professional clinical services for addictive disordered as well as other patient populations.

2. Practicum and clinical supervisors as well as fieldwork and internship supervisors in educational, agency, hospital, and mental health or various addictions focused treatment settings are also encouraged to provide training, education, and experimental alliance and relational evidence-based clinical practice experiences and supervision for their trainees. Supervisors, and academic and clinical staff who supervise and train students involved in graduate level addictions counseling and behavioral health programs that are offered in academic settings are encouraged to consider placing all of their trainees in addictions specific training and treatment settings (i.e., detox facilities, residential and out-patient settings, mental health and psychiatric facilities, or private practice settings) whenever possible. Within the context of many clinical settings providing comprehensive and more extended care addictions training opportunities, clinical supervisors and faculty are also encouraged to develop student rotations involving placements or rotations on different addiction units and provide clinical experiences and educational opportunities for their trainees.

RESEARCH SUGGESTIONS AND RECOMMENDATIONS FOR ADDICTION THERAPISTS, COUNSELORS, AND TREATMENT CARE PROGRAMS

1. Research and faculty involved in both under-graduate and graduate level programs as well as counselor education, clinical counseling psycho-

therapy, psychology, and social work programs are encouraged to initiate faculty studies associated with an expanded spectrum of variables related to addictions specific alliance-relationship and psychotherapy outcomes.

2. Researchers, educators, and clinical supervisors are also encouraged to utilize basic clinical practice and empirical advanced methodological design models specific to addictions related alliance-relationship and treatment outcomes via their training, education, and supervision work with graduate level addictions therapists and clinicians.

3. Researchers are likewise encouraged to train their addictions students, clinicians and therapists to utilize the observational perspective in studies and reviews of addictions outcomes and "what works" in psychotherapy work within the context of the therapeutic relationship and alliance, as well as therapist expertise, outcomes, and therapeutic interventions phrase here for diverse addiction populations (Hill et al., 2017) (Klemperer et al., 2017)

4. Organizations such as APA (Division 50, ACA, NAA, DAC, NASW) are also encouraged to educate, train, and supervise their students, therapists, and clinicians in their benefits of evidence-based therapy relationships and the alliance context.

5. All addictions treatment provider organizations, education and training programs, including NAADAC and mental health organizations are encouraged to educate, train, and supervise their addictions treatment providers and other behavioral health providers about the improved therapeutic outcomes associated with using evidence-based therapy relationships and alliances.

6. All behavioral health organizations and professional health care service providers are encouraged to actively advocate for the use of training, education, supervision and research-based benefits of nurturing, and responsive and supportive human relationships in psychotherapy.

7. All administrators, directors and corporate bodies engaged in the process of providing clinical health care services in addictions, mental health, and behavioral health treatment settings are engaged to attend to the relational features of the various professional services they provide their patients, and attempts to improve quality of care should account for treatment relationships and adaptations.

COMMENTS OF "WHAT WORKS" AND "WHAT DOES NOT WORK" IN ADDICTIONS PSYCHOTHERAPY AND ADDICTIONS TREATMENT PROGRAMS

The content of this text focuses almost exclusively upon the clinical and empirical evidence-based research data that has been published over the past sixty-five years related to the therapeutic alliance, psychotherapy relationship and the process, outcome and effectiveness of therapy. Clinicians and researchers have conducted thousands of investigations over the past several decades in order to foster enhanced treatment outcomes and develop more efficacious therapeutic practice intervention techniques and strategies.

As noted throughout the text all contemporary behavioral scientists, educators, supervisors, practicing clinicians, and treatment providers, can utilize the information and therapeutic knowledge that has been gleamed from the psychotherapy alliance and relationship literature to improve psychotherapy outcomes. Sadly, a sizeable segment of professional addictions psychotherapy, counseling and treatment providers are either unaware or relatively unaware of the various alliance-related dynamics and facets that are directly related to the process, outcomes and effectiveness of their treatment work. In this context, addiction professionals also need to remain aware of the reality that addictions specific psychotherapy and counseling clinical studies and research investigations have never, in fact, encompassed a major component of the historic psychotherapy alliance, relationships, and outcome studies data base. Nonetheless, the over-all body of alliance-focused literature does include numerous studies and investigations that address a spectrum of addictive disordered behaviors and a diversity of addictive disordered patient populations. There has also been a continually expanding body of empirical psychotherapy treatment alliance related to addictions studies in behavioral health and psychotherapy research arena over the past twenty years.

The author's clinical practice experience encompasses some forty-five years of alliance focused addiction specific psychotherapy and treatment with and as delineated via the inclusion of a multiplicity of clinical publications, case studies, text works, as well as the content of this volume. The Norcross and Wampold (2011) "What works," demonstrates effective alliance categories including the alliance in individual psychotherapy, alliance in youth psychotherapy, alliance in family therapy, cohesion in group therapy, empathy and collecting client feedback. These constitute the heart and soul of effective therapeutic work with various patient populations. From a strictly clinical practice perspective, this author would add support, positive reward, non-possessive warmth and genuineness to the list.

The Norcross and Wampold (2011) "What works" category also includes effective goal consensus, collaboration and positive regard as additional core ingredients in all psychotherapy and treatment relationships including addictions-focused psychotherapy and treatment work in the author's (Forrest, 2016) clinical practice experience. The Norcross and Wampold (2011) meta-analysis research data related to these qualities reflects that they "are probably effective" but they are not demonstrably effective via the preponderance of previous investigations..

Finally, The Norcross and Wampold (2011) "what works" category *promising but insufficient research to judge* including congruence/genuineness, repairing alliance ruptures and managing countertransference are additional central factors in effective addictions focused therapeutic work in the author's (Forrest, 2016) clinical practice experience. However, the author views therapist congruence or genuineness a first order clinical characteristic of highly effective addictions therapists, and would also add managing patient transference as a first or second order clinical characteristic or skill set of effective addictions psychotherapists and clinicians.

With regard to the earlier Norcross and Wampold (2011) "What does not work" in psychotherapy investigation, this author (Forrest, 2015, 2016) would certainly concur from an experiential perspective involving extensive psychotherapy work with addictive disordered patients that "a low quality alliance in individual psychotherapy, lack of cohesion in group therapy, discordance in couple and family therapy, paucity of empathy, collaboration, consensus, and positive regard predict treatment drop out and therapeutic failure" (p. 101). Ineffective addictions therapists also frequently "resist client feedback, ignore (or remain unaware of) alliance ruptures, and discount his or her countertransference" (p. 106). Ineffective addiction therapists fail to address significant patient transference and dissonance (Forrest, 2002). Many, if not most, addictive disordered patient present in therapy with floridly active addictive disease. As a result, early stage psychotherapy and treatment work with these individuals can be rife with transference and countertransference management issues and can result in therapy treatment failures and acute or incipient alliance ruptures. These addictive disordered patients also frequently manifest co-morbid boarder line and antisocial personality disorders, bi-polar disorder, and other more severe adjustment disorders or varieties of psychopathology which contributes significantly to the outcropping of strong transference and countertransference reactions in psychotherapy.

Norcross and Wampold (2011) address six additional psychotherapy factors that "do not work" in therapy: (1) *Confrontations,* including "controlled research trails, particularly in the addictions field, consistently find a computational style to be ineffective—by contrast, expressing empathy, rolling with resistance, developing discrepancy, and supporting self-efficacy, and characteristics of motivational interviewing have demonstrated large effects with a small sample sessions (Lundahl and Burke, 2009, p. 101). Addictions psychotherapists and treatment professionals always need to avoid the use of angry hostile, pejorative and destructive confrontation-based relational dynamics and interventions with their clients. Per the earlier discussion on confrontation work with addictive disordered persons in this chapter and elsewhere in the text (Forrest, 1982, 1991, 2002, 2012), supportive, empathic, sensitive, warm, nurturing, and insightful and timely confrontations that often include the use of humor and paradoxes which the client can both understand and usefully employ in the service of his or her recovery process can be very constructive as well alliance and recovery enhancing. Experienced and well-trained addictions therapists, counselors and clinicians are best qualified to use supportive types of confrontation strategies in their therapeutic relationships, and to the contrary, neophyte therapists and early-career therapists may be wise to generally or totally refrain from the use of confrontation strategies in their work with addictive disordered clients. (2) *Negative processes,* including "warning therapists to avoid comments or behaviors that are hostile, pejorative, critical, rejecting, or blaming— Therapists who attack a client's dysfunctional thoughts or relational patterns need, repeatedly, to distinguish between attacking the person verses his or her behavior" (Norcross and Wampold, 2011; Lambert and Barley, 2002) Addictions therapists and all other addictions focused behavioral health providers need to curtail all forms of noxious relational and verbal transactions and interventions with their clients. Blaming, cursing, attacking, hostile and otherwise threatening relational communicative interventions constitute iatrogenic measures that should never occur in psychotherapy or other helping relationships (p. 101). (3) *Assumptions,* including "psychotherapists who assume or intuit their client's perceptions of relationship (alliance) satisfaction and treatment success are frequently inaccurate. By contrast, therapists who specifically and respectfully inquire about their client's perceptions frequently enhance the alliance and prevent premature termination" (Lambert and Shimokawa, 2011, p. 101).

Addictions therapists and counselors as well as treatment program administrators and office staff, educators, and supervisors also need to avoid comments and patterns of behavior that communicate a rejecting, demeaning, beaming, hostile, over-critical or pejorative attitudinal set toward addictive disordered patients. Blaming and segregating therapeutic alliance focused relational transactions are perhaps most frequent associated with patient relapses, transference and countertransference dynamics related to resistance, passive-aggressive or antisocial behaviors and border line personality issues. Addictions therapists and all addictive treatment providers need to remain aware of these issues, and training and clinical staff supervisors need to repeatedly adhere these matters with the context of their training and supervisory relationship with trainees and clinical staff and program administrators.

Likewise, "assumptions" including therapist based and other treatment program staff member perceptions related to alliance, relationship and treatment success or failure also need to be avoided. Addictions therapists, clinical staff, and treatment program administrators also need to be encouraged to actively, specifically and respectfully inquire about the client's personal beliefs, perceptions and feelings pertaining to such matters as the alliance, potential termination issues, rupture repair and various other facets of the therapeutic relationship and process, (4) *Therapist-centricity*, including a recurrent lesson from process-outcome research is that *the client's observational perspective on the the*rapy relationship best predicts outcome (Orlinsky, Ronnestad and Willutzki, 2004). Psychotherapy practice that relies on *the therapist's observational perspective,* while valuable, *does not predict outcome as well.* Therefore, privileging the client's experiences is central" (Norcross and Wampold, 2011, p. 101). Addictions therapists, educators, supervisors, program administrators and researchers need to remain cognizant of this reality in all of their various professional notes, and continuously reinforce the need to include direct patient or client involvement and evaluative feedback in all of their treatment process-outcome professional activities including program reports consumer-based information resources and marketing efforts, (5) *Rigidity*, including " by inflexibility and excessively structuring treatment, the therapist risk empathic failures and inattentiveness to clients experiences. Such "therapists are" likely to overlook a breach in the relationship (alliance dissonance and potential rupture dynamics) and mistakenly assume he or she has not contributed to that breach, (6) *Dogmatic reliance on particular relational or therapy methods, incompatible with the client, imperils treatment"* (Ackerman and Hilsenroth, 2001, p. 101). Addictions professionals, in general, need to remain especially vigilant in their efforts to avoid particular pitfalls associated with personal and program inflexibility, rigidity and "dogmatic reliance on particular relational and treatment methods" that can be incompatible with patient's beliefs, values, culture and other factors which may limit or imperil the alliance relationship, treatment process, and outcome of therapy or care. Historically, these dynamics have not uncommonly been played out within the explicit context of mandated patient engagement in treatment programs and psychotherapy models or paradigms that have been essentially constituted around the Alcoholics Anonymous (AA) or self-help model and ideology of recovery and treatment. Contemporary addictions treatment providers, clinicians, and programs are encouraged to provide integrative services that are provided by a diversity of well-trained and skilled therapists who utilized a broad range of therapeutic tools and resources which are adopted and utilized to meet the specific treatment needs of individual patients. Effective and well-trained addictions therapists consistently employ selective therapeutic strategies, resources and tools in their therapeutic work with addictive disabled persons. They also remain flexible in their therapeutic interactions with patients, and are able to adaptively shape alliance relationships which encompass evolving therapeutic goals and tasks, as well as the frequent use of ancillary therapeutic strategies, interventions and recovery-based resources. These dynamics generally foster continued alliance growth, diminished and reduce potential patient sources of resistance, foster patient motivation for care and embrace psychotherapy and treatment outcomes (Forrest, 2015, 2016). In effect, all addictions treatment providers and therapists need to remind themselves from time to time that there are "many roads to recovery and change;" over essential relational roles and tasks in the recovery process involve helping addictive disordered persons discover and consistently utilize to the best of their abilities the various tools, strengths and resources we have to foster the ongoing recovery and change process, and (6) Procrustean bed, including "as the field of psychotherapy (and addictions therapy and treatments) has matured, *using an identical therapy relationship (and treatment method) for all clients is more recognized as inappropriate and, in select cases, even unethical.* The efficacy and applicability of psychotherapy (and other treatments) will be enhanced by tailoring it to the unique needs of the client, not by imposing a Procrustean bed onto unwilling consumers of psychological services (addictions psychotherapy and other addictions treatments and care modalities) We should all avoid the crimes of Procrustes, the legendary Greek giant who would cut the long limbs of clients or stretch short limbs to fit his one-sized bed.

We can optimize therapy relationships by simultaneously using "what works" and studiously avoiding what "does not work" (Norcross and Wampold, 2011, p. 101).

Again, addictions therapists and treatment providers need to also avoid the pit falls of both Rigidity and the Procrustean bed that Norcross and Wampold (2011) have delineated in their list of six therapist behaviors or qualities to avoid in psychotherapy.

These researched-based and identified ineffective therapist qualities pertaining to the alliance and relationship (Duncan et al., 2010; Norcross, Koocher and Garofalo, 2006).

Within this context, addictions therapists, educators, clinical supervisors and other treatment providers also need to remember that this body of empirical and clinical knowledge may be skewed or limited to the relatively unique realities associated with the limited number of addiction-specific psychotherapy treatment investigations historic and current limiting parameters of the addictions psychotherapy and treatment profession and industry, including past and present educational and training limitations, previously segregated mental health and addictions or substance abuse governmental, state, and local agencies and programs, issues, patient characteristics and dynamics, liability risk factors, funding, lack of behavioral health parity in American health care industry, persistent stigmas, dogma and also collective erroneous beliefs related to many facets of treatment and also to the process of therapy and other treatments associated with the complex co-morbid pathology and behaviors that can be related with the addictions treatment profession.

It should also be noted that contemporary behavioral health education, training, research and practice settings continue to provide relatively limited opportunities for students and persons who wish to pursue addictions specific psychotherapy and treatment focused careers. Indeed, even the majority of graduate level education, training and research in the behavioral health professions of social work, counseling and clinical psychology, counseling and clinical psychology, counselor education, addictions counseling, and psychiatry typically provide very limited professional development experiences for their addictions focused students.

Addictions therapists and treatment providers need to be encouraged to actively strive to enhance the over-all development of optimal educational, training, research, supervision, clinical practice, and treatment opportunities for all health professionals engaged in the various behavioral health professions.

SUMMARY AND CONCLUDING REMARKS

Per the earlier work of Norcross and Wampold (2011) pertaining to "what works" and "what does not work" in psychotherapy, it was noted that the "culture wars of psychotherapy that pit the therapy relationship against the treatment method (or model), it is easy to close sides, ignore disconfirming research, and lose sight of our super ordinate commitment to patient benefit" (p. 101). These authors go on to stress the importance of continued research and work in the realm of "what works" and "what does not work" in the psychotherapy relationship, and also "what works when we adapt that relationship to non-diagnostic patient characteristics." Norcross and Wampold also emphasize the importance of our collective behavioral health aim of "improving patient success, however measured and manifested in a given case" (p. 101).

These core psychotherapy relationships and treatment models related issues have also remained germane to the addictions treatment profession since the time of our conception in the mid-late 1930s. Contemporary addictions therapists, clinicians, educators, supervisors, and program administrators continue to manifest a diversity of often conflicting viewpoints related to "what works," "what does not work," and which treatment approaches, models and methods work within the relatively specific realm of addictions psychotherapy and treatment. Many contemporary clinicians, therapists, researchers and other professional addictions treatment providers strongly advocate for the use of CBT, brief therapy, group therapies, family therapy or residential care, intensive outpatient care, individual therapy and self-based (Alcoholic Anonymous, Narcotics Anonymous, etc., "therapies") treatment preferences.

Some addictions clinicians continue to believe, based primarily upon their personal and professional treatment-based exercises, that the "only way" or "only thing that works" in addictions treatment and therapy is limited to one or two of these specific treatment models. Many of these clinicians continue to manifest very little awareness or knowledge pertaining to

The research evidence and clinical salience of the relationship and alliance in their personal therapy work as well as the lives and potential recoveries of their patients. To this end, all addictions professionals need to continue to explore "what works" and "what does not work" within the therapeutic relationship and alliance context as well as "what works" and "what does not work" within psychotherapy and treatment work when they adopt the relationship to a number of other variables including non-diagnostic patient-therapist relationship characteristics.

All addictions clinicians and treatment providers additionally need to embrace the basic collective good of "improving patient success and outcomes, however measured and manifested in a given case."

Addictions therapists and other behavioral health professionals also need to embrace the concept that psychotherapy "is at root a human relationship" (Norcross and Wampold, 2011). In a more global sense, all forms of psychotherapy including "mechanistic therapies" (Forrest, 2012) have historically evoked and taken place via the medium of human relationship. As also noted by Norcross and Wampold (2011), even when "delivered via distance or on a computer, psychotherapy is irreducibly human encounter—both parties (or multiple parties) being themselves—their origin, culture, personalities, psychotherapy, expectations, biases, defenses, and strength—to the human relationship" (p. 101). This author (Forrest, 2012) would further add that therapists and patients ultimately and mutually being, and potentially express their total human exponential histories within the context of the therapeutic relationship. Norcross and Wampold further state "some will judge this relationship a precondition of change and others a process of change, but all agree that it is a relational enterprise."

Again, these essential precepts need to remain at the forefront of the addiction therapist's conscious awareness and throughout the course of every stage and facet of the therapeutic process involving addictive disordered persons.

Finally, addictions therapists and treatment providers need to realize and integratively accept that how we create and cultivate the human relationship—the psychotherapy relationship, can be enhanced and guided by empirical research findings. Norcross and Wampold (2011) note that Rogers (1980) "compellingly demonstrated that there is no inherent tension between a relational approach and a scientific approach. Science can, and should inform us about what works in psychotherapy, be it a treatment method, an assessment measure, patient behavior, or yes, a therapy relationship" (p. 101).

Understandably, many, if not most addictions therapists, and practicing clinicians and other behavioral health professionals in general tend to regressively divorce themselves from the psychotherapy research evidence-based literature over the course of their extended careers in the helping professions. In particular, psychotherapists and other behavioral health clinicians and professionals throughout the United States as well as the world have been confronted with the task of providing care and therapy for an ever-increasing number of disturbed and emotionally conflicted patients during the past fifteen to twenty years. The personal strain and emotional realities of seeing 6-8 psychotherapy patients a day, four or five days a week, conducting therapy groups, crisis interventions, conducting clinical assessments and evaluations, providing consultation services, academic notes, and the various tasks and demands of family life and the basic process of daily living can over-ride or erode the practicing psychotherapist's continued on-going and active efforts to remain objective relative to the empirical psychotherapy research studies and investigations related to a multiplicity of process, outcome and relational factors. Therapists and clinicians who sustain active and productive practices for twenty-five to fifty years usually understand their "practice dilemmas" quite well!

Nonetheless, within the context of our ethical and collective goal as addictions imperative to therapists, clinicians, treatment providers and behavioral health professionals relative to improving patients successes and outcome, the conclusions of the Norcross and Wampold (2011) Task Force and content of this chapter, implore all of us to not only be guided by the ever-present evolving fruits of our psychotherapy research evidence by also by the findings, data and privileges that have been delineated in this chapter as well as the text all addictions therapists and treatment providers will be able to enhance their treatment outcomes and therapeutic relationship by utilizing this information within the context of their therapeutic alliance and relationship work with addictive disordered patients.

In juxtaposition to much of the context of this chapter, addictions therapist and professionals also need to recognize that as a profession we have made considerable progress over the past 30 years to the various issues that have been presented, discussed and recommended in this chapter. However, we must continue to evince a strong collective motivation to strengthen our professional development in the specific areas of (1) developing more enhanced didactic and clinical experimental addictions focused graduate education and training programs (2) conducting more and increasing psychotherapy and other treatments sophisticated addictions focused empirical research investigations, including an emphasis on (3) alliance and relational factors and dynamics in addictions psychotherapy as well as addictions treatment models related to the full spectrum of addictive disordered patients. Furthermore, the results of these evolving professional activities, endeavors and findings need to be made readily available to our professional colleagues as well as the general public via the mediums of professional publications including professional journal articles and continuing education, training, and supervision for all addictions treatment providers.

Education, training, supervision and clinical practice guidelines and recommendations for addictions therapists and counselors should generally chemical dependency match those of graduate level (MAIMS, PhD, PsyD, EdD, and MSW) programs that are offered by fully accredited Colleges and Universities through the United States. These programs most typically involve counseling psychology and clinical psychology departments, counselor education departments, and marriage and family therapy, counseling and guidance, mental health, social work, rehabilitation counseling and addictions specific degree programs. Several graduate level training programs in the field of addictions therapy and treatment currently exist in these various professional behavioral health programs in America, and such programs also need to "provide addition specific focused practice internships, field-work, clinical and possibly post-doctoral supervision training experiences for their students. Addictions education and training programs also need to include research design, methodology, and statistical course work and experiential involvement for all of their graduate students. These educational and training experiences are optimally conducted by graduate level faculty, staff and supervisors who ideally have explicate personal expertise in the area of addictions treatment and psychotherapy, and also manifest considered and ongoing clinical practice experience with the spectrum of addictive disordered persons.

Ethical practice and training requirements and standards, state certificates and license issues, supervision requirements, continuing education requirements, professional memberships, and a myriad of other addiction counselors-therapist professional development matters have also been delineated via the various education, training, supervision and practice standards and regulations that have evolved through the efforts of the American Psychological Associations, American Counseling Association, National Association of Social Workers, and National Association of Alcohol and Drug Addiction Counselors (NAADAC). However, it also needs to be emphasized that the paramount focus of all addictions education and training programs involve the development of students' global professional skill set specific to the psychotherapy and treatment of addictive disordered persons.

Our current addictions training programs clearly need to provide enhanced therapist trainee research and general empirical science skills, and actively reinforce the consistent use of these particular skill sets withing the explicit realm of the psychotherapy relationship, clinical practice settings, and all addictions treatment programs.

Chapter 10

ALLIANCE UNIVERSALITY: THE HEART AND SOUL OF CHANGE AND RECOVERY

INTRODUCTION

The extensive empirical data base pertaining to a wide range of alliance related psychotherapy factors including therapeutic outcomes, therapy retention rates, various measures of constructive change including patient, therapist, and independent rater assessments as well as therapist psychotherapy treatment modality related measures rather compellingly demonstrate the universal relevance and salient role of the alliance in virtually all forms of psychotherapy—for better or worse. The alliance of therapeutic "bond" and human relationship dimensions of therapy constitute the bedrock foundation for constructive human growth, adaptive change, and successful psychotherapy outcomes.

As noted and referenced throughout the text, this body of evidence-based psychotherapy research has expanded and consistently demonstrates the robust relationships between strong therapeutic alliances, specific alliance ingredients and characteristics, and successful therapeutic outcomes pertaining to diverse patient populations receiving forms or models of therapy in a variety of treatment settings. This body of empirical evidence spans a course of seventy years. The vast majority of these research and clinical investigations have also included the author's and researchers' various observations pertaining to the limitations, caveats, methodological and other reservations that are related to the results of their studies.

Many of these empirical psychotherapy studies have included clinical practice based case studies and actual therapy vignettes that have also been used to demonstrate the various therapeutic facets of change, evolving patient-therapist relational dynamics and interactions, patient pathology or more global relational change dimensions, and time related outcomes. In this context, alliance universality becomes a core construct in all clinical practice settings and all forms and facets of psychotherapy work!

315

Much of this book focuses upon the direct clinical observations, psychotherapy practice experiences, publications, and clinical work of the author (Forrest, 1975-2016) related to the alliance and alliance universality in successful addictions psychotherapy work and treatment. This chapter examines (1) the meaning and definitional parameters of the alliance universality construct in psychotherapy from both a scientific or empirical perspective, and (2) a broad range of clinical practice perspectives that several highly esteemed, experienced and widely recognized therapists, academicians, and scientist-practitioners have expressed or alluded to via their publications and scholarly contributions to the counseling and psychotherapy literature over the past several decades. In many respects, much of this clinical discourse ultimately amounts to a redundant expression of the constructive and multi-faceted universal impact and relevance of the alliance as a central ingredient in the process and outcome of most, if not all, human psychotherapy relationships. However, this alliance data-base and framework far transcends the topical arena of process and "for better, or worse" outcome dimensions of psychotherapy research.

DEFINING AND MEANING PARAMETER OF ALLIANCE UNIVERSALITY IN PSYCHOTHERAPY

Alliance universality can be defined as a core therapist-patient focused ingredient, quality or relational characteristic of most, if not all, effective psychotherapy relationships. Furthermore, successful therapy outcomes and effective therapy relationships essentially and universally evolve and take place as a function of the development of therapist-patient alliances or "bonds" which involve mutually strong, resilient, flexible and personal commitments between therapists and patients.

The ongoing psychotherapy relationship and process helps patients actualize positive growth, development, and constructive personality and behavioral change associated with a wide range of behavior dysfunction and patterns of living or thinking. From a human relationship perspective, the alliance relationship may constitute the most universal or fundamental prerequisite for all forms of significant constructive therapeutic change. Weak and fragile alliances as well as the lack of ability or inability of the therapist and patient to routinely form working and productive therapeutic alliances generally contribute to poor therapeutic outcomes, deterioration in therapy, and premature therapy terminations. Furthermore, alliance universality in the context of effecting successful psychotherapy outcomes has also been consistently and repeatedly demonstrated to be rather specifically associated with the therapist's ability to provide consistently high-levels of relatively specific core relational ingredients or qualities throughout the course of therapy. As discussed throughout the text, these essential therapist relational ingredients or qualities include (1) non-possessive warmth or positive regard, empathy, and genuineness or congruence (Rogers, 1957; Truax and Carkhuff, 1967; Horvath et al., 2011). Other positive ingredients also contribute to the therapist's ability to provide high-level therapeutic relationships which contribute to successful therapeutic outcomes. These alliance-based qualities or ingredients include effective communication skills, concreteness, self-disclosure or transparency, unconditional positive regard, affirmation, and support. However, it should be noted that Rogers (1957) originally indicated that the therapist's ability to provide non-possessive warmth (unconditional positive regard), congruence (genuineness), and empathy were *the essential and sufficient conditions* for therapeutic change.

The relevance and meaning of the alliance universality construct in psychotherapy and addictions therapy can also be associated with the realization that the alliance is currently "one of the most intensely researched subjects in psychotherapy research literature" (Horvath et al., 2014; Eubanks-Carter, Muran and Safran, 2015; Fisher et al., 2016). The relevance and interest in the alliance, and discussion related to the concept of alliance universality, "is probably due to its pan theoretical nature as well as its well-documented and robust relationship with the outcome of psychotherapy" (Norcross, 2011; Ulvenes et al., 2012). These authors also note "the alliance seems to be critically important across therapeutic approaches."

Fluckiger et al. (2012) further investigated moderators of the alliance-outcome relationship in a meta-analysis study and found that neither research design, use of disorder-specific manuals, type of treatment, or specificity of outcome measures affected the alliance-outcome relationship. Several studies (Baldwin, Wampold and Imel, 2007; Eubanks-Carter, Muran and Safran, 2015; Ulvenes et al., 2012) indicate that therapists vary in their ability to form alliances with their patients, and this variability accounts for the correlation between alliance and outcome—"therapists who are better able to form strong alliances with their patients have better outcomes than therapist who are less able to form alliances with their patients." Furthermore, it appears that the patient's contribution to the alliance did not affect the outcome. The importance of therapists' ability to form alliances for improved outcomes in psychotherapy has also been replicated in a variety of settings (Zuroff et al., 2010).

The Project MATCH Research Group (1998) found that some therapists have a majority of patients with successful outcomes, and other therapists have a high percentage of patients who did not improve or get worse over time. Truax and Carkhuff (1967) also reported these findings in psychotherapy studies over 50 years ago. The personal attributes of therapists (warmth, empathy, openness, genuineness, support, capacity for attachment, etc.) positively impact the therapeutic alliance, regardless of the clinician's theoretical orientation. Therapeutic techniques (i.e. listening skills, here and now focus, accurate interpretations, affect awareness, and exploring patient experiences) also positively impact the alliance (Ackerman and Hilsenroth, 2003; Clemente et al., 2012).

Laska, Gurman and Wampold (2014) likewise report that "therapists' contributions" to the alliance predicted outcome rather than patients' contributions, that is, therapists who were able to form better alliances generally with their patients had better outcomes. These authors additionally indicate that "there is accumulating evidence that the alliance is predictive of patient change after controlling for early symptom change—the alliance is not weaker in EST's (empirically supported treatment), in disorder-specific manualized treatments, for symptom measures, for cognitive or behavioral treatments, or RCT's (vs. naturalistic studies), nor is it weaker in family therapy, with one hallmark study (Alexander et al., 1976) of the behavioral treatment or delinquent adolescents finding therapists' relationship skills accounted for 59 percent of the outcome variance" (p. 472). Once again, the authors (Laska, Gurman and Wampold, 2014) report that recent meta-analysis studies involving "hundreds of studies" reveal "a robust and moderate correlation (between .25 and .30) between the alliance and outcome, also noting this may be an underestimate owing to measurement issues" (p. 471).

The universality of the alliance construct is further defined and supported vis-à-vis the recent work of Zack et al. (2015) which examined attachment history and the alliance outcome relationship in adolescent therapy. These authors again indicate "the therapeutic alliance has a well-established history as a factor predicting treatment outcome across various treatment approaches, findings are robustly replicated in more than 7,000 studies of adult psychotherapy, demonstrating an effect size of .275" (p. 258). It is also noted in this study that "compared with the adult literature, youth alliance research is sparce—however, it has grown exponentially over the past two decades, and findings replicate adult effects—for example, a meta-analysis of (youth) studies with alliance measurement on par with investigations of adults found an alliance outcome association of r=.22—not only is the working alliance a robust predictor of symptom reduction, the alliance and therapeutic relationship are the areas identified as most important by youth practitioners, clients, and parents and are the most frequently endorsed reason for discontinuing treatment" (p. 258).

Zack et al. (2015) point out that the alliance-therapy outcome link is viewed by some as "curative in and of itself, and by others as a necessary, but insufficient, condition to allow techniques to have their effect." The findings of the Zack study (2015) suggest that "attachment to the primary caretaker moderated the impact of the working alliance on treatment outcome, such that for youth with the poorest attachment history, working alliance had a stronger relationship with outcomes. Conversely, for those with the strongest attachment histories, alliance was not a significant predictor of symptom reduction—our findings replicated the established alliance-outcome link demonstrated in earlier psychotherapy meta-analysis studies (Shirk and Karver, 2011); stronger alliance was associated with greater symptom reduction at the end of treatment, a small to moderate effect—poorer attachment was negatively associated with alliance scores and treatment scores individually" (pp. 258, 264).

Friedlander et al. (2011) note that the working alliance in couple and family therapy (CFT) was recognized over 20 years ago, and their meta-analytical review of 24 studies in which alliances, self-reported and observed, were used to predict treatment retention, improved mid-treatment, and/or outcomes concludes that "(1) the therapeutic alliance is a critical factor in the process and outcome of CFT, (2) shared sense of purpose within families, a particularly important dimension of the alliance, involves establishing overarching systemic goals, (3) evaluating the alliance based on observation is a skill that can be taught, and (4) in short, each person's alliance matters and alliances are not interchangeable—thus, clinicians should build and maintain strong alliances with each party and be aware of the ways in which, depending upon the family's dynamics, the whole alliance is more than the sum of its parts" (p. 31).

These authors (Friedlander et al., 2014; Friedlander, 2015) also report a wide range of couple and family therapy alliance specific resource findings related to treatment retention, therapy outcomes, couples therapy, family therapy, types of treatment and limitations of this research. This body of clinical and empirical data does include a number of studies involving adolescent substance abuse. Addictions therapists will find this information to be particularly useful, as adolescent alliance evidence is wide-ranging and rather complex.

Group therapy or cohesion (alliance) related studies (Burlingame, McClendon and Alonso, 2011) likewise contribute to the body of relational related clinical and empirical evidence which can be used to support the alliance universality construct in psychotherapy. The "cohesion" construct has essentially become synonymous with the alliance or therapeutic relationship in more recent group therapy literature. The Burlingame et al. (2011) group therapy/cohesion literature evidence supports two fundamental dimensions of cohesion: relationship structure and relationship quality. The relationship quality of the cohesion construct includes a two-factor definition of the therapeutic relationship in group therapy: (1) belonging and acceptance factors (cohesion and member-leader alliance) and (2) interpersonal work factors/group working alliance, individual working alliance, and group climate.

Based upon their review of multiple group therapy meta-analysis studies, Burlingame et al. (2011) indicate "past reviewers have concluded that cohesion has shown an overwhelming positive relation with patient improvement—the overall conclusion from 40 studies published across a four-decade span is a positive relation between cohesion (alliance) and outcome." It is significant to note that 58 percent of the group therapy cohesion studies were published after 2000, and over one-fourth of the studies appeared before 1990.

These authors also conclude that cohesion (alliance) is related to outcome defined as symptom reduction, improvement in interpersonal functioning, involves groups treated in different clinical settings (inpatient, outpatient, etc.), various diagnostic classifications (including substance abuse and other addictions), and cohesion (alliance) is most strongly involved with patient improvement in groups using interpersonal, psychodynamic or cognitive-behavioral orientation, involving group leaders emphasizing member interaction irrespective of theoretical orientation, and post higher cohesion (alliance) links. These groups were less focused on process in cohesion (alliance) and explains outcome regardless of the length of the group, but is strongest when a group lasts more than 12 sessions and is composed of 5 to 9 members. Younger group members experience the largest changes when they are present within these groups. The authors further conclude that "cohesion (alliance) is integrally related to the success and outcomes of group therapy, and this research and clinical data base also identifies specific behaviors that enhance group cohesion and therapeutic outcomes" (Burlingame et al., 2011).

Other studies (Burlingame et al., 2002; Dinger and Schauenburg, 2010; Sternberg and Trijsburg, 2005; Tschuschke and Dies, 1994) report similar findings relative to the impact of cohesion or alliance in the practice of group therapy.

Alliance in individual psychotherapy has also remained one of the most intensely researched subjects in the psychotherapy research literature for several decades (Horvath and Symonds, 2001; Luborsky, Singer, and Luborsky, 1975; Meltzoff and Kornreich, 1970; Truax and Carkhuff, 1967; Smith and Glass, 1977; Stiles, Shapiro and Elliot, 1986). These studies have also reached the general conclusion that diverse therapies provided similar beneficial effects to psychotherapy clients.

As touched upon earlier in this chapter, Horvath et al. (2011) add additional support for the universality facet of the alliance construct in efficacious psychotherapy work when they note that "perhaps the most potent force responsible for the sustained growth of interest in the alliance was the consistent findings of a moderate but robust relationship between the alliance and treatment outcome across a broad spectrum of treatments in a variety of client/problem contexts" (Horvath and Symonds, 1991; Martin, Garske and Davis, 2000; Horvath and Bedi, 2002). These authors also indicate the "most distinguishing feature of the modern pan-theoretical reconceptualization of the alliance is its emphasis on collaboration and consensus—the 'new' alliance concept emphasizes the conscious aspects of the relationship (as opposed to the unconscious processes), and the achievement of collaborative, working together aspects of the relationship" (p. 10).

The fundamental alliance-universality dimensions and overall results of the Horvath et al. (2011) study related to therapeutic practices and clinical work involving individual psychotherapy patients include: (1) the positive relationship between quality of the alliance and diverse outcomes for many types of psychological therapies is confirmed in the meta-analysis study, (2) the overall ES or $=.275$ accounts for a relatively modest proportion of the total variance in treatment outcome, and (3) the overall magnitude of this correlation along with therapist effects, *is one of the strongest and most robust predictors of treatment success empirical research has been able to document* (Wampold, 2001).

As discussed earlier in the text, these authors (Horvath et al., 2011) also actively advocate that therapists implement seven clinical practice-based strategies related to the alliance-outcome evidence associated with the findings of recent studies. Briefly, these clinical practice guidelines and recommendations encompass clinical, alliance and relational dynamics that emphasize "(1) developing and fostering the alliance is not separate from the interventions therapists implement to help their clients, (2) development of a 'good enough' alliance early in therapy is *vital for therapy success,* (3) early in therapy, modulating the methods of therapy (tasks) to suit the specific client's needs, expectations and capacities is important in building the alliance, (4) therapist and client perceptions of the alliance, particularly early in treatment, do not necessarily match, (5) strength of the alliance, within and between sessions, often fluctuates in response to a variety of in-therapy factors, (6) therapist non-defensive responses to client negativity or hostility are critical for maintaining a good alliance, and (7) therapists contributions to the quality of the alliance are critical. Therapists who are good at building a strong alliance tend to have better alliances with most of their clients. The reverse is also true. This suggests that alliance development is a skill and/or capacity that therapists can and should be trained to develop, just as they are trained to attend to other aspects of their practice" (p. 15).

Once again, the reader needs to be reminded that the authors of these various alliance focused investigations, studies and clinical articles also include numerous caveats, research limitations, methodological limitations and other moderating factors associated with their reported research evidence and clinical findings. The limitations of correlational studies and data, meta-analysis studies, definition of terms, assessment instruments and tools, moderator analysis, type of treatments, therapists and patients, outcome measures, and even "halo effect" phenomena issues have repeatedly been addressed in this body of psychotherapy literature.

Nonetheless, Horvath et al. (2011) again conclude that "aggregate alliance-outcome correlations are statistically significant beyond P less than .001—*this result strongly supports the claim that the impact of alliance on therapy outcome is ubiquitous irrespective of how the alliance is measured, from whose perspective it is evaluated, when it is assessed, the way the outcome is evaluated, and the type of therapy involved—The quality of the alliance matters*" (p. 13). These conclusions are generally endorsed by the other alliance researchers and clinicians who have contributed to the overall content of this chapter as well as this clinical text.

Lingiardi et al. (2011) state that the "*therapeutic alliance is probably the most vital common factor in psychotherapy, and one of the most investigated constructs in psychotherapy research*" (p. 392). Escudero, Friedlander and Heatherington (2011) indicate that "of the many technique–and relationship—related factors that account for change in successful psychotherapy, *the working alliance is undoubtedly the most robust*—the felt sense of collaboration between therapist and client, including an *emotional bond* and negotiation of therapy tasks and goals, has consistently predicted favorable outcomes in study after study, and in multiple literature reviews and meta-analyses—with sufficient evidence that the working alliance matters across modalities" (p. 138).

Additional recent research and clinical evidence (MacFarlane, Anderson and McClintock, 2015) supporting the universality of the alliance construct point out that "although the working alliance is among the best predictors of outcome, much debate remains about how to properly define this complex construct—clients and psychotherapists appear to understand the quality and strength of the alliance differently, as evidenced by a weak correlation between client and therapist rating of the alliance. These authors (MacFarlane, Anderson and McClintock, 2015) further report that (1) collaborative factors may be less integral to alliance development, (2) clients seem to attribute responsibility to the psychotherapist and rarely acknowledge their own contributions to the alliance, (3) clients value the psychotherapist's supportive behaviors and perceive that this support plays a role in alliance development, (4) clients often make reference to their psychotherapist's use of encouraging statements, friendliness, respect, validation, and even personalized greetings and farewells, and that (5) three particular psychotherapist behaviors (making encouraging statements, making positive comments about the client, and greeting the client with a smile) accounted for 62 percent of the variance in client ratings of the working alliance. These seemingly simple, yet supportive behaviors were, according to clients, critical to a strong working alliance. Clients also report, when interviewed, that treatment techniques are intimately linked with the alliance and contribute to its development" (p. 363).

MacFarlane, Anderson, and McClintock (2015) conclude that the results of their study suggest that "clients may be unaware of the role they play in alliance development, although this does not necessarily negate their contributions to its development, clients' efforts to communicate their troubles early in therapy, along with their psychotherapist's assistance in this task, may often be the foundation for alliance development—early interactions are critical for the process of psychotherapy—according to the clients in this study, it is through the work of therapy that the alliance is developed, and clients engage in this work, even when it is difficult" (p. 370). The present study provides evidence that communication, supportive behaviors, and technical activities facilitate alliance development.

A recent study investigating the role of the alliance in treating alcohol problems (Cook et al., 2015) indicates that "a factor common to all treatments is the collaborative relationship between therapist and client, known as the therapeutic or working alliance." These authors also note that less is known about the role of the working alliance in treatment for alcohol problems, in terms of what factors are important for the development of a strong working alliance, and the outcome impact of the working alliance. The authors of the study also point out that analyses of Project MATCH data found that "whether working alliance predicted drinking outcomes after 12 months depended upon study setting; both therapist and client working alliance predicted drinking outcomes among outpatients but in the aftercare patients the only statistically significant relationship found was between therapist-rated working alliance and percentage of days abstinent at follow-up. Therapist but not client ratings of the working alliance predicted drinking outcomes" (p. 371). A subsequent Project MATCH study (Cook et al., 2015) also found that client-rated alliance "did predict less drinking after six months but not 12 months, and did not interact with motivation. However, therapist-rated alliance predicted lower alcohol use at both intervals, and interacted with motivation such that alliance was more important for those with low motivation" (p. 372).

Cook et al. (2015) further note that "it is surprising in light of the strength and consistency of findings available for other psychological problems that this has been limited to previous study of the role of the working alliance in the successful treatment of alcohol problems and its possible importance is unclear" (p. 372). However, the results of their recent study "support ratings of working alliance as important in explaining differences in outcome following treatment for alcohol problems, and perhaps for differences in the mechanisms of effects of different treatments." The authors also report this is the "first study to include effects of the working alliance on post treatment motivation to change, in addition to longer-term treatment outcomes. For all outcomes, clients' perceptions of the working alliance were more important than those of therapists" (p. 380).

Another recent investigation of therapeutic alliance as a predictor of DBT vs. non-behavioral psychotherapy for Borderline Personality Disorder (BPD) reports that in the treatment of BPD, the "therapeutic alliance has been identified as one of the few replicated core change processes associated with positive outcomes" (Bedics et al., 2015). Therapist ratings of the alliance were predictive of reduced suicide attempts in both treatments. Client and therapist rating of the alliance were not significantly associated with changes in depression across both treatments, but the study supports theoretically predicted relationships between facets of the therapeutic alliance in DBT and suicidal behavior (p. 67).

Additionally, recent studies (Brown et al., 2015; Miller et al., 2015) addressing contemporary tools for increasing the value of psychotherapy and realizing the potential for feedback-informed treatment, indicate that "studies in psychotherapy have clearly demonstrated that significantly larger amount of variance in treatment outcomes is due to the therapist than to the method of treatment, therapists are not the best judge of their own outcomes, what therapists claim they are doing in treatment (theoretical orientation) provides no substantial evidence, outcomes for clinics serving as training sites for graduate students found significant differences between therapists, but no evidence that the experienced and licensed clinical staff has better outcomes than the graduate trainees, and the belief that graduate training and traditional supervision alone will produce effective therapists is not supported by the evidence, the evidence supports the conclusion that whatever factors do contribute to the therapist's effectiveness are not being enhanced by traditional training, and finally, clients whose therapists had access to the progress and alliance information were less likely to deteriorate, more likely to stay longer, and twice as likely to achieve a clinically significant change" (p. 419).

Miller et al. (2015) and Wampold and Imel (2015) concordantly indicate that "the evidence has consistently shown that the therapist effects dwarf the contribution made by the perennially popular treatment models and techniques, accounting for five to nine times more variance in outcome. Furthermore, studies show that higher levels of commitment led to faster rates of client progress (DeJong et al., 2012), openness to feedback has been shown to affect outcome in several studies, and effective therapists were found to be more self-critical and report making more mistakes (Najavits and Strupp, 1994), higher levels of 'professional self-doubt' positively impacted client ratings of the working alliance (Nissen-Lie, Monsen, and Ronnestad, 2010), and highly effective psychotherapists reported being 'surprised by client feedback' more times in a typical work week than their less effective counterparts" (pp. 451–452).

Miller et al. (2015) report that "to date, perhaps the most persuasive evidence bearing on therapist effects in ROM (routine outcome monitoring in clinical practice) comes from research demonstrating clinicians do not get better at what they do as a result of monitoring and measuring—over a five-year period, despite the routine and systematic use of outcome measures, clinicians not only did not become more effective, they got worse—erosion in performance could not be explained by clients' initial severity, length of treatment, rates of early termination, size of caseload, or various other factors (therapist's age, years of experience)" (p. 452). (See Goldberg et al. [2016)], *Journal of Clinical and Consulting Psychology,* confirming Lambert report tracking the performance of 170 therapists and more than 6,500 clients over a five-year period.)

Finally, a study by Baldwin, Wampold and Imel (2007) indicated that "97% of the difference in outcome between therapists was attributable to clinician variability in the working alliance. Anderson et al. (2009) subsequently provided evidence this variability could be explained by differences among therapists in the depth of their domain-specific knowledge—the more effective the clinician, the more they interacted empathetically and collaboratively with a more diverse group of clients—Their comments were much less likely to create distance or cause offense."

Stronger therapeutic alliance and higher therapist competence in the delivery of 12-step facilitated care (TSF) intervention were recently demonstrated to be associated with better treatment retention whereas treatment adherence was not, and the therapeutic alliance was also significantly associated with better retention (Campbell et al., 2015). Furthermore, "the alliance predicts emotional experience, and alliance strength indirectly predicts client level of functioning—emotional experience and the therapeutic alliance are important determinants of the therapeutic process, which contribute to predict client improvement in functioning within psychodynamic treatment" (Fisher et al., 2016, p. 105).

Perhaps these general findings further confirm of at least bring us back to the core reality of the alliance universality construct; all forms of psychotherapy are human relational enterprises, and the alliance or human "bond" component of the therapeutic relationship encompasses the additional clinical reality that all therapists (and all patients) are not created equal, and as such, any tool, no matter what its evidence base, will only be as good as the therapist who uses it (Kiesler, 1988; Forrest, 2016).

SUMMARY AND CONCLUDING REMARKS

Universality most generally refers to the quality or state of being universal in nature, or universal comprehensiveness in range. In essence, universality as a global construct encompasses the notion that universal facts can be discovered, and is therefore understood as being in opposition to relativism. This construct also suggests a presence in all places and all times.

Psychotherapists, counselors, and the vast majority of addictions therapists and behavioral health care providers have long recognized the universality of substance abuse and addictions via all individuals and human beings, ethnic groups, and world-wide cultures and diverse populations (Forrest, 1975–2014, 2016; Kelly, 2016). Kelly (2016) has recently addressed the universality of substance abuse in a comprehensive text along with specific ethnic and cultural differences.

The content of this chapter as well as the empirical and clinical evidence provided throughout the book provides compelling support of the alliance universality construct as a significant facet most, if not all forms, of constructive and successful psychotherapy relationships as well as successful therapeutic outcomes. Psychotherapy research and practice literature of the past 60 years certainly supports the notion that the therapeutic alliance has a "presence in (almost) all places, and all times" within the context of this extensive empirical data and knowledge base.

Alliance universality was defined earlier in this chapter as a core therapist-patient ingredient, quality or relational characteristic of most, if not all, effective psychotherapy relationship and successful therapeutic outcomes. While this particular facet of the therapeutic alliance relationship universally transcends therapeutic models and approaches, diverse patient populations, treatment settings and other psychotherapy process outcome related variables and factors, the author has also repeatedly noted throughout this text with a rather wide range of patient-therapist and situation life-related issues and events or circumstances can also impact, effect and sometimes either terminate or radically change the therapeutic relationship at any juncture in the therapy process. Thus, the caveat of alliance universality within the context of "most, if not all" effective therapeutic relationship and outcomes. All events and things in life may also be characterized in the context of including various types or degrees of relativity, and "exceptions" to most, if not all, events or realities also appear to involve some degree of relativity.

Addictions psychotherapists, researchers and clinicians, are especially encouraged to pursue further investigations, clinical evaluations and examination parameters of their work. This text represents the first alliance addictions psychotherapy, counseling and treatment focused work that the author is aware of, and thus, it also needs to be viewed as an initial or early contribution to the realm of the addiction psychotherapy and treatment profession. The greater part of the alliance psychotherapy, counseling and treatment data and empirical alliance related literature that has been presented in this work does not include addictions specific investigations, and has also been noted, the evidence related to substance abuse, addictive disorder, and alliance process-outcome evidence has been historically both limited and suggestive mixed salience in some complex domains.

Clearly, further research and clinical work needs to become in the arena of alliance and realities of alliance universality in the psychotherapy and treatment of the addictive disorders spectrum. This work will hopefully stimulate further heuristic efforts within the alliance relationship realm of professional addictions education, training, supervision, clinical practice and noted earlier in the text, the author has long espoused that addictions therapists and counselors frequently find themselves dealing with various thorny alliance related transference and context transference dynamics and issues that can contribute to alliance countertransference dynamics and issues that can contribute to alliance ruptures, conflicts and adverse therapeutic outcomes that may differ significantly from alliance related work and outcomes with other psychotherapy populations (Forrest, 1974–2016). Current empirical psychotherapy evidence (Friedlander et al., 2011, 2014, 2015) certainly suggests that therapeutic alliance dynamics involving substance abusing and addictive disordered patients can be more complex and multifaceted in nature than with other populations. Treatment modalities, therapist characteristics and other factors may also impact these variables differently. In this respect, the personal equation related to therapists' experience and skills may also significantly impact alliance dynamics and psychotherapy outcomes. Again, further addictions specific psychotherapy research and clinical investigation related to a diversity of alliance factors is indicated.

Addictions therapists and treatment providers also need to remain cognizant of the following contemporary science-based realities and difficulties that continually play important roles within context of their psychotherapy and treatment relationships with addictive disordered persons. These empirical evidence-based realities potentially impact the therapeutic alliance and every facet of the treatment process and outcomes of therapy in a multiplicity of often unpredictable ways.

As Volkow (2015) suggests, addictions treatment providers are confronted with a wide range of clinical realities associated with facilitating and encouraging the process of continued recovery associated with contemporary scientific evidence which indicates that (1) "addiction is a brain disease, (2) addiction is complex and involves a wide range of brain circuits, neurotransmitters, brain changes, and regions and structures, (3) addicts require medical management (often including various therapies, medications, and interactive biopsychosocial treatments), (4) relapse is a basic characteristic of the addictive disease process, and (5) the ability to follow through on the choice to not use drugs (or actively engage in other patterns of addictive disordered behavior) has been compromised by their disease—the cycle of relapse and the shame and self-disappointment this disease produces can rob a person of hope and even, in extreme cases, the will to continue living."

Thus, clinicians need to remember that the alliance always remains vulnerable to regression, requires reparative work, and can be subject to rupture as a result of a variety of biologic, genetic and other factors related to the brain disease process. These realities are also potentially reinforced by the impact of computer use on the therapeutic alliance and continuance in care during the early mental health or addictions psychotherapy and treatment process (Rosen, Nakash, and Alegria, 2016).

REFERENCES AND BIBLIOGRAPHY

Ackerman, S.J., and Hilsenroth, M.J. (2001). A review of therapist characteristics and techniques negatively impacting the therapeutic alliance. *Psychotherapy, 38,* 171–185.

Ackerman, S.J., and Hilsenroth, M.J. (2003). A review of therapist characteristics and techniques positively impacting on the therapeutic alliance. *Clinical Psychology Review, 23*(1), 33.

Alcoholics Anonymous. (1939). *The big book.* New York, NY: Alcoholics Anonymous World Service Inc.

Alexander, F.M. (1956). *Psychoanalysis and psychotherapy.* New York: W.W. Norton.

Alexander, J.F., Barton, C., Schiavo, R., and Parsons, B. (1976). Behavioral intervention with families of delinquents: Therapist characteristics and outcome. *Journal of Consulting and Clinical Psychology, 44,* 656–664.

American Psychiatric Association. (2000). *Diagnostic and statistical manual of mental disorders* (4th ed., Text Revision). Washington, DC: Author.

American Psychiatric Association. (2013). *Diagnostic and statistical manual of mental disorders* (5th ed.). Arlington, VA: Author.

Anda, R.F., Felitti, V.J., Bremner, J.D., Walker, J.D., Whitfield, C., Perry, B.D., and Giles, W.H. (2006). The enduring effects of abuse and related adverse experiences in childhood: A convergence of evidence from neurobiology and epidemiology. *European Archives of Psychiatry and Neuroscience, 256,* 174–186.

Anderson, S.M., and Przybylinski, E. (2012). Experiments on transference in interpersonal relations: Implications for treatment. *Psychotherapy, 49,* 370–383.

Anderson, T., Ogles, B.M., Patterson, C.L., Lambert, M.J., and Vermeersch, D.A. (2009). Therapist effects: Facilitative interpersonal skills as a predictor of therapist success. *Journal of Clinical Psychology, 65,* 755, 768.

Arachtingi, B., and Lichtenberg, J.W. (1998). The relationship between clients' perceptions of therapist-patient similarity with respect to empathy, regard, and unconditionality and therapists' rating of client transference. *Journal of Counseling Psychology, 45,* 143–149.

Auerbach, S., May, J., Stevens, M., and Kiesler, D. (2008). The interactive role of working alliance and counselor-client interpersonal behaviors in adolescent substance abuse treatment. *International Journal of Clinical and Health Psychology, 8*(3), 617–629.

Axline, V. (1947). *Play therapy.* Boston: Houghton Mifflin.

329

Baldwin, S.A., Wampold, B.E., and Imel, Z.E. (2007). Untangling the alliance-outcome correlation: Exploring the relative importance of therapist and patient variability in the alliance. *Journal of Consulting and Clinical Psychology, 75,* 842–852.

Barber, J.P., Connolly, M.B., Crits-Christoph, P., Gladis, L., and Siqueland, L. (2000). Alliance predicts patients' outcome beyond in-treatment change in symptoms. *Journal of Consulting and Clinical Psychology, 68,* 1027–1032

Barber, J.P., Gallop, R., Crits-Christoph, P., Frank, A., Thase, M.E., Weiss, R.D, and Connolly, M.B. (2006). The role of therapist adherence, therapist competence, and alliance in predicting outcome of individual drug counseling. Results from the NIDA collaborative cocaine treatment study. *Psychotherapy Research, 16,* 229–240.

Barber, J.P., Luborsky, L., Crits-Christoph, P., Thase, M.E., Weiss, R., Frank, A., and Gallop, R. (1999). Therapeutic alliance as a predictor of outcome in treatment of cocaine dependence. *Psychotherapy Research, 9,* 54–73.

Barber, J.P., Luborsky, L., Gallop, R., Crits-Christoph, P., Frank A., Weiss, R.D., and Siqueland, L. (2001) Therapeutic alliance as a predictor of outcome and retention in the NICA Collaborative Cocaine Treatment study. *Journal of Consulting and Clinical Psychology, 69,* 119–124).

Barrett-Lennard, G. (1962). Dimensions of therapist response as casual factors in therapeutic change. *Psychological Monographs, 76*(43), 1–36 (Whole Number 562).

Barrett-Lennard, G.T. (1964). The Relationship Inventory. Form OS-M-64 and OS-F-64 and MO-F-64, University of New England, Australia.

Barrett-Lennard, G.T. (1978). The Relationship Inventory: Later development and applications. JSAS: Catalog of Selected Documents in Psychology, 8, 68 (MS. NO. 1732, p. 55).

Barrett-Lennard, G.T. (1981). The empathy cycle: Refining of a nuclear concept. *Journal of Counseling Psychology, 28,* 91–100.

Beach, K., and Power, M. (1996). Transference: An empirical investigation across a range of cognitive-behavioral and psychoanalytic therapies. *Clinical Psychology and Psychotherapy, 3,* 1–4.

Berger, T. Boettcher, J., and Caspar, F. (2014). Internet-based guided self-help for severe anxiety disorders: A randomized controlled trail comparing a tailored with a standardized disorder-specific approach. *Psychotherapy, 51*(2), 207–219.

Berggraf, L., Ulvenes, P.G., Oktedalen, T. Hoffart, A., Stiles, T., McCullough, L., and Wampold, B. J. (2014) Experience of affects predicting sense of self and others in short-term dynamic and cognitive therapy. *Psychotherapy (Chic.), 51*(2), 246–257.

Bergin, A.E., and Garfield, S.L. (Eds.). *Handbook of psychotherapy and behavior change: An empirical analysis.* New York: Wiley.

Beutler, L.E., Crago, M., and Arizmendi, T.G. (1986). Research on therapist variables in psychotherapy. In S.L. Garfield and A.E. Bergin (Eds.), *Handbook of psychotherapy and behavior change* (3rd ed., pp. 257–310). New York: Wiley.

Bhatia, A., and Gelso, C.J. (2017). The termination phase: Therapists' perspective on the therapeutic relationship and outcome. *Psychotherapy, 54*(1), 76–87.

Bien, T.H., Miller, W.R., and Tonigan, J.S. (1993). Brief interventions for alcohol problems. A review. *Addiction, 88,* 315–336.

Binder, J.L., and Strupp, H.H. (1997). "Negative process": A recurrently discovered and underestimated facet of therapeutic process and outcome in the individual psychotherapy of adults. *Clinical Psychology: Science and Practice, 4,* 121, 139.

Blalock, J.A., Nayak, N., Wetter, D.W., Schreindorfer, L., Minnix, J.A., Canul, J., and Cinciripini, P.M. (2011). The relationship of childhood trauma to nicotine dependence in pregnant smokers. *Psychology of Addictive Behaviors, 25*(4), 652–663.

Blum, H. (1987). Countertransference: Concepts and controversies. In E. Slatker (Ed.), *Countertransference* (pp. 87–104). Northvale, NJ: Jason Aronson, Inc.

Bordin, E.S. (1955). *Psychological counseling.* New York: Appleton-Century-Crofts.

Bordin, E.S. (1975, September). *The working alliance: Basis for a general theory of psychotherapy.* Paper presented at the society for Psychotherapy Research, Washington, DC.

Bordin, E.S. (1989, June). *Building therapeutic alliances: The base for integration.* Paper presented at the society for psychotherapy research, Berkley, CA.

Bordin, E.S. (1994). Theory and research on the therapeutic working alliance: New directions. In A.O. Horvath and L.S. Greenberg (Eds.), *The working alliance: Theory, research, and practice* (pp. 13–37). New York: Wiley.

Bourgeois, L., Sabourin, S. and Wright, J. (1990). Predictive validity of therapeutic alliance in group marital therapy. *Journal of Consulting and Clinical Psychology, 58,* 608–613.

Bowlby, J. (1969). *Attachment and loss, Vol. 1: Attachment.* New York, NY: Basic Books.

Bradley, R., Heim, A., and Western, D. (2005). Transference patterns in the psychotherapy of personality disorders: Empirical investigation. *British Journal of Psychiatry, 186,* 342–349.

Brammer, L.M., and Shostrum, E.L. (1953). *Therapeutic psychology: Fundamentals of counseling and psychotherapy.* Englewood Cliffs, NJ: Prentice-Hall.

Bratter, T.E., and Forrest, G.G. (Eds.). (1985). Alcoholism and substance abuse: Strategies for clinical intervention. In G.G. Forrest (Ed.), *Psychodynamically oriented treatment of alcoholism and substance abuse.* New York, NY: The Free Press.

Brenner, C. (1997). *Psychoanalytic technique and psychic conflict.* New York: International Universities Press.

Breuer, J., and Freud, S. (1895). Studies on hysteria. In J. Strachey (Ed.), *The standard edition of the complete psychological works of Sigmund Freud* (Vol. 2). London, England: Hogarth Press.

Bridges, N.A. (2001). Therapist's self-disclosure: Expanding the comfort zone. *Psychotherapy: Theory, Research, Practice and Training, 38*(1), 21–30.

Brorson, H.H., Arnevik, E.A., Rand-Hendricksen, K., and Duckert, F. (2013). Dropout from addiction treatment: A systematic review of risk factors. *Clinical Psychology Review, 33,* 1010–1024.

Brown, L.S. (1994). *Subversive dialogues.* New York: Basic Books.

Burlingame, G., Fuhriman, A., and Johnson, J. (2002). Cohesion in group psychotherapy. In J.C. Norcross (Ed.), *Psychotherapy relationships that work* (pp. 71–87). Oxford University Press.

Burlingame, G.M., Mackenzie,K.R., and Strauss, B. (2004). Evidence-based small group treatments. In M. Lambert, A.E. Bergin, and S.L. Garfield (Eds.), *Handbook of psychotherapy and behavior change* (5th ed.). New York: Wiley.

Burlingame, G.M., McClendon, D.T., and Alonso, J. (2011A). Cohesion in group therapy. *Psychotherapy, 48*(1), 34–42.

Burlingame, G.M., McClendon, D.T., and Alonso, J. (2011B). Group therapy. In J.C. Norcross (Ed.), *Psychotherapy relationships that work* (2nd ed.). New York: Oxford University Press.

Burns, D.D., and Nolen-Hoeksma, S. (1992). Therapeutic empathy and recovery from depression in cognitive-behavioral therapy: A structural equation model. *Journal of Consulting and Clinical Psychology, 60,* 441–449.

Cameron, N. (1963). *Personality development and psychotherapy: A dynamic approach.* Boston: Houghton Mifflin Co.

Campbell, B.K., Guydish, J., Thao, L., Wells, E.A., and McCarty, D. (2015). The relationship of therapeutic alliance and treatment delivery fidelity with treatment retention in a multisite trial of twelve step facilitation. *Psychology of Addictive Behaviors, 29*(1), 106–113.

Cappas, N.M., Andres-Hyman, R., and Davidson, C. (2005). What psychotherapists can begin to learn from neuroscience: Seven principles of brain-based psychotherapy. *Psychotherapy, 42,* 374–383.

Carkhuff, R.R. (1969). *Helping and human relations: A primer for lay and professional helpers* (2 vols.). New York: Holt, Rinehart, and Winston.

Carruth, B. (2002). Foreword. In G.G. Forrest, *Countertransference in chemical dependency counseling.* Binghamton, New York. The Haworth Press, Inc.

Cohen, J. (1988). *Statistical power analysis for the behavioral sciences* (2nd ed.). Hillsdale, NJ. Erlbaum.

Cohn, A., Hagman, B.T., Moore, K., Mitchell, J., and Ehlke, S. (2014). Does negative affect mediate the relationship between daily PTSD symptoms and daily alcohol involvement in female rape victims? Evidence from 14 Days of Interactive Voice Response Assessment. *Psychology of Addictive Behaviors, 28*(1), 114–126.

Constantino, M.J., Coyne, A.E., Luukko, E.K., Newkiek, K., Bernecker, S.L., Ravits, P., and McBride, C. (2017). Therapeutic alliance, subsequent change, and moderators of the alliance-outcome association in interpersonal psychotherapy for depression. *Psychotherapy, 54*(2), 125–135.

Crits-Christoph, P., Connolly Gibbons, M. B., Crits-Christoph, K., Narducci, J., Schamberger, M., & Gallop, R. (2006). Can therapists be trained to improve their alliances? A preliminary study of alliance-fostering psychotherapy. *Psychotherapy Research, 16*(3), 268–281.

Crits-Christoph, P., Johnson, J. E., Connolly Gibbons, M. B., & Gallop, R. (2013). Process predictors of the outcome of group drug counseling. *Journal of Consulting and Clinical Psychology, 81*(1), 23–34.

Culbreth, J.R., and Borders, L.D. (1999). Perceptions of the supervisory relationship: Recovering and nonrecovering substance abuse counselors. *Journal of Counseling and Development, 77*(3), 330–338.

Darchuk, A.J. (2007). The role of the therapeutic alliance and its relationship to treatment outcome and client motivation in an adolescent substance abuse treatment setting. (ProQuest Information and Learning). *Dissertation Abstracts International: Section B: The Sciences and Engineering, 68*(5-B), 3392.

DeJong, K., van Sluis, P., Nugter, M.A., Heiser, W.J., and Spinhoven, P. (2012). Understanding the differential impact of outcome monitoring: Therapist variables that moderate feedback effects in a randomized clinical trial. *Psychotherapy Research, 22,* 464–474.

DiClemente, C.C. (1993). Changing addictive behaviors: A process perspective. *Current Directions in Psychological Science, 2,* 101–106.

DiClemente, C.C. (2006). Natural change and the troublesome use of substances: A life-course perspective. In W.R. Miller and K.M. Carroll (Eds.), *Rethinking substance abuse: What the science shows and what we should do about it.* New York, NY: Guilford.

Dillon, D. (2014). Evolving Self-Help Care and Change Models. Presented at Psychotherapy Associates, PC 40th "Addictive Disorders, Behavioral Health and Mental Health" Annual Winter Symposium, January 28th, 2014, Colorado Springs, CO.

Dillon, D. (2016). The Connected Leader. Presented at Psychotherapy Associates, PC 42nd "Addictive Disorders, Behavioral Health and Mental Health" Annual Winter Symposium, February 2nd, 2016, Colorado Springs, CO.

Dinger, U., and Schauenburg, H. (2010). Effects in individual cohesiveness and patient interpersonal style on outcome in psychodynamically oriented inpatient group psychotherapy. *Psychotherapy Research, 20,* 22–29.

Divino, C.L., and Moore, M.S. (2010). Integrating neurobiological findings into psychodynamic psychotherapy training and practice. *Psychoanalytic dialogues, 20,* 337–355.

Dozier, M., Sovall-McClough, K.C., and Albus, K.E. (2008). Attachment and psychopathology in adulthood. In J. Cassidy and P. Shaver (Eds.), *Handbook of attachment: Theory research, and clinical applications* (2nd ed., pp. 718–743). New York, NY: Guilford Press.

Duan, C., and Hill, C.E. (1996). A critical review of empathy research. *Journal of Counseling Psychology, 43,* 261–274.

Duncan, B.L., Miller, S.D., Wampold, B.E. and Hubble, M.A. (Eds.). (2010). *The heart and soul of change in psychotherapy: Delivering what works in therapy* (2nd ed.). Washington, DC: American Psychological Association.

Dundon, W.D., Pettinati, H.M., Lynch, K.G., Xie, H., Varillo, K.M., Makadon, C., and Oslin, D.W. (2008). The therapeutic alliance in medical-based interventions impacts outcome in treating alcohol dependence. *Drug and Alcohol Dependence, 95,* 230–236.

Elliott, R., Bohart, A.C., Watson, J.C. , and Greenberg, L.S. (2011). Empathy. In J. Norcross (Ed.), *Psychotherapy relationships that work* (2nd ed.). New York: Oxford University Press.

Ellis, A. (1979). *Rational-emotive therapy training.* Lecture presented at Psychotherapy Associates, PC Fifth Annual Advanced Winter Workshop, Treatment and Rehabilitation of the Alcoholic, Feb.1, Colorado Springs, Colorado.

Ellis, A., and Harper, R. (1961). *A guide to rational living.* Englewood Cliffs, NJ: Prentice-Hall.

Emrick, C.D. (1975). A review of psychologically oriented treatment of alcoholism. Part I: The use and interrelationship of outcome criteria and drinking behaviors following treatment. *Quarterly Journal of Studies on Alcoholism, 35,* 523–549.

Emrick, C.D. (1975). A review of psychologically oriented treatment of alcoholism. Part II: The relative effectiveness of different treatment approaches and the effectiveness of treatment vs. no treatment. *Quarterly Journal of Studies on Alcoholism, 36,* 88–108.

Escudero, V., Friedlander, M.L., and Heatherington, L. (2011). Using the E-SOFTA for video training and research on alliance-related behavior. *Psychotherapy, 48*(2), 138–147.

Eubanks-Carter, C., Muran, J.C., and Safran, J.D. (2015). Alliance-focused training. *Psychotherapy, 52*(2), 169–173.

Eysenck, H. J. (1967). The effects of psychotherapy. *Int. J. Psychiat, 1,* 97–178.

Farber, B.A. (2006). *Self-disclosure in psychotherapy.* New York, Guilford Press.

Farber, B.A. (2007). On the enduring and substantial influence of Carl Rogers not-quite essential nor necessary conditions. *Psychotherapy, Theory, Research, Practice, Training, 44,* 289–294.

Farber, B.A., and Doolin, E.M. (2011). Positive regard. *Psychotherapy, 48*(1), 58–64.

Farber, B.A., and Sohn, A.E. (2007). Patterns of self-disclosure in psychotherapy and marriage. *Psychotherapy: Theory, Research, Practice, and Training, 44*(2), 226–231.

Farber, B.A., Brink, D.C., and Raskin, P.M. (1996). *The psychotherapy of Carl Rogers: Cases and commentary.* New York: Guilford Press.

Faw, I., Hogue, A., Johnson, S., Diamond, G.M., and Liddle, H.A. (2005). The Adolescent Therapeutic Alliance Scale: Development, initial psychometrics, and prediction of outcomes in family-based substance abuse prevention counseling. *Psychotherapy Research, 15,* 141–154.

Fenichel, D. (1945). *The psychoanalytic theory of neurosis.* New York: W.W. Norton

Fiedler, F.E. (1950). The concept of an ideal therapeutic relationship. *J. Consult. Psychol., 14,* 339–345.

Fisher, H., Atzil-Slonim, D., Bar-Kalifa, E., Rafaeli, E., and Peri, T. (2016). Emotional experience and alliance contribute to therapeutic change in psychodynamic therapy. *Psychotherapy, 53*(1), 105–116.

Fleming, J.L. (2017). The yin and yang of brain networks: Relevance to addiction. depression, schizophrenia, autism and ADHD. Presented at Psychotherapy Associates, PC. 43rd "Addictive Disorders, Behavioral Health and Mental Health" Annual Winter Symposium, January 29th, 2017, Colorado Springs, CO.

Flicker, S.M., Turner, C.W., Waldron, H.B., Ozechowski, T.J., and Brody, J.L. (2008). Ethnic background, therapeutic alliance, and treatment retention in functional family therapy with adolescents who abuse substances. *Journal of Family Psychology, 22,* 167–170.

Forrest, G.G. (1970). *Transparency as a prognostic variable in psychotherapy.* Unpublished doctoral dissertation. University of North Dakota, Grand Forks, ND.

Forrest, G. G. (1975). *Diagnosis and treatment of alcoholism* (p. 12). Springfield, IL: Charles C Thomas, Publisher, Ltd.

Forrest, G.G. (1975, 1978, 2nd parts). *The diagnosis and treatment of alcoholism.* Springfield, IL: Charles C Thomas, Publisher. (Paperback editions, 1994, 1997, Northvale, NJ: Jason Aronson, Inc.: The Master Work Series.)

Forrest, G.G. (1978). *Alcoholism and family psychodynamics.* Presented at Psychotherapy Associates, PC. 4th annual "Treatment and Rehabilitation of the Alcoholic" Winter Workshop, January 30, Feb. 1, Colorado Springs, Co.

Forrest, G.G. (1978). *Motivating alcoholic patients for treatment.* Presented at the 4th Annual Colorado Summer School on Alcoholism, June 11, 1978, Glenwood Springs, Co.

Forrest, G.G. (1979). Negative and positive addictions. *Family and Community Health, 2*(1), 103–112.

Forrest, G.G. (1979). Setting alcoholics up for therapeutic failure. *Family and Community Health, 2*(2), 59–64.

Forrest, G.G. (1980). *How to live with a problem drinker and survive.* New York, NY: Atheneum. (Subsequent paperback printings, Charles Scribner and sons, Simon and Schuster, Learning Publications, 1984–2001.)

Forrest, G.G. (1982). *Confrontation in psychotherapy with alcoholics.* Holmes Beach: Learning Publications. (2nd edition paperback printing through 2002.)

Forrest, G.G. (1983). *Alcoholism and human sexuality.* Springfield, IL: Charles C Thomas, Publisher. (Paperback editions, 1994, Northvale, NJ: Jason Aronson, Inc: The Master Work Series.)

Forrest, G.G. (1983). *Alcoholism, narcissism and psychopathology.* Springfield, IL.: Charles C Thomas, Publisher. (Paperback editions, 1994, 1997, Northvale, NJ: Jason Aronson, Inc: The Master Work Series. 2nd pages back editions, 2002–2017, Lanham, MD: Roman and Littlefield Publishers, Inc.)

Forrest, G.G. (1983, 1999). *Alcoholism, narcissism and psychopathology.* New York: Jason Aronson, Inc.

Forrest, G.G. (1984). *Alcoholism, narcissism and psychopathology.* Presented at psychotherapy Associates, PC. 10th annual "Treatment and Rehabilitation of the Alcoholic" Advanced Winter Workshop, February 1, 1981, Colorado Springs, Co.

Forrest, G.G. (1984). *How to cope with a teenage drinker.* New York, NY: Atheneum. (Subsequent paperback printings, Bahlantine and Denmark, 9186–1988.)

Forrest, G.G. (1984). *Intensive psychotherapy of alcoholism.* Springfield, IL: Charles C Thomas, Publisher. (1st paperback editions, 1994, 1997, Northvale, NJ: Jason Aronson, Inc: The Master Work Series. 2nd paperback editions 2002–2017, Lanham, MD: Roman and Littlefield Publishers, Inc.)

Forrest, G.G. (1984). Outcome Assessment revisited: Psychotherapy of alcoholics and substance abusers. *Family and Community Health, 2*(1), 40–50.

Forrest, G.G. (1984). Psychotherapy of alcoholics and substance abusers: Outcome assessment revisited. *Family and Community Health, 2*(1), 40–50.

Forrest, G.G. (1985). Behavioral contracting in psychotherapy with alcoholics. In T.E. Bratter and G.G. Forrest (Eds.), *Alcoholism and substance abuse: Strategies for clinical intervention.* New York, NY: Free Press.

Forrest, G.G. (1985). Antabuse treatment. In T.E. Bratter and G.G. Forrest (Eds.), *Alcoholism and substance abuse: Strategies for clinical intervention.* New York, NY: Free Press.

Forrest, G.G. (1985). Psychodynamically oriented treatment of alcoholism and substance abuse. In T.E. Bratter and G.G. Forrest (Eds.), *Alcoholism and substance abuse: Strategies for clinical intervention.* New York, NY: Free Press.

Forrest, G.G. (1989). *Common sexual problems in chemically dependent clients.* Presented at the 31st International Summer School of Alcohol Studies, University of North Dakota, July 19th, 1989, Grand Forks, ND.

Forrest, G.G. (1989). *Guidelines for responsible drinking.* Springfield, IL: Charles C Thomas, Publisher. (2nd paperback edition, 1994, Northvale, NJ: Jason Aronson, Inc.: The Master Work Series.)

Forrest, G.G. (1989). *Therapist-patient relationship dynamics in the psychotherapy of substance abusers and addicted psychopaths.* Presented at Psychotherapy Associates, P.C. 15th annual advanced international Winter Symposium on the treatment of Addictive Disorders, February 8, 1989, Colorado Springs, Co.

Forrest, G.G. (1991). Role slippage and adaptation in the alcoholic family system. *Family Dynamics of Addiction Quarterly, 1*(3), 315–339.

Forrest, G.G. (1992). *Managing the dual-diagnosis patient: Chemical dependency and persistent and chronic severe mental illness.* Presented at Prairie View, Inc. Psychiatric Hospital, March 26, 1992, Newton, KS.

Forrest, G.G. (1995). *Chemical dependency and antisocial personality disorder: Psychotherapy and assessment strategies.* Binghamton, NY: The Haworth Press. (2nd paperback editions, 2006–2017, London, England: Taylor and Francis Group.)

Forrest, G.G. (1997). *Intensive psychotherapy of alcoholism.* Northvale, NJ: Jason Aronson, Inc.

Forrest, G.G. (1999). *Countertransference in chemical dependency counseling.* Presented at Psychotherapy Associates, PC. 25th annual advanced international "Treatment of Addictive Disorders" Winter Symposium, January, 26, 1999, Colorado Springs, Co.

Forrest, G.G. (2002). *Countertransference in chemical dependency counseling.* Binghamton, NY: The Haworth Press, Inc. (2nd Paperwork editions, 2009–2017, London, England: Taylor and Francis Group.)

Forrest, G.G. (2008). *Training, supervising and mentoring chemical dependency counselors.* Presented at Psychotherapy Associates 34th annual advanced international "Addictive Disorders and Behavioral Health" Winter Symposium, February 1, 2008, Colorado Springs, CO.

Forrest, G.G. (2011). *The therapeutic alliance, transference, countertransference, self-disclosure and relational dynamics in addictions psychotherapy.* Presented at Psychotherapy Associates, PC. 37th annual advanced international "Addictive Disorders, Behavioral Health and Mental Health" Winter Symposium, February 4, 2011, Colorado Springs, CO.

Forrest, G.G. (2012). *Self-disclosure in psychotherapy and recovery.* Lanham, MD: Jason Aronson, Rowman and Littlefield Publishing Group, Inc. (paperback edition).

Forrest, G.G. (2014). *Alliance Rupture and Repair in Addiction-Focused Psychotherapy.* Presented at Psychotherapy Associates, PC 40th "Addictive Disorders, Behavioral Health and Mental Health" Annual Winter Symposium, January 27th, 2016, Colorado Springs, CO.

Forrest, G.G. (2014). *Alliance university in psychotherapy and addictions treatment.* Presented at Elements Behavioral Health Continuing Education Workshop, Antlers Hotel, October 17–14, Colorado Springs, CO.

Forrest, G.G. (2014). Alliance University in Psychotherapy and Addictions Treatment. CEU Training and Education Presentation, Elements Behavioral Health, Antlers Hilton, October 14, Colorado Springs, Co.

Forrest, G.G. (2015). *Psychogenic etiology of addictive disorders and alliance dynamics.* Presented at Psychotherapy Associates, P.C. 41st annual international "Addictive Disorders, Behavioral Health and Mental Health" Winter Symposium, January 26, 2015, Colorado Springs, CO.

Forrest, G.G. (2016). Alliance Universality in Psychotherapy and Behavioral Health Care: The Heart and Soul of Change and Recovery. Presented at Psychotherapy Associates, PC 42nd "Addictive Disorders, Behavioral Health and Mental Health" Annual Winter Symposium, February 1, 2016.

Forrest, G.G. (2016). *Alliance universality in psychotherapy and behavioral health care: The heart and soul of change and recovery.* Presented at Psychotherapy Associates, PC 42nd Annual International Addictive Disorders, Behavioral Health and Mental Health Winter Symposium, February 1, Colorado Springs, CO.

Forrest, G.G., and Gordon, R. (1990). *Substance abuse, homicide, and violent behavior.* New York: Gardner Press.

Fortune, A.E. (1987). Grief only? Client and social worker reactions to termination. *Clinical Social Work Journal, 15,* 159–171. https://psycnet.apa.org/doi/10.1007/BF00752909

Frank, J.D., and Frank, J.B. (1991). *Persuasion and healing: A comparative study of psychotherapy* (3rd ed.). Baltimore, MD: Johns Hopkins University Press.

Freud, A. (1946). *The psychoanalytic treatment of children.* New York: International University Press.

Freud, S. (1888). Hysteria. In J. Strachey (Ed.), *The standard edition of the complete psychological works of Sigmund Freud* (pp. 41–57). London, England: Hogarth Press, Inc.

Freud, S. (1910). Future prospects of psychoanalytic therapy. In J. Strachey (Ed.), *The standard edition of the complete works of Sigmund Freud* (pp. 139–151). London, England: Hogarth Press.

Freud, S. (1912/2002). Recommendations to physicians practicing psychoanalysis. In *The standard edition of the complete psychological works of Sigmund Freud* (Volume 12, pp. 111–112). London: Vintage; Hogarth Press; The Institute of Psycho-Analysis, 2001.

Freud, S. (1959). Fragment of an analysis of a case of hysteria. In J. Riviere (Ed. and Trans.), *Collected papers of Sigmund Freud* (Vol. 3, pp. 13–146) (Original work published in 1905). London, England: Hogarth.

Freud, S., (1912, 1913, and 1958). The dynamics of transference [Zur Dynamik der Übertragung] (J. Strachey, Trans.). In J. Strachey (Ed.), *The standard edition of the complete psychological works of Sigmund Freud* (12, 99–108). London: Hogarth Press.

Freud,S. (1953). The future prospects of psycho-analytic therapy. In *Collected papers: Vol. II.* London: Hogarth.

Fried/Ander, M.L. (2015). Use of relational strategies to repair alliance ruptures: How responsive supervisors train responsive psychotherapists. *Psychotherapy, 52*(2), 174–179.

Friedlander, M.L. (2015). Use of relational strategies to repair alliance ruptures: How responsive supervisors train responsive psychotherapists. *Psychotherapy, 52*(2), 174–179.

Friedlander, M.L., Lambert, J.E., and Muniz de las Peña, C. (2008b). A step toward disentangling the alliance improvement cycle in family therapy. *Journal of Counseling Psychology, 55,* 118–124.

Friedlander, M.L., Lambert, J.E., Escudero, V., and Cragun, C. (2008a). How do therapists enhance family alliances? Sequential analyses of therapist client behavior in two contrasting cases. *Psychotherapy: Therapy, Research, Practice, Training, 45,* 75–78.

Friedlander, M.L., Lee, H.H., Shaffer, K.S., and Cabrera, P. (2014). Negotiating therapeutic alliances with a family at impasse. *Psychotherapy, 51*(1), 41–52.

From ER Visits, US Center for Disease Control, June, 2010, JAMA (2013): 30901657-659, and Institute of Medicine (2011), Relieving Pain in America.

Fromm-Reichmann, F. (1949). Note on the personal and professional requirements of a psychotherapist. *Psychiatry, 12,* 361–378.

Fromm-Reichmann, F. (1950). *Principles of intensive psychotherapy.* Chicago: University of Chicago Press.

Fromm-Reichmann, F. (1952). Some aspects of psychoanalytic psychotherapy with schizophrenics. In E. Brody and F.C. Redlich (Eds.), *Psychotherapy with schizophrenics.* New York: International Universities Press.

Fromm-Reichmann, F. (1959). *Psychoanalysis and psychotherapy.* Chicago: University of Chicago Press.

Gelso, C.J. (2011). *The real relationship in psychotherapy: The hidden foundation of change.* Washington, DC: American Psychological Association.

Gelso, C.J., and Bhatia, A. (2012). Crossing theoretical lines: The role and effect of transference in nonanalytic psychotherapies. *Psychotherapy, 49,* 3, 384–390.

Gelso, C.J., and Carter, J.A. (1985). the relationship in counseling and psychotherapy: Components, consequences, and theoretical antecedents. *The Counseling Psychologist, 13,* 155–243.

Gelso, C.J., and Carter, J.A. (1994). Components of the psychotherapy relationship: Their interaction and unfolding during treatment. *Journal of Counseling Psychology, 41,* 296–306.

Gelso, C.J., and Hayes, J.A. (1998). *The psychotherapy relationship: Theory, research and practice.* New York: Wiley.

Gelso, C.J., and Samstag, L.W. (2008). A tripartite model of the therapeutic relationship. In S. Brown and R. Lent (Eds.), *Handbook of counseling psychology* (pp. 267–283). New York: Wiley.

Gelso, C.J., Kelley, F.A., Fuertes, J.N., Marmarosh, C., Holmes, S.E., and Costas, C. (2005). Measuring the real relationship in psychotherapy: Initial validation of the therapist form. *Journal of Counseling Psychology, 52,* 640–649.

Gendlin, E.T., and Geist, M. (1962). The relationship of therapist congruence to psychological test evaluations of personality change. Wisconsin Psychiatric Institute, University of Wisconsin, Brief Research Reports, 24.

Genovese, M. (2016). *Treatment of doctors with addiction.* Presented at Psychotherapy Associates, PC. 42nd "Addictive Disorders, Behavioral Health and Mental Health" Annual Winter Symposium, February 2nd, 2016, Colorado Springs, CO.

Gilbert, A. (2015). Confessions of a seduction addict. *New York Times Magazine.* New York, NY, pp. 47–49.

Glasser, W. (1965). *Reality therapy: A new approach to psychiatry.* New York: Harper and Row.

Glidewell, R.N. (2015). *10 Laws of Insomnia: Solve the puzzle of poor sleep and reclaim your best life.* Colorado Springs, CO: The Insomnia Clinic™ Press.

Goldberg, S.B., Rousmaniere, T., Miller, S.D., Whipple, J., Nielsen, S.L., Hoyt, W.T., and Wampold, B.E. (2016). Do psychotherapists improve with time and experience? A longitudinal analysis of outcomes in a clinical setting. *Journal of Counseling Psychology, 63*(1), 1–11.

Gorski, T.T. (1976). *The denial process and human disease.* Hazel Crest, IL: Ingalls Memorial Hospital, The CENAPS Corporation.

Gorski, T.T., and Grinstead, S.F. (2010). *Relapse prevention therapy workbook* (2nd ed.). Independence, MO: Herald House/Independence Press.

Gorski, T.T., and Miller, M.M (1979). *Counseling for relapse prevention: The workshop manual.* Hazel Crest, IL: Human Ecology Systems, Inc.

Gorski, T.T., and Miller, M.M. (1982). *Counseling for relapse prevention.* Independence, MO: Herald House Press.

Gorski, T.T., and Miller, M.M. (1986). *Staying sober: A guide for relapse prevention.* Independence, MO: Independence Press.

Greenson, R.R. (1965). The working alliance and the transference neuroses. *Psychoanalytic Quarterly, 34,* 155–181.

Gregg, L., Haddock, G., Emsley, R., and Barrowclough, C. (2014). Reasons for substance use and their relationship to subclinical psychotic and affective symptoms, coping, and substance use in a nonclinical sample. *Psychology of Addictive Behaviors, 28*(1), 247–256.

Grinstead, S.F. (2016). *Medication management dilemmas that often lead to relapse.* Presented at Psychotherapy Associates, PC. 42nd "Addictive Disorders, Behavioral Health and Mental Health" Annual Winter Symposium, February 2nd, 2016, Colorado Springs, CO.

Grinstead, S.F., and Cabaret, J.A. (2017). *Chronic pain management and the American heroin epidemic.* Presented at Psychotherapy Associates, PC. 43rd "Addictive Disorders, Behavioral Health and Mental Health" Annual Winter Symposium, January 30th, 2017, Colorado Springs, CO.

Grossmann, K.E., Grossman, K., and Waters, E. (Eds.). (2005). *Attachment from infancy to adulthood: The major longitudinal studies.* New York, NY: Guilford Press.

Gurman, A.S. (1977). The patient's perception of the therapeutic relationship. In A.S. Gurman and A.M. Razin (Eds.), *Effective psychotherapy: A handbook of research* (pp. 503–545). New York: Pergamon Press.

Hahn, W.K. (2000). Shame: Countertransference identifications in individual psychotherapy. *Psychotherapy: Theory, research, practice, and training, 37*(1), 10–21.

Haller, M., and Chassin, L. (2014). Risk pathways among traumatic stress, posttraumatic stress disorder symptoms, and alcohol and drug problems: A test of four hypotheses. *Psychology of Addictive Disorders, 28*(3), 841–851.

Hardy, J. A., & Woodhouse, S. S. (2008, April). How we say goodbye: Research on psychotherapy termination. [Web article]. Retrieved from https://societyfor psychotherapy.org/say-goodbye-research-psychotherapy-termination

Hare, R.D. (1970). *Psychopathy: Theory and research.* Wiley: New York.

Hatcher, P.L., and Barends, A.W. (2006). Thinking about the alliance in practice. *Psychotherapy, Theory, Research, Practice, and Training, 41,* 7–10.

Hayes, J.A., Gelso, C.J., and Hummel, A.M. (2011) Managing countertransference. *Psychotherapy, 48,* 1, 88–97

Hayes, J.A., Nelson, D.L.B., & Fauth, J. (2015). Countertransference in successful and unsuccessful cases of psychotherapy. *Psychotherapy, 52*(1), 127–133.

Helzer, J.E., and Pryzbeck, T.R. (1988). The co-occurrence of alcoholism and other psychiatric disorders in the general population and its impact on treatment. *Journal of Studies on Alcoholism, 49*(E), 219–224.

Hill, C., and Knox, S. (2013). Training and supervision in psychotherapy. In M.E. Lambert (Ed.), *Bergin and Garfield's handbook of psychotherapy and behavior change* (6th ed., pp. 775–811). New York, NY: Wiley.

Hill, C.E., and Knox, S. (2001). Self-disclosure. *Psychotherapy, 38,* 413–417.

Hill, C.E., Mahalik, J.R., and Thompson, B.J. (1989) Therapists self-disclosure. *Psychotherapy, 26,* 290–295.

Hilsenroth, M., and Cromer, T. (2007). Clinician interventions related to alliance during the initial interview and psychological assessment. *Psychotherapy: Theory, Research, Practice, Training, 44,* 205–218.

Hogue, A., Dauber, S., Stambaugh, L.F., Cecero, J.J., and Liddle, H.A. (2006). Early therapeutic alliance and treatment outcome in individual and family therapy for adolescent behavior problems. *Journal of Consulting and Clinical Psychology, 74,* 121–129.

Horney, K. (1936). *The neurotic personality of our time.* New York: W.W. Norton and Company.

Horney, K. (1939). *New ways in psychoanalysis.* New York, NY: Norton.

Hornsey, M., Dwyer, L., Oei, T., and Dingle, G.A. (2009). Group processes and outcomes in group therapy: Is it time to let go of cohesiveness? *International Journal of Group Therapy, 59,* 267–278.

Horowitz, M.J., and Möller, B. (2009). Formulating transference in cognitive and dynamic psychotherapies using role relationship models. *Journal of Psychiatric Practice, 15,* 25–33.

Horvath, A.O., Del Re, A.C., Flückiger, C., and Symonds, D. (2011). Alliance in individual therapy. *Psychotherapy, 48*(1), 4–16.

Horvath, A.O., and Bedi, R.P. (2002). The alliance. In J.C. Norcross (Ed.), *Psychotherapy relationships that work.* New York: Oxford University Press.

Hountras, P.T., and Forrest, G.G. (1970). Personality characteristics and self-disclosure in a psychiatric outpatient population. *University of North Dakota College of Education Record, 55,* 206–213.

Hunsley, J., Aubry, T.D. Verstervelt, C.M., and Vito, D. (1999). Comparing therapist and client perspectives on reasons for psychotherapy termination. *Psychotherapy, 36,* 380–388.

Hustad, J.T.P, Eaton Short, E., Borsari, B., Barnett, N.P., O'Leary Tevyaw, T., and Kahler, C.W. (2011). College alcohol citations result in modest reductions in student drinking. *Journal of Substance Abuse Treatment, 40,* 281–286.

Ilgen, M.A., McKellar, J., Moos, R., and Finney, J.W. (2006). Therapeutic alliance and the relationship between motivation and treatment outcomes in patients with alcohol use disorder. *Journal of Substance Abuse Treatment, 31,* 157–162.

Jellinek, E.M. (Ed.). (1945). Heredity of the alcoholic. In *Alcohol, Science and Society.* Westport, Connecticut: Greenwood Press, pp. 105–114.

Jellinek, E.M. (1960). *The disease concept of alcoholism.* New Haven: College and University Press.

Jellinek, E.M. (1962). Phases of alcohol addiction. In D.J. Pittman and C.R. Snyder (Eds.), *Society, culture and drinking patterns.* New York: Wiley, pp. 356–368.

Johansson, R., Hesslow, T., Ljótsson, B., Jansson, A., Jonsson, L., Färdig, S., Karlsson, J., Hesser, H., Frederick, R.J., Lilliengren, P., Carlbring, P., and Andersson, G. (2017). Internet-based affect-focused psychodynamic therapy for social anxiety disorder: A randomized controlled trial with 2-year follow-up. *Psychotherapy, 54*(4), 351–366.

Johnson, S.M., and Talitman, E. (1997). Predictors of success in emotionally focused marital therapy. *Journal of Marital and Family Therapy, 23,* 135–153.

Jourard, S.M. (1964). *The transparent self.* Princeton, NJ: Van Nostrand.

Jourard, S. M. (1968). *Disclosing man to himself.* Princeton, NJ: Van Nostrand.

Jourard, S.M., and Lasakow, P. (1958). Some factors in self-disclosure. *Journal of Abnormal and Social Psychology, 56,* 91–98.

Jun, H.J., Rich-Edwards, J.W., Boynton-Jarrett, R., Austin, S.B., Frazier, A.L., and Wright, R.J. (2008). Child abuse and smoking among young women: The importance of severity, accumulation, and timing. *Journal of Adolescence Health, 43,* 55–63.

Kaysen, D., Atkins, D.C., Simpson, T.L., Stappenbeck, C.A., Blayney, J.A., Lee, C.M., and Larimer, M.E. (2014). Proximal relationships between PTSD symptoms and drinking among female college students: Results from a daily monitoring study. *Psychology of Addictive Behaviors, 28*(1), 62–73.

Kelly, J.F., and Greene, B. (2010). Diversity within African American, female therapists: Variability in clients' expectations and assumptions about the therapist. *Psychotherapy* (Chicago, IL), *47,* 186–197.

Kelly, V.A. (2016). *Addiction in the family, what every counselor needs to know.* Alexandria, VA: American Counseling Association.

Kernberg, O.F. (1993). *Severe personality disorders.* New Haven: Yale University Press.

Kernberg. O.F. (1975). *Borderline conditions and pathological narcissism.* New York: Jason Aronson.

Kessler, R.C., Crum, R.M., Warner, L.A., Nelson, C.B., Schulenberg, J., and Anthony, J.C. (1997). Lifetime co-occurrence of DSM-III-R alcohol abuse and dependence with other psychiatric disorders in the National Comorbidity Survey. *Archives of General Psychiatry, 54,* 313–321.

Kessler, R.C., McGonagle, K.A., Zhao, S., Nelson, C.B., Hughes, M. Esleman, S. and Kendler, K.S. (1994). Lifetime and 12-month prevalence of DSM-III-R psychiatric disorders in the United States. *Archives of General Psychiatry, 51,* 8–19.

Kevorkian, S., Bonn-Miller, M.O., Belendiuk, K., Dever, M.C., and Robertson-nay, R. (2015). Associations among trauma, posttraumatic stress disorder, cannabis use, and cannabis use disorders in a nationally representative epidemiologic sample. *Psychology of Addictive Behaviors, 29*(3), 633–638.

Khantzian, E.J. (2003). Understanding addictive vulnerability: An evolving psychodynamic perspective. *Neuro-Psychoanalysis, 5,* 5–21.

Khantzian, E.J. (2014). A psychodynamic perspective on the efficacy of 12-step programs. *Alcoholism Treatment Quarterly, 32*(2–3), 225–236.

Khantzian, E.J., and Albanese, M.J. (2008). *Understanding addiction as self-medication: Finding hope behind the pain.* Lanham, MD: Rowan and Littlefield Publishers.

Khantzian, E.J., and Treece, C. (1985). DSM-III psychiatric diagnosis of narcotic addicts. *Arch. General Psychiatry, 42,* 1067, 1071.

Kiesler, D.J. (1988). *Therapeutic metacommunication: Therapist impact disclosure as feedback in psychotherapy.* Palo Alto, CA: Consulting Psychologist Press.

Kirschenbaum, H., and Jourdan, A. (2005). The current status of Carl Rogers and the person-centered approach. *Psychotherapy: Theory, Research, Practice and Training, 42,* 37–51.

Knight, R.P. (1937). Psychodynamics of chronic alcoholism. *J. Nerv. Ment Dis., 86,* 538–548.

Knoblock-Fedders, L.M., Pinsof, W.M., and Mann, B. (2004). The formation of the therapeutic alliance in couple therapy. *Family Process, 43,* 425–442.

Knox, S., Adrians, N., Everson, E., Hess, S., Hill, C., and Crook-Lyon, R. (2011). Clients' perspective on therapy termination. *Psychotherapy Research, 21,* 154–167. http://dx.doi.org/10.1080/10503307.2010.534509

Knox, S., Hess, S.A., Peterson, D.A., and Hill, C.E. (1997). A qualitative analysis of client perceptions of the effects of helpful therapist self-disclosure in long-term therapy. *Journal of Counseling Psychology, 44,* 274–283.

Koob, G.F., and Volkow, N.D. (2010). Neurocircuitry of addiction. *Neuropsychopharmacology, 35,* 217–238.

Ladislac, T., McElvaney, J., Keogh, D., Martin, E., Clare, P., Chepukova, E., and Greenburg, K.S. (2017). Emotion-focused therapy for generalized anxiety disorder. *Psychotherapy, 54*(4), 361–366.

Lambert, J.E., and Friedlander, M.L. (2008). Relationship of differentiation of self to adult clients' perceptions of the alliance in brief family therapy. *Psychotherapy Research, 43,* 160–166.

Lambert, M.J, and Barley, D.E. (2002). Research summary on the therapeutic relationship and psychotherapy outcome. In J.C. Norcross (Ed.), *Psychotherapy relationships that work* (pp. 17–32). New York, NY: Oxford.

Lambert, M.J., and Shimokawa, K. (2011). Collecting client feedback. *Psychotherapy, 48,* 72–79.

Lasika, K.M., Gurman, A.S., and Wampold, B.E. (2014). Expanding the lens of evidence-based practice in psychotherapy: A common factors perspective. *Psychotherapy, 51*(4), 467–481.

Latts, M.G. (1996). *A revision and validation of the Countertransference Factors Inventory* (Unpublished doctoral dissertation). University of Maryland, College Park, MD.

Lazarus, A.A. (1981). *The practice of multi-modal therapy.* New York: McGraw-Hill Book Company.

Lehavot, K., Stappenbeck, C.A., Luterek, J.A., and Kaysen, D. (2014). Gender differences in relationships among PTSD severity, drinking motives, and alcohol use in a comorbid alcohol dependence and PTSD sample. *Psychology of Addictive Behaviors, 28*(1), 42–52.

Levin, J.D. (1991). *Treatment of alcoholism and other addictions: A self-psychology approach.* Northvale, NJ: Jason Aronson, Inc.

Levy, K.N., and Scala, J.W. (2012). Transference, transference interpretations, and transference-focused psychotherapies. *Psychotherapy, 49*(3), 391–403.

Levy, K.N., Meehan, K.B., Kelly, K.M., Reynoso, J., Weber, M., Clarkin, J.F., and Kernberg, O.F. (2006). Change in attachment patterns and reflective function in a randomized control trial of transference-focused psychotherapy. *Journal of Consulting and Clinical Psychology, 74,* 1027–1040.

Lietaer, G. (1993). Authenticity, congruence, and transparency. In D. Brazier (Ed.), *Beyond Carl Rogers: Toward a psychotherapy for the twenty-first century* (pp. 17–46). London: Constable.

Lingiardi, V., Colli, A., Gentile, D., and Tanzilli, A. (2011). Exploration of session process: Relationship to depth and alliance. *Psychotherapy, 48*(4), 391–400.

Little, M. (1951). Countertransference and the patient's response to it. *International Journal of Psychoanalysis, 32,* 32–40.

Lo Coco, G., Gullo, S., Prestano, C., and Gelso, C.J. (2011). Relation of the real relationship and the working alliance to the outcome of brief psychotherapy. *Psychotherapy, 48*(4), 359–367.

Luborsky, L. (1976). Helping alliances in psychotherapy. In J.L. Cleghorn (Ed.), *Successful psychotherapy* (pp. 92–116). New York: Brunner/Mazel.

Lundahl, B., and Burke, B.L. (2009). The effectiveness and applicability of motivational interviewing: A practice-friendly review of four meta-analyses. *Journal of Clinical Psychology, 11,* 1232–1245.

Mamodhoussen, S., Wright, J., Tremblay, N., and Poitras-Wright, H. (2005). Impact of marital and psychological distress on therapeutic alliance in couples undergoing couple therapy. *Journal of Marital and Family Therapy, 31,* 159–169.

Markin, R.D., McCarthy, K.S., and Barber, J.P. (2013). Transference, countertransference, emotional expression, and session quality over the course of supportive expressive therapy: The raters' perspective. *Psychotherapy Research, 23,* 152–168. doi:http://dx.doi.org10.1080/10503307.2012.747013

Marlatt, G.A., and Gordon, J.R. (1985). *Relapse prevention: Maintenance strategies in the treatment of addictive behaviors.* New York, NY: Guilford Press.

Marlatt, G.A., and Witkiewitz, K. (2010). Update on harm-reeducation policy and intervention research. *Annual Review of Clinical Psychology, 6,* 591–606.

Marmarosh, C.L. (2012). Empirically supported perspectives on Transference. *Psychotherapy, 49*(3), 364–369.

Marmarosh, C. L., Gelso, C., Markin, R.D., Majors, R., Mallery, C., and Choi, J. (2009). The real relationship in psychotherapy: Relationships to adult attachments, working alliance, transference, and therapy outcome. *Journal of Counseling Psychology, 56,* 337–350.

Maroda, K. (1994). *The power of countertransference: Innovations in analytic technique.* Northvale, NJ: Jason Aronson, Inc.

Martin, D.G. (2000). *Counseling and therapy skills* (2nd ed.). Prospect Heights, IL: Waveland Press.

Martin, D.J., Garske, J.P., and Davis, K.M. (2000). Relation of the therapeutic alliance with outcome and other variables: A meta analytic review. *Journal of Clinical and Consulting Psychology, 68,* 438–450.

Martin, J.L., Burrow-Sanchez, J.J., Iwamoto, D.K., Glidden-Tracey, C.E., and Vaughan, E.L. (2016). Counseling psychology and substance use: Implications for training, practice, and research. *The Counseling Psychologist, 44*(8), 1106–1131.

Marx, J.A., and Gelso, C.J. (1987). Termination of individual counseling in a university counseling center. *Journal of Counseling Psychology, 34,* 3–9. http://dx.doi.org10.1037/0022-0167.34.1.3.

Maslow, A.W. (1954). *Motivation and personality.* New York: Harper and Row.

Masterson, J.F. (1981). *The narcissistic and borderline disorders: An integrated developmental approach.* New York: Brunner/Mazel.

Mattos, L.A., Schmidt, A.T., Henderson, C.E., and Hogue, A. (2017). Therapeutic alliance and treatment outcome in the outpatient treatment of urban adolescents: The Role of callous-unemotional traits. *Psychotherapy, 54*(2), 136–147.

May, R. (1958). Contributions of existential psychotherapy. In May, R., Angle, E., and Ellenburger, H. (Eds.), *Existence.* New York: Basic Books.

May, R. (1973). Psychotherapy and the daimonic. In A. Mahrer and L. Pearson (Eds.), *Creative developments in psychotherapy.* New York: Aronson.

May, R. (1983). *The discovery of being.* New York: Norton.

McGowan, J.F., and Schmidt, L.D., (1962). *Counseling: Readings in theory and practice.* New York: Holt, Rinehart and Winston.

Meier, P.S., Barrowclough, C., and Donmall, M.C. (2005). The role of the therapeutic alliance in the treatment of substance misuse: A critical review of the literature. *Addiction, 100,* 304–316.

Meier, P.S., Donmall, M.C., McElduff, P., Barrowclough, C., and Heller, R.F. (2006). The role of the early therapeutic alliance in predicting drug treatment dropout. *Drug and Alcohol Dependence, 83,* 57–64.

Meissner, W.W. (2000). Reflections on psychic reality. *The International Journal of Psychoanalysis, 81,* 1117–1138.

Menninger, C. (1958). *Theories of psychoanalytic technique.* New York: Basic Book.

Menninger, K. (1938). *Man against himself.* New York: Harcourt, Brace and World, Inc.

Miller, S.D., Hubble, M.A., Chow, D., and Seidel, J. (2015). Beyond measures and monitoring: Realizing the potential of feedback-informed treatment. *Psychotherapy, 52*(4), 449–457.

Miller, W.R., and Rollinick, S. (2002). *Motivational interviewing: Preparing people for change* (2nd ed.). New York: Guilford Press.

Miller, W.R., Sovereign, R.G., and Krege, B. (1988). Motivational interviewing with problem drinkers: II. The drinker's check-up as a preventive intervention. *Behavioral Psychotherapy, 16,* 251–268.

Miller, W.R., Wilborne, P.L., and Hettema, J.E. (2003). What works? A summary of alcohol treatment outcome research. In R.K. Hester and W.R. Miller (Eds.), *Handbook of alcoholism treatment approaches: Effective alternatives* (3rd ed., pp. 13–63). Boston, Ma: Allyn and Bacon.

Mitchell, K.M., Truax, C.B., Bozarth, J.D., and Kraft, C.C. (1973). *Antecedents to psychotherapeutic outcome.* NIMH grant Report (12306). Hot Springs, AR: Arkansas Research and Training Center, AR Rehabilitation Services.

Munroe, R. L. (1955). *Schools of psychoanalytic thought.* New York: Dryden Press.

Myers, S. (2000). Empathic listening: Reports on the experience of being heard. *Journal of Humanistic Psychology, 40,* 148–173.

Nace, E.P. (1990). Substance abuse and personality disorder. In D.F. O'Connell and E.P. Beyer (Eds.), *Managing the dually diagnosed patient: Current issues and clinical approaches* (2nd ed.). New York: The Haworth Press.

Najavits, L., and Strupp, H. (1994). Differences in the effectiveness of psychodynamic therapists: Process-outcome study. *Psychotherapy: Theory, Research, and Practice, 31,* 114–123.

Nissen-Lie, H.A., Monsen, J.T., and Ronnestad, M.H. (2010). Therapist predictors of early patient-rated working alliance: A multilevel approach. *Psychotherapy Research, 20,* 627–646.

Norcross, J.C. (2010). The therapeutic relationship. In B.L. Duncan, S.D. Miller, B.E. Wampold, and M.A. Hubble (Eds.), *Heart and soul of change in psychotherapy* (2nd ed.). Washington, DC: American Psychological Association.

Norcross, J.C. (Ed.). (2002). *Psychotherapy relationships that work: Therapist contributions and responsiveness to patient needs.* New York: Oxford University Press.

Norcross, J.C. and Wampold, B.E. (2019). Relationships and responsiveness in the psychological treatment of trauma: The tragedy of the APA clinical practice guideline. *Psychotherapy, 56*(3), 301–399.

Norcross, J.C., and Camembert, M.J. (2018) Psychotherapy relationships that work III. *Psychotherapy, 55*(4), 303–315. http://dx.doi.org/10.1037/pst0000193.

Norcross, J.C., and Lambert, M.J. (2011). Psychotherapy relationships that work II. *Psychotherapy, 48*(1), 4–8.

Norcross, J.C., and Wampold, B.E. (2011). Evidence-based therapy relationships: Research conclusions and clinical practices. *Psychotherapy, 48*(1), 98–102.

Norcross, J.C., Beutler, L.E., and Levant, R.F. (Eds.). (2006). *Evidence-based practices in mental health: Debate and dialogue on the fundamental questions.* Washington DC: American Psychological Association.

Norcross, J.C., Koocher, G.P., and Garofalo, A. (2006). Discredited psychological treatments and tests: A Delphi poll. *Professional Psychology: Research and Practice, 37,* 515–522.

Norcross, J.C., VandenBos, G.R., and Freedheim, D.K. (Eds.). (2011). *History of psychotherapy: Continuing and change* (2nd ed.). Washington, DC: American Psychology Association.

Ochsner, R. (2016). Medically Assisted Addictions Care. Presented at Psychotherapy Associates, PC. 40th "Addictive Disorders, Behavioral Health and Mental Health" Annual Winter Symposium, January 27th, 2016, Colorado Springs, CO.

Olivera, J., Challa, L., Gomez-Pendo, J.M., and Roussos, A. (2017). Client-therapist agreement in the termination process and its association with therapeutic relationship. *Psychotherapy, 54*(1), 88–101.

Orlinsky, D.E., Ronnestad, M.H., and Willutzki, U. (2004). Fifty years of psychotherapy process-outcome research: Continuity and change. In M.J. Lambert (Ed.), *Handbook of psychotherapy and behavior change* (5th ed., pp. 307–390). New York, NY: Wiley.

Oshri, A., Rogosch, F.A., Burnette, M.L., and Cicchetti, D. (2011). Developmental pathways to adolescent cannabis abuse and dependence: Child maltreatment, emerging personality and internalizing versus externalizing psychopathology. *Psychology of Addictive Behaviors, 25*(4), 634–644.

Patterson, C.H. (1984). *Theories of counseling and psychotherapy* (3rd ed.). New York: Harper and Row

Pereira, T., Lock, J., and Oggins, J. (2006). Role of the therapeutic alliance in family therapy for adolescent anorexia nervosa. *International Journal of Eating Disorders, 39,* 677–684.

Perls, F.S. (1958). *Gestalt therapy.* New York, NY: Julian.

Peterson, Z.D. (2002). More than a mirror: The ethics of therapist self-disclosure. *Psychotherapy: Theory, Research, Practice, and Training, 39*(1), 21–31.

Philips, B., and Wennberg, P. (2014). The importance of therapy motivation for patients with substance use disorders. *Psychotherapy, 51*(4), 555–562.

Pinsof, W.B., and Catherall, D. (1986). The integrative Psychotherapy alliance: Family, couple, and individual therapy scales. *Journal of Marital and Family Therapy, 12,* 137–151.

Prochaska, J.O., DiClemente, C.C. and Norcross, J.C. (1992). In search of how people change: Applications to addictive behaviors. *American Psychologist, 47,* 1102–1114.

Rabinovich, M., and Kacen, L. (2009). Let's look at the elephant: Metasynthesis of transference case studies in psychodynamic and cognitive psychotherapy integration. *Psychology and Psychotherapy: Theory, Research and Practice, 82,* 427–447.

Rank, O. (1999, 1929). *The trauma of birth.* (Reprinted), Routledge: London, England, New Fetter, Ln. Originally published in 1929: Kegan, Paul, Trench, Trubner and Co; London England.

Read, J.P., Colder, C.R. Merrill, J.E., Ouimette, P., White, J., and Swartout, A. (2012). Trauma and posttraumatic stress symptoms predict alcohol and other drug consequence trajectories in the first year of college. *Journal of Consulting and Clinical Psychology, 810,* 426–439.

Reich, W. (1961). *Character analysis.* New York: The Noonday Press.

Reik, T. (1948). *Listening with the third ear.* New York: Pyramid Books.

Robbins, M.S., Mayorga, C.C., Mitrani, V.B., Turner, C.W., Alexander, J.F., and Szapocznik, J. (2008). Adolescent and parent alliances with therapists in brief strategic family therapy with drug-using Hispanic adolescents. *Journal of Marital and Family Therapy, 34,* 316–328.

Rochlen, A.B., Rude, S.S, and Baron, A. (2005). The relationship of client stages of change to working alliance and outcome in short-term counseling. *Journal of College Counseling, 8,* 52–64.

Roe, D., Dekel, R., Harel, G., Fennig, S., and Fennig, N. (2006). Clients' feeling during termination of psychodynamically oriented psychotherapy. *Bulletin of the Menninger Clinic, 70,* 68–81. https://psycnet.apa.org/doi/10.1521/bumc.2006 .70.1.68

Rogers, C.R. (1951). *Client-centered therapy.* Boston: Houghton Mifflin.

Rogers, C.R. (1980). *A way of being.* Boston: Houghton Mifflin.

Rogers, C.R., and Dymond, R. (1954). *Psychotherapy and personality change* (Eds.). Chicago: University Press.

Rogers, C.R., and Truax, C.B. (1966). The therapeutic conditions antecedent to change: A theoretical view. In C.R. Rogers, E.T. Gendlin, D. Kiesler, and C.B. Truax (Eds.), *The therapeutic relationship and its impact: A study of psychotherapy and schizophrenics.* Madison, WI: University of Wisconsin Press.

Rogers, C.R., Gendlin, E.T., Kiesler, D.J., and Truax, C.B. (Eds.). (1967). *The therapeutic relationship and its impact: A study of psychotherapy with schizophrenics.* Madison, WI: University of Wisconsin Press.

Rosario, M., Reisner, S.L., Corliss, H.L., Wypij, D., Calzo, J., and Austin, S.B. (2014). Sexual-orientation disparities in substance use in emerging adults: A function of stress and attachment paradigms. *Psychology of Addictive Behaviors, 28*(3), 790–804.

Rosen, D.C., Nakash, O., and Alegria, M. (2016). The impact of computer use on therapeutic alliance and continuance in care during the mental health intake. *Psychotherapy, 53*(1), 117–123.

Rounsaville, B.J., Eyre, S.L., Weissman, M.M., and Kleber, H.D. (1983). The antisocial opiate addict. *Advances in Alcohol and Substance Abuse, 2*(4), 29–42.

Ryan, V.L., and Gizinski, M.N. (1971). Behavior therapy in retrospect: Patient's feelings about their behavior therapy. *Journal of Counseling and Clinical Psychology, 37,* 1–9.

Schaffer, J.A. (2007). *Transference and countertransference in non-analytic therapy: Double-edged swords.* New York: University Press of America.

Searles, H.F. (1987). Countertransference as a path to understanding and helping the patient. In E. Slakter (Ed.), *Countertransference* (pp. 131–163). Northvale, NJ: Jason Aronson, Inc.

Shaffer, H.J. (1994). Denial, ambivalence, and countertransferential hate. In J.D. Levin and R.H. Weiss (Eds.), *The dynamics and treatment of alcoholism: Essential papers* (pp. 421–437). Northvale, NJ: Jason Aronson, Inc.

Shapiro, J.L., and Gust, T. (1974). Counselor training for facilitative human relationships. *Counselor Education and Supervision, 13,* 198–206.

Shaw, S., and Murray, K. (2015). Incorporating feedback-informed treatment into counseling practice. *Counseling Today, 57*(12), 44–51.

Shelef, K., and Diamond, G.M. (2008). Short form of the Vanderbilt Therapeutic Alliance Scale: Development, reliability, and validity. *Psychotherapy Research, 18,* 433–443.

Shirk, S.R., and Karver, M.S. (2011). Alliance in child and adolescent psychotherapy. In J.C. Norcross (Ed.), *Psychotherapy relationships that work: Evidence-based responsiveness* (2nd ed., pp. 70–91). New York, NY: Oxford University Press.

Shirk, S.R., and Russell, R.L. (1996). *Change processes in child psychotherapy: Revitalizing treatment and research.* New York: Guilford Press.

Shostrom, E.L. (1965). *Three approaches to psychotherapy* [Part I, Film]. Orange, CA: Psychological Films.

Smerud, P.E., and Rosenfarb, I.S. (2008). The therapeutic alliance and family psychoeducation in the treatment of schizophrenia: An exploratory prospective change process study. *Journal of Consulting and Clinical Psychology, 76,* 505–510.

Smith, M.L., and Glass, G.V. (1977). Meta-analysis of psychotherapy outcomes studies. *American Psychologist, 32,* 752–760.

Sommer-Flanagan, J., and Lewis, K. (2017). Building better counselors. *Counseling Today, 60*(5), 58–63.

Stekel, W. (1943). *The interpretation of dreams.* New York: Liveright.

Stekel, W. (1949). *Sadism and masochism* (Vol. 1). London: Liveright Publishing, Co.

Stekel, W. (1952). *Patterns of psychosexual infantilism.* New York: Washington Square Press.

Sterba, R.F. (1934). The fate of the ego in analytic therapy. *International Journal of Psychoanalysis, 115,* 117–126.

Sternburg, S., and Trijburg, W. (2005). *The relationship between therapeutic interventions and therapeutic outcome.* Unpublished manuscript, Department of Clinical Psychology, University of Amsterdam, Netherlands.

Stiles, W.B., Shapiro, D., and Elliot, R. (1986). Are all psychotherapists equivalent? *American Psychologist, 41,* 165–180.

Strupp, H. (1973). *Psychotherapy: Clinical, research and theoretical issues.* New York: Aronson.

Sullivan, H.S. (1953). *The interpersonal theory of psychiatry.* New York: W.W. Norton and Company.

Sullivan, H.S. (1954). *The psychiatric interview.* New York: W.W. Norton.

Sutker, P.B. (1971). Personality differences and sociopathy in heroin addicts and non-addict prisoners. *J. of Abnormal Psych, 78,* 247–251.

Symonds, B.D., and Horvath, A.O. (2004). Optimizing the alliance in couple therapy. *Family Process, 43,* 443–455.

Szapocznik, J., Perez-Vidal, A., Brickman, A., Foote, F.H., Santisteban, D.A., Hervis, O., and Kurtines, W.M. (1988). Engaging adolescent drug users and their families into treatment: A strategic structural approach. *Journal of Consulting and Clinical Psychology, 56,* 552–557.

Szasz, T.S. (1974). *Ceremonial chemistry.* New York: Doubleday.

Szasz, T.S. (1976). *Schizophrenia: The sacred symbol of psychiatry.* New York: Basic Books, Inc.

Tansey, M.J., and Burke, W.F. (1989). *Understanding countertransference: From projective identification to empathy.* Hillsdale, NJ: The Analytic Press.

Tellides, C., Fitzpatrick, M., Drapeau, M., Bracewell, R., Janzen, J., and Jaouich, A. (2008). The manifestation of transference during early psychotherapy sessions. *Counseling and Psychotherapy Research, 8,* 85–92.

Thomas, J. (2015). *Addiction through an attachment lens.* Presented at Psychotherapy Associates, P.C 41st annual international "Addictive Disorders, Behavioral Health and Mental Health" Winter Symposium, January 26, Colorado Springs, Co.

Thomas, S.E.G., Werner-Wilson, R.J., and Murphy, M.J. (2005). Influence of therapist and client behaviors on therapy alliance. *Contemporary Family Therapy: An International Journal, 27,* 19–35.

Timulak, L., and McEvaney, J. (2017). *Transforming generalized anxiety: An emotion-focused approach.* Hove, England: Routledge.

Town, J.M., Salvadori, A. Falkenström, F., Bradley, S., and Hardy, G. (2017). Is affect experiencing therapeutic in major depressive disorder? Examining associations between affect experiencing nad changes to the alliance and outcome in intensive short-term dynamic psychotherapy. Psychotherapy, 54(2), 148–158.

Truax, C.B. (1961A). The process of group psychotherapy: Relationship between hypothesized therapeutic conditions and intrapersonal exploration. *Psychol. Monogr., 75,* 7 (Whole No. 511).

Truax, C.B. (1961B). *A scale for the measurement of accurate empathy.* Psychiatric Institute Bull., Wisconsin Psychiatric Institute, University of Wisconsin, 1, 2.

Truax, C.B. (1962). Variations in levels of accurate empathy offered in the psychotherapy relationship and case outcome. *Brief Research Reports,* Wisconsin Psychiatric Institute, University of Wisconsin, 1962, 38.

Truax, C.B. (1963). Relationship quality: Relationship between conditions offered in psychotherapy and relationship quality between constructive personality change and relationship quality. *Brief Research Reports,* Wisconsin Psychiatric Institute, University of Wisconsin, 83.

Truax, C.B. (1965). Personality change in hospitalized mental patients during group therapy as a function of alternate sessions and vicarious therapy pretraining. *J. Clin. Psychol., 21,* 225–228a.

Truax, C.B. (1966). Therapist empathy, warmth and genuineness and patient personality change in group psychotherapy: A comparison between interaction unit measures, time samples, and patient perception measures. *Journal of Clinical Psychology, 22,* 225–229.

Truax, C.B. (1969). Relationship quality: Relationship between conditions offered in psychotherapy and relationship quality and between constructive personality change and relationship quality. *Brief Research Reports,* Wisconsin Psychiatric Institute, University of Wisconsin, 83. In C.B. Truax and R.R. Carkhuff (1967). *Toward effective counseling and psychotherapy: Training and practice.* Chicago: Aldine.

Truax, C.B. (1971). Perceived therapeutic conditions and client outcome. *Comparative Group Studies, 2,* 301–310.

Truax, C.B., and Carkhuff, R.R. (1963). For better or for worse: The process of psychotherapeutic personality change. Chapter in *Recent advances in the study of behavior change.* Montreal, Canada: McGill University Press.

Truax, C.B., and Lister, J.L. (1971). Effects of short-term training upon accurate empathy and non-possessive warmth. *Counselor Education and Supervision, 10,* 120–125.

Truax, C.B., and Mitchell, K.M. (1971). Research on certain therapist interpersonal skills in relation to process and outcome. In A.E. Bergin and S.L. Garfield (Eds.), *Handbook of psychotherapy and behavior change* (pp. 299–344). New York: Wiley.

Truax, C.B., and Wargo, D.G. (1966). *Antecedents to outcome in group psychotherapy with juvenile delinquents: Effects of therapeutic conditions, alternate sessions, vicarious therapy pretraining and patient self-exploration.* Unpublished manuscript, University of Arkansas, Arkansas Rehabilitation and Training Center, Hot Springs, Arkansas.

Tryon, G.S., and Winograd, G. (2011). Goal consensus and collaboration. *Psychotherapy, 48*(1), 50–57.

Tschuschke, V., and Dies, R.R. (1994). Intensive analysis of therapeutic factors and outcome in long-term inpatient groups. *International Journal of Group Psychotherapy, 44,* 185–208.

Ulvenes, P.G., Berggraf, L. Hoffart, A. Stiles, T.C., Svartberg, M., McCullough, L., and Wampold, B.E. (2012). Different processes for different therapies: Therapist actions, therapeutic bond, and outcome. *Psychotherapy, 49*(3), 291–302.

Van Wagoner, S.L., Gelso, C.J., Hayes, J.A., and Diemer, R. (1991). Countertransference and the reportedly excellent psychotherapist. *Psychotherapy, 28,* 411–421.

Vittengl, J.R., Clark, L.A., Thase, M.E., and Jarrett, P.B. (2015). Predictors of longitudinal outcomes after unstable response to acute-phase cognitive therapy for major depressive disorder. *Psychotherapy, 52*(2), 268–277.

Volkow, N.D. (2015). Can science of addictions help reduce stigma? *Advances in Addiction and Recovery, 3*(3), 16–19.

Volkow, N.D. and Koob, G. (2015). Brain and disease model of addiction: Why is it so controversial? *Lancet Psychiatry, 2,* 677–679.

Wampold, B.E. (2001). *The great psychotherapy debate: Models, methods, and findings.* Mahwah: Erlbaum.

Wampold, B.E., and Imel, Z.E. (2015). *The great psychotherapy debate: The evidence for what makes psychotherapy work.* New York, NY: Routledge.

Watson, J.C., Greenberg, L.S., and Lietaer, G. (1998). The experimental paradigm unfolding: Relationship and experiencing in therapy. In L.S. Greenberg, J.C. Watson, and G. Lietaer (Eds.), *Handbook of experiential psychotherapy* (pp. 3–27). New York: Guilford Press.

Weinhold, J.B. (2016). *Developmental trauma: The game changer in mental health professions.* Presented at Psychotherapy Associates, P.C 42nd annual international "Addictive Disorders, Behavioral Health and Mental Health" Winter Symposium, February 2, Colorado Springs, Co.

Weiss, R.H. (1994). Countertransference issues in treating the alcoholic patient: Institutional and clinical reactions. In J.D. Levin and R.H. Weiss (Eds.), *The dynamics and treatment of alcoholism: Essential papers.* Northvale, NJ: Jason Aronson, Inc.

Wells, T. (1994). *Therapist self-disclosure: The use of self in psychotherapy* (2nd ed.). Baltimore: University Park.

Westmacott, R., Hunsely, J. Best, M., Rumstein-McKean, O., and Schindler, D. (2010). Client and Therapist views of contextual factors related to termination from psychotherapy: A comparison between unilateral and mutual terminators. *Psychotherapy Research, 20,* 423–435. http://dx.doi.org/10.1080/1053301003645796

Wetzler, S. (1993). *Living with the passive aggressive man.* New York, NY: Fireside.

Widom, C.S., DuMont, K., and Czaja, S.J. (2007). A prospective investigation of major depressive disorder and comorbidity in abused and neglected children grown up. *Archives of General Psychiatry, 64,* 49–56.

Wiprovnick, A.E., Kuerbis, A.N. and Morgenstern, J. (2015). the effects of therapeutic bond within a brief intervention for alcohol moderation for problem drinkers. *Psychology of Addictive Behaviors, 29*(1), 129–135.

World Health Organization. (1992). *International classification of diseases and related health problems* (10th rev., ICD-10). Geneva, Switzerland: Author.

Xu Li, Kivlighan, D.M., Hill, C.E., Zhi-Jin, H. and Xu, M. (2018). Helping skills, working alliance, and session depth in China: A multilevel analysis. *The Counseling Psychologist, 46*(3), 379–405.

Yalom, I.D. (2002). *The gift of therapy: An open letter to a new generation of therapists and their patients.* New York: Harper Collins.

Young-Joo, H., and O'Brien, K.M. (2014). Critical secret disclosure in psychotherapy with Korean clients. *The Counseling Psychologist, 42*(4), 524–551.

Zack, S.E., Castonguay, L.G., Boswell, J.F., McAleavey, A.A., Adelman, R., Kraus, D.R., and Pate, G.A. (2015). Attachment history as a moderator of the alliance outcome relationship in adolescents. *Psychotherapy, 52*(2), 258–267.

Zane, N., Hall, G.N., Sue, S., Young, K., and Nunez, J. (2004). Research on psychotherapy with culturally diverse populations. In M.J. Lambert (Ed.), *Bergin and Garfield's handbook of psychotherapy and behavior change* (5th ed., pp. 767–804). New York: Wiley.

Zeig, J. (2017). *Advanced techniques of psychotherapy: The foundations of empathy, hypnotic response and attunement.* Presented at Psychotherapy Associates, PC. 43rd "Addictive Disorders, Behavioral Health and Mental Health" Annual Winter Symposium, January 31st, 2017, Colorado Springs, CO.

Zetzel, E.R. (1956). Current Concepts in transference. *International Journal of Psychoanalysis, 37,* 369–376.

Zuroff, D.C., Kelly, A.C., Leybman, M.J., Blatt, S.J., and Wampold, B.E. (2010). Between-therapist and within-therapist differences in the quality of the therapeutic relationship: Effects on maladjustment and self-critical perfectionism. *Journal of Clinical Psychology, 66,* 681–697.

INDEX

12-step, 325, 342

A

academic training, 31
addiction treatment, xiii, 105, 135, 168, 249, 289, 301–302, 331
alcohol problem(s), 12, 323–324, 331
alliance-focused, 4, 31, 41, 47, 181, 185, 205, 211, 287, 305, 334
alliance ingredient(s), xv, 6, 9, 51–52, 124, 204, 229
alliance issues, 29
alliance qualities, 16, 79, 100
alliance rupture(s), 10, 33–34, 41, 52, 58, 83, 88, 105, 109, 111–116, 123–124, 160, 188, 199, 205, 208, 214, 220, 222, 245–246, 271, 291, 296, 306, 327, 337–338,
alliance universality, xvi, 11, 315–317, 319, 325–327, 337
assessment(s), vii, 7, 15, 21–22, 30–31, 39–40, 44, 107–108, 128, 155, 160, 163–165, 167, 169–175, 186, 191, 206, 235, 249–250, 287–288, 298, 301–302, 312, 315, 322, 332, 335–336, 340
assumption(s), 72, 297, 307, 342
attachment, 24, 32, 35, 39, 44, 47, 55, 74, 82, 126, 130, 134, 144, 152–158, 163, 169, 175, 178, 257, 261, 261, 277, 279, 282, 318–319, 331, 333, 340, 343–344, 347, 349, 351
authentic, 8, 66, 68, 73–75, 100, 119
authenticity, 9, 57, 68–69, 75, 77–78, 82, 98, 100–101, 165, 187, 199, 343

B

behavioral health, v, vii, ix, 6–8, 13–14, 16, 18–22, 27, 48–49, 80, 98, 106, 116, 125, 127, 135, 137, 140, 149, 154, 166–168, 172–174, 210, 231, 250, 252, 256, 300–305, 307, 309–313, 326, 333–334, 336–337, 339–340, 346, 349, 351–352
bias(es) 72, 74, 85, 298, 311
biopsychosocial, 7–8, 18, 24, 128, 141, 157, 168, 170, 174–175, 177, 191, 211–212, 214, 217, 240, 258, 276, 278, 288, 328
Borderline Personality Disorder (BPD), 47, 65, 127, 135, 138, 142, 146, 324

C

case study, 177, 216, 230, 240, 242, 282
challenge(s), 10, 43, 45, 65, 158, 207, 220, 233, 236, 264
clinical
clinical data, 9, 21, 82, 320
clinical evidence, 26, 78, 80, 293, 322, 326
clinical practice, v, xiii, xv, xvi, 6, 8, 10–12, 15, 21, 28, 30, 48, 50, 53, 56, 58–59, 74, 78, 80, 83, 95, 100, 110, 115, 124, 127, 152, 155, 159–160, 197, 279, 288, 292, 298–300, 302–306, 310, 313–316, 321, 325, 327, 346
clinical research(ers), 12, 15, 27, 31, 59, 98, 137
clinical training, 15, 52, 139
cognitive behavioral, 3, 51, 56, 115, 204, 210

cohesion, 44–46, 82, 126, 143, 292, 296, 305–306, 319–320, 331–332
collaborative, 29–30, 32–33, 38–39, 83, 109, 116, 215, 321–323, 325, 330
commitment to change, 10, 116–117, 124, 175
communication(s), 8–9, 34, 52, 57, 60, 66, 76–77, 79, 83, 96, 109, 123, 164, 166, 180, 193, 205, 256, 317, 323, 342
communication style, 9
complex trauma, 47
concreteness, 9, 24, 31, 52, 58, 61, 76–79, 114, 187, 197, 246, 317
confrontation(al), vii, 10, 73, 92, 95, 110, 115, 197–200, 242, 245–246, 250, 287, 306–307, 335
consultation, 11, 48, 166, 169–170, 176, 185, 272, 286, 288, 312
contemporary belief systems, 12
correctional, 11, 40, 117, 140, 144
counseling and therapy, 19, 81, 105, 168, 237, 344

D

daily living, 10, 15, 248, 254, 312
definition(s), 9–10, 15, 29–30, 32–33, 45, 70, 81, 84, 89, 96, 122–123, 154–155, 197, 319, 322
depression, 7–8, 57, 107–108, 127, 133–134, 141, 145, 148–149, 155, 183, 186, 191–192, 195, 200, 208, 212, 214, 218, 222, 230–232, 242, 253, 257–258, 262, 272, 290, 324, 332, 334
detox, 11, 18–19, 82, 104, 115, 117, 136, 160, 162, 164, 175, 177, 209, 212, 216–217, 224, 228, 257, 271, 303
detoxification, 113, 141, 145, 161, 203, 250, 302
DSM, 7, 37, 127, 135, 137–139, 147–148, 150, 154, 172–173, 287, 342
"doctor-patient" relationship(s), 4, 279
dogmatic reliance, 297, 308
duration, 6, 13, 18, 23–24, 150, 176, 204

E

early stage(s), 10, 30, 36, 88, 92, 114–115, 160, 163, 172, 174–175, 178–179, 181, 186, 189, 191, 194, 198–200,

204–207, 212, 214, 216, 218, 220–221, 223, 225–226, 228, 235, 237, 245–246, 248, 257, 261–262, 287–288, 306
eclectic therapy, 3, 73–74, 204, 210, 212, 216, 270, 287
effective therapy, 54, 79, 82, 115, 254, 316
efficacy, 5, 13, 16, 21–23, 35, 38, 42, 49, 63, 78, 94, 100, 116, 160, 168, 211, 297, 309, 342
empirically, 52, 67, 94, 123, 318, 344
ethical(ly), 95, 115, 213, 250, 272, 312–313
evidence-based psychotherapy, xv, 3, 8, 9–11, 15–16, 23, 28, 78, 80, 298, 300
evolution, 4, 9, 23, 26, 28, 31, 49, 59, 98, 125, 142, 157, 191, 252, 259, 270, 301
evolutionary, 50, 301

F

failure(s), 3, 9, 12–13, 45, 57, 83, 91, 103, 109, 114, 130, 133, 138–139, 144–145, 193, 220, 223, 225–227, 261, 275, 291, 296–297, 306, 308, 335

G

genetic reconstruction, 10, 175, 181–183, 185–186, 198, 206, 287
guideline(s), vii, xv, 10–11, 26, 38, 40, 44, 48–49, 58, 66, 83, 94–95, 107, 111, 114, 246, 270, 292–293, 298, 300, 313, 321, 336, 346

H

healing process, 21, 24
"heart and soul of change," xvi, 315, 333, 337, 345
"here and now," 88, 146, 166, 183, 206–208, 254, 318
"how and why" therapy, 13

I

identity consolidation, 254, 256–260, 262–263, 266, 287
ineffective, 81, 104, 117, 211, 293, 296–297, 306, 309

intensive outpatient (IOP), xiii, 11, 21, 104–105, 117, 160, 164, 230, 266, 271, 311
interpretation(s), 10, 30, 36, 61, 66, 68, 76, 79, 85, 88, 94, 112, 115, 123, 146, 183, 185, 187–188, 197, 203, 213, 215–216, 245, 255, 257, 287, 318, 343, 348

L

late stage(s), 10, 141, 225, 252, 253–266, 269, 271, 273–274, 279, 287–288
life issues, 170, 286

M

medication assisted treatment, 177
middle stage(s), 86–87, 89, 95, 192–293, 204–210, 212–216, 219–223, 225–226, 228–230, 233, 236–238, 241, 245–250, 253–255, 257, 261, 265, 271–272, 279, 287
miracles, 18–19
modalities, xiii, 4–5, 9, 16, 21–23, 27, 32, 35, 49, 67, 94, 112, 118, 145, 149, 160–161, 177, 184, 205, 210, 212, 219–220, 222, 226, 229–231, 234, 242, 249, 264, 277, 282, 286, 288–289, 301, 309, 322, 327
modality, 5, 28, 37, 49, 68, 73, 109, 315
motivation for change, 23, 116–117, 124, 170, 175, 178, 187, 270, 284

N

neurotransmitters, 129, 327
non-possessive warmth, 9, 24, 31, 52–57, 59, 62–63, 70, 77–80, 100, 114, 180, 187, 197, 246, 305, 317, 350

O

outcome data, 22–23, 48
outcome research, 31, 53, 55, 78, 205, 297, 308, 345–346

P

patient
    patient readiness, 10, 52, 116–117, 124, 165
    patient variables, 5, 12, 38
persuasion(s), 20, 21, 24, 53, 337
poor therapeutic outcomes, 13, 91, 188, 222, 316
poor therapy outcomes, 127, 199
practice
    practice setting(s), 6, 11, 303, 310, 314, 315
    private practice, v, 6, 11, 22, 40, 98, 105, 135, 161, 288, 303
projective identification, 10, 256, 261–263, 266, 288, 349
Project MATCH, 317, 323
psychodynamics, xv, 10, 125–127, 129, 133–134, 144, 149, 155, 158, 335, 342

R

random, 9–10, 16, 22, 24, 62, 120–121, 145, 151, 157
randomized, 74, 330, 333, 341, 343
recommendation(s), xvi, 11, 58, 66, 74–75, 100, 113, 270, 286, 292–294, 300–301, 303, 313, 321, 337
regression, 87–88, 93, 102–103, 121, 193, 208, 328
relapse dynamics, 105, 225
repair work, 10, 41, 52, 83, 105, 112–116, 123–124, 208, 271
reparative work, 328
residential care, ix, xiii, 13, 19, 21–22, 24, 40, 82, 104–105, 117, 123, 135, 147, 160–162, 164, 177, 185, 216–217, 237, 250, 258, 266, 271–272, 288, 303, 311

S

schools of therapy, 76, 168
self-awareness, 69, 94, 96, 133, 182, 186–189, 193, 197, 205, 215–216, 221, 287
self-disclosure, vii, 8, 24, 33, 43, 52, 67, 69, 74, 82, 97–102, 118, 122–123, 187, 209, 216, 317, 331, 334, 336, 340–342, 346, 351

sex therapy, 233, 235, 237, 287
stages of therapy, 89, 185, 188, 193, 220,
     223, 225, 248, 254, 260, 273, 289–290
successful outcomes, 40, 58, 178, 317
suggestions, xvi, 11, 83, 114, 299–301, 303
suicidal, 7, 91, 121, 137, 147, 324
suicide, 8, 34, 91, 121, 143, 164, 229, 240,
     324
   suicide attempts, 34, 121, 229, 324
supervision, 11, 15, 18, 51–52, 64, 91, 95–
     96, 106, 113, 123, 222, 237, 288, 300,
     303–304, 310, 313, 324, 327, 340,
     348, 350
symptom reduction, 318–320

T

therapeutic constructs, 59, 79
therapist-centricity, 297, 308
therapist characteristics, 3, 23, 36, 52, 69,
     327, 329
therapist disclosure, 82, 94, 99
therapy termination(s), 28, 34, 82, 113, 120,
     162, 208, 270–276, 278–279, 283–
     284, 286, 288–291, 316, 340–342

time structuring, 128, 180, 245, 247, 249–
     250, 277, 287
treatment modalities, 5, 22, 27, 49, 67, 112,
     118, 145, 149, 160–161, 220, 226,
     231, 234, 242, 301, 327
treatment modality, 5, 37, 49, 109, 315
treatment outcomes, 3, 9, 11–12, 17, 22, 40,
     42, 71, 112, 148, 184, 208, 222, 237,
     278, 289–290, 294, 300, 302, 304–
     305, 309, 312, 324, 341
treatment retention, 41, 44, 112, 319, 325,
     332, 334
treatment setting(s), 4, 6, 18, 20–21, 65, 67,
     79, 81, 98, 121, 147, 149, 160–162,
     167, 303–304, 315, 326, 333

U

uncommon, 18, 102, 249, 271–273, 278
unconditional positive regard, 54, 62–63,
     76, 114, 161, 317
unethical, 297, 309